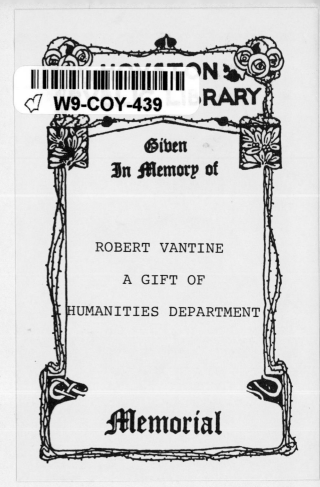

BURT FRANKLIN: RESEARCH & SOURCE WORKS SERIES 522
American Classics in History & Social Science 135

THE PURITAN AGE

IN

MASSACHUSETTS

PURITAN AGE AND RULE

IN THE

Colony of the Massachusetts Bay

1629—1685

BY

GEORGE E. ELLIS

BURT FRANKLIN
NEW YORK

Published by BURT FRANKLIN
235 East 44th St., New York, N.Y. 10017
Originally Published: 1888
Reprinted: 1970
Printed in the U.S.A.

S.B.N. 10540
Library of Congress Card Catalog No.: 75-122838
Burt Franklin:Research and Source Works Series 522
American Classics in History and Social Science 135

PREFACE.

THE Preface of a book is usually that part of it which is the last to be written, and the first to be read. The author makes use of it to supply any possible oversight in his pages in the statement of his purpose, or to anticipate any misapprehension of it. The reader turns to it with a view to find in it a brief and comprehensive exposition of the design of the book, and the reason why it has been written and put forth. A few words here may answer both these intents.

The author some half century ago began the reading of our local history in the then most recently published volumes which dealt with it. From these he read back through the many books which had preceded them, till, having favorable opportunities for so doing, he found his way to many of the original and primary sources of it in print and manuscript. It may safely be affirmed that proportionally more pages have been written and put into print concerning the early history of Massachusetts — including the Commonwealth, the municipalities which constitute it, the incidents and events, the men and the institutions identified with it — than those concerning any other like portion of the earth's territory. And to this mass of written and printed literature we must add the larger mass of ephemeral matter which has simply been spoken, to be remembered or forgotten. This community is generally regarded as acceding to the repute of the ancient Athens in its interest to hear news, with the additional proclivity for delivering and listening to oratory. Our abounding commemorations and celebrations, historic and festive, have furnished themes from our early annals, in prose and poetry. Alike in our digested histories and in these ephemeral utterances there is a large variety in the qualities of accuracy, fidelity, good sense, and judgment, as well as of good taste and candor. Nor are there lacking tokens of superficial knowledge and flightiness of mind and pen in gibes and satires which may amuse but which do not instruct. But having in view all these contributions to our information about our early annals, we may say that our knowledge is full, if not exhaustive, and that (there is a general consent in judgment, among all intelligent and fair-minded persons, as to the harshness, austerity, intolerance, and repulsive features of the earliest legislation and administration of government by the founders of Massachusetts. No right-minded and right-hearted person of our time would attempt to reverse that judgment. But some may find in the motives and principles of the responsible parties an integrity and sincerity of purpose, and in the stage of political and religious development on the way to something larger and better at which wise and good men then rested, an explanation of much that cannot be approved or justified.)

It is in the original documentary sources of our early history, written by those who made that history, not in even the best digests and compends of it, that we are brought into the most communicative relations with the founders and early legislators of our Commonwealth. There we learn from themselves their motives and principles, in the matters in which they are most at variance with the light and advancement to which we have attained.

The historic judgment passed upon these austere and arbitrary rulers is expressed in the two familiar statements, — that they sought liberty of conscience for themselves and denied it to others; and that they exiled themselves to escape persecution for their religious beliefs and practices, and then proceeded to persecute all who questioned or opposed their own principles. It was not till I had carefully read and reflected upon their own autograph documents above referred to, — letters, journals, and public records, — that I was made to realize to what qualifications those statements must be subjected in order to be true to them and true to us. It is exactly and precisely in the difference of meaning and interpretation which those statements have for us, and which they would have had to those exiles, that we are to find, — not the justification nor the palliation, but the explanation of their course as in their view a righteous one. "Liberty of conscience," in the full significance and range which the phrase covers for us, was never claimed or exercised by our early Puritans. They held in supreme dread what it stood for in their time. The spiritual and mental liberty which they demanded and employed, was a right and duty to release themselves from all humanly imposed authority in religion, and all indulgence of their own devices and inclinations, in order that they might put themselves directly under the Divine rule found in "the Word of God." Then, as to escaping persecution for themselves and inflicting it on others, the following pages will abundantly offer us their plea, alike

justifying their self-exile from England and their administration here. The constraints, disabilities, and penalties
from which they sought to release themselves were all of
human device and imposition. Whether Papal or Prelatical, these ecclesiastical impositions and exactions were, as
they believed, wholly without warrant. They were traditions, priestly conceits, and inventions, mingled with falsehoods, frauds, and superstitions, ensnaring conscience and
violating individual rights and freedom, planting themselves between God and the direct approach of his children to him. Turning from all these human devices and
obstructions, the Puritan committed himself to a Book
which Papists and Prelatists, with himself, professed to
believe and accept as of Divine authority, — "the Word of
God." The Puritans argued that it could not be wrong
to obey God rather than men. Putting themselves under
the authority of that Book, as revealing "the laws, statutes, and ordinances of God," the Puritans persuaded themselves that there was also no wrong in holding all under
their government to obedience to it; for "the government
was God's, not theirs."

My aim in the following pages is to set forth with more
fulness and method than I have met with elsewhere the
motives of estrangement and grievance which prompted
the exile of the Puritans to this Bay, and the grounds on
which they proceeded to exercise their severe and arbitrary
rule here. (The points to be chiefly emphasized in this historic exposition are these: the relations of the Puritans, as
Nonconformists, to the Church of England at the period of
its reformation and reconstruction in the transition from
the Papacy to Protestantism ; the peculiar estimate of and
way of using the Bible, characteristic of the Puritans under

the critical circumstances of the time which had substituted the Book for the authority of the Papal and the Prelatical Church; their finding in that book the pattern and basis for a wholly novel form of government in civil and religious affairs, with an equally novel condition of citizenship; their attempt at legislation and administration on theocratic principles ; and the discomfiture of their scheme as involving injustice, oppression, and intolerance.

The reader will find throughout the volume, and especially on pages 525, 536–538, with what strength and explicitness of statement the authorities of Massachusetts urged the religious motives of their scheme and enterprise. These earnest and plaintive utterances were called forth in their painful struggle to preserve the Charter, which they believed covenanted to them the rights they had exercised. They say to the king that they are ready to comply with his Majesty's demands for altering their laws, " *except such as the repealing whereof will make us to renounce the professed cause of our first coming hither.*"

MARCH, 1888.

CONTENTS.

I.

BOSTON, AND PUBLIC MEETINGS.
PAGES 1-44.

Boston settled. Capital of Massachusetts. Meetings there. Its
original Area and Features. Changes in them. Changes in Population. Domestic and Social Qualities and Habits. Recent Foreign
Elements. Simplicity and Integrity of its early Municipal Government. Changes in the Country Towns of Massachusetts. Pu-
ritan Legislation on the Sabbath. Modern Statutes upon it. The
Founders of Massachusetts. Their Religious Aims and Motives.
A Novel Basis for Government and Citizenship. An Ideal Com-
monwealth administered by the Bible. Severity of Rule and Dis-
cipline. John Winthrop the Master Spirit. His Elevated and
Noble Character. His Virtues and Services. Criticisms upon him.
His Death and Funeral. Tribute of the General Court to him.
Taken as the Exponent of the Aims of his Associates. Historical
Judgments upon their Spirit and Administration. The Claims of
Truth and Candor. Liberty of Conscience, how understood. A
Biblical Commonwealth or Theocracy. Restraints upon Individual
Liberty; Domestic and Social Life. Trial of their Scheme. Treat-
ment of Dissenters. Stages in the Progress of Liberal Principles.
Fanaticism and Enthusiasm displaced by Rationalism, the Effect
not necessarily leading to Indifference, Laxity, and Degeneracy.

II.

THE GOVERNOR AND COMPANY OF THE MASSACHUSETTS BAY.
PAGES 45-62.

Charter and Territory of, as a Trading Company. Members of it.
Endicott at Salem, 1628. Cradock, Governor. Transfer of Charter
and Government here. Alleged Illegality of the Measure. "General Considerations" for the Plantation. Design for a " Particular

III.

THE NONCONFORMISTS AND THE CHURCH OF ENGLAND.
PAGES 63–124.

IV.

THE PURITANS AND THE BIBLE.

PAGES 125–166.

V.

THE BIBLICAL COMMONWEALTH.

PAGES 167–199.

IX.

MRS. HUTCHINSON AND THE ANTINOMIAN CONTROVERSY.

PAGES 300–362.

X.

A Jesuit enjoys Puritan Hospitality.

Pages 363–374.

XI.

The Baptists under Puritan Discipline.

Pages 375–407.

XII.

The Intrusion of the Quakers.

Pages 408–491.

XIII.

The Downfall of the Colony Charter.

Pages 492–555.

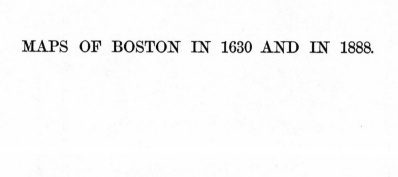

MAPS OF BOSTON IN 1630 AND IN 1888.

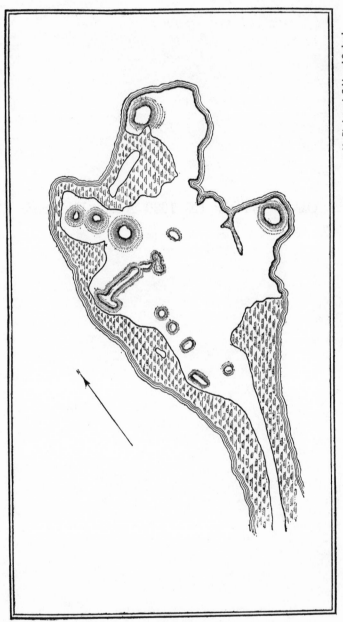

BOSTON IN 1630.

× Mr. Blackstone's Cabin and Orchard.

BOSTON IN 1888.

THE PURITAN AGE AND RULE

IN THE

COLONY OF MASSACHUSETTS BAY.

————◆————

I.

BOSTON, AND PUBLIC MEETINGS.

" THE Governor and Company of the Massachusetts Bay in New England," composed of the Magistrates and those who up to that date had been made Freemen, sometimes called " the Commons,". meeting in Boston, Oct. 3, 1632, passed the following vote : —

"It is thought by generall consent that Boston is the fittest place for publique meetings of any place in the Bay."

This vote gave its Capital to the future Commonwealth of Massachusetts.[1]

Those who have acceded to their heritage, either by birth or adoption, in this Commonwealth, in whatever else they

[1] During some jealousies in 1644, which brought about changes in the magistracy, there were omens that the Court might be removed to Ipswich, then a formidable rival to Boston. In 1650, a petition in behalf of the town of Boston was presented to the General Court that it might be made a Corporation, — a " Mayor Town." The Court deferred decisive action to its next session, with an intimation that the request should be granted conditionally, if reasons could be given for it consistent with "the meane condition of the country." (Records, iii. 207.) Nothing further was done in the matter, as the people proved unwilling to part with their town-meeting privileges. It was not till a hundred and seventy years after that date, that Boston became a "Mayor Town."

1

have retained or yielded of the principles and ways of its
founders, have faithfully agreed with them in opinion and
practice in the matter of that vote. The Court had met
here previously, on Oct. 19, 1630, "For the Establishinge
of the Government."

And what was the Boston of that time, when a company
of exiled Englishmen thus laid in the wilderness the foundations in law and policy of a new commonwealth? It was
a rough, rugged, and irregular peninsula, not exceeding a
mile and a half square of land area, of six abrupt eleva-
tions with valleys, slenderly clad with trees, but strewn
with thickets, bushes, and reeds ; with wide, flat, oozy sea-
margins, inlets of river and ocean, and a few sunken depos-
its of fresh water. Many pure and limpid springs gushed
to the surface. One white occupant, a lonely Englishman,
ordained in the Church, but with no flock in the wilderness,
had here a cabin, with an orchard and tilled-ground. The
peninsula was united at the south to the mainland by a
neck about two miles in length, often washed over by the
bays on either side.

"The fittest place in the Bay for publique meetings."
And so it has proved. Where, upon any spot on the surface of the earth, within the same limits of time, has there
been held as here such a succession of public meetings, in
number, variety of occasion and purpose, in constituency of
membership, in the gravity and consequences of the business, the movements, and the results decided in them?
From edicts going forth from the Court meeting in the
town all the other municipalities making up the Commonwealth have been created. Here levies for wars with Indians, France, and England have been exacted, and armies
have been equipped and victualled. Here municipal, State,
and National Constitutions have been debated and ratified.
Here patriotic assemblies, political parties, meetings for
every interest of commerce, trade, education, art, science,
enterprise, benevolence, — in recent years including women

with men, — have been gathered, to give and hear plain counsel, and to be stirred by eloquence.

A simple, chronological list of the " publique meetings " which have been held in Boston, with the dates and occasions and the doings of them, since the Court decreed its " fitness " for them, would in itself be a history of the series of developments and events covering all the highest interests of men in society. We have but to add the fact, that alike in serious and in satirical repute Boston has been accredited with ingenuity, inventiveness, and eccentricity in the variety, fertility, novelty, and extravagance of the " isms " which have had birth and furtherance here, — and then we have the completed inventory of what has come from the confiding vote of our first legislators.

Is there not reason then for asserting that no portion of the area of Christendom has witnessed such varied and radical changes as have been realized here ? And as the narrative which is to engage us is to bring before us scenes, actors, and subjects with which everything now before our eyes and in our living experience is so marvellously in contrast, we may note in full the transition from the wilderness town to the cosmopolitan city. An ingenious and admirably drawn map now lying before me represents, by an artistic arrangement of lines and colors, the original outlines of the peninsula and its present bounds.

The following description of Boston, probably written in 1649, is from Johnson's " Wonder-Working Providence,"[1] London, 1654 : —

" Boston — invironed it is with the *Brinish* flouds, saving one small Istmos, which gives free access to the Neighbour Townes ; by Land on the South side, on the North west, and North East. The forme of this Towne is like a heart, naturally scituated for Fortifications, having two Hills on the frontice part thereof next the Sea, — the one well fortified on the superfices thereof, with store of great Artillery well mounted ; the other hath a very strong bat-

[1] Chapter xx.

tery built of whole Timber, and filled with Earth. At the descent
of the Hill in the extreme poynt thereof, betwixt these two strong
armes, lies a large Cove, or Bay, on which the chiefest part of this
Town is built, over-topped with a third Hill : all three like over-
topping Towers keepe a constant watch to foresee the approach of
forrein dangers, being furnished with a Beacon and lowd-babling
Guns, to give notice by their redoubled eccho to all their Sister-
townes. The chiefe Edifice of this City-like Towne is crowded on
the Sea-bankes, and wharfed out with great industry and cost, the
buildings beautifull and large, some fairly set forth with Brick, Tile,
Stone, and Slate, and orderly placed with comly streets, whose con-
tinuall inlargement presages some sumptuous City. The wonder
of this moderne Age, that a few yeares should bring forth such
great matters by so meane a handfull, and they so far from being
inriched by the spoiles of other Nations that the states of many
of them have been spoiled by the Lordly Prelacy, whose Lands
must assuredly make Restitutions. But now behold the admirable
Acts of *Christ!* at this his peoples landing, the hideous Thickets in
this place were such that Wolfes and Beares nurst up their young
from the eyes of all beholders, — in those very places where the
streets are full of Girles and Boys sporting up and downe, with a
continued concourse of people."

Allowance must be made in this description for the enthusiasm of the military officer, surveyor, law-maker, town
clerk, court deputy, and commissioner on all miscellaneous business, — Capt. Edward Johnson, the anonymous
author of the " Wonder-Working Providence of Zion's
Saviour in New-England." He was a Puritan of the
Puritans, historian — after a sketchy, uncouth, and fragmentary fashion — of affairs of State and Church identified
with each other. His prose is to a degree intelligible, but
his attempts at poetry are distressing, suggestive of cramps
and dyspepsia in the writer.

What was once the narrowest point of the peninsula is
now its broadest stretch of land between two inner bays.
The costliest edifices are reared on sand and gravel brought

in from the country twenty miles distant, on foundations
of piling and granite from forest and quarry. Its land
area has been nearly trebled. Its sea-margin has been
fringed successively by piers and wharves extending farther into deep water, and giving to it on the map the appearance of a centipede. We need not exempt even the
amphibious territory of Holland from the sweep of the
statement, that more of expense and labor and artificial
construction has been laid out on the land surface of Boston than upon any other equal space of the earth. The
levelling of hills, the reclaiming of alluvial and marshy
basins, the grading of declivities, the opening and broaden-
ing of highways, and the coating of stone and brick laid
over the original soil, present visible evidences to the eye
of continued and still uncompleted processes. Of the bur-
rowings beneath the surface, the disused wells, the pipes
for water, drains, sewerage, and gas, and for conveying
heated water, the labyrinthine perforations, with their
" man-traps," and their risks of miasmatic exhalations
and explosions, convert it into a mined citadel or a slum-
bering volcano.

If we should attempt to trace the changes of two and a
half centuries on this peninsula in the character and composition of the people, their occupations and resources,
their habits of life, their amusements, their opinions, their
distribution into classes, their political and religious parties and sects, and their inherited traditional or alien beliefs and proclivities, — we should be led into discursions,
interesting indeed, but having no other relation to the subject of these pages than the possible connection we might
find between operating causes in the past and their results
in the present.

As the end of life draws near to some, who with zeal,
ability, and earnestness have been leaders in some of the
revolutionary experiments and movements in human affairs,
more strong in their breasts than the desire for the prom-

ised bliss of the hereafter is the craving that they might have the privilege of consciously watching the development, the fate or fortune, of their enterprises and aims on the earth. How have time and changing generations wrought with them? Have their plans and schemes, into which they threw their noble, heroic, and self-sacrificing pride and hope, been led on to triumph and fruition; or have they failed, been repudiated, mocked over, and consigned to the category of the fallacies and follies through which true progress has ever made its impeded advance? If one might call back for companionship and converse a veritable Puritan magistrate or elder of our first age, and while in the use of eye and thought on this same old soil, with its border of the sea, he unites the past with the present, the sadness with which he would pronounce upon the failure of his devout scheme could be relieved only by the comments and explanation which you could offer him of the methods and the results. Three classes of public buildings, belonging respectively to the City, the State, and the Nation, would furnish you the guides for explaining to him the great historic developments which have left such marked memorials of their course. Next, you would be glad to withdraw his gaze and his curiosity from objects which you know would grieve him, by naming to him the generous, refining, and benevolent uses of the long array of public edifices, hospitals, asylums, refuges, homes, libraries, halls of culture and of art, set off by sumptuous and luxurious private homes. It will furnish for each intelligent citizen a good test of the extent and method of his information of the past among these transformed scenes, and the changes which time has wrought in them, if he asks himself how far he is qualified to interpret the processes which have wrought here, and to estimate them on the scale of the progress of humanity in all things.

It would have been a subject of instructive interest for one engaged in tracing the results of heredity and the de-

velopments of lineage in a class of distinctly marked social and racial characteristics, if he could have had before
him now in Boston and in Massachusetts only the descendants of the original Puritan stock. At the period marked
as the limit for the treatment of the subject of the following pages, the population of the town and colony was substantially indigenous and homogeneous. There was then
lingering on the stage, as the Nestor of the original type
of magistrates, the venerable Simon Bradstreet, allowed,
after a shock of revolution, to preside for a brief term
over the flickering after-glow of the expiring old régime,
with a faint conceit of a revival. Judge Sewall, in his
journal, utters his piteous laments as one by one the first
worthies, "who loved the old ways," fell in their lot, till
the last was gone. But their children — of which were he
and his — and their grandchildren, with replenishments
of like beliefs and ways from the old home, still held the
ancient rule. The Puritans of their time combined the
melancholy and the softened elemental vigor of the Indian
summer of their region. By recognizing two significant
facts which would enter into the inquiry, we are aided in
conceiving what would have been the inherited, yet reduced
and qualified, characteristics of their successive generations
restricted to the development from the original stock, with
no admixture. First, we should recognize just at the close
of the Puritan age the presence and working of some softening, liberalizing influences in the old rigidity of doctrinal belief, in the constraint of religious observance, and in
the austerity of manners and habits of life. The second
fact to be held in mind is, that there yet survive among us
sturdy specimens of those of Puritan lineage, training, and
spirit, who still rejoice in their inheritance, and under whatever enfranchisement or enlargement they may have found
for it stand for the essentials of the old belief and principles. Taking those two facts together, — the liberalizing
and softening of the old austerities, and the survival in

life and practical influence of Puritan principles, — we might with some facility have traced the developments of Puritanism from its own stock, on its own soil.

There are still secluded towns and villages of the Commonwealth, not accessible by railroads and not occupied by manufacturing corporations, in which the old Puritanism has, so to speak, "gone to seed," without change of crops. The original sandy and stony soil has known no fertilizers, and those who till it still have to live on its root and surface products. But within the memories of those still in life here in Boston, elements and influences, peoples and institutions, have been subjected to such radical and marvellous changes as to make it equally futile and vain to ask what the place, its condition and circumstances, would have been if left to the developments from its own lineage and stock. One might almost say that the inheritance has lapsed, from the failure of heirs of lawful succession, and by alienation, into the hands of strangers. The descendants of the Puritans are in the minority here, nor is the rule nor the tone of life with them. Slight respect of recognition or courtesy is paid to them or their traditions, such as is thought to be due from some fine and generous natures to the representatives of a decayed, but once formidable family. We put the sum and substance, the facts and their import, of all the transformation that has been wrought here in a single sentence, when we say that men, principles, habits, and institutions have now the ascendency in the Puritan heritage of which the fathers intended and hoped to have rid themselves and their posterity for all time. The process and the results of this transformation may here be glanced at, not in a partisan or sectarian spirit, nor with intimations of personal preferences or regret, nor even with references to gains or losses, improvement or deterioration, — but simply in their character as changes.

At the close of the seventeenth century a foreign element for the first time came in to mingle with our native Puritanism. It was not large or influential in its substance, nor in any way disturbing by its presence, but on the contrary, welcome and congenial. It was that of the French Huguenots, whose doctrinal beliefs and religious usages were mainly in harmony with those of the Puritans, though the rigidity and strictness of the Puritan discipline led many of them afterward to prefer the forms and worship of the English Church. Even the convulsions, innovations, and relaxation of restraints and morals attendant and consequent upon the struggle of the Revolutionary War, did not radically transmute or largely impair the inherited Puritanism of Massachusetts, in its religious habits, principles, or institutions. The foremost of its patriots in the cause of liberty — Samuel Adams — was through and through, in spirit and habit of life, in scruples and in observances, a Puritan. It is to the second quarter of the present century that we must assign the entrance into the life and population of Boston of those foreign elements which now hold the mastery here. Expansion, prosperity, the development of the resources of the country, the introduction of the factory system, the demands for vigorous and cheap labor, the needs of domestic service, and the renaissance of art, literature, and every form of culture, amusement, recreation, and enjoyment are all to be recognized as presenting the reasons and occasions for the wonderful transmutation — we cannot call it development — which has been witnessed by those still living on this peninsula. The process has certainly not been "evolution," and it remains to be proved whether it is a case of the "survival of the fittest." The fathers had left us a noble, free, and inviting heritage. The heritage was as free and inviting — and in contrast with their former condition and surroundings more enviable — to the foreigners who have flooded it, as it was to the natives. The terms of the franchise and of the full rights of citizenship were of the most generous laxity; and party policy, with its strategies of caucuses and elec-

tion frauds, have put offices, patronage, and the control
and use of the public treasury in the hands of those who
in any other country would have been aliens.

Breaking abruptly the line of reflection and remark in
which this subject would engage us, I turn to the notice
of some of the more striking manifestations of change here.
Some of these may be regarded as legitimate developments
from the old Puritanism, to be referred to the enlargements
of view, the increased intelligence, and freedom of thinking
and acting of those in its direct lineage. But the most
radical and subversive and effective of them all are of
importation from foreign peoples and principles, habits,
tastes, and institutions.

In not a single one of the many scores of the places for
Sunday worship in this city is the old Puritan creed in its
literal rigidness — followed by its discipline in the fellowship — heartily, loyally, consistently accepted and honored.
In the consecrated and unconsecrated churches and halls
there is an unchallenged and peaceful — and who will presume to say that it is not prevailingly an instructive,
edifying, and practically good — dispensation of religious
and moral teaching and observance, desired and turned to
account by believers in all creeds and in no creeds. Six
synagogues engage the devotions of ten thousand Israelites
in our population. The largest and most thronged of the
places of worship are those of the Roman Catholics, of
which there was but one in the State at the opening of this
century. The head and the majority of the members of
our city government are Roman Catholics of a foreign
stock. Curiously enough, the same year which finds an
Irishman of that creed in the Mayor's chair in Boston,
finds a foreign-born Roman Catholic — the first since the
Reformation — with the honors of Lord Mayor of London.
Dutifully did our chief municipal magistrate observe the
original and time-honored usage that the organization of
his government, like that of the annual town-meeting,

should be opened with prayer; and the service was duly and reverently rendered by a priest.

Any one who now or at any future time shall be interested in noting the stages and phases of change and development through which this community has passed, will find most suggestive information in a series of volumes published by authority of the city government, and edited by the Record Commissioners. These, beginning from the first settlement, report to us the proceedings of the authorities, selectmen, school committees, overseers of the poor, of the highways, and of all public affairs. The most interesting point of view, as giving us instruction on the subject now before us, is that we have in these volumes, chronologically presented to us, such striking illustrations of the firm hold which Puritan methods and principles had taken in the administration of secular affairs, — all that concerned the economic, thrifty, and protective welfare of the town and its inhabitants. We see that the foremost of the citizens in character, social position, and influence were invariably intrusted with these interests, however trivial in details. And this class of citizens, to whom their time and what little of leisure they could command was of the highest value, were always found ready to discharge these trusts. Petty, irksome, and vexatious were many of the matters committed to their oversight; but the responsibility which they tasked was always faithfully, if not cheerfully, met. True, these were the days of small things, compared with the expansion of our own times; but none the less they afforded a field for the exercise of great principles, and for the unchanging rules of rectitude and duty. And the abiding or lingering sway of Puritanism animated and controlled them. There was a rigidity, a scrutinizing watchfulness, a severe regard for economy and yet a generous exercise of liberality, an expanded public spirit, and always a sense of accountability to the highest exactions of integrity characteristic of, if not peculiar to, these municipal magistracies. The original, self-protective, self-defensive, legal method of warning out of the town any undesirable stranger of doubtful antecedents, and who under any circumstances might prove a burden or a nuisance to the community, was continued for more than a century. Places of doubtful repute for resort, revelry, and idleness were under sharp oversight. The reckless-ness and extravagance of outlay of public funds have come in among us through the license of casting the burden of debt on posterity. But that is of modern license, unknown to the fathers. The word " juncate," which Shakspeare uses for " a stolen entertainment," was not in their civic speech, still less was it recognized in their habits. It is amusing to note the meagreness of the diet charged as paid for by the treasurer during the service of special committees.

Now that Civil Service Examinations are in vogue, it might be judicious to require henceforward, as the city government has printed these proud and instructive rec-ords of the noble principles of their predecessors, that all candidates for municipal office should faithfully read them. In the day of hard and small things, the beginnings in all public provisions — highways, bridges, churches and schools, mills and forts — certainly impose heavier bur-dens than do later works under the name of improve-ments. The fathers bore the former; we lay the charges of the latter on posterity. The General Court in 1646, when occasion called for it, made this cogent statement : —

" We spend nothing superfluously in buildings, feastings, pen-sions, public gratuities, officers' fees, or the like; nay, we are ashamed sometimes at our penuriousnes, but that we had rather beare shame and blame than overburden the people. Such as are in chief office amongst us are content to live beneath the honour of their places, that they might ease the common charge." [1]

1 Hutchinson's Collection of Papers, p. 209.

Some of the changes most obvious to the eye, and most significant in their meaning to those whose memory takes in the first infusion of a foreign element into our indigenous population, may be noted in their simple aspect of facts, without reflections or comments upon them. There has been an enormous increase of the dependent, indigent, and criminal classes. Dating from the first settlement of this and of other towns, the authorities, as has been mentioned, warned and expelled from it any unwelcome stranger who might become a burden on the industry of others, or a public nuisance. For more than two centuries each town had provided a refuge, or poor's farm, for the support of every forlorn, orphaned, or reduced person who by citizenship or through parentage could claim a "legal residence" in it. At first, in the influx of needy persons from abroad, they were naturally distributed in these refuges. But their legitimate occupants, who "had known better days," complained grievously of such forced companionship. This compelled the State to provide and maintain enormous costly institutions for the orphans, the insane, and the diseased who had no legal residence.

For more than two centuries the public school system, "the boast and glory of Massachusetts," was sustained to the satisfaction of the citizens, supplying the generations of both sexes with such education as suited their needs and condition in life. The methods in which religion and morality were taught in them met the demands of parents and guardians. The religious guides of the incoming foreign element of the population making complaint of this established method in our schools, it was modified to meet their scruples. Then followed a fresh complaint from them that the schools were "irreligious and godless." The priests are now compelling the parents of their youth, under penalty of discipline, to withdraw them, and to set up schools of their own. This subject is engaging public discussion that is earnest and

apprehensive. The objection is, that this jealously separate method of education of the young will tend to impede
the assimilation of the diverse elements of our population,
which is greatly to be desired. There have been many
manifestations of sensitiveness when our Irish fellow-citizens are distinguished by their nationality, as indicating
a race or sectarian prejudice; yet more demonstratively
than any other class of our adopted citizens do they keep
their nationality before the notice of the community.
Considering their alienation of feeling from England, one
might suppose that the Irish here would heartily enter into
the commemoration of that most signal incident in the
patriotic history of Boston, on March 17, when Washington compelled the evacuation of the town by the British
army, which had had military possession of it for a year.
But, no! the Irish prefer on that day to commemorate
their national Saint, who is to their fellow-citizens a
purely mythical character. Their procession, the most
demonstrative annual parade in the city, with its national
emblems and regalia, has liberty to obstruct the streets;
and the youth of the city are allowed by the Mayor a
holiday from their schools, that they may see the show.
And this in the old Puritan town of Boston!

It is in some of the country towns in Massachusetts, the
planters of which received their grants from the General
Court, that we may trace the most marked change which
has come in with the recent generation. The first condition of the grant was that the settlers should be under the
care of a competent and approved Orthodox minister. He
was a citizen with others, casting his vote with them; but
he was the guardian and good genius of the settlement.
The tenure of his office was character and ability, with the
conditions of the good-will and approval of his townsmen.
He was not sent and billeted upon them; he answered
to their call to come to them. As a husband and a father
he had a home and all domestic ties. His home and the

homes of his flock made one circle of intimacies and responsibilities in all sympathies and helpfulness. He had no official, clerical superior, and it was for his people only to appoint his means of support and to receive his record of his trust. In all that related alike to the secular and religious charges, business, and interests of the town, all the inhabitants had the disposal of affairs from the initiative. They planned, built, and furnished the place of worship ; they took the oversight of the poor, fixed the occasions and seasons for religious observance, asked counsel from their minister when they wished for it, intrusted him with their confidences when they pleased to do so, and differed with him and called him to account when they had grounds for it. As a man who had received the best education of his time, he was to represent among his people the good cause of learning, from its essential primary elements for every child, on to an oversight of the best training for professional life of any promising youth that he might find in the most frugal home.

In contrast with these developed principles and usages from Puritanism in town, village, and hamlet, we have set before us now, especially in manufacturing places thronged with Irish and French Canadian immigrants, quite a different state of things, especially as regards religion and education. A foreign celibate priest, with no local or traditional interest in the scenes of his work, is sent, uncalled and unknown, by his ecclesiastical superior. He owes no account and renders none to the people that he calls his parish. The Curia for his supreme allegiance is across the sea. He shares no domestic ties, no parental feelings ; in the Puritan sense he has no home, either for his flock or for himself. Such solaces and intimacies as he has must be found among fellow-priests, with their professional confidences and secrets. No one of his flock may bring him under questioning. Their relations to him are very like what they are to their physicians and legal ad-

visers : they have to receive instructions and follow pre-
scriptions. They are appealed to and assessed for money
for religious purposes, but they have nothing to say as to
its use, for the exchequer of the Roman Church makes no
return to the laity. Its laity have no voice in its economical
or professional administration. Its priests may demand admission to the very secrets of their souls, and it is for the
priests to decide for each layman what is the realm of conscience and religion over which they have supreme sway.
The withholding of the last sacraments is the ghostly
thrall over those who fail of spiritual obedience.

Here, certainly, are two quite different types of the
Christian ministry. When Puritanism, even in its reduced
forms, is thus brought into contrast with the ecclesiastical
sway from which it thought to release itself once for all,
the contrast has its significance. The history, from the
beginning, of very many of these towns has been published:
the continuation of it will have many new features.

Without following further into general or detailed conditions the aspects of things around us, marking the amaz-
ing changes from the sway of old Puritanism, we may take
a single subject as significant and typical of very many of
them. Let it be the observance of the Sabbath, Sunday, or
Lord's Day. Of the whole body of distinctive Puritan
legislation in the support of religion and the Church, there
remains now upon our statute book but a single subject,
which almost from year to year, in its changed relations to
social and civil life, comes up for discussion with a view to
the modification and adaptation of existing laws. It is the
observance of the first day of the week, guarded by restrictions and penalties. The Puritan legislation on the subject
will come before us in its fit place. Whenever an appeal has
been made for a relaxation of the old restraints, or for a
larger individual or social freedom on that day, — as for
the carrying of the mails, facilities of travel, the transaction of secular business, the opening of museums and

libraries, the allowance of public amusements, — the lovers
of what is sacred in the past, cherishing its ways through
reverential or traditional sentiments, warmly utter their
pleading protests. They are met by counter protests against
the conserving or reviving the rigid usages of the old
Puritanism. The inference then is that that stern type of
religion, with all its characteristic features and methods, is
antiquated and repudiated. On this subject a middle party,
with a somewhat undefined shape and office of mediation,
presents itself. There still lingers and hovers over us from
the past the fond and fragrant benedictive spell from " the
blessing of the Sabbath," than which no richer or more
potent influence has mingled in the sum of all earthly
sanctities. The most sacred memories and joys of home,
the lyric ballads and essays of our choicest literature, have
gathered and retain the aroma of that blessing. The once
quiet streets and highways, the hush of noise, the renewal
which by the law of periodicity comes to man and beast
from rest, the limit on servile toil, the better garb, and the
generous motive that individuals merge their own private
liberties in a regard for a universal good, — these are the
strong resources of argument for that mediating party on
the observance of the Lord's Day. They would retain all
that is conservative of good in this inheritance from the
past, while generously considerate of the concessions to be
made on account of the changed circumstances of society
and the conflicting demands of social life in the present.
It is in debating and deciding what these concessions are
to surrender, that we are most made to realize how heterogeneous in its elements and composition is the population
which accedes in this city to its once homogeneous constituency. "Works of necessity and mercy " is the familiar
phrase which the old laws used as allowed in exemption
from the rigid rule of Sabbath observance. The calling of
the doctor out of the meeting-house during service, a fire-
alarm, or a rally to some case of danger or suffering, covered

2

all the indulgences intended in that phrase. Scarcely did it allow of summer or harvest labor in the fields when the clouds were threatening. But how shall we in these days and circumstances define works of necessity and mercy, which have become so multiplied and varied ? It is generally admitted that the statutes, in some liberal yet not lax way, must adjust themselves by a deference to a sentiment which has planted itself strongly, if not devoutly, in the minds and hearts of all considerate persons ; that an inherited social safeguard and blessing, that might be defined by a great variety of terms, is conditioned for all our generations upon the perpetuity of the red-letter mark upon the one day out of seven, assigning to it special uses, all of which shall have the sanction of law and custom, on the one single exacted condition that they seek and serve some form of good, and are restrictive of evil.

It has been with facility and without opposition or remonstrance, save from a remnant of old survivors in narrow surroundings of place or fellowship, that the stern and gloomy sway of the old Puritan Sabbath was broken. The morbid austerity and scrupulosity of their type of piety had created for them a rule and standard for the Sabbath which exceeded in its demands even the letter and spirit of the Bible, — their supreme authority. The Old Testament gave but partial sanction to the Puritan Sabbath, and the New Testament gives it none whatever. As the old regards of bugbear superstitions and strained Scripture interpretations are discredited, the Lord's Day is an inheritance to be retained, enjoyed, and improved by those whose gain it will be to preserve it, whose loss it will be to part with it.

From this scarcely more than a superficial and very incomplete review of some of the changes, by time and the succession of seven or eight generations, effected in the town which, through its public meetings, planted and legislated for this Commonwealth, let us go back to the beginnings of our subject.

These pages are, for the most part, concerned with the proceedings, measures, and results of " public meetings " held in Boston by governing authorities during the first half century of its occupancy by English colonists. There are many matters of local and of broader historic interest to be found in the methods and results of their legislation and administration which cannot be noticed here. The heritage and the institutions which time, with its changes, has developed from those beginnings have come to engage the attention of the civilized world. That fact alone would make the seed-planting, from which has grown such a harvesting, worthy of a retrospective study. It has indeed won to it the keen inquiries and discussions of many well-trained minds. A mercantile company, formed in the Old World for trade and colonization here, transported itself and its Charter, with more or less of legality in the proceeding, to establish itself with its covenant of proprietorship and its rights of administration, to this then virgin soil on the edge of a wilderness, washed by the ocean waters of a fair bay. We are to keep in view from the start that their proceedings would necessarily, to a large extent, be without the guidance and the limitations of precedent. There was so much that was original and independent in their experiment that they would naturally be compelled, even perhaps beyond the borders of right and safety, to be a law to themselves. Here they established a form of government, a mode of rule, a style of citizenship, and a method of administration such as had never been put on trial in any part or in any previous age of the world. We have before us a narrative, with episodes, which though not wholly lacking in the interest of adventure and enterprise is in the substance of it painfully trying to the sensibilities of readers, and provocative of sharp censure and stern indignation. It is a narrative of a grim and iron rule of bigotry, austerity, and intolerance ; of a harsh and cruel dealing, not with crime and wickedness, but with what were called heresies, — novel, offensive, and dangerous opinions held as matters of conscience. And what further complicates and embarrasses any fair dealing with the subject, is, that these heresies were themselves forms of Puritan intolerance, — were not peaceful and harmless in utterance, but aggressive and turbulent. What the founders of Massachusetts did under the promptings of intolerance and bigotry has often been told to their discredit and condemnation ; but why they did it, through what instigation of motive, for what intent and purpose, and by what mastery and subjection of their own free-will under an authority recognized by them as supreme, has not always been fairly told. It may be that in coming to a better apprehension of the motive and prompting of their enterprise, as found not in any wilful conception of their own, but in what they believed to be a divine inspiration, we may transfer some of our reproach from them and their acts, and attach our judgment to the delusion which misguided them.

As the writer seeks to set forth more fully in the following pages, the founders of Massachusetts attempted here a wholly novel scheme and experiment in civil government. It was adopted in entire and lofty sincerity of purpose, demanding from them first of all several of the highest qualities of character, — self-consecration, fortitude, constancy, — and various forms of sacrifice. The novelty of the scheme, and its vital connection with a particular religious creed and type of piety were its distinctive characteristics ; worldly profit, and all other mundane ends, were subordinated to an ideal object. The experiment was in a continuous line with others which preceded and have followed it, — alike ideal and practical, in the development of social, civil, and industrial schemes for human progress. It was entitled in that series of experiments to have had its trial. The especial and peculiar quality in it was in the place given to, and the use made of, the Bible in legislation and administration, under a joint form of civil and ecclesiastical order. The opportune time for the trial of the experiment came when the Bible was held as it never had been before, and never has been held since, not only as sufficient for the use that was then made of it, but as authoritatively requiring, by positive divine injunction, that it should reverently and faithfully be put to that use.

No thought of what is to us so obvious in the impracticability of the experiment seems to have presented itself to those who put it on trial. The sanction of divine authority made it obligatory. Begun by one generation, it was continued into another. It was clung to tenaciously,—we may even say, defiantly. Two conditions were pre-eminently requisite for its successful trial. One was, full persuasion, conviction, resolute adherence, and constancy by those who had adopted it, under all perplexities and opposition. These were human impediments, while the scheme was God's ; the issue then was between the purpose of God and the resistance of men. This condition we shall find engaged spirits of zeal and courage to meet it. The other condition was a strong and stern hand of rule over those who not being parties to the experiment, were none the less to be compelled by authority, laws, and penalties to conform to it. And here the experiment was wrecked,— some may even say, disgraced, brought under contempt, as it involved oppression, harsh and cruel measures, not distinguishable from spiritual tyranny working through merciless and inhuman barbarities.

The only claim which the experiment, as we review its method and working, has upon our study, our discriminating judgment and possibly upon our restraint of censure, is in its devout sincerity of purpose, in the unfaltering belief of those engaged by it that they were not following any fancy or hallucination of their own, but were graciously and potently taken into the service of the Being whom they revered with a submission that was rather awe and dread than love.

One may be prompted to ask, What relative place in the series of schemes and experiments which have helped to instruct us in civil and political science is to be assigned to this of a Puritan Commonwealth? We are to study the trial of it after its failure and utter discomfiture. Its chief value then for us, as a lesson, is as it bears upon the fundamental principles of government. What have we come, after all previous trial and theorizing, to accept as the basis of civil government and legislation? The Puritan found it, as common law, in a Book containing the revealed will and commandments of God. We may safely affirm that the failure of the Puritan experiment has discredited that basis, and that it will never again be adopted or sanctioned. Whatever may be the regrets, the affirmings, or the denials of those whose beliefs are inherited from the Puritans on having to face the following statement, candor requires its utterance, — that neither from natural nor revealed religion will any people in Christendom henceforward be satisfied to draw their constitutions, laws, or principles of government. There is much debating the question whether this or that people make up "a Christian nation," and whether we have, or ought to have, "God in our Constitution." In vain should we name Him in the Constitution if He is not in the hearts and minds of the people: if He be there, His name may be omitted from the paper. The practices of so-called Christian nations, in their jealousies, diplomacy, oppressions, outrages, and wars, are hardly redeemed by a complimentary phrase. If the failure of the Puritan experiment, so sincerely tried, has taught the world one great lesson, it is that all governments must be, as they really are, administered on human and mundane principles and sanctions.

I have defined in strong terms, and without qualifications, what I fully believe to have been substantially the religious aim, with its Biblical model and statute-book, adopted by the founders of Massachusetts. Any qualifications which that statement may require as to the date, the distinctness of purpose, the avowal of it, the clearness with which all its conditions were apprehended and accepted, — and especially the proportion of the whole number of the first comers here who were in hearty sympathy with it, — will engage attention further on. I have stated the consecrated aim and scheme as the basis of the enterprise, and as mastering the responsible, confidential, and controlling leaders and guides of it.

And here I may frankly avow, with the reasons which have persuaded and convinced me in my decision, that I take John Winthrop as the witness and exponent of the leading aim in the planting and early administration of this Colony. He was for a score of years its chief citizen, and for eleven years its Governor. Among many men of lofty, devout, and pure spirits, it seems to me that he was the noblest and the best, — the one of them all to be loved and honored for religious graces and human virtues, for his fine simplicity of sincerity, and for his grand vigor of constancy. No writer on our early history has grudged or failed to pay to him an exalted tribute. Some of them have dropped censures or strictures upon some traits of his character and some incidents of his administration with which I cannot fully sympathize, and the justice of which I cannot admit without qualification. Any shadow cast upon him as sharing in the limitations and superstitions of his time and surroundings is that part, it may be, of a faithful portraiture which comes from floating clouds, and not from the rays which illumine character. In one of the public squares of this city is a statue of John Winthrop as the "Founder of Massachusetts," with the Bible in one hand, and the Charter in the other. Another, a seated statue of him in Puritan garb, the habit in which he lived, is in the Chapel of the cemetery of Mount Auburn,

where now repose the ashes of thousands of those of the
lineage of the fathers. A third statue of him, one of the
two of its foremost men furnished by several States of
the nation, is in the Capitol at Washington. The public
highway, the cemetery chapel, and the marble halls of the
palatial centre of our government thus distribute and
gather the tributes of posterity to one than whom no wor-
thier of our race ever lived on the earth. His Vandyke
portrait hangs in the chamber of our State Senate. His
Journal, or History, from his own hand and pen, is the
earliest, the most communicative, and the most precious
of our historical relics. We know him more thoroughly,
more searchingly, in thought, heart, and life, than we do
any one of his contemporaries. When we note the serious,
grave, and sober earnestness of Winthrop, the fond and
tender yearnings of his affection and lofty devotion to
wife, children, and friends, we must recognize elevated
and manly qualities which are not to be depreciated by
the limitations of temporary superstition. In his writings
we meet the utterance of all the pious emotions and sentiments, and all the words and phrases, which have come to
be called *cant;* but no considerate person would apply
that term to anything from his pen, except in the better
meaning of the word, as the *singing* of a devout soul.
There are shocking entries in his Journal in the exposure
of vice, folly, and poor, wretched delusions ; but they were
written in a chaste spirit, and will harm only unchaste
eyes and hearts.

Our respect for Winthrop is warmly engaged by the
candor and magnanimity of spirit manifested by him in the
treatment of even some of the most truculent of those who
brought plausible or only censorious complaints against
his acts or policy. The reader's admiring regard is frequently drawn to him by his modest humility in admitting
his own mistakes and occasional excesses of a spirit of self-
confidence. We know of the particulars of the sharp con-

tention which he had with the testy Dudley only from what
he has himself written about it. In a manly tone he con-
fesses that for some things he was censurable. And when
he records in other cases that opinion and judgment were
not on his side, he adds no plea for self-justification, and
never yields to rancor. We find in his Journal such
avowals as these, in recording some disputatious passages:
" He had been over-sudden in his resolutions ; " " he did
arrogate too much to himself, and ascribe too little to
others ; " he had dropped " an expression which was not
becoming him, but a fruit of the pride of his own spirit ; "
and his hope was that he might be " more wise and watchful hereafter." [1] A judicial estimate of character and of a
full and closed career will lay its stress, not upon the frail-
ties which led to error, but upon the nobleness of spirit
which confessed them.

Hutchinson, without naming his authorities,[2] writes :
" Some writers say that upon his death-bed, when Mr.
Dudley pressed him to sign an order of banishment of an
heterodox person he refused, saying, ' he had done too
much of that work already.' " So far as the testimony of
that unsavory character Capt. John Underhill — who had
stood before Winthrop both in court and in church as
a moral culprit and a heretic — is of worth, it is to the
same effect. Writing in 1660 to John Winthrop, Jr.,
who refused to approve the severest measures against the
Quakers, Underhill says: " Gife me lefe for your forther
incorrigement from percekuchon, to mind you of my fare
well words from your nobell father, of happi memori, to
me, and hafe taken such imprschon throg the sperrit of
God in mee, that I dare not meddel with that pepell [the
Quakers] ; but lefe them to there libberti grantted by the
gud ould Parlement of Eingland." [3] The same valuable

[1] Vol. ii. p. 117.
[2] History of Massachusetts, i. 151.
[3] Winthrop Papers, 4 Mass. Hist. Coll. vii. 186.

military officer, but dubious citizen and church-member, had before written to the elder Governor Winthrop, as follows : " Sir, give me leave to make a serious protestation for you. I have seene thatt in you thatt hath confirmed me that you are as deare to God as the aple of his eye; though these late passages [the Antinomian] have much stumbled me, yett I hould you the same as before, as deare to God as ever, though perhaps for the tyme being you were left to temptation, as Hezechia, &c." [1]

There is a most pertinent suggestion to be made in reference to those shocking and revolting details about " monstrous births " and other dismal occurrences, not needing closer report here, which the pure and devout-souled Winthrop entered in his Journal. They had all their significance to him solely from the reverent and awe-stricken point of view in which he regarded them, as direct indications of the startling judgments of a special providence in designating offenders and their bold sins. In fact, this is simply one of the many evidences of his supreme veneration for the Bible, in which he read of many similar cases of the judgment of God upon sinners in sudden deaths, startling calamities, and loathsome diseases. Nor those in the Old Testament only, but also in the New, — as in the case of Herod (Acts xii. 23), where " the angel of the Lord smote him, and he was eaten of worms." We may call it stark superstition in Winthrop, but it was not a finding satisfaction in such sad tragedies, nor a vengeful temper, that moved him to record them.

The severest reflections that have been cast upon Winthrop have been for his loss of poise and equanimity in the trial of Ann Hutchinson. In that dismal dissension he did not wholly surmount the personal aggravations which it had brought to him. We may well realize how he had been badgered, vexed, and grieved by misconstruction, and by the pitting against him of a rival whose abettors

[1] Winthrop Papers, 4 Mass. Hist. Coll. vii. 171.

were less lovable than himself. More than any other of the parties concerned, Winthrop viewed the matter and the results of Mrs. Hutchinson's schism, when they reached the minds of common people, as a muddle of unintelligible absurdities, with a mingling of mean personal preferences and prejudices. The tongue of a woman is the sharpest of all the weapons with which even the calmest of men in an encounter of grievances has to deal; and Winthrop thought he saw duplicity and prevarication in the inexhausted persistency of that harassed woman. But after all just allowance and abatement, Winthrop stands as not only the founder and the real promoter of this Colony, but also as its wisest, most faithful counsellor, fosterer, and ever loyal friend, the sincerest, purest spirit of the Puritan Theocracy. He met with a clear conscience and a calm dignity all misapprehensions and buffetings of rivalry from his associates, and all the temporary chills of popularity from an inconstant but finally a revering constituency. He sank his whole inherited and acquired estate in the support of the Colony, so completely, that it had to assume the support of his infant son after his decease in penury. The pathetic letter written near his death-chamber, signed by magistrates and elders in tender consultation, to be sent by an Indian runner through the woods to his son in Connecticut, is a touching and loving tribute of mourning hearts to his virtues and services.[1] The reference in the Records of the Court to his death and character is brief, but it is sufficient. Some of the Colony's powder had been used without official authority in volleys at his funeral: "The Courte doth think meete that the powder spent on the occasion should never be required againe, & thankfully acknowledg Boston's great, worthy, due love and respects to the late honored Governor, which they manifested in solemnising his funerall, whom wee accompted worthy of all honor."[2]   Had he been called

---

[1] The letter is given in *facsimile* in "Life and Letters of John Winthrop," vol. ii. p. 395.   [2] Records, ii. 270.

upon for that service, Roger Williams would have been the most willing, as well as the most gifted, in offering for Winthrop — never to him but a friend, though a censuring magistrate — the richest and sweetest of epitaphs.

In stating, therefore, as I have done in such positive terms, the paramount and constraining purpose of the responsible leaders of the Massachusetts Colony, to try an experiment of government not of their own devising, for the exercise of their own authority or for their own thrift, but one of which God should be the supreme magistrate and the Bible the statute book, I rely mainly and with entire conviction on the repeated and emphatic avowals of Winthrop, that such was his aim and the aim of his chief associates. Of this the evidence and witnesses will come before us in the following pages. (And I lay stress upon the distinctive and fundamental point, that they were acting under the constraint of a divine obligation and covenant, and not as being at perfect liberty to use their own wit or wisdom in plans of their own. They followed instructions; they obeyed commands; they accepted with loyal reverence a pattern and model not merely given to but imposed upon them as literally, in its principles and details, as was the Jewish Commonwealth founded and administered on in- spired directions to Moses.) If this view be correct, as for myself I fully believe that it is, then the responsibility of the Puritan authorities for the practical working of the experiment is certainly, to a degree, qualified. They could say, as in fact they did say, to many victims of their severe discipline, " You are not simply withstanding us, breaking our laws, defying our authority, — you are rebelling against God; and as we have put ourselves under His rule and statutes, we intend to hold you to the same subjection." In the forecast of our great civil convulsion the plea of obedience to " the higher law " was advanced by those who set at nought civil statutes and ordinances. The Govern- ment neither recognized that " higher law " itself, nor would allow its citizens to prefer it for their following. But the Puritan magistrates did not only accept, they revered, that higher — the highest — law themselves; and one of its requisitions on them was to compel other people to obey it. It would follow, therefore, that those who censure and condemn these Puritans should go below their bigotry, austerity, and severity, and challenge them for their credulity, their folly, even their impiety, in committing themselves to a belief and covenant their allegiance to which would compel them to unjust and barbarous dealings with their fellow-men.

Before proceeding further in the development of the scheme and experiment here put on trial, and following it into the processes and measures of a stern rule which make our Puritan annals so unattractive and even repulsive to many who have studied them, the writer of these pages would avail himself of the privilege of stating distinctly his own aim and purpose, to which he will endeavor strictly to confine himself. His sole intent is to narrate historically, with but little of criticism or censure, and nothing of advocacy or vindication, the incidents and proceedings attendant and consequent upon the formation and administration of a Biblical form of government in Massachusetts. Often enough will occasion force itself upon a reader, prompting him to comment censoriously and even bitterly upon the severities of the Puritan rule. The reader is free to make these criticisms; the writer will try for himself to restrain the expression of them : his purpose is faithful and candid narration, not criticism or judgment. Such as have written upon the early history of Massachusetts with a view of setting forth the principles and measures of its government in the light of its contemporary era, and of allowing the Puritan convictions and purposes to have a fair presentation, have been very unjustly charged with a championship of them, with palliating their severity and intolerance, and defending them against the reproaches and judgments pronounced upon them. More common, on the other side, are the free expressions of contempt, of harsh invective, and even of abhorrence, which have been visited on the Puritan rule, — as our early missionaries to India, China, and Japan sent home hideous idols as symbols of the whole religion and life of those countries. It is enough to say that no intelligent and candid person of our own times, whose opinion is of any worth or weight, would undertake to vindicate the Puritan policy as practicable, reasonable, or righteous. The problem to be dealt with is simply this: The scheme put on trial here was one that offered itself in utmost sincerity and loftiness of purpose to a company of men for their own faithful and heroic acceptance, at whatever cost of zeal, sacrifice, and self-denial. The integrity, purity, and devotion of the prime agents in the scheme is beyond all question. The scheme itself, in its own age, so far from seeming impracticable and sure to involve oppression and injustice, — as at its very first view it appears to us, — presented itself as one that carried with it a divine obligation and command that it should be put on trial, with earnestness and resolution. So far away are we from the tone of thought and the use of words characteristic of the Puritans, that we may hardly apprehend the idea, which was none the less in their minds, that the scheme they were putting on trial here was not theirs but God's.

The only possible attraction which an historical student in these days can find in rehearsing the policy and rule of Puritanism in early Massachusetts, and the only relief of which he can avail himself in facing its repelling features, is in the attempt to trace the chronological and philosophical relations of Puritanism in the development of theories, beliefs, and experiments in human society and in government. If one who has but a superficial knowledge and apprehension of the principles and spirit of Puritanism is disposed to pronounce upon their rule that they must have been inborn inquisitors and fiends of cruelty, he must be left free to hold that opinion or advised to enlighten it. The writer will here frankly anticipate the statement of his own strong conviction — to be subsequently more fully set forth — that the Puritans were ill-guided and misled by their estimate of, and way of using, the Bible.) Let it be allowed — for in reason no one will deny the proposition — that in their age and under their circumstances they held, and had reasons satisfactory to themselves for holding, that the Bible was the statute book of God for the rule of human life, and offered the only means of man's salvation. Influences which had long been working in the currents of thought, and the repudiation of the authority of church and priesthood, had as a substitute brought the Bible into supreme and well-nigh idolatrous regard, as the sole means of communication between God in heaven and men on the earth. How the Puritans formed their exalted estimate of it and to what uses they applied it, will by and by invite our attention. I can but repeat now the statement, even at the risk of shocking some readers, that the Puritans were beguiled into the worst of their errors of policy, bigotry, and intolerance, by their belief in and their attempt to follow the teachings which they found in the Bible. A single illustration of what is meant in this frank statement may be offered here. Everything in the Bible had to them the inspiration and infallibility of God. In that book are these two positive prohibitions: "Thou shalt not suffer a witch to live" (Ex. xxii. 18); "There shall not be found among you a witch" (Deut. xviii. 10). Belief in witchcraft is an extinct delusion for all intelligent and enlightened persons; they do not hesitate to pronounce it impossible that a man or woman should enter into a covenant with the Devil, who on his part should invest them with an infernal power of mischief. Those who seek to conserve anything of the literal authority of the Bible interpret those passages, not as positively warranting a belief in witchcraft,

but as interdicting all pretenders to necromancy or the
" black art." But the Puritans — and, for that matter,
all who had the same belief as theirs about the Bible —
took no such liberties with its letter and teaching. They
believed it to be as possible for a man or a woman to
enter into a covenant with the Devil as it was for them
to enter into a covenant with God. Mark the words of
that high authority in English law, Sir William Blackstone,
written nearly three-quarters of a century after the last
trial of a witch in New England, though such trials still
continued in Europe. Blackstone wrote : " To deny the pos-
sibility — nay, actual existence — of witchcraft and sorcery
is at once flatly to contradict the revealed Word of God in
various passages in both the Old and New Testaments."

(The inane assertion, so often flippantly repeated, that the
Massachusetts colonists came here to seek and to provide a
field for the enjoyment of liberty of conscience, and then
proved faithless to their profession by securing the right
for themselves and denying it to others, is simply false to
all the facts of the case. What is now really meant by the
phrase " liberty of conscience " was something which those
Puritans regarded with shuddering abhorrence. It might
with much more truth be said that the leaders of the colony
came here to be rid of the liberty of conscience, which was
working and showing its fruits in England, as will appear
on our future pages. Nor is it an adequate interpretation
of their errand here to say that they were seeking liberty
even for their own consciences. That liberty was already
pledged and fettered, — put under bonds and limitations ;
it was held in subjection to a stern and exacting rule of
life and duty, found not in their own thinkings and will-
ings, but in the " Word of God." This complete abnega-
tion of the privilege and license which we associate with
liberty of conscience, must be kept in mind in all our
reading about the beliefs and doings of these Puritans.
Fallen and wrecked as in their belief the nature of man

was, they would not entertain the thought that any one, however earnest he might be, could find his rule within his own resources of thinking and believing. They read the sentence repeated several times in the Book of Judges, that in the lack of any supreme authority "every man did that which was right in his own eyes," as equivalent to saying that he did what was wrong in the eyes of everybody else. It may thus appear that a championship of Puritan legislation and administration, leaving nothing weak or defective in it, would involve a defence of their estimate of and way of using the Bible. One who has faith and disposition for that argument may undertake it; it is not intended here.

The first object of a government established in civil society, allowed to be alike needful and lawful, is to provide for its own security and peace. Reflection would at once suggest what experience has so abundantly illustrated, — that this aim and function of government, instead of presenting at any time fixed and permanent conditions for its discharge, must be constantly adjusted to changing circumstances. The question, always a practical one for discussion and decision, is, How much of individual liberty must be denied or restrained for the common safety and welfare? In other words, we have to ask, What portion of the whole range, action, and use of human life — beginning even with the holding and utterance of opinions and beliefs, and including private conduct, habits, all individualities of character, use of time, relaxations, amusements, and self-indulgences — can rightfully be brought under the surveillance and control of civil law, or may safely be exempt from its oversight? In no civilized community which has a continuous history in its progress and development can this question be opened, discussed, and traced through more striking and interesting phases of its practical trial than through the two and a half centuries of Massachusetts.

The curious fact is at once presented to our notice that

civil government on the soil of Massachusetts began with the very utmost stretch of restraint upon every exercise of the liberty of the individual, and has been brought on by the development of circumstances to the utmost indulgence of freedom — some think even to a dangerous laxity — in loosening that restraint by law. If one was concerned to trace in details and stages that process from restraint to laxity in the relations between law and individuals, the records and the statute book of this State would furnish him with exhaustive materials. Legislation and government here, enforced by the sanction and approbation of those whom the first, and ever since the most honored, of our governors called the wisest and the best, though the fewest,[1] began with the maximum of control, interdiction, and exaction exercised over each individual inhabitant. Admitting, evidently grudgingly, that it could not interfere with opinions and beliefs privately held, it positively, and with penalties, interdicted the utterance of them in any way of dissent or protest against those which authority had pronounced to be right and true. The acting according to these individual dissents of belief and opinion was visited by a gradation of inflictions even up to capital punishment.

There was no incident, circumstance, or experience of the life of an individual, personal, domestic, social, or civil, still less in anything that concerned religion, in which he was free from the direct or indirect interposition of public authority. His civil rights depended upon his acceptance

---

[1] In a letter written by Winthrop to Hooker — not now extant, but contemporaneously quoted — in reference to the establishment of government in Connecticut, Winthrop says: "The best part of a community is always the least; and of that least part the wiser are still less." Another equally strong statement of the Governor is this: "Democracy is among most civil nations accounted the meanest and worst of all forms of government, . . . and histories record that it hath always been of least continuance and fullest of troubles." (Life and Letters, ii. 427.) Yet, under his lead was born a Commonwealth the completest of democracies.

of a covenant of faith and fellowship in a church with a formulated system of doctrine; and in that fellowship he subjected himself to a rule of discipline additional to the secular code which bound him to obedience. If he could not obtain membership in a church, or preferred to remain outside, he was none the less taxed for its support, and mulcted if he did not attend regularly upon its teaching and worship. There was no secrecy allowed for his home and domestic privacies. If husband and wife preferred to live apart, or were resigned to having an ocean flow between them for any extended period of time, they were reckoned with by an inquisition, and compelled to an "orderly disposal of themselves." There was not a child in any house that was not also a ward under public guardianship to make sure of the faithful performance of parental duty. A fractious and rebellious child might by law be brought to the gallows. Men and women were watched and dealt with if apparently living beyond their means or station, or with no visible and profitable " calling " or occupation, or if idling, gossiping about, or giving the least suspicion of scandal. Sumptuary laws forbade gay or luxurious apparel, lascivious freedom of manners, and light speech, especially in those of the humbler sort. All "affairs of the heart" in young people must be gravely laid before their elders. From sunset of Saturday to sunset of Sunday were solemn Sabbath hours, during which all noise must be hushed, all toil, and especially all worldly pleasure, must cease. No strolling was to be allowed in street or field, no social visiting. During the whole Puritan era there was no place for a public game or amusement. All revelry and carousing were prohibited. The only chance for anything like rollicking and fun was in connection with military trainings, though these began and ended with prayers. The first indulgences which perseveringly asserted themselves at the College Commencement season it was vainly attempted to arrest in their development by an interdict

of " plum-cake " on the occasion, grimly enforced by a sup-
plementary edict against those who " went about to evade
it " by introducing " plain cake." House-raisings and
harvestings gave vent for the repressed impulses of the
elders ; corn-huskings, in the places and materials of them,
afforded opportunities, always however " on the sly," for
the irrepressible vivacities of the young.

Obvious enough to us is it that this Puritan experiment
of government, as making the magistrates the interpreters
and representatives of the divine will and authority, involved elements of spiritual tyranny and the suppression of
soul liberty. But it was not so to them, nor would they at
once have admitted that the ill-working of their rule discredited its sovereignty. In the four episodes under their
administration, to be rehearsed in these pages, we shall
find that their severities were exercised upon two quite
different classes of offenders. One of these were trespassers, intruders, who not having any proprietary rights
in the Company, not freemen or citizens, could not claim
protection, indulgence, or privilege, but might be disposed
of by being ordered out of the jurisdiction. Of this class
was Roger Williams, who was not a member of the Company, nor a citizen with the franchise. So also were the
missionary Quakers, regarded by the authorities as tramps,
or vagabonds. This class of persons, the Puritans argued,
had no right to complain of the laws, because they were
free to find release from them by going elsewhere. More
serious, however, was the case when they had to deal with
quite another class. These were full partners and proprietors in their enterprise, enfranchised citizens, vowed
and pledged to one another under the same religious covenant, full believers in the principles of the Theocracy,
with their homes, their property, their kinships, and all
their affections and interests identified with the community. Among those arose dissent and variance about some
doctrinal beliefs and religious usages, breaking the unity

of the faith and the uniformity of discipline. Such as these were the Antinomians and the Baptists. In dealing with these the Puritan administration was put to the severest trial, and proved to be utterly hostile to soul liberty, intolerant, and sooner or later intolerable.

These exposures, however, were to be reached by experience, not anticipated. Nor were they to be at once accepted as rightful and not avertible, till an effort and a struggle, however painful and ineffective, had been made to bring the whole power of the Theocratical government to sustain its legislation. Do not the resolution, the persistency, even the defiant blinding of their own eyes to the distressing consequences of their measures, move us to recognize the loyalty of the magistrates to their own covenanted obligations? Certainly theirs was no skin-deep, superficial attachment to their principles. These had struck down into conscience and faith, and would have been fictions and follies had they not been fought for. Only an actual demonstration of the impracticability of their scheme, and that demonstration enforced by externally disabling them from persevering in it, could effect its discomfiture. Conscientious errors in belief and practice bring with them their own penalties; and these have a self-corrective influence. Very little satisfaction or justice is there in visiting our censure or contempt on those who in the light — or rather the darkness — of their own times were beclouded with delusions and falsehoods from which the progressive illuminations of our age, to which the wisest of us have individually contributed so little, but of which we all enjoy the results, have released us. Truth and freedom advance by the interlocking of the largest and the smallest wheels of the mechanism of time. If our laments and reproaches must be pronounced upon those who have been the agents of error, dissension, and discord in any age, we must be sure to go so far back as to reach as near as possible to the original offenders. It would be some satisfaction, for

example, if we could summon before us as culprits some
of the earliest, the most ancient, and conspicuous agents of
this mischief, — say, for instance, those who planned and
began to build the Tower of Babel for the avowed intent of
circumventing God. On them we might charge the sources
of all the ills and discordances that have followed the
baffled attempts of men to work in harmony, with consent
of purpose and a common plan. Those thwarted builders,
falling out in their plans, and by the confusion of their
speech no longer able to understand one another, are responsible for the long and infinite succession of embar-
rassments and difficulties, not only about words, but about
meanings and ideas. It is they who are blamable for the
confusion of languages, the need of translators and interpreters, the verbosity and tautology of legal documents
and litigation, and the misunderstandings in conversation
and correspondence.

The Massachusetts Puritans acceded to their place and
stage in this development of truth struggling to outgrow
error. We can in part understand and interpret our own
age. But if we wish candidly and fairly to understand
them, we must not throw back two and a half centuries
the standards of intelligence and judgment of our own
time as applicable to them. Amid the resources and appliances, the comforts and luxuries, of our own mode of life
we may sometimes, turning from the records which the
fathers have left us, and with the easy help of the imagination, fall into musings upon their external lot and experiences. The contrasts will be strong and strange. Even
in their native country there had been much of rudeness
and hardness in their physical, social, and domestic conditions. But for the first generation here how numerous
were the wants and needs, how deficient the resources and
supplies! A grim wilderness environed them, with real
and visionary dangers in its dark shadows. Marshes,
morasses, unbridged streams, and devious trails made in-

tercourse difficult and all travel tedious. The numerous inventories left to us of household goods, of farm implements, and of apparel are often amusing illustrations of simple thrift, and of the frugality, paucity, and rudeness of their furnishings, which still were of such relative value as to be carefully appraised. The tortures of the medical and surgical practice of those days were fearful for endurance. Our light foot-gear and water-proof protection for snow-storms and tempests found substitutes for them in boots of hide smeared with grease, and doublets of leather which drank in the water, so that they had to be cast aside as the weight increased. The spoils of the hunter and safety from the Indian foe were won by the long gun, supported by a " rest," and fired by a match-lock. What would the housewife and the forest-traveller of those days have been ready to give for a bunch of friction-matches, the price of which for us is one cent ! The lack of any currency, save Indian shell-peage, caused all traffic to be by barter of produce or labor at shifting values. The entire lack of all the delights of intellectual intercourse and of literature, save those of the most lugubrious character, must have had a most depressing influence upon the spirits of those who were so intently brooding over dismal theological problems.

Now, it never occurs to us to blame those whose time and conditions of life subjected them to these external limitations and hardships ! we simply commiserate them, while we complacently enjoy our own often unappreciated resources. Can we not indulge some of the same commiserating but uncensorious sentiments toward those who were two or three centuries before us in the hard, slow tasks of delving in the mines of intellectual, moral, and religious truth ? Unhappily, all men and all things in this world, at least, are judged by their faults. If we ourselves hope for a more considerate or a more lenient judgment at another tribunal, we ought to give the benefit of

it to those whom we bring from the distant past to be tried
by ourselves. There are some of generous and tolerant
minds, even under our severest contempt of bigotry and
utmost deliverance from it, through liberality and radical
freedom, who will try at least to distinguish devoutness
and earnestness of purpose, in consecrating themselves to
a sacrificial work, though it presented itself clouded in
error and delusion.

The Puritan rule has been almost exclusively censured
for the severity with which it bore upon those outside of
and hostile to its covenant. But one who is familiar with
its internal and secret workings can hardly fail to notice its
restless, morbid, and afflictive influence, even upon its most
loyal and devout disciples. Its strain upon human nature
was intense, rigid, and unrelaxing. Fidelity to the covenant rule was constantly requiring more and more of constraint, suggesting self-reproaching dreads of a falling
away of faith and zeal. To have found any cheering,
radiant delight in their communings and conferences, they
must have been trained to conceptions like those which
that logical Calvinist Jonathan Edwards had reached,
when he set forth that among the qualities of the happiness of the redeemed would be the satisfaction of witnessing the sufferings of the damned. Whence, then, came
the sincerity, the earnestness, and constancy of the Puritans? Through that very able and profoundly thoughtful
work of Mr. Lecky, on the " Rise and Influence of Rationalism in Europe," runs the sad and depressing strain, in
assertion and evidence of the statement, that errors connected with religion have had vastly more power over
human beings than its grandest and most illuminating
truths. His line of proof for his assertion may be readily
conceived. Beginning with the most grovelling and besotted superstitions, and following down all false and
craven dreads which have enslaved and tormented human
beings through delusions, credulities, and clouded imagina-

tions, he shows how the thrall and spell of sway which they have exercised over men has been measured by their foulness, their falsity, their unreality. Men have been willing to suffer and bear and do the most, in the name of religion, for what was most unworthy of their sacrifices. The hook-swingers of India, the immolators and victims of human offerings, ascetics of every type, pilgrims, self-flagellants, monks, nuns, hermits, and also Puritans, have graduated their zeal by the form and phase of error which have beguiled them. And Mr. Lecky presents, as the converse of this sad recital, the chilling and disheartening view, that the effect of all enlarging, expanding, elevating, and liberalizing tenets of religion is to quench enthusiasm and earnestness, to induce apathy, sybaritism, self-indulgence, and to repress many noble impulses. Happily his lament is subject to this very serious qualification, which relieves its dismal burden. Superstitions, delusions, and falsities, accepted as religious beliefs and prompting to actions of obedience conformed to them, have indeed had a more constraining power over men than have lofty and liberalizing truths substituted for them. But this power has not been a power for good; rather has it been a power for evil, working fatefully and malignantly on the passions of men, clouding their intelligence, perverting their natural human instincts, and enslaving them to mean and debasing practices. Enthusiasm, earnestness, full sincerity, and painful self-inflictions may prove the power that has had sway over men through these superstitions, credulities, and delusions; but the mere potency of their influence in no way relieves its dismal workings. And as to the converse statement held before us by Mr. Lecky, that emancipation from these religious errors, by enlarged, liberal, and rational views, seems to reduce earnestness and enthusiasm, to foster laxity and self-indulgence, — one may well ask if truth, when substituted for falsity in religious tenets, does not displace false and baneful super-

stitions, not merely to leave the heart and mind empty of
all quickening activity and fervors, but to fill the vacancy
with cravings for something worthy of belief and loyal
service ? Liberalism and rationalism in religion have certainly proved the efficiency of their power over men in
having released them from the thrall of poor and craven
superstitions, in breaking galling fetters, in lighting up the
chambers of thought and imagination, and, though still
leaving the deep mysteries of existence in shadow, substituting hope and trust for gloom and despair.

Nor is it to be wondered at, still less grieved over, if the
relief found in liberal and rational views, displacing credulities and superstitions, reduces the intensity of belief,
of self-sacrifice for visionary ends, and relaxes the constraint upon personal freedom, even to the borders of
self-indulgence. Religion, in its deeper and most serious
influences, finds its opportunity of power over individuals
in trying and sorrowful and bereaving experiences ; and
so in companies of human beings, times of persecution, of
endurance, of exile, and of enterprises of grave moment
repress all lighter sentiments, and give to life and effort a
sombre tone and aspect. The heart resumes its cheer
when these restraints are withdrawn, as the rustic whistles
when he has cleared the dark woods or passed the ghostly
grave-yard. The grievous complaints and regrets which
fill the sermons of the preachers in Massachusetts a century after the settlement, over the decay of the early piety
and the decline of the ancient fervor, are simply lugubrious
comments upon, instead of grateful recognitions of, the
release of beliefs and life from the gloom and severities,
the bugbears and delusions of the early age. Further on
in these pages we shall have to admire the heroic and
high-pitched fervors of constancy, even to the scaffold,
with which the missionary Quakers bore their testimony ;
and we shall note how large a part of that testimony, with
the buffetings which it brought upon them, consisted in

oddities and extravagances of conduct which had no vital connection whatever with their noble and illuminating principles. But mark how one of their writers, glowing with the old spirit, mourns their degeneracy just one hundred years after their first coming to Massachusetts. He thus draws a censorious contrast " concerning the difference between the former Quakers, that suffered Persecutions, and these in this day " : —

" If we may know them by their Fruits, they were two manner of People: the first often going to Meeting Houses and bearing a godly testimony after the Speaker had done [not always waiting for that, however] ; also Teaching and Exhorting at other public places, for which they suffered much Persecution, which they took joyfully, being upheld by the Power of God. And these, only holding Meetings of their own in a formal way, as other Professors do ; having a form of Godliness, and not the Power and Life thereof, as the suffering Quakers had ; minding earthly things, being adulterated and living in the friendship of the World, which is enmity with God. So these, not having the spirit as the first Quakers had, are no more to be compared with them than a dead Tree may be compared to a living Tree." [1]

Which signifies, that when the Quakers, losing their original fervors, ceased to annoy other people, and quietly pursued their own way of life, they became degenerate and dead.

In following the tracks of the early navigators to our side of the great ocean, we note their long voyages, through tempests, fogs, and ice-barriers, in their cramped vessels, with salt food and foul water, and watch them, as without charts, save such as they make themselves, they lie-to and send off the shallop to feel their way through reefs and soundings. They were the pioneers of passengers in the shuttles which now cross the seas in a week with their

---

[1] "An addition to the book, entitled ' The Spirit of the Martyrs revived,' " by Joseph Bolles.

luxuries and pleasure-seekers. Chemical science keeps the record of its votaries who have been smothered or blown up by their own gases; medical science shows us a long trial of experiments for killing or curing. All along through the ages we can trace the lines, divided and contrasted, drawn by those who in the profoundest sincerity of earnest conviction received as the intensest realities what to us have not the interest even of traditions. The same process is realized in many extended human lives, and we call it one of disillusioning.

We are to trace this process as illustrated in the Puritan experiment here. There are many facts which might be adduced to prove that only the iron hand of a stern rule and discipline could have carried the colony over the ventures and risks of its beginning. It is not worth any one's time or skill to open special pleadings for the limitations, excesses, or severities of the Puritans. A portion of them may be accounted to exigencies of time and circumstance. If beyond this it comforts any one to visit upon them objurgatory epithets, he is free to do so; the doing it may relieve his own feelings, and his blows will fall upon insensate and unrevenging victims.

We are now, after introducing the actors with their principles and purposes, to review a stern and tragic period of history. My own sensitiveness of nerves, and resources and allowances of sympathy and tolerance have been so heavily taxed by much that I have had to read and think about in preparing these pages, that I shall not apologize or ask pardon for anything in them that may wound or offend others.

II.

THE GOVERNOR AND COMPANY OF THE MASSACHUSETTS BAY.

IN view of the outcome of the experiment put on trial by the founders of Massachusetts, in setting up here a Commonwealth patterned after a Biblical model, a question presents itself to us equally interesting and important in our judgment of their motives and of their scheme. The question is, whether at the start, before coming hither, they had the intent in their minds, essentially and substantially matured, with a plan and method for accomplishing it; or whether the scheme was developed by stages, as new impulses moved them and new means and opportunities were offered to be used by them. In trying to dispose of the alternative views here suggested, we shall have to trace the process by which what was originally organized in England as a company for pursuing objects of trade in this Bay, became transformed into an agency for establishing a Commonwealth in which religion should predominate in civil affairs. In tracing this process we shall have to note that the transfer of the patent and the setting up of administration under it on this soil were first prompted by religious motives coming in to influence the chief movers in the enterprise, and that these religious motives steadily acquired the ascendency.

The territory included in the Massachusetts Bay patent had been at the disposal of the Council for New England. After having been held by various individuals and associates as grantees and proprietors, it was transferred to the Governor and Company of Massachusetts Bay. Originally there were but six grantees; of these, only Humphrey and Endicott appear in our local history. These six admitted additional associates as members of their Company, and through the influence of friends at Court the Company obtained a royal charter in 1628-29. Endicott was sent with companions, ministers, and servants of the Company to establish a local government here, in subordination to that in England; he was furnished with a copy of the charter, and received advice and orders from his superiors. We can trace on the records of the Company nearly every stage and incident in the councils and motives which led to the transfer of the patent and government. Where there is obscurity, light comes from other sources. The proposition for removal, however it may have been privately agitated, was first made by the Governor (Cradock) at a meeting of the Company July 26, 1629. In the debate upon it the seriousness of the proposition was realized, and the decision was deferred. The members present were desired " privately and seriously to consider thereof," to set down each his reasons, to be reduced afterward to heads; meanwhile " they are desired to carry this business secretly, that the same be not divulged." August 28 a special meeting of the Company was held to consider the proposition; committees were designated to weigh the reasons on either side, and to present the results on the morrow. August 29, reports having been listened to and considered, the question was put as to transfer of patent and government, " soe it may be done legally." " Erection of hands " showed " the general consent of the Company " in favor. September 29 an order was passed " to take advice of learned counsell whether the same may be legally done or noe."

There is no record as to any consultation of counsel or of advice given on this point. Hence it has long passed current in the history and in incidental notices of these important proceedings, that without a shadow of legality, and in daring contempt of authority, the Company surreptitiously stole away from England with its patent to set up an unlicensed authority on the soil of New England, — thus beginning that series of usurpations and wrongs which were matters of complaint and hearing at Court, and which have been discussed in charges and defences by our historians.

This imputation has been satisfactorily set aside. Among a mass of valuable family and public documents which came to light after long oblivion in 1860, belonging to the Winthrops, was a very remarkable paper written by the first Governor, in which he positively and distinctly states that when the charter was in preparation it was sought " to keepe the chief Government in the hands of the Company residinge in England, and so this was intended; and with much difficulty we got it abscinded." [1] This effectually disposes of a plausible charge, and accounts for the absence in the charter of any provision of the place of administration under it. It may also be mentioned here in anticipation, that when, in 1633, Gardiner, Morton, and Radcliffe stirred up Gorges and Mason to bring charges before the Privy Council on account of rough treatment which they had received, and Humphrey and Saltonstall appeared to defend the Company here, — the result was that the Council, thus fully informed as to the administration in the Bay colony, made no complaint of the transfer from England. So far from it, the Council promised that if the government here was administered as was professed when the charter was granted, it should receive the royal favor.

We must leave the records here for a moment to take note of a transaction having a very significant relation to the matters to be brought to our notice when we return to them. We know well what came of the enterprise consequent on the transfer of patent and government. We are

---

[1] Life and Letters of John Winthrop (2d ed.), vol. ii. p. 443.

concerned now to trace the coming into the affairs of
a trading company of that strong religious leaven which
was first to build and then to subvert a Biblical commonwealth.

In July, 1629, John Winthrop, not yet even a member
present at any meeting of the Company, was riding with
his brother-in-law Downing to Semperingham to visit Isaac
Johnson to confer about the Massachusetts enterprise. To
his son John in London, just returned from foreign travel,
he communicates his thoughts about emigration. There
had been in circulation among a group of congenial friends
a certain very pregnant paper entitled "General Considerations for the Plantation of New England, with an Answer
to several Objections." This paper, to which reference
will be made in another connection, has a most vital relation to the enterprise in hand, and to what came of it. It
begins thus: "It will be a service to the Church of great
consequence to carry the Gospel into those parts of the
world." It complains that all the churches of Europe are
brought to desolation and calamities; there are troubles,
corruptions, decays of piety, disturbances, and threatenings of evil in England. Objections are orderly presented
and answered from Scripture, and largely Old Testament
authorities. To an objection drawn from the failure of
previous attempts at colonization, it is replied that their
"mayne end was carnall and not religious." Let note be
taken of the stress laid in the argument "to raise and
support a *particular* church," — repeated afterward thus:
"The service of raysinge and upholdinge a particular church
is to be preferred before the betteringe of some parte of a
church alreadye established." Here is certainly an intimation of — what afterward was so fully realized on this
soil — the views working in the minds of Winthrop and his
sympathizers as to the relations between the sort of church
which they had in mind and that to which they then belonged, which they believed needed "betteringe." The

authorship of this paper has by some been attributed to White, the Puritan rector of Dorchester. But the weight of evidence would seem to assign it to Winthrop, as found in its fullest form among his documents.

While the question of the transfer was pending before the Court, a most decisive step was taken to advance the projected enterprise of removal to New England. A meeting was held at Cambridge, Aug. 26, 1629, in which — undoubtedly preceded by full and earnest discussion — an agreement bearing twelve signatures was signed. This agreement is simple but positive in its terms. It was entered into by all " upon the joint confidence we have in each other's fidelity and resolution herein, so as no man of us would have adventured it without assurance of the rest." In order that each of those thus to be pledged, with others who may join them, " may without scruple dispose of his estate and affairs as may best fit his preparation for this voyage, it is fully and faithfully AGREED amongst us, and every one of us doth hereby freely and sincerely promise and bind himself, in the word of a Christian and in the presence of God," to be ready in person and family, with provisions, etc., to embark for the Plantation by the first of the next March at such port as the Company should agree upon, "to pass the Seas (under God's protection), to inhabit and continue in New England : Provided always, that before the last of September next the whole Government, together with the Patent for the said Plantation, be first, by an order of Court, legally transferred and established to remain with us and others which shall inhabit upon the said Plantation." A forfeit of £3 for every day's default is to be paid by each, except those detained by reason accepted by three-fourths of the signers.

Of the twelve names subscribed, John Winthrop's stands the ninth. Those of the others best known to us are Richard Saltonstall, Thomas Dudley, William Vassall, Isaac Johnson, John Humphrey, Increase Nowell, and

4

William Pynchon.[1] How much of negotiation, conference, correspondence, and balancing of reasons and arguments had been engaged in maturing this covenant we can well conceive, though it is known to us only fragmentarily. The conditions were exact, the decision summary. The legal transfer of government and patent; the parting with estates in England to meet the charges of emigration and the new settlement; the removal of families and the identification henceforward of life and hope and service with a spot in the wilderness beyond the dread ocean, — these were the chief terms of the covenant religiously entered into by men of lofty integrity and high and devout purpose. Each put his whole confidence in the possession of such qualities by his associates. It may be that our minds will revert to these conditions of sacrifice and obligation when further on in these pages we shall have to note the ingenuity, the persistency, and even the keen strategy by which they defended themselves against plotters to their harm in England and the harsh severity of their dealings with troublers within.

After the resolve for the transfer of the government there were immediate and marked changes in the membership of the Company, — a selling out of stock by some and a purchase by others. The name of John Winthrop appears for the first time on the records, Sept. 19, 1629. He was not then present at the meeting, but was named as on a committee for business of the Company. That the changes in membership and ownership of stock were largely due to the coming in of the serious and religious movements of the Company, by which those who had been wont to meet to discuss matters of traffic were coming under the spell of piety, is not a mere inference. At a meeting of the Court, Nov. 25, 1629, on motion of Mr. White, it was resolved —

" That this business might be proceeded in with the first intention, which was cheifly the glory of God, and to that purpose that their

---

[1] Life and Letters of John Winthrop, vol. i. pp. 344, 345.

meetings might bee sanctyfied by the prayers of some faithfull ministers resident heere in London, whose advice would bee likewise
requisite upon many occasion, the Court thought fitt to admitt
into the freedome of this Company Mr. Jo : Archer and Mr. Phil-
lip Nye, ministers heere in London, who being heere present kindly
accepted thereof.   Also Mr. Whyte did recommend unto them Mr.
Nathaniell Ward of Standon."

These ministers voted into the freedom of the Company
were earnest Puritan divines. And then and there, at a
meeting of the Company in London on the eve of its transfer hither, was initiated the sacred custom — ever since
perpetuated in what has succeeded to that Company as the
Colony, the Province, and the State of Massachusetts — of
opening the proceedings of its Legislature with prayer. Nor
only this, for in every rapidly multiplying municipality derived by authority of that parent Legislature, the same
usage has prevailed at the opening of town-meetings.

On August 29 the decision had been made by the Court
that the government of persons should be set up in New
England, while the government of trade was retained in
London. But this arrangement was compromised. Winthrop was present at the Court for the first time October
15 ; and on the 20th, as Cradock could not go to New
England, it was necessary to choose a new Governor. The
Court "having received extraordinary great commenda-
tions of Mr. John Winthrop, both for his integritie and suf-
ficiencie," his name was put in nomination, with those of
Saltonstall, Johnson, and Humphrey ; and "Mr. Winthrop
was, with a generall vote and full consent of this Court,
by erection of hands, chosen to bee Governor."

He wrote to his wife — as he afterward said in public
with modest dignity, — that he was taken by surprise, and
thought himself unequal to the high trust committed to
him. But the Court had judged wisely in their estimate of
the man, and his career and service for the score of years
yet left to him proved that for virtues and capacities, for

consecration of heart, and for the heroisms of patience and sacrifice, his election had a higher ratification. From the hour in which Winthrop assumed this leadership in labor and responsibility to the day of his embarkation, his cares and efforts were equally varied and exacting. There is enough extant of his correspondence at the time to show with what tender affection he wrote to members of his family when separated from them by his business and when preparing for parting with his wife and such of his children as he had to leave to follow after him; also, his letters widely scattered to enlist others in his enterprise, among them the humble and dependent as well as those needful as mechanics, engineers, and physicians, — indeed, to those of a wide and inclusive range, who were in sympathy with or could be inspired by his own motives. He was then forty-two years of age.

The fleet was to consist of eleven ships, and included the "Mayflower," whose fame was won ten years before. We must leave to our imagination to analyze and dispose the elements of character and qualities which marked individuals and classes in that company of two thousand souls. Care and caution had been exercised to the utmost possible extent in selecting healthful, honest, capable, and well-disposed persons; but what was needed and what had to be accepted were not correspondent terms. We shall doubtless be safe in surmising that there were less of the incongruous and mischievous elements of humanity gathered in that fleet than have ever before or since been massed together in enterprises that have lured men in flocks, — from the voyages of Columbus, through the early settlements of Virginia, down to the rushing swarms to the gold mines of California. Nor can we infer, except through the developments afterward realized here, what proportion of the whole company, below the rank of the most earnest and responsible leaders of the enterprise, were in full or partial sympathy with their aims. The

voyage began April 8, 1630.   Such reports as we have
of conduct and experience on board the vessels would indicate that it was without turbulence, with orderly and
serious observances.

Before the leaders of the Company sailed away, they had
left to be printed and circulated in England a document
which has been the subject of much critical discussion
among historians, and has been turned into matter of
grave censure against Winthrop and his associates.   The
ground of this censure is, that the professions of tender
and affectionate attachment and gratitude to the Church
of England expressed in the document, were strangely inconsistent with, and utterly slighted by, the course which
the signers at once adopted in the church-method instituted and administered by them on their arrival here.
The reflection cast upon them has not stopped short of the
charge of insincerity and hypocrisy.   We must seek to
throw such light on the matter as a dispassionate statement of the facts will admit, with such comments as may
suggest themselves.   The paper is entitled, —

" The Humble Request of His Majesty's Loyall Subjects, the
Governor and the Company late gone for New-England, to the
rest of their Brethren in and of the Church of England, for
the obtaining of their Prayers, and the removal of suspicions and
misconstructions of their Intentions."

It may be remarked, in passing, that the publication and
free circulation of this paper disposes effectually of the absurd charge that the Company, with such a fleet on such
an enterprise, stole away covertly from England.   The
paper is addressed, " Reverend Fathers and Brethren," and
it proceeds upon the general rumor and knowledge of their
enterprise as a reason for asking prayers and blessings
upon it.   It seems to me, after the full thought and study
which I have given to the various bearings of the subject,
that we may wisely begin here to recognize the fact — to

be further on more fully illustrated·— that Winthrop's
Company, like the other Nonconformists, made a distinction between certain prime elements and qualities and certain secondary matters in the institution and administration of the Church of England, to some of which they were
heartily attached, while with others they were not in sympathy.   And further, that the Nonconformists regarded
those essentials to which they clung as infinitely tran-
scending those incidental features which they rejected
in their relations to the ends of religion and piety.   However this may have been, the candid reader must judge
when he reviews the facts and professions to be soon set
forth, not as a plea, but as an historical summary.   The
most emphatic statement in the paper before us is as
follows : —

"And howsoever your charity may have met with some occasion of discouragement through the misreport of our intentions,
or through the disaffection or indiscretion of some of us, or
rather amongst us (for we are not of those that dream of perfection in this world), yet we desire you would be pleased to take
notice of the principals and body of our Company, as those who
esteem it our honour to call the Church of England, from whence
we rise, our dear mother, and cannot part from our native Country, where she specially resideth, without much sadness of heart
and many tears in our eyes, ever acknowledging that such hope
and part as we have obtained in the common salvation we have
received in her bosom and sucked it from her breasts.   We leave
it not, therefore, as loathing that milk wherewith we were nourished there; but blessing God for the parentage and education, as
members of the same body, shall always rejoice in her good and
unfeignedly grieve for any sorrow that shall ever betide her, and
while we have breath sincerely desire and endeavour the continuance and abundance of her welfare, with the enlargement of her
bounds in the Kingdom of Christ Jesus."

There is a sentence in this Address which does not
appear to have engaged the attention of some who have

most severely judged the signers of it, — the leaders of the Company. It is this: "If any there be who through want of clear intelligence of our course, or tenderness of affection towards us, cannot conceive so well of our way as we could desire," etc. They then had "a way" of their own; and this may have had some relation to that idea of "a particular church," referred to on a previous page in the "Considerations."

It is not out of place here to interrupt the course of comment on this language used by the exiles touching their feelings and relations to the Church of England, by quoting a similar expression of those in religious sympathy with them. The Rev. Francis Higginson, a graduate of St. John's College, Cambridge, while settled at Leicester became a Puritan, and on account of his scruples declined many attractive livings offered him under the Establishment. He had been invited by the Bay Company in 1628 to go in its service as minister to the preparatory settlement at Salem. Dreading a summons before the High Commission Court, he accepted, and arrived at Salem, June 29, 1629. On his passage hither, as he left the shores of England, he called his family and other passengers around him, and said: —

"We will not say, Farewell Babylon! Farewell Rome! but we will say, Farewell dear England! Farewell the Church of God in England, and all the Christian friends there! We do not go to New England as Separatists from the Church of England, though we cannot but separate from the corruptions in it; but we go to practise the positive part of the Church reformation, and to propagate the Gospel in America." [1]

The voyage of Winthrop hither, begun April 8, 1630, was closed on June 22. Frequent and constant religious exercises of catechism, prayer, and preaching on Sundays and week-days must have equally tried the patience of

[1] Mather's Magnalia, book iii. p. 74.

mariners and servants, and fed the joys of piety in the consecrated hearts of the exiles. One is left to infer that they did not follow the forms of the Liturgy. Higginson, the minister at Salem, who as just noted came over the preceding year, tells us in his Journal that his ship's company marked their watches "with singing a psalm, and prayer that was not read out of a book." [1]

Among the papers of Winthrop was found one entitled "A Modell of Christian Charity," written on the ocean on board the "Arbella." As he was wont "to exercise in the way of prophesying," it was doubtless made by him to serve the use of a sermon. It is in a strain of gentle and elevated piety; and while it confirms all our estimate of the sweetness and nobleness of his spirit, it reveals most significantly his own strengthening conception of the religious intent of his enterprise. The paper is crowded with Scripture references. If the careful and candid study of our history leave any of its readers in doubt as to whether the religious and Biblical character of the Commonwealth here established was intended from the first conception of it, this paper should help the decision. Winthrop wrote : —

"The work we have in hand is by a mutuall consent, through a special overvaluing providence and a more than an ordinary approbation of the Churches of Christ, to seek out a place of cohabitation and Consorteshipp under a due forme of Government, both civill and ecclesiasticall. In such cases as this, the care of the publique must oversway all private respects. . . . Thus stands the cause between God and us. We are entered into covenant with Him for this worke. We have taken out a commission. The Lord hath given us leave to drawe our own articles. We have professed to enterprise these and those accounts upon these and those ends. We have hereupon besought Him of favour and blessing. Now if the Lord shall please to heare us, and bring us

---

[1] Young's Chronicles of Massachusetts, p. 237.

in peace to the place we desire, then hath hee ratified this covenant and sealed our Commission, and will expect a strict performance of the articles contained in it." [1]

We certainly can be at no loss to discover what was the
master motive of Winthrop in his enterprise, nor to conceive what sort of a Church and State he had in view.
He believed that his Company had entered on a covenant
with each other which was at the same time a Covenant
with God : constancy and fidelity exhibited in mutual
love were the terms pledged.   The enterprise demanded
resolution of spirit, for it was hazardous, and might end
in disaster ; but he would abide by it.   He never looked
backward ; he never saw his native land again.   Twelve
years after the arrival here, at a crisis of discouragement,
very many of his associates, under the same pledges as
himself, went back to England, or to more promising
scenes.   Winthrop's plaint in his Journal [2] over this defection is pointed in rebuke of them, but of noble manli-
ness as to his own constancy.   " Ask thy conscience if
thou wouldst have plucked up thy stakes and brought thy
family three thousand miles if thou hadst expected that
all, or most, would have forsaken thee there."

Bearing in mind the expressions of tender attachment
to the Church of England with which the leaders of the
Company had parted from their native land, we wait with
interest for information on the proceedings and measures
first adopted on this foreign shore in church institution,
communion, and worship.   That information is full as to results, which, however, were of so marked and unlooked for
a character as to lead us to believe that they were preceded
by some deliberation and discussion, — possibly some variance of opinion.   But of this we know nothing.   So far
as appears from the record, the proceedings and conclu-

[1] The whole sermon is printed in Mass. Hist. Coll., 3d Series, vol. vii.
pp. 33–48.
[2] Vol. ii. p. 87.

sions were all spontaneous and harmonious. While they naturally cause more or less surprise to all who have traced with care the history developed to this point, they have excited much severity of criticism and censure, as not only done without any recognition of " the ways " of the Church of England, but so as effectually to initiate a breach and rupture with it.

Gathered under a tree, or within the fresh rude timbers of the " Great House " built in Charlestown for the miscellaneous uses of defence, storage, and meetings, the leaders of the Company had " set apart the 30th of July, 1630, as a day of fasting and prayer." After religious exercises, Governor Winthrop, Deputy-Governor Dudley, Mr. Isaac Johnson, and Mr. John Wilson, " with many others, both men and women," put their names to the following Covenant : —

" In the Name of our Lord Jesus Christ, and in Obedience to His holy will and Divine Ordinance, —

" Wee whose names are hereunder written, being by His most wise and good Providence brought together into this part of America in the Bay of Massachusetts, and desirous to unite ourselves into one Congregation, or Church, under the Lord Jesus Christ our Head, in such sort as becometh all those whom He hath Redeemed and Sanctifyed to Himselfe, do hereby solemnly and religiously (as in His most holy Proesence) Promisse and bind ourselves to walke in all our wayes according to the Rule of the Gospell, and in all sincere Conformity to His holy Ordinannces, and in mutuall love and respect each to other, so neere as God shall give us grace."

The completion of their church proceedings, which was not made till the 27th of August, is thus related by Winthrop : [1] —

" We of the congregation kept a fast, and chose Mr. Wilson our teacher, and Mr. Nowell an elder, and Mr. Gager and Mr. Aspinwall,

[1] Vol. i. p. 31.

deacons. We used imposition of hands, but with this protestation by all, that it was only a sign of election and confirmation, not of any intent that Mr. Wilson should renounce his ministry he received in England."

The points to be specially noted in these proceedings are that " conformity " is pledged to Christ, not to the Church of England, and that the words " elder " and " deacon " are used in a sense unknown to that Church. These points will call for further notice. Substantially the same method of church organization had been previously recognized in Plymouth and in Salem ; but it is the more significant here, as having the authority and sanction of the responsible leaders of the Bay Company. Whether so intended or not, it proved to be the initiation of a mode of church institution alienated from and not in accord with the Church of England ; as such it became the model to be copied in the thousands of Congregational churches which cover the land. This alienation of the Boston church from the Church of England had been significantly anticipated a year previous in the setting up of the church in Salem. When this was gathered, under the Congregational form, two brothers, John and Samuel Browne, — men much honored by their associates as members of the Council, — taking offence at the disuse of the Common Prayer and the ceremonies, at once put them to service in a small congregation made up of those who were in sympathy with them. Endicott for this offence summoned the Brownes before the Council. The brothers pronounced the minis-ters Separatists, and likely to become Anabaptists. Endicott told them that New England was not a fit place for them, and they were summarily sent back to England. This measure of high-handed authority seemed to settle the point that the colony was to be one of Nonconformists. Mr. Doyle[1] says : —

---

[1] The English in America, i. 129.

"If the colony was to become what its promoters intended, unity, not merely of religious belief, but of ritual and of ecclesiastical discipline, was, at least for the present, a needful condition of existence. We must not condemn the banishment of the Brownes unless we are prepared to say that it would have been better for the world if the Puritan colony of Massachusetts had never existed."

We shall see further on that the Boston church would not, when challenged to do so, renounce its communion with the Church of England, nor express its penitence for having been in its fold. But by its own act it was cut off from recognition by that mother church. Its ways from its beginning were in accordance with the Nonconformity professed by its members; its usages were at once and continuously distinctive. The liturgy, the read prayers, the responsive services, days of observance other than the Sabbath, the official relation of the minister, were all dispensed with. This pattern for a New England church was of course regarded as exactly set by Scripture, and variances from it were unscriptural. Strangely enough, it was to come about in from fifty to sixty years,—when habit and usage and the coming upon the stage of a new generation had made this New England pattern traditional, and civil law had conferred on it the privilege and dignity of an Establishment,—that when the old mother church presented itself here for recognition it was regarded not only as a stranger, but as a trespasser and intruder, unwelcome and odious. Yet the fathers had expressed to it their yearning love and gratitude; Winthrop and his associates had never renounced its communion in England, though there is evidence that they had sought religious sympathy and nourishment in independent services of conference and prayer. Still, as already noticed, the spontaneity and harmony with which they entered into their innovating ways,—without, as we can discover, any variance or opposition,—would seem to indicate some previous mutual understanding of plan and purpose before leaving England. It has been suggested that under the circumstances of the exile the Congregational institution and discipline was a matter of exigency and necessity. But this does not appear ; for the first ten pastors here had been Episcopally ordained. The Book of Common Prayer might have been obtained as easily as the Bible. They might have chosen vestrymen, wardens, and a clerk; they might have set up an altar and a rail; they might have followed the Scripture lessons orderly. There was nothing here in soil, climate, or physical condition to hinder but that Englishmen might have brought hither their sacred forms and usages, had they wished to do so. Had they wished to do so : but they evidently did not. Unless, therefore, one is prepared to say that the professions of attachment and gratitude with which they parted from the Church in their native land, when followed by the course at once adopted here, indicate artifice, insincerity, and hypocrisy, he must seek for a reconciling explanation.

Winthrop makes a significant entry in his Journal [1] within three years after his arrival here. Referring to a hearing before the Council in England of some friends of the Colony in answer to some complaints by its enemies, he writes that " the defendants were dismissed with a favorable order for their encouragement, being assured from some of the Council that his Majesty did not intend to impose the ceremonies of the Church of England upon us ; for that it was considered that it was the freedom from such things that made people come over to us."

Here it may be that we find relief in the perplexity before us. Nonconformists might be fond of their lineage through the Church of England and express their attachment to it, because they distinguished broadly between what was vital to its being, the divine essentials of its life and power, and certain unessential, indifferent, and even injurious elements

[1] Vol. i. p. 103.

in its discipline, organization, and administration. The Scriptures and the Faith were the essentials. The Puritans revered the Scriptures, and held the doctrinal belief of the Thirty-nine Articles more rigidly than did many of those who did not share their scruples. It is for such as so believe to maintain that the glory of the Church of England consists in the ceremonial and forms which distinguish it from other churches rather than in its inheritance and enjoyment of the Scriptures and the Gospel of Jesus Christ. The Puritans did not so believe. This will appear as we now proceed to set forth the principles of their nonconformity. Higginson, in the words of his already quoted, has clearly intimated the difference, well understood at the time, between " Separatists " and " Nonconformists."

III.

THE NONCONFORMISTS AND THE CHURCH
OF ENGLAND.

As the two terms "Nonconformists" and "Separatists" were found necessary to express the different relations of parties toward the English Church after its rupture with Rome, the difference between their meaning and use must be clearly drawn. The term "Separatist" carried its own explanation with it. It described those who put themselves wholly outside of the ecclesiastical fold, renouncing membership, and assuming toward it an attitude of repugnance, with more or less of active hostility to it. Of these were the congregations which left England for Holland and other parts of the Continent, and one of which came to Plymouth. The Nonconformists did not wish or intend to sever themselves from the English Church, nor to remain in it as internal enemies, but rather as its warm and faithful members. An attempt will soon be made to define their views and wishes. Here it may be said in general, that, in adhering to the Church and shrinking from renouncing their heritage in it, they put themselves in an attitude of distinguishing between certain of its elements and others, some of which they approved, others of which troubled their consciences. This attitude of theirs was somewhat similar to that of a man who allows himself to be ranked in a great political party, yet disapproves of and will not comply with some of its measures or tactics; or, as one may mingle in the social life around him, and yet object — even to eccentricity — to some of its standards or customs. The point before us is to explain — if any one thinks an explanation worth the while — how Winthrop and his Company, after leaving England with such warm professions of attachment to the mother church, should immediately on reaching their new home institute " a particular church " of their own, so unlike it and so independent of it as effectually to sever themselves and their posterity from its communion. And further, we must keep in view the fact that under the novel church institution in which they had placed themselves, they stoutly refused, when challenged to do so, to renounce their mother church and express penitence for having communed with it.

I will try to put to service the fruits of some considerable study which I have given to this period and subject of history, with the purpose of stating as impartially as I may the case of the Puritans, simply, however, as an expositor, not as its champion. The positions to be taken and the arguments to be set forth are theirs, — the measure of my own approval of or sympathy with them is a wholly irrelevant matter here.

If at this present time there were no " dissenters " in England, and if the Established Church, thoroughly organized and settled in its government and administration, were peacefully and harmoniously pursuing its work, there should start forth within its fold a considerable body of men to impugn or assail it, raising division and discord, we might well look to them to give us reasons and grounds of great weight and of manifest urgency to justify them in their course. They might be able, under the circumstances supposed, to vindicate themselves in the judgment of fair-minded persons by offering sufficient, or if but seeming, warrant for their course; for all human organizations and institutions are open to inquisition, review, and readjustment. But if these critics and dissentients should show themselves as moved simply by a restless and factious spirit to breed discord where there was peace, and could offer for their justification only perverse and inflammatory complaints, imaginary grievances, angry objections to things "indifferent," trivial scruples and crotchets engendered in their own conceits, they might expect to draw upon themselves not only the censure and disapprobation of good men, but even some forms of a severer retribution.

Now, there are in print countless volumes and pamphlets, dating soon after the Reformation in England and coming down to our own time, which represent the Nonconformists and the Puritans in general as not only pursuing the course described in the former of these suppositions, but as adding to it all that is perverse and odious in the latter. The fact that the Puritan party not only failed to secure a triumph for its own principles, but also suffered humiliation in its defeat, is used as reflecting back upon it a just judgment for its factiousness and unreasonable antagonism.

The description given of the English Nonconformists in many pages that stand for history, is as follows : That they started forth under a well-settled order of constitution and discipline in the Church of England, which had the general assent and approval of the mass of the people of the realm, and factiously fomented variance and discord with a contentious and malignant spirit, working themselves into a morbid activity of conscience which, while rendering them disagreeable to others, proved them to be without reason, judgment, and true Christian sentiment.

How wide of the truth, how grievously erroneous, and how false to all the verities of the case this representation of the principles and course of the Puritans is, will appear from a simple statement of the well attested facts of history. This view of the Puritans as introducing strife and discord in a well-settled order in the Church, and of urging factious and perverse methods, whims, and scruples in things indifferent under the plea of advancing a pure reformation, proceeds upon two assumptions. First, that when the Puri-

tans present themselves actively and earnestly within the
fold of the English Church, its constitution and organization
were well settled, its order and discipline were satisfactory
to the people of the realm, and its sacred offices were in
peaceful administration. The second assumption is, that
after the rupture with Rome called the Reformation, a
standard had been recognized as fixed in reason and the
nature of things for deciding at once the compass, range,
and details of the changes to be made in the organization,
discipline, ritual, and worship of the renewed Church, —
as to what in the Roman heritage was to be retained and
honored, and what was to be repudiated and disused. How
utterly opposed these bold assumptions are to historic
truth, will reveal itself to any one who reads any ten out
of the thousands of the volumes upon the subject which
have claims to our trusty perusal.

What date in the period of the opening and vigorous
prosecution of the English Reformation will any one venture to fix upon as marking the condition of settled order,
and, but for the factious spirit of the Puritans, of quietude
in the English Church? Let him run through the whole
period covered by the reigns of Henry VIII. and of his
three children, — Edward, Mary, and Elizabeth, — and of
the four Stuart kings. Through that whole space of time
the Church was, to use the mildest term for description,
unsettled, in process of reconstruction and of internal and
external organization and pacification.

The reign of Henry VIII. found the Pope of Rome the
head of the Church of England, with more of power and
rule in the realm than had its sovereign. His spiritual
authority had become so mixed and so transcendent in
secular affairs as to be undistinguishable from a temporal
sway. He was the head of a hierarchy, which in its gradations and orders gathered all classes, ranks, and estates
of the people, from the monarch and nobility down to the
peasant, into subordination to it. Every ecclesiastic in the

realm — cardinal, prelate, abbot, rector, monk, and friar — received commission from and owed allegiance to him. The Pope through his ministers constituting the Church, apart from its lay membership, was the largest landholder in the kingdom, holding by the dead hand, in *mortmain*, enormous endowments for religion, education, and charity. The Pope could put the kingdom under interdict, and absolve all the King's subjects from their allegiance. The quarrel of the King with the Pope, on personal grounds, led the monarch to deny and renounce the Pope as the head of the English Church, and to claim that prerogative for himself. This was the whole of the work of Reformation effected by the King; in all else he lived and died a good Roman Catholic.

But what of the Church of England in this crisis, with only a change from an ecclesiastical to a lay headship? The Church bearing the name of Christ had grown, been developed, or evolved from the simplicity of its primitive institution to a towering and grasping dominancy over its willing and unwilling discipleship. If one should say to us that the Church of St. Peter in Rome "was built by God," we should understand him as so affirming because God furnished the materials and endowed the human skill that reared the structure. And this would not make us oblivious of the fact that unconsecrated stones from heathen edifices had been built into the walls, that fables and falsehoods entered into its symbolism, and that artifice, greed, extortion, rapacity, and fraud in the traffic of "Indulgences" had furnished the funds for an enormous outlay. In much the same way, one who is not in the communion of the Papal Church regards its claims to a divine origin and authority. He knows from what original and germ it started, and the method of its growth, accretion, and claim to supreme authority in spiritual things, and, so far as it pleases, to extend the compass of the spiritual, in temporal things. It requires no great profundity

of scholarship in ancient lore for an inquirer to trace the
processes of corruption, fraud, ingenuity, the artful use of
opportunities, forged documents, towering ambitions, and
an adroit playing upon human credulities and weaknesses
by which the Papal Church gathered to it, and then assimilated, the elements and methods of its thrall over men.
The power and skill of organization, through multiplied
and graded representatives of its unity, explain to us the
secret of its marvellous and stupendous sway.   It has
wrought into its ecclesiastical fabric the noblest and the
meanest materials ; its discipleship has included saints
and devils, and it has been served by both of them.
Lordly prelates, puffed with ambition, intrigue, and sensuality, have been its statesmen ; men of the loftiest zeal
and the humblest spirit in its service have been its missionaries ; and women of meek and all self-sacrificing graces
and virtues have been the ministers of its holy charities.
As we study that Church in the contrasted aspects which
it presents in history and in life, we are moved to affirm
that there is nothing too good to be said of it, and nothing
too bad to be said of it.   But when the papal head of the
Church of England had been repudiated and displaced, the
Church itself was left under the organization and administration, discipline and ceremonial, to which many centuries
of authority and obedience had trained the people of the
realm.   The problem now presented was, what was to be
done with a papal church deprived of its papal head ?
Henry VIII. opened that problem, and left it to be disposed of by his royal successors through the reigns already
mentioned.   During a large part of that period the question whether the Reformation itself should abide, should
advance or recede, depended upon the education which
the successive sovereigns had received, and whether they
would uphold the old church or the new.   Roman Catholics and Protestants took turns at roasting at the stake,
and at being committed to the Tower, the prisons, and the

headsman's axe. Will any one fix for us the date when
the present established Church of England came into existence, and had finally settled its constitution and order?
The Books of Homilies adopted by that Church in the
reigns of Edward VI. and Elizabeth, were ordered to be
read in every church in the kingdom. The "Homily
against the Peril of Idolatry" pronounces this judgment
upon the Roman Church, under which the kingdom had
previously been in obedience: "Laity and clergy, learned
and unlearned, all ages, sects, and degrees of men, women,
and children of the whole of Christendom, had been at
once drowned in abominable idolatry, and that for the
space of eight hundred years and more." Here certainly
was a good start and reason for reform. But so vacillating and inconstant was the work as it went on for a
century that the statement often repeated by Roman
Catholic writers is substantially true, — that the English
Parliament, or Convocation, has alternately approved and
repudiated such Roman doctrines and usages as Transubstantiation, Invocation of the Saints, Extreme Unction,
Prayers for the Dead, and Auricular Confession. In 1559
the Mass was pronounced to be "a blessed privilege," and
in 1632 it was condemned as "a blasphemous fable." In
1534 Parliament denied that the Pope had rightful jurisdiction in England; but two years afterward the Convocation at York affirmed that "the King's Highness, nor
any temporal man, may not be the head of the Church by
the laws of God," and that "the Pope of Rome hath been
taken for the head of the Church and Vicar of Christ, and
so ought to be taken." [1] Eighteen years afterward this
judgment was condemned, and the King was substituted
for the Pope as the head of the Church. In 1559 the ball
was thrown to and fro. Both houses of Convocation asserted the Pope's supremacy; Parliament denied it, and
gave the Queen the headship. The royal head of the

[1] Strype's Ecclesiastical Memorials, vol. i. part ii. pp. 266, 267.

Church promulgated successively the two following opposite doctrines; namely, in 1537, this : —

"As touching the sacrament of the altar, we will that all bishops and preachers shall instruct and teach our people committed
by us unto their spiritual charge, that they ought, and must, constantly believe that under the form and figure of bread and wine,
which we there presently do see and perceive by our outward
senses, is verily, substantially, and really contained and compre-
hended the very self-same body and blood of our Saviour Jesus
Christ, which was born of the Virgin Mary and suffered upon the
cross for our redemption; and that under the same form and figure
of bread and wine the very self-same body and blood of Christ is
corporally, really, and in the very substance exhibited, distributed,
and received of all them which receive the same sacrament."

And this in the Articles of 1552 : —

"Transubstantiation (or the change of the substance of bread
and wine), in the Supper of the Lord, cannot be proved from
Holy Writ; but it is repugnant to the plain words of Scripture, and hath given occasion to many superstitions. . . . And
since (as the Holy Scriptures testify) Christ hath been taken up
into heaven, and there is to abide till the end of the world, it
becometh not any of the faithful to believe or profess that there
is a real or corporal presence (as they phrase it) of the body and
blood of Christ in the holy eucharist. The sacrament of the
Lord's Supper was not, by Christ's ordinance, reserved, carried
about, lifted up, or worshipped."

Bishop Burnet, an historian of the Reformation, tells us
of a kindly attempt to allow a free choice between these
two beliefs : —

"In 1559 it was proposed to have the communion-book so contrived that it might not exclude the belief of the corporal presence; for the chief design of the Queen's Council was to unite
the nation in one faith, and the greatest part of the nation continued to believe such a presence." [1]

[1] History of the Reformation, p. 573.

On one point only was Elizabeth decided and positively fixed; that was the fundamental principle of the Reformation, the denial of any rightful exercise of the papal power within her realm. She was tolerant of some of the principles and practices of the Papacy which had so long held sway in some of the details of government, and which were not readily to be discredited for the mass of her subjects. Her policy was shrewd and artful. There were Catholic sovereigns and princes whom she had either to conciliate or to render impotent in any measures they might attempt for strengthening the papal power against her. The diplomacy of her reign, as it has been revealed to us in State Papers, is a most marvellous disclosure of crooked intrigues and wily ingenuities, with tricks of falsehood which baffle all attempts at classification.

When the first act was done in the work of reform in the English Church, even the wisest in the realm could have had but the faintest apprehension of the scope and substance of the revolution that was to be wrought. Under Romanism an elaborate and highly artificial ceremonial had engaged the senses and sentiments of the people, leaving thought and intellect at rest. The Lord's Supper, from what we read of it in the New Testament, where the gathered disciples remembered their Master " in the breaking of bread," had become — as one may regard it, either an august or a deceiving ceremonial — an altar-service by the priest, with symbols, incense, robings, gestures, genuflections, and adorations, the wafer serving as an amulet or a charm. Baptism, with its consecrated water and its chrism, was an exorcising spell. The mendicant orders — filthy and covered with vermin — infested the highways and by-ways, the village purlieus, market-places, and hostelries. The land was skinned and plundered for Peter's pence. Fees and exactions were extorted for every incident and experience of life; the humblest hut or cottage could not be occupied till by ghostly exorcism the Devil had been warned out of it. Birth, baptism, the churching of mothers, confirmation, confession, communion were assessed by a scale of fees. Even death did not secure a release from these priestly extortions; for not even the saintliest soul, as it parted with the body, went direct to heaven, but was delayed in the limbo of Purgatory, needing altar masses for its release. And as in the transition from time to eternity dates and periods are immeasurable, and it was impossible to know when a soul had been prayed out of the half-way house, it was but a measure of prudence to provide for " perpetual masses."

From the complete and ubiquitous oversight and sway of this system in belief, usage, and authority, it was the ultimate end of the Reformation to secure deliverance for all who would avail of it. In place of it was to come an intense activity of such intellectual force as each individual might possess, a craving for instruction, an illumination and direction of conscience by divine guidance, a rejection of sacerdotal mediation, and a reliance upon reason. It was a process of slow and lengthened stages. Where was this exercise of independent thought and reason to be trammelled or arrested? The full, complete claim of ecclesiastical authority being repudiated, how could a portion or fragment of it be reclaimed? How could Protestantism in its development recognize a natural or artificial bound for its free activity? Those who would have us believe that the work and standard for the Reformation were settled at the start are blind to what they will not see.

These are but fragmentary tokens — they might be indefinitely multiplied — of the distractions of that formative period of the English Church alternating between the old and the new order, into whose alleged composure and tranquillity the Puritans are charged with introducing strife and discord. And who were these Puritans? They constituted fully one-half of the most sincere, scholarly, learned, high-minded, and every way noble men among the reformers of

England. They were heads and professors in her universities, eminent divines in her pulpits, exiles on the Continent during the vacillations of Henry VIII. and the martyrdoms under Mary. They initiated the very first processes of the Reformation, and were the most constant, consistent, and resolute adherents to and advancers of it. More than once in the alternations and developments of the protracted strife, the mastery in the direction of affairs seemed as if it would find them in the majority. In the developments of the long and bitter conflict between the Puritans and the Conformists, some heated, factious, and unreasonable spirits did indeed aggravate the contention about the original, fundamental, and wholly pertinent principles which were in conflict. But these principles were worthy of and gave dignity to the noble, earnest scholars, divines, and statesmen who, as composing the leaders of the Puritans, aimed for a thorough and consistent reformation and reconstruction of the Church.

Macaulay[1] thus states the views of some prelates, none of whom " belonged to the extreme section of the Protestant party " : —

" Many felt a strong repugnance even to things indifferent, which had formed part of the polity or ritual of the mystical Babylon. Bishop Hooper, who died manfully at Gloucester for his religion, long refused to wear the episcopal vestments. Bishop Ridley, a martyr of still greater renown, pulled down the ancient altars of his diocese, and ordered the eucharist to be administered in the middle of churches, at tables which the Papists irreverently termed ' oyster-boards.' Bishop Jewel pronounced the clerical garb to be a stage dress, a fool's coat, a relic of the Amorites, and promised that he would spare no labor to extirpate such degrading absurdities. Archbishop Grindal long hesitated about accepting a mitre from dislike of what he regarded as the mummery of consecration. Bishop Parkhurst uttered a fervent prayer that the Church of England would propose to herself the Church of Zurich as the

---

[1] History of England, chap. i.

absolute pattern of a Christian community. Bishop Ponet was of opinion that the word 'bishop' should be abandoned to the Papists, and that the chief officers of the purified church should be called 'superintendents.' Cranmer, indeed, plainly avowed his conviction that in the primitive times there was no distinction between bishops and priests, and that the laying on of hands was altogether unnecessary."

Roger Williams [1] in his quaint style presents the oscillations of the Church of England in its efforts to find an equilibrium : —

"To seeke no further than our *native* Soyle, within a few scores of years how many wonderfull *changes* in *Religion* hath the *whole Kingdome* made, according to the *change* of the *Governours* thereof in the severall *Religions* which they themselves imbraced! *Henry* the 7 finds and leaves the *Kingdome* absolutely *Popish. Henry* the 8 casts it into a *mould* half *Popish,* halfe *Protestant. Edward* the 6 brings forth an *Edition* all *Protestant.* Queen *Mary* within a few yeares defaceth *Edward's* worke, and renders the *Kingdome* (after her Grandfather Hen. 7 his pattern) all *Popish. Maries* short *life* and *Religion* ends together ; and *Elizabeth* reviveth her Brother *Edward's* Modell — all Protestant. And some eminent *Witnesses* of God's Truth against *Anti-Christ* have enclined to believe that before the downfall of that Beast, England must once againe bow down her faire Neck to his proud usurping yoake and foot."

It is idle to regard the work and crisis of the Reformation in the English Church as if it were assignable to a date in time, or to any decisive step or measure. It was a work of degrees, stages, and methods, running through several reigns, — not continuous in them, — and with retrogressive as well as with resisted and repressive incidents. Henry VIII., though regarded as taking the lead in it, can be called a " religious reformer " only under serious qualifications of the phrase as we use it. He was a political reformer, in that he extinguished the thraldom of the Papacy

---

[1] Bloody Tenent (Narragansett Club ed.), pp. 136-137.

in its claim to supreme authority in the realm in ecclesiastical affairs and in appointments to all benefices, and that he cut off the greedy revenue — at times exceeding the royal revenue — which the Popes had extorted from the King's subjects.   He was a social reformer, in that he had broken up many of those vile dens called "religious houses." But no change was made by him in the doctrine, ritual, or discipline of the Church during his reign.   Save that he was not a Papist, he was no heretic, but lived and died, as before stated, a good Roman Catholic.   The extinction of the Papal dominancy in the realm was indeed the primary and signal act of the Reformation, from which all else followed.   Henry might at any time have made his peace with the Pope, and been left free for a vast deal of purifying and revolutionary and reconstructing work, simply by yielding his headship of the English Church to the Bishop of Rome.   And many years afterward when the work of reform had greatly advanced, though the Pope had declared Elizabeth to be illegitimate, and had denied her hereditary right to the crown, he offered to retract his judgment and sentence, and to allow her subjects the use of the English liturgy, if she would reinstate him in his old authority.[1]

One can but marvel at what we may call the versatility of the English people, their easy and amiable way of accommodating themselves to the rapid changes, the advances and the arrests of the work of reform during the successive reigns.   A few prominent in station, or bold and unquailing in standing for personal convictions, paid the penalty of the prison, the gibbet, or the stake ; but the mass of the people moved as do the flowing and the ebbing tides. After the six years of the reforming reign of Edward VI., the Papacy resumed its sway under the brief and bloody rule of Mary, and the majority of Edward's bishops and clergy turned with the tide.   But the Pope, during the brief resumption of his authority, had had the satisfaction in the

[1] Sharon Turner, Modern History of England, vol. iv. p. 165.

four years of Mary's reign of burning the first reformed
Archbishop of Canterbury and three reformed bishops, and
of putting to death other victims, two hundred and seventy-
seven in number. When Elizabeth came to the throne the
number of ecclesiastics in the realm, all nominally Roman
Catholics, was nine thousand and four hundred. All of
these, except about two hundred, freely and uncompelled
transferred their allegiance to the Queen, peacefully enjoyed their benefices, and used the new English forms of
service and worship in the very places where they had just
been celebrating the Mass.

And now as to that supposed standard to be found in the
reason and nature of things for marking the extent and
thoroughness of the reform to be instituted in the organization, discipline, and ritual of the Church. Was there such
a standard? Could such be found; and if so, should it be
assumed, even though by a majority, as in itself so just
and reasonable, so suited to advance the ends of piety and
morality in the realm, as to warrant its legal establishment
and enforcement?

Among the various schools and parties included more
or less tolerantly in the Church of England, has been a
class of men who have thought it to be wise and true to
minimize the extent and nature of the dominancy of the
Papacy in England at the period of the Reformation. They
maintain that an English Church, with an all but complete autonomy, existed in the realm, with its own organization and means of independent administration, which had
been gradually encroached upon, impaired, and tyrannously
brought under the sway of Rome. Nothing, therefore, was
needed but to renounce that foreign usurpation, to deny the
headship of the Pope, to respond to his interdict by despising it, and to resume the original ecclesiastical order and
system which Rome had temporarily perverted.

There is an easy plausibility in this assumption. But
how does it stand in view of the strife, the alternating

fortunes, the royal and parliamentary measures, the controversies and persecutions through which the present English Establishment was substituted for the old Church of the realm? By no means during the age of the Reformation, either in England or on the Continent, were the whole import and consequences of it realized. It has taken the succession of many generations, developments of experiment, thought, and opinion, and dynastic and political convulsions and revolutions, to draw out the full results of the substitution of individualism in the whole field of religion for mediævalism and the sway of a priesthood. And Puritanism in its various stages and methods has been the continuous force and agency for working that stupendous process. The effort has been to open for free investigation, to discredit and make impotent, every dogma, assumption, and institution which has wrongfully and tyrannously brought men under intellectual, spiritual, and ecclesiastical bondage, and to verify and give free course to substantial and wholesome truths that can win the convictions of intelligent minds, and conserve all the transcendent interests of social, civil, political, domestic, and private life.

Even the Puritans saw but a tract of the long way before them in which their principles would find a development; but they recognized clearly that part of it on which they were to advance, and they were resolute in following it. They did not take that complacent view of the Church into which they were born, — that all that it needed of reform was to substitute their own lay king for a papal ecclesiastic as its head. The Church of Christ which was so dear to them, and which claimed their whole love and service, had an invisible head in Him, and no vicegerent could represent Him on the earth. It gives definiteness and force to the general and comprehensive position on which the Puritans planted themselves, to assert of them that their nonconformity consisted in this, — that everything of doc-

trine, hierarchy, institution, and discipline in the Church
of England to which they objected and which they renounced, had come into it as corruption and imposition
from the dominancy of the Papacy. All their fellow-sub-
jects of the realm who sympathized with the Reformation
became in fact Nonconformists. That this name and the
position which it defined should have come to be restricted
to the Puritans, simply indicated an arrest in the process
of the Reformation.

In the reconstruction of the reformed Church of England
as a substitute for the Papal Church, an alternative presented itself to statesmen and ecclesiastics, and the choice
which decided between the two methods which were offered settled from that time to this the relations between
conformity and nonconformity. Those statesmen and ecclesiastics, for reasons which had a prevailing weight with
them, chose a method of compromise and eclecticism. They
wished to conserve some of the elements of the hierarchical
and ceremonial system of the Papal Church, — not, however, because inherited from that Church, but upon other
grounds for approving them. In deference to the prime
authority of the Scriptures, they affirmed that nothing was
to be enjoined or imposed for belief or practice but what
could be deduced from those Scriptures, or proved to be
not inconsistent with their teachings. Thus a range of
liberty was left in instituting the reformed Church for the
adoption of certain practices and usages of the "primitive"
Church, which as being traceable in the age immediately
following upon that of the Apostles, might be claimed to
have had their institution or sanction. Those who accepted
this side of the alternative presented at the reconstruction
of the Church, became conforming members of it.

On the other side of the alternative, the fundamental,
unqualified, unyielded position tenaciously assumed by the
Puritans in the opening of their strife, and constantly
maintained ever since by those of their religious lineage,

was the sole and sufficient use and authority of the Scriptures for all that concerned the institution, organization, and discipline of the Christian Church, its ministry, its doctrinal teaching, its ritual, and government. They would not be led outside of the Bible for precedents, arguments, or usages. The rightfulness or expediency of the position thus taken by the Puritans was by no means obvious, and was fairly open to weighty objections raised against it. The Bible, it was urged in answer to their position, came to us as a deposit and legacy from the " Church." That Church might have more to give us for faith, for edification, and for directing the Christian life in individuals and in their sacred fellowships. What, it was asked, could be more natural and reasonable, more to be expected, recognized, and welcomed by us, than that the Apostles, where Gospel and Epistle closed, should have left to those who were to succeed them unwritten directions and counsels to be reverently transmitted in tradition and usage, and which, having been carefully identified and verified, should go down with the Scriptures as comment or supplement to guide the Church ?

Most certain it is that the Puritans would have gladly welcomed and reverently obeyed all such Apostolical teaching and usage of this character as admitted of being distinctively certified to them. It was indeed but reasonable to have looked for it; but when it came to the search for original and certified Apostolical tradition the result was disappointing. Many of those Puritans were profoundly learned and scholarly men, far surpassing the scholars of our age in their skill and mastery of the lore for the study of antiquity, of primitive times, of the works of the Fathers, and of ecclesiastical history. For learning and its materials were then mostly confined to such themes, instead of gathering into it the present enormous wealth of literature and science. The Puritans searched earnestly and patiently through those ancient stores which now pass,

even among their descendants, as rubbish. We have in
use a symbol called the "Apostles' Creed;" but it can be
traced back only to the fourth century. What a boon
would millions have esteemed it if there had been certified
to us a real Apostles' Creed, — a summary, distinct statement, in simple language, of the cardinal teachings for a
living, devout, and edifying belief! What a resource and
substitute would this have been for the dismal and unsatisfactory task of searching through the Bible, fractured into
fragments, for sentences, half-sentences, and words to be
patched into mosaics for setting forth a creed! But the
wheat and the chaff of patristic divinity were threshed and
winnowed ; the results are to be found in folios which
would bridge the ocean. That "primitive" Church literature was found by the Puritans to be bitterly disappointing.
In the mass it proved to be an extended and humiliating
commentary upon hints dropped by the pens of the Apostles about those who in their time were corrupting "the
simplicity of the Gospel," "causing divisions and strifes,"
"seeking to have the pre-eminence." The Puritan Milton
had studied with equal zeal the classic authors and the
antiquities of the Church. He pronounced the latter to be
the gatherings of "the drag-net of tradition." Whatever
else is to be said of this primitive and patristic literature,
this is to be affirmed,— that fertile as have proved the contents of the Scriptures for word controversy, textual strife,
and doctrinal variance, the conflicts, heresies, and contentions of Christians have found more abounding and distracting material in patristic and ecclesiastical theology.
When we consider how small is the nucleus of positive and
certified truth as to documents, persons, and facts with
which we have to start, and then realize the enormous ac-
cretions and developments accumulated and transmitted as
justly or erroneously held to share their value and authority, we no longer wonder over the dismal and fearful materials of Church history. It would be a relief if we could

assure ourselves that as the trunk, boughs, branches, twigs, and leaves of the gigantic and spreading oak all partake of the essence and quality of the tiny acorn, so all that now stands to represent the outgrowth of the original Gospel of Jesus Christ bears with it the virtue and power of the germ.   Many men of the clearest intellect and most sincere in purpose, with the learning of sages and the skill and acumen of judicial minds, have set to themselves the fond task, probing the question to its depths, to reach to and verify the root-facts about the personal life, history, and teaching of Jesus Christ.   Some of these seekers have given forth the results of their search for the help of others.   The effort resembles somewhat the retrospective musings of an aged person in an attempt to cast aside the impressions and experiences gathered from long years, that he may revive the freshness of his early childhood.

But the way was clear for the Puritans, under their exalted estimate of and way of using the Bible, — which will be further defined in following pages, — to plant themselves upon the Scriptures as the sole authority for them in matters of faith and Church institution and discipline. When they were told that their attempt to confine themselves strictly to a simple Scriptural model was unreasonable and impracticable, they were content to reply that it ought not to be so, and that on the face of the statement they detected false lures and risks of error.   There were questions enough, they said, opened within the Scriptures which all professed to believe ; but that outside of the Holy Book they were all adrift.   Puritanism, then, as represented by the Nonconformists, — loving and clinging to their mother church, which had come under usurped and corrupting foreign thraldom, — stood for a return to the simplicity of the first discipleship and fellowship among Christians as set forth in the New Testament.   If the Puritan scholars and champions were drawn into controversy outside those pages, they were ready, with a secondary earnestness, as if defending only outworks, to follow their adversaries into what they regarded as the bogs and swamps of the post-Apostolic centuries. But their zeal and their primary efforts were spent in maintaining that the Scriptures were the sole and sufficient authority for them, and in searching through them for the light and guidance which they needed. One of the most interesting and effective methods by which Puritanism wrought its earliest and most radical work, was one which came into practical and earnest use at the Reformation, and one which has ever since — coming down through the heritage of Puritanism — been a most popular and edifying usage among the non-prelatical and independent fellowships of Christians. The Roman Church knew nothing of lay-conferences, or of the intermeddling of the laity in any way with religious debatings. Still less had there been under the old priestly rule even a trace of what immediately after the rupture of unity became so familiar as " Bible reading," — the solace, joy, and soul sustenance of the Puritans. The Church had taught its confiding children that it was not for them to concern themselves with questions of faith, or discussions of religious mysteries ; she alone had knowledge, wisdom, and authority in these matters. They were simply to accept her teachings ; she was charged with the sacred deposit, and would dispense its treasures to all her docile children.

Puritanism found its early nurture and vigor in private assemblies for conferences, prayer, and Scripture exposition ; and in these earnest meetings, led by men among the ablest of their time in learning and loftiness of purpose, they sought to revive the primitive simplicity of the Apostolic ministry. They traced through the inspired records, into most minute particulars and with a microscopic study of texts, the usages of the first generation of disciples, and drew from them a model of what the Church ought to be for all time. It was thus that they were made

to realize what a stupendous, towering, and oppressive system of priestly and ecclesiastical enthralment had substituted itself, through the Papacy, for the original fellowship
of Christian disciples. Their amazement first, and then
their indignation, was excited by the contrast. It was but
the natural working of the elements of human nature that
their revolt from Rome should pass into hatred of all that
it had devised of superstition, priestcraft, imposition, and
tyranny in doctrine, rite, and discipline, in trifles as well
as in the most august observances. The hatred grew to
bitterness, finding its expression in the well-worn phrases,
" the rags of Popery," " the mark of the Beast," " Anti-
christ," and " the Scarlet Woman."

From the leading rule of the Puritans — that they would
follow in all things the model and precedent of Scripture —
were deduced all their other principles. There they found
the " pattern " for the composition and institution of a
fellowship or church among disciples of Christ. The minister or teacher was in no sense a priest. The line of
teachers would follow from the Apostles, certified by the
transmission — not through the touch of human hands, but
through oracles of truth — of what they themselves had
taught. One of these Apostles had thus instructed a beloved disciple of his own: " The things that thou hast
heard of me among many witnesses, the same commit thou
to faithful men who shall be able to teach others also." [1]
" Faithful men," " able to teach," — there, for the Puritan,
lay the qualification and the function of the Christian minister. From that simple model the Puritan asserted another of his root-principles, — the parity and equality of
Christian ministers. There was no occasion or warrant for
orders or ranks among them. They were all " brethren ; "
they were to have no " master." With what amazement,
then, would the Puritan turn to study the process by
which a domineering and haughty hierarchy, with all its

[1] 2 Timothy, ii. 2.

gradations of dignity, its prerogatives, its robings, its mitres, its crosiers, and its pride of power, had substituted itself for the early fellowship of "the ministers of the Word"! There was no court in Christendom, no feudal distribution of ranks of nobility down to serfdom, which from the loftiest to the lowliest, in the allotment of prerogatives and privileges, could compare itself with the priesthood of the Roman Church. With Pope and cardinals at the head, closing with a retinue of friars, it represented a power in the temporal affairs of men which well-nigh made them forget the stages of its growth and aggrandizement. The circumstances of their own time and experience caused the Puritans in England to suffer from the arrogance and oppressions of those whom they called the "Lord Bishops," — temporal and spiritual peers, with baronial rights and ecclesiastical courts and processes. So here again the Puritans turned back to Scripture, and found there no warrant for these clerical dignitaries succeeding to such as in the Roman Church had been high ministers of State, planning and executing military campaigns. They could not believe that the Christian ministry, consistently with the original simplicity of its purpose and service, could offer a field of graded honors and dignities parallel to that in social ranks and relations in the civil state. The prizes were to be won, also, by ambition, corruption, patronage, and intrigue; and when so won would be worn arrogantly and offensively.

The Preface to the Ordinal of the English Book of Common Prayer opens with this sentence: "It is evident unto all men diligently reading Holy Scripture and ancient authors, that from the Apostles' time there have been these Orders of ministers in Christ's Church, — bishops, priests, and deacons." In dealing with this sentence the Puritans, for reasons already stated, would leave unnoticed the reference to "ancient authors," whom they ruled out of the case, and they would substitute *in* for *from* "the Apostles'

time." Of the sentence thus qualified, leaving it to express what alone had pertinency for them, they would
offer a sturdy and positive denial, which would be approved by all who represent them on this point at the
present day, who would urge that in the sentence the assertion of its being "evident to all men" would have
required large exceptions, amounting even to a majority
on the other side. The Puritans, recognizing the special
dignity and functions of the Apostles, in which they could
have no successors, could find but a single Order of ministers in the New Testament. They found the terms
"bishop," or "overseer," and "presbyter," or "elder," to
be used interchangeably and synonymously, as designating
the same persons. As for deacons being an "Order of the
ministry," they turned to the record for the plain evidence
that so far from being an Order of the ministry, having
advancement in office in view, they were chosen for the
express purpose of filling a different service, — namely, to
relieve others discharging "the ministry of the Word"
from a burdensome task which did not belong to them.
They sought for the first selection of deacons in the first
planting of the Christian Church. This they found in the
Acts of the Apostles, chap. vi. verses 1-6, together with a
charming disclosure of the jealousies of human nature,
even in the freshness of the first Christian generation.
The early fellowship embraced alike Jewish and Gentile
converts. A murmur arose among the latter that the
Apostles, in allotting distributions from a common fund
for the relief of those who needed aid, showed a partiality
for the widows of their own Jewish race. Seeming to re-
sent the charge, "the Twelve called the multitude of the
disciples unto them," — afterward known as "the laity,"
without any function in such matters, — and spoke to
them as follows: "It is not reason that we should leave
the Word of God and serve tables. Wherefore, brethren,
look ye out among you seven men of honest report, full of

the Holy Ghost and wisdom, whom we may appoint over this business. But we will give ourselves continually to prayer and to the ministry of the Word. And the saying pleased the whole multitude; and they chose "— seven men named — "whom they set before the Apostles : and when they had prayed, they laid their hands on them." The Puritans, with acuteness and force of argument, drew many inferences from this plain statement, which proved embarrassing to their opponents. Here was distinctly recognized the right and privilege of those afterward called "the laity" to make the primary selection of officers in their churches, — a right of which they were wholly deprived in the Church of Rome and in the Church of England, and which, having been sturdily stood for by the Puritans and other Dissenters, was recovered by the lay members of the Episcopal denomination when organized in the United States. Again, it appeared from the text that the first seven "deacons," [1] so far from being chosen as an initiatory "order" preparatory to an advancement to higher grades in the ministry, were elected for a service quite distinct from the ministry, and in order to release those charged with the ministry from a vexatious task which did not belong to them, — namely, that of distributing charity gifts and having care for widows. After they had been chosen by the people, the Apostles transferred the funds to them. The Puritans also argued that the "laying

[1] It is true that the title "deacons" is not attached to the seven persons thus chosen. But the functions and offices here assigned them identify them with the officers afterward so named. Jerome calls deacons "attendants on tables and widows." There is not a single case mentioned in the New Testament of promotion from one Order in the ministry to a higher one. There is a single sentence from the pen of Saint Paul (1 Tim. iii. 13) : "For they that have used the office of a deacon well, purchase to themselves a good *degree*," — which has been used as intimating stages and ranks in a line of promotion in the ministry. The word βαθμὸς has, indeed, for one of its meanings, a *step*, or a *stair*. But it also means a *standing*. The Revised Version renders the text, — "they that have served well as deacons gain to themselves a good standing."

on of hands" by the Apostles was simply a formal designation of the candidates, and did not imply a "gift to them
of the Holy Ghost," inasmuch as a primary condition of
their nomination and selection as "deacons," or servants,
was that they should be known already to the community
as men "full of the Holy Ghost." The qualifications required, and the service to be performed seem on the face
of them rather suggestive of that class of grave and elderly
men known in Congregational churches as "deacons,"
overseers of charities, and helpers of ministers in temporal
matters, having no view to advancement in the ministry,
than of the young and inexperienced candidates for the
ministry in the Episcopal communion. It is true that
some of these first deacons afterward exhorted in meetings of the disciples; but Congregational deacons have
always been free to do this, according to occasion and
ability. The first of these deacons soon became the first
martyr, — Stephen. But was either one of the seven by
subsequent "ordination" advanced in the ministry as a
presbyter or bishop? The writer may incidentally state
here, that, so far as his memory serves him, he cannot
recall a case in the early or more recent history of New
England in which a deacon of a Congregational Church
became an ordained minister. Of course, there may have
been such cases, but as an almost universal rule there
was a well understood recognition of distinctive sets of
gifts and qualities had in view in the selection of pastors
and deacons. It was no bar to the appointment of one of
the latter officers that he had not been well educated, that
he was lame in speech and lacking in personal graces,
and so disqualified for the ministry. There were also
"deaconesses" in the early Church. These, however, did
not make an "order" in the ministry, though they were
beloved and honored in the fellowship. It has proved no
easy task for prelatists to invalidate the Scriptural argument of the Puritans on this point.

Then if, as the Puritans insisted on grounds of Scripture, bishops and presbyters were only two names for designating indifferently one and the same class of ministers, — all in a parity, there being several of them, whom we should now call pastors of churches in one city, as in Ephesus, — the Puritans asked how it came about that the word "bishop" had been accepted as the title of a superior among his brethren, with special and exalted functions over them, and the clerical or spiritual head of all "the inferior clergy" of a diocese or province? They read in the "Acts" that the Apostles made renewed visits to the disciples in the cities where they were gathered, "confirming the churches."[1] This conveyed to Puritan readers the idea that these visits were designed for further and fuller teaching of imperfectly trained companies of early disciples. But the word "confirmation," without the slightest warrant for such a use of it, was selected and emphasized in that text as the basis of the rule that only the bishop of a province or diocese, no matter how many able and faithful ministers were serving churches in it, had authority to admit a candidate to the Lord's Supper. The Puritans being referred to "ancient authors" on these points, declined, for reasons given, to recognize those warring and conflicting writers, and insisted upon a reference to the "Word," which was silent upon these pretensions. But as to the "Lord Bishops" of the Church of England, the Puritans put themselves in a very decided position of disapproval and antagonism. At the time of the Reformation every one of the English bishops was under an oath of obedience to the Pope, and held office under that obligation. When the authority of the Pope was prostrated and repudiated, the lay monarch became the "head of the Church." The Puritans came to regard the process by which bishops obtained tenure of their exalted offices as a mere farce. The

[1] Acts xiv. 22; xv. 41.

monarch appointed them, leaving to the Chapters a pretended right of choice, which amounted merely to the absurd privilege of ratifying the choice already made. These
bishops became literally " lords over God's heritage," of
the highest order of nobility, introducing into the Church
all the passionate rivalries and jealousies of worldly ambition. From the towering pride and rule of these functionaries the Puritans turned back again to their stronghold of
Scripture, and planted themselves on the Gospel rule of the
parity of ministers, whether serving in a palace or in a
hovel, whether having the ear of a monarch or laboring in
the humblest hamlet. If some Christian ministers affected
the state of nobles, others must accept the lot of vassals.
It would be difficult to express in the same number of
words an idea more discordant with the spirit and letter of
the primitive teaching of Jesus Christ, than goes with the
phrase " the inferior clergy," used to designate all ordained
clergymen below the rank of prelates. It has even come
into use in the Episcopal fellowship on this side of the
ocean. Evidently its only significance must attach to it as
designating a lower degree of rank, dignity, and office, —
all inapplicable in the Christian ministry. For, as a matter of fact, the inner history of the English Church has
abundantly proved that among " the inferior clergy " have
ever been found its most devoted, laborious, consistent, and
faithful ministers. To this claim of lordly rank and pre-
eminency for the bishops was added the exclusive power of
ordination for the ministry, to continue in the Church " the
Apostolical succession." [1] The reformed churches on the
Continent did not commit themselves to this theory as
necessary for the continuance of " a valid ministry." For
the English Puritans it was enough to assure themselves,

---

[1] The translators of our English version of the New Testament contrived
not only to assign a " bishopric " to Judas, but also to quote the Psalmist as
prophesying of him in that dignity (Acts i. 20). The revised version substitutes the word " office."

through their mastery of the historical learning bearing on the subject, that it would have been — as Archbishop Whately in our own time forcibly and candidly urged — utterly impossible for any bishop or prelate to have traced his official lineage back to the Apostles. What with the lay bishops and the "boy bishops" of mediævalism, there would have been many missing links and also many rotten links in the chain. But the Puritan protest struck deeper than that; it refused to confound the vitalities of the Christian religion with a form or ceremonial restricting the gift of Apostolic grace to the hands of a prelate. The cogency of the Puritan argument on this point has been candidly yielded in these calmer times of controversy and discussion. For though among the divines and champions of the English Church there are those who insist that "a valid ministry" of the Christian religion can be secured only through prelatical ordination, the assumption is modified and diminished in more moderate assertions of it, till Episcopal ordination is content to present itself as simply a police method for the orderly introduction of proper candidates into the ministry.

The Presbyterians equally claim an Apostolical succession in their ministry, — a presbyterial episcopate, descending through the line of presbyter-bishops. Indeed, a series of recent historians, divines, and lecturers on foundations in the Church of England might be cited here, as yielding the strength of the position taken by the Puritans on these formerly sharply-contested questions of prelacy and the Apostolical succession. The change in the spirit as regards impartiality and candor in which Church writers now deal with themes once so unfairly and passionately treated by them, is so marked and so commendable that it will not be a digression to illustrate it here. The reformers of the conservative party in the Church of England, standing between the Romanists and the Puritans, had to deal with both horns of a dilemma. In disputing with the Puri-

tans, who planted themselves strictly and exclusively upon
the Christian Scriptures and the Apostolic age, their opponents had to justify themselves for trespassing outside of
those Scriptures and into the post-Apostolic period, and insisting that for an undefined and undefinable period called
" primitive," and in certain accredited patristic writings,
they could find materials for creed and polity which had
substantially the authority of the commissioned founders
of the Christian Church. But in dealing with the champions of the old unreformed Church, they were rightfully
challenged for a merely arbitrary selection of a line and
standard in accepting or rejecting matters which were
claimed to be of primitive tradition and usage. The leading spirits of the work of reformation under Edward VI.
were guided by a sincere purpose of conforming the Church,
its formularies and services, as closely as possible to the
letter and spirit of the Scriptures. But this purpose was
not followed in subsequent revisions of the formularies and
in adaptations of the ecclesiastical system in the reign of
Elizabeth. James I. was fond of all Romanism except the
Pope. How all attempts at inclusion and comprehension
of the Christian people of the realm under one fold with
a common worship and discipline have failed since, even
when propitious opportunities have been offered for them,
need not here be reviewed. A fresh opportunity, with helpful provocatives to the improvement of it, seems now to be
offering itself. The existing English Church is the construction or residuum — whichever we may choose to call
it — of a compromise betweeen Puritanism and the old
Romanism. Whether that result of compromise was, or
was not, the only way of disposing of the issues of the
times and circumstances under which it was reached, need
not be here discussed. But that church of compromise
finds matters to-day very much in the same condition as
they were in the reign of Elizabeth ; and the question now
is whether compromise shall be extended under new terms

and adjustments, or yield to more radical measures. The threatened disestablishment of the Church of England, with the intent to deprive it of the exclusive privileges and monopolies which it has enjoyed for three centuries, revives — indeed, they have never been in abeyance — the same pleadings, arguments, and principles which were so resolutely maintained by the Puritans of the sixteenth and seventeenth centuries. As a matter of fact the English Church is but one sect among many sects of the realm. The arguments so ingeniously, not to say artfully, plied to disguise the fact are in part perversions of history, and in part deductions from the actual privileges of favoritism which the Church enjoys. Civil enactments have made over to her exclusively the vested ecclesiastical property of the realm, — cathedrals, parish-churches, and benevolences, representation in the upper house of Parliament, patronage at the Court, in the Army and the Navy, — while half the subjects of the realm stand outside the fold. The case stands thus: The clergy of the Church of England, with no advantage or superiority whatever over the Nonconformists, or Dissenters, in learning, character, abilities, or any of the best qualifications for the Christian ministry, or of fidelity and success in its work, have as of worldly advantage just what is secured to them by privilege and patronage, by Parliamentary law. The unsettled legacy of the controversy with Dissent still prevents unity or comprehension in the Church, while "Romanizing" tendencies preserve the full vitality of the uncompromising Church of the Papacy.

Under these circumstances it is gratifying to read, as coming numerously from the press during the last score of years, volumes from the pens of learned, able, and candid divines and scholars of the Church of England, which not only allow, but even urge and insist upon, the position and principles of the Puritans as to the supreme and exclusive authority and sufficiency of the New Testament Scriptures and of the Apostolic age for deciding all matters of Christian belief and church institution and discipline. I have imagined the satisfaction and delight with which John Winthrop or John Cotton would have read one such volume which I have now in my hands.[1] Nothing but the official designation of the author on the titlepage and a few incidental allusions would persuade a reader that the book was not written by an original Puritan. Winthrop or Cotton would have exclaimed on reading it, " Why could not the English churchmen of our time have recognized the force and validity of these arguments as they came from our lips and pens?" A few passages from the pages of this learned and candid Puritan Conformist in the Church of England in the latter part of the nineteenth century, will show the identity of his views with those of the Puritan Nonconformists of the beginning of the seventeenth century. Referring to the assumption that besides the Scriptures of the New Testament and the usages authorized by the Apostles themselves in the institution and discipline of the Church, the following post-Apostolic age furnishes for two or more centuries, called "primitive," certain other usages which may be presumed to have had the sanction of the Apostles, Dr. Jacob writes : —

" The opinion that we are bound dutifully to submit to the authority, and ought to be guided by the practice and example, of the Church as it was in the first three, four, or any other centuries, however prevalent and plausible, is delusive and ensnaring. The Church of the Apostolic period is the only Church in which there is found an authority justly claiming the acknowledgment of Christian bodies in other times. And such authority is found in this Church, not because it was possessed of a truer catholicity or a purer constitution or a more primitive antiquity than belong to

[1] The Ecclesiastical Polity of the New Testament. A Study for the present Crisis in the Church of England. By the Rev. G. A. Jacob, D.D., late Head-Master of Christ's Hospital. Fifth American Edition. New York: Thomas Whitaker. 1878.

succeeding ages, — for neither antiquity, nor purity of form, nor catholicity confers any right to govern or command, — but because it was under the immediate rule and guidance of the Apostles; and it is their infallible judgment alone, as exhibited in this Church, which has a legitimate claim to our submission. Of the Church of no other period can the same be said, because the Apostles had no successors in their office. They stand alone. They stand alone as the divinely inspired teachers, legislators, and rulers in Christ's Church and kingdom. They stand alone as men appointed and commissioned by Christ himself, and not by man; whereas all Christian ministers since their time, of whatsoever order or degree, have been fallible men, and have been appointed and commissioned by man, — by the authority of the particular Church in which they were to minister. The promise of our Lord that He would be with the Apostles even to the end of the world, as it did not secure to them a continuance on earth beyond their own generation, so neither did it engage or imply that others with a similar power and authority should succeed them. With faithful preachers of Christ, and sound teachers of His word and doctrine, and diligent pastors of His flock, their divine Master has in all ages been present by His spirit. But no Christian ministers having received the commission or inspiration of the Apostles, none of them could inherit the Apostolic office, nor could they individually or in any collective body ever possess the Apostolic authority. And as no Church ministers, so neither the Church itself of any post-Apostolic time — in whatever mode we may suppose it to have uttered a united voice — has ever had any Apostolic or divine authority to which after-ages owed submission. The opinion that such submission is due to the Church of any given period can be justified only on the supposition that the Church of that period was infallible; that, in fact, our Lord was then so present with the visible Church as miraculously to exempt it from error in the exercise of its legislative and administrative functions, in doctrine and in practice. But if so, is there any ground whatever for rejecting the claims of infallibility such as are persistently and consistently put forward by the Church of Rome? Is there any ground whatever for ascribing this sanction to the Nicene period, and denying it to the modern Papacy? For surely it is impossible, with any show of reason or truth, to draw the line at any one place in the history of the Church after the Apostles had been withdrawn, and to say, Before this the Church was divinely preserved from error; after this, it was fallible and erred. There is unquestionable evidence that soon after the Apostles disappeared the Church was no longer always guided by the spirit of truth and wisdom, but on the contrary gradually yielded to the seductions of error. I appeal, therefore, from the Nicene Fathers to the Apostles of Christ, from patristic literature to the New Testament, from ecclesiastical authorities and practices of post-Apostolic centuries to the primitive Church of the Apostolic age. To go back to that time and to endeavor as far as possible to reproduce the Church of the New Testament is most needful for us now, if we would preserve a faithful and distinct acknowledgment of Christian truth among our people. . . .

"Most interesting, though not without its sadness, it is to trace the characteristic features of the Church of Christ in its primitive and Apostolic state; and then to mark how its grand and spiritual simplicity, preserved awhile after the departure of the Apostles, began even in the earliest centuries to be marred by the doctrines and inventions of men, and to be overlaid with imposing but superstitious ceremonials. . . .

"The Lord's Supper, in its original institution the most simple of all religious ordinances, became in the hands of men a most awful mystery. In its Apostolic use a pledge of soundness in the faith, it was made in the hands of men an example of gross superstition and idolatry. In its divine intention a bond of brotherly love and mutual kindness, it was changed in the hands of men into an occasion of the most cruel persecution. No idea of a sacrifice was attached to its celebration; no change was supposed to take place in the sacred elements; no virtue to be imparted to them or through them by the administrator; no presence of Christ *in* them or *with* them in any especial or peculiar manner. But in the post-Apostolic Church all this was gradually changed, until at last the service was represented as a sacrifice offered upon an altar by a priest, the elements were spoken of and worshipped as if they were Christ himself; and other gross superstitions naturally ensued. . . .

" The authority to which alone we should appeal is that of the
Divine Head of the whole Church, as it may be gathered from
the words and actions of His inspired Apostles. The only safe
and legitimate course in all our Church reforms is to go to the
New Testament as our guide." [1]

What a responsive assent would our old Puritan Nonconformists have given to the following statement: —

" The clergy, not being a priestly caste, or a mediating, sacri-
ficing, absolving order, but Church officers appointed for the
maintenance of due religious solemnity, the devout exercise of
Christian worship, the instruction of the people in divine truth,
and their general edification in righteous living, are the acting
representatives of the Church to which they belong, and derive
their ministerial authority from it. In the words of Archbishop
Whately, the clergy are merely the functionaries of the particular
Church of which they are members; it is in that capacity only
that they derive their station and power from Christ, by virtue of
the sanctions given by Him to Christian communities. Their authority, therefore, comes direct from the society so constituted, in
whose name and behalf they act as its representatives, just to that
extent to which it has empowered and directed them to act." [2]

As regards prescribed forms and liturgical services in
worship in the early Church, Dr. Jacob writes: —

" All the evidence directly deducible from the New Testament
is against the use of such formularies in the Apostolic age. Nor
throughout the second century is any reliable testimony to be
found indicative of any considerable alteration in this respect.
On the contrary, the prayers of the Church, described by Justin
Martyr, seem to have depended upon the ability and discretion
of the officiating minister as much as they did in the preceding
century." [3]

[1] The Ecclesiastical Polity of the New Testament, pp. 25–29, 285, 324,
337, 348.
[2] Ibid., p. 123.
[3] Ibid., pp. 221–222.

As I am writing these pages, the religious journals of the various denominations are largely discussing propositions to advance the promotion of " Christian Unity " among them. The subject had a hearing in the last Convention of the Protestant Episcopal denomination, which set forth the requisite conditions for its own engagement in the object. Its response was indeed more courteous than would have been an absolute refusal to be a party to the end proposed; but it could not be more effective than would have been such a refusal in utterly discouraging any expectation of sympathy or help from that denomination in the advancement of Christian Unity.[1]

That response exacted a condition with which not a single one of the other Christian fellowships — whether much larger than the Episcopal, or smaller — will ever comply. The condition was that all these other fellowships should conform themselves to the theory that " Episcopal ordination " is indispensable for the valid ministry of Christ's Gospel. To all outside the Episcopal communion this assumption is either a puerile conceit, or a pompous assertion of some exclusive right or sacramental grace which eludes all demands upon it for a clear, frank, and intelligible definition of what the claim covers. The assertion of the Roman Church that salvation is impossible outside of its communion, defines a position about which there can be no misunderstanding. But though there has been such voluminous discussion and controversy about the " Apostolical succession " and the exclusive prerogatives of " Episcopal ordination," one may look in vain — except it may be in the pages of some extravagant champion — for a clear strong statement of the loss, the

---

[1] One might be tempted here to dilate upon the utter inadequacy of the conception of "Christian Unity" as really concerning heart sentiments of sympathy, love, diffusive and comprehensive Christian effort, by persons holding an infinite variety of beliefs and opinions ; which seems to be had in view by those who are proposing "an organic unity," — a thing undesirable, even if possible.

7

harm, the peril, or penalty which is risked by a Christian outside of the Episcopalian communion. Is Gospel truth thus deprived of its power over his heart and life, or does he expose himself to a reduced share in the blessing going with it ? In other words, what covenant privileges, immunities, and securities are monopolized by Episcopalian Christians ? Till something more than vague and clouded oracular assumptions and intimations are defined as assuring the exclusive claims of Episcopacy, they will be likely to be regarded as they are now by non-Episcopalians, as simple bugbears. Protestants generally acquiesce placidly in the slight cast upon their ministry by the Roman priesthood, because it is so sweeping and impartial; for in the view of that priesthood a Protestant bishop or archbishop is of no more account than a field preacher. But while most non-episcopal Protestants pass with a smile of indifference — if not with a more pronounced look — the exclusive claims of the Episcopacy, some take the matter to heart, and are grieved and irritated by those claims. If the discussion that has been opened proceeds, it will be necessary to define those claims more sharply. They are covered by the general statement, that Episcopacy "has the only valid ministry." Now, *valid* is a word of vague and dubious meaning in this connection. Those who so use it might hardly venture to substitute "the only *efficient* ministry." Yet efficiency is the all-essential thing in the Christian ministry. That claim of sole validity, which is not backed by any superiority of character, ability, moral or spiritual excellence, or success in the sacred work, in the view of some who are aggrieved by it, can hardly be relieved of the charge of assumption, pretentiousness, and official arrogance.

But what is more to the point in the matter before us — if the old controversy is to be opened for fresh discussion — is the recognition of the fact, that while the Nonconformists of the seventeenth century argued their cause solely with the New Testament Scriptures in their hands, their successors in this age need only to quote from the writings of learned and candid Episcopalians concessions and affirmations that Episcopacy finds no basis in the Scriptures; was not known in the age of the Apostles, or established by them; is not essential to the institution or administration of the Christian Church; and came into some portions of that Church in post-Apostolic times, on indifferent reasons of convenience or assent.

A few more passages may here be quoted from the pages of Dr. Jacob: —

"In order to obtain a correct conception of the Christian ministry in its primitive state, it is necessary to distinguish clearly between what the Apostles themselves established in the Church, and what was afterward found to be expedient as a further development of their polity. That which may justly claim to be a legitimate and beneficial extension of Apostolic order must not on that account be confounded with ordinances of Apostolic institution. I have, therefore, thought it necessary to omit all notice of Episcopacy in considering the offices of presbyters and deacons. These were established in the churches by the Apostles themselves, while the Episcopate, in the modern acceptation of the term, and as a distinct clerical order, does not appear in the New Testament, but was gradually introduced and extended throughout the Church at a later period." [1]

The author shows how the Episcopal office came in as a presidency or superintendency, like that of a chairman, when several presbyters, all on an equality, were in one city or neighborhood. Sometimes there was a rotation in the office.

"The churches which like our own have retained the Episcopate and Episcopal ordination, may reasonably prefer this form of government, and justly consider that it is one of all but Apostolic antiquity, and one which having been found desirable, or even

---

[1] The Ecclesiastical Polity of the New Testament, p. 67.

necessary, after the departure of the Apostles, and having been well-tried by long experience, should never lightly be given up. But, on the other hand, the government and the ordinations of Presbyterian churches are just as valid, Scriptural, and Apostolic as our own." [1]

" The authority of the Christian minister in any place is given to him by the Church in which and for which he acts ; and this authority is *Apostolic*, if his teaching is sound in Apostolic truth ; this authority is from *Christ*, if His Church is a legitimate Christian community formed in obedience to Christ's command." [2]

Certainly the best way to identify a river must be by the water which flows continuously through it from its source.

" The doctrine of the Apostolical succession is not the doctrine of the Church of England, as the following proofs distinctly testify :

" A doctrine so important and fundamental, if it is believed to be true, could not have been omitted as it is from our Articles and Prayer Book, if it had been held by our Church ; whereas it is not only omitted, but the wording of Art. 23 is quite incompatible with it.

" The Statute of Elizabeth, 1570, — ' An Act for the Ministry of the Church to be of sound Religion,' — only requires those who had received ordination in ' any other form of Institution, Consecration, or Ordering,' than that of the Church of England, to subscribe to the ' Articles of Religion,' in order to hold ecclesiastical preferment in this country ; no objection at all being raised to the validity of such ordinations." [3]

The author gives other grounds for his statement, among them the allowance of Hooker, " that there might be very just and sufficient reason to allow ordination made without a bishop."

If more evidence were needed in illustration of the fact that the positions taken by Puritan nonconformists on the Scripture model for the institution of a church, now

---

[1] The Ecclesiastical Polity of the New Testament, p. 115.
[2] Ibid., p. 422.   [3] Ibid., pp. 422, 423.

find full support in the works of churchmen, many other volumes might be quoted here.   One of these [1] is almost radical in its tenor.   The author states his object to be to account for "the apparently wide differences between the primitive and the modern forms of some Christian institutions."   He endeavors to trace "the gradual steps by which the congregational system of early times passed into the diocesan system of later times." [2]

While reason and occasion enough were found in the serious points already referred to to give significance to the term "nonconformity" as applied to the principles of the English Puritans when claiming their rights and privileges in the reform and reconstruction of their own church, it was in matters and details of lesser significance that their name, not as Separatists, but as Nonconformists, received its popular and familiar use.

It is difficult for us to realize the stupendous change to which the whole people of England had to be reconciled and trained in the transition from the mode of worship and instruction and religious discipline under the Roman observance to the Protestant institution.   The English language was to take the place of the Latin in all the services. Public worship, in which all the people could intelligently take a part, was to be substituted for the altar service so largely performed by the priest.   The Lord's Supper, according to the account in the New Testament as a sacrament to be perpetuated, — was it the re-enactment of a sacrificial offering of a victim, or a fraternal service of communion at a common table for a share in a commemorative observance ? [3]

---

[1] The Growth of Church Institutions.   By the Rev. Edwin Hatch, M.A., D.D., Reader in Ecclesiastical History in the University of Oxford.   1887.

[2] Ibid., p. 7.

[3] When one whose training has been under the simple services of the Puritanism of our modern days sees for the first time the service of the Mass, — with what is to him a dumb show, with the attitudes, the bowings, and genuflections of the priest, as he consecrates and lifts the wafer for adoration, —

The people were to have a manual for worship and the Bible in their own English tongue. Perfection and satisfaction could not be reached at once, but required tentative stages, opening many subjects for intelligent differences in matters of opinion and conscience. The first prayer-book, the contents of which were gathered and translated by a company of divines from previous service-books, was published under Edward VI. in 1549, and a second one with changes appeared in the same reign. It was again altered in 1558, in 1603, and 1661. The last prayer-book differs from the first principally in the omission of the name of the Virgin Mary in the prayers offered to saints ; of prayers for the dead ; of the mixing of wine and water in the cup ; and of all the elaborate ceremonies in baptism except the crossing of the forehead. Queen Mary suspended all the reforming acts previous to her reign, so that they had to be renewed under Elizabeth. The psalter had been published in Latin and English, and the Bible " lessons " had been read in English in 1540. In 1544 Cranmer translated the Litany into English. The English Bible called by his name was the first used in the churches till the Bishops' Bible was substituted in 1604.

The rapacity of courtiers and nobles to share and appropriate the spoils of the " religious houses," their wealth in treasures and lands, when they were suppressed by Henry VIII., had a most disastrous effect upon the moralities of the Church. These spoils fed the pride, the rivalry, and the worldliness of those who were enriched by them, and

he may be moved to ask himself if, by any effort of the imagination, he can conceive of an apostle as going through that observance before the early disciples ? Some readers may have shared the wonder of the writer on witnessing the observance of the Mass in the Church of St. Peter at Rome, with all the pomp and gorgeousness of the scenic show. The thought that rose to his mind was whether, if the dome of the superb temple could have been riven and the Apostle to whom it is dedicated could have descended into it, he would have understood what was going on there. It would have been interesting to have heard his successor explain the situation to him.

plundered the common people of many resources and appliances which the piety of earlier ages had consecrated
to their use.

The next great and vital question to engage the zeal
of the Puritans, as they rightfully claimed to exercise it
in the reconstruction of a reformed church, was the internal constitution and administration of the Church itself.
Their own principles and views on this subject will come
before us subsequently when we have to follow the course
pursued by that representation of the Puritan body which
instituted in the Massachusetts colony the "particular
Church," so designated by Governor Winthrop.   It is
sufficient to anticipate here, by saying, that while every
baptized person in the realm was held to be a member of
the Church of England, the Puritans maintained that a
Church must consist only of "Actual Believers, True Disciples, such as can give some account how the Grace of
God hath appeared unto, and wrought that heavenly change
in them."

The Puritans gladly recognized the advance made by
radically reforming principles in substituting a service of
prayer in English and intelligent worship and instruction,
for what in their view were "the mumblings and bowings
of the priest, with his back to the people, in his own idolatrous mummeries."   But an attachment and reverence for
all entailed and endeared usages and observances, curiously
mingled with superstitions, charms, and legends, had a
strong hold upon the minds and hearts of the common
people.   It was in rude and unsympathizing dealings with
these, — the observance of saints' days, praying with the
rosary, the use of the cross as a talisman, the repetition
for scores of times of the Pater Noster and the Ave,
and many other lingerings of the traditionary piety, — that
the Puritans drew upon themselves odium as over-scrupu-
lous precisians, and radicals.   For example, the Puritans
"scrupled the Cross in Baptism."   They did so, and they

gave reasons for their scruples. Among all the parties
and sects of Christians there were none to whom the
Cross of Christ had a more august or holy significance than
to the Puritans ; but it was as a reality, and not as a symbol, that they prized it. They believed that in the Roman
observance the cross had been turned to idolatrous, unintel-
ligent, and merely formal uses, as a charm or phylactery.
They " scrupled " its trivial and mechanical desecration.
The ritual for the baptism of an infant by a priest of the
Roman Church was then — and is now, unchanged — very
elaborate in its method, designed to signify the transcendent
importance and efficacy assigned to it. Godfathers and god-
mothers to assume or share the responsibilities of parents
were to be present. The priest blows thrice on the face
of the child, bidding the devil in it "to give place to the
Holy Ghost." Then he makes the sign of the cross on
the forehead and breast, with words of exhortation. Then,
after prayer, the priest blesses some salt and puts a grain
of it into the mouth of the child, with more exhortation,
and exorcism of the Evil Spirit, and repetition of the
cross. The service so far was in the porch of the church ;
then coming into the church, the priest with spittle from
his mouth touches the ears and the nostrils of the infant,
with further exhortation and exorcism. Then with holy
oil he anoints the infant on the breast and between' the
shoulders, and while the god-parents are holding or touching him, the priest names the child, and thrice pours water
on or dips it, repeating the formula. There is another
anointing with oil and balm, or "holy chrism ;" a linen
cloth is put upon the head of the child, a lighted candle
is put into its hand, and there is a concluding exhortation. Every act and element of the service is symbolic,
with explanatory comment. Those who prepared the
English Prayer Book " scrupled " and omitted every part
of this ritual except the use of the cross. The Puritans
carried their scruples one step further, and " scrupled "

the cross. They asked, " Why omit all the rest and retain this ? "

The position taken by the Puritans as to the sign of the
cross — because of its superstitious use — may well be
regarded as suggesting their general and comprehensive
objections to all mere " ceremonials." They wished to
displace them by plain, intelligible, direct instruction that
should be enlightening and edifying, engaging the thoughts
and reaching the consciences of the people. Our concern
in these pages is with that class of the Puritans, the
founders of Massachusetts, who themselves defined their
relation to the English Church as one not of open hostility, antagonism, or separation, but of nonconformity. Acknowledging their birthright and heritage in it as the
source of their Christian nurture, they mourned over the
corruptions, superstitions, and enslavement to which it
had been subjected under the Papal dominancy, and they
wished to rid it of everything foreign and inconsistent in
its institution and discipline. They came to look upon the
usages and ceremonies of the Church which they renounced
as precisely answering to those " traditions of the elders"
for which Jesus rebuked the Jews, as nullifying or depre-
ciating the positive commandments of God. And at this
point we must broadly distinguish between this class of
Nonconformists and the Sectaries of the period, with
whom they are often strangely confounded. In the ferment and distraction, chiefly among the ranks of the common people, the illiterate, husbandmen and artisans, which
followed upon the general enfranchisement of thought, and
the free use of the Scriptures, individualism in opinion and
belief ran to the wildest extremes. Enthusiasm and fanaticism, with every form of eccentricity and extravagance,
came in to unsettle order and breed confusion. The dingy
old volumes, now gathered in the proper receptacles for
them, remain to us as exponents, attempted classifications,
or definitions and descriptions of all the strange fancies,

conceits, devices, heresies, and delusions, any one of which sufficed as raw material for a sect, a congregation, or even a "church." Many of these freely avowed an open hostility to civil government, magistracy, and the laws of morality and common decency. "Antinomians," "Familists," "Libertines," and "Adamites" are the embers left in English speech, for which one has to seek the definitions in old tractates, but which, when in living use, were brands threatening fearful conflagrations. The stock basis of Bible sanction for one of these sects, the "Adamites," is thus stated: "Their joint issue is, that clothes were appointed not so much to cover shame, as to discover sin; and that therefore, they being such as Adam was in his innocency, ought to goe naked, and not to be ashamed." [1]

It would be unprofitable to concern ourselves further with the extravagances of individualism and sectarism in this period of distraction in England. Reference to it has been in place here, solely to distinguish every form and manifestation of this spirit from the nonconformity of the founders of Massachusetts. The relations to be given further on in these pages of the way in which every excess of individualism and sectarism was dealt with by court and magistracy, will themselves suffice to show the breadth of that distinction. Sir Ferdinando Gorges, thoroughly familiar as he was with the character and purposes of those founders, and their keenly watchful enemy at the Court, thus fairly defines their motive in their exile. He says that the Puritans had become discouraged as to any further pressure of reform in the Church, and therefore that "some of the discreeter sort, to avoid what they found themselves subject unto, made use of their friends to procure from the Council for the affairs of New England to settle a Colony within their limits."

After John Cotton had been the Vicar of St. Botolph nearly a score of years, he came under the hand of Laud

[1] The Dippers Dipt, etc. By Dr. Daniel Featley. London, 1651, p. 35.

for nonconformity. He was informed against at the High
Commission for " refusing to kneel at the Lord's Supper." [1]
Cotton says : " When the Bishop of Lincoln Diocese [Dr.
Mountaigne] offered me liberty upon once kneeling at the
Sacrament with him the next Lord's Day after, I durst not
accept his offer of liberty upon once kneeling." [2] Cotton
" scrupled kneeling " as a remnant of the " idolatrous sacrifice of the Mass." The Earl of Dorset, his warm friend,
interceded in vain in his behalf, assuring him " that if he
had been guilty of drunkenness, uncleanness, or any such
lesser fault, he could have obtained his pardon ; but as he
was guilty of Puritanism and nonconformity the crime was
unpardonable, and therefore he advised him to flee for his
safety."

The hundred scholars and divines who, from the training of the English universities, and many of them from
incumbency of parishes and service in the pulpits of the
English Church, came to New England in its first age to
lay the foundations here, were the peers in every respect
of their conformist fellows whom they left behind. Their
nonconformity in matters of discipline and ritual had
drawn upon them the processes of the bishops and their
spiritual courts. Bands of earnest laymen, who had enjoyed and valued their ministry, preceded, accompanied, or
welcomed them here. The model for church institution,
which they established, when free in the wilderness to follow their own consciences and preferences, exhibits in its
divergences the character and quality of their nonconformity. The laymen improved their opportunity to select
and institute their own religious teachers, which they had
had no power of doing under the parochial system of England. They could constitute their churches of " covenanted
believers." Instead of the " dumb reading " of the Scriptures by appointed lessons, they could accompany the read-

---

[1] Neal, Puritans, i. 317.

[2] Way of Congregational Churches, p. 19.

ing with exposition. They could observe the sacraments according to what they believed to be their original purpose and method. They were free in offering prayer, and not bound to a service-book. All the changes and modifications made in the Book of Common Prayer had not reconciled the Puritans to its use. It fettered their spirits and their tongues. It was to them formal and mechanical in its effect, routine, and rigidity.[1] Experience ever since, however, has proved that it is rather by taste and temperament than by conscience, that individuals gathered for public worship prefer freedom or formality in its exercise. It appears that at this time in England, where neither restraint nor obligation interposes, of those who habitually engage in public worship, nearly an equal number accept and disuse the Church forms. Calvin, the chief religious guide for the Puritans, gave three reasons for set prayers, which might have had weight with them, but did not : (1) To provide for the weakness of some ministers ; (2) For general consent and agreement in churches ; (3) To cross the liberty of some ministers who affect novelties.

Under the rule of the Roman Church there had been an ingeniously devised scheme to permeate secular life with a course of religious observances additional to those of the weekly Sabbath. A calendar of the year was prepared designating events and methods in Christian history and training. Just and beautiful in conception and purpose, this system became burdensome, perverted, and overladen.

---

[1] The objections of the Nonconformists to the Common Prayer Book, and some of the ceremonies of the Church, are stated forcibly, but temperately, and with dignified restraint of language, in the Preface to the Directory for Worship, prepared by the Westminster Assembly. As lack of sympathy so readily becomes antipathy, these objections soon passed into alienations and strong dislikes often expressed with bitterness. Some of the Puritan party still attending the parish churches were wont to stay outside during the preliminary services, and then go in to listen to the sermon. Every reference to a service of prayer in the New Testament suggested to them a free outpouring of sentiment and utterance. They could not conceive of a book being used on such occasions.

Festivals and fasts, saints' days, revels, games, fairs, pilgrimages, holy places, exorcisms, and puerile and debasing legends and superstitions were inextricably mixed in this system, with results and influences both good and bad. The English Church thought it wise to retain some of the usages which had come into it from Rome, for the same reason that the Roman Church retained some of the sanctities of Paganism, because of fond attachments and associations holding the common people. But the Puritans, with an indiscriminating aversion and contempt, cast aside all the sweet and grateful sentiments and associations wrought in with the heart tendrils of affection in these Church observances in secular things.

In this connection reference should be made to one of the least attractive traits or principles of the Puritans as shown afterward in their intense aversion to the observance of holy days, which were in fact holidays, including Christmas, and which prompted them to pass an interdict upon them in their legislation here. But it was by no means only the Nonconformists who complained of and sought to reduce the elaborate system of semi-sacred observances which crowded the calendar of the year, and seriously interfered with the performance of the regular duties and labors of life in the home, the field, and the workshop. The administrators of the Church found their discretion and efforts severely taxed in dealing with the popular habits of idleness and dissipation encouraged by this usage of holy days. Archbishop Cranmer, in a letter to Cromwell, complains of " having found the people of my diocese very obstinately given to observe and keep with solemnity the holidays lately abrogated, and that the people were partly animated thereto by the curates." [1] Before the Reformation Cromwell had drafted for the Commons a complaint to the King of the harmful interference with trade and agriculture caused by the use of holy days as

[1] No. 198, of "Letters of Cranmer," collected by Rev. Henry Jenkyns.

holidays. The complaint recites that "A great number of holy days now at this present time, with very small devotion, be solemnized and kept throughout this your realm, upon the which many great, abominable, and execrable vices, idle and wanton sports, be used and exercised, — which holy days might be made fewer in number." [1] As a result of this complaint, Convocation on July 15, 1536, "by the King's Highness' authority as supreme head on earth of the Church of England," declared that the number of these holy days was —

"The occasion of much sloth and idleness, the very nourish of thieves, vagabonds, and divers other unthriftiness and inconveniences and loss of man's food, many times being clean destroyed through the superstitious observance of the said holy days, in not taking the opportunity of good and serene weather in time of harvest; but also pernicious to the souls of many men, which being enticed by the licentious vacation and liberty of those holidays, do upon the same commonly use and practise more excess, riot, and superfluity than upon any other days." [2]

The Nonconformists, with the thoroughness which they demanded in the work of purification, required that all these trivial, superstitious devices of the Roman domination should be discredited and disused, and that the Sabbath alone should be held to be a holy-day, and reverently observed as such. The delusions, frauds, and superstitions connected with these holy days outweighed in their minds any possible service they could have for edification. It was the repudiation or discountenance by the Puritans of all these lighter, gentler agencies and influences for fostering religion in church and home, on the village green and in popular festivals, that drove them into a grimness and austerity wholly unnecessary to the vitality of their own faith, and repulsive to all genial persons. We may look in this

[1] Froude's History of England, i. 208.
[2] Stephen's Ecclesiastical Statutes, p. 333 ; Strype's Cranmer, i. 122.

direction to find an explanation of a fact which presses itself upon the notice of every one versed in the details of New England history during its Puritan age, and the contemporary history of the Puritans who remained in England. The influences of their exile, with deprivations and hardships, and their freedom to follow out to extremes their own proclivities, prejudices, and fancies, tended to an exaggeration of the natural austerity of Puritanism here, while it was held in restraint among Puritans at home. The ivy-clad churches and towers, the chime of bells, the sports on the green, the village festivals, the bridal revelries, and the holiday delights, all entering into the heritage of "merry England," were not without their softening and amiable working upon the sentiments even of those least in sympathy with them because of their Puritan spirit.

But the exiles here parted with all these mute or pleading influences which soften and enrich the heart and cheer the routine of toil and brighten the family home. The first generation born from the Puritans on this soil were of stiffer and sterner fibre than their parents, and such of them as found their way to the old home always became mellowed, even if their fellowship there was confined to the dissenting households. The Puritans remaining in England, still under the influence of traditional beliefs and ecclesiastical observances, were less repelling in their austerity than their brethren who had gone into the wilderness. The former still maintained neighborly and companionable intercourse with many who were not in sympathy with their own ways. The exiles were isolated from all liberalizing and expanding influences, and restricted to a fellowship — and that a very close one — whose necessity it was to be all of one mind, in full accord as to purposes and methods. They were compelled to discover by their own experience that this was impracticable. The highest rule of guidance which they recognized was that of the individual conscience "enlightened by the Word." But this enlightened conscience was not a common luminary. Individuals most tenacious of their own consciences were most grudging of the consciences of others.

One is almost disposed to think that "consciences" first came into recognition and use under those times and circumstances. Consciences thenceforward claim a part and influence in affairs of truth and duty, and in collisions of authority and controversy such as had not before enlisted them. Certainly the range and province of conscience were widened, and its activity and tenderness were intensified. Very many matters not before wonted to engage, much less to disturb it, came under its cognizance. The claim of "liberty of conscience" came in with the Reformation. The world had not heard of it before in the relations in which it was now asserted. Under the old church discipline the office of conscience in some of its sternest and some of its most delicate exercises was assumed by the spiritual director. Often did he create, or reconstruct, or adapt a conscience for matters not within the province of the natural conscience. He could generally prescribe satisfactorily what was to be believed and what was to be done. The Protestant was put into a largely changed position and relation to his conscience, which was set under a divine direction, — silent, not communicated by speech, except through Scriptural help, but left to thought and serious interpretation.

The conscience of a man like Roger Williams, and that of a woman like Mary Dyer, were original and rich in their processes. There had previously been many consciences as profoundly earnest, as highly illuminated. But theirs were engaged on new materials, exercised upon new subjects, and made keen and aggressive by sharp activity in their collisions with other sorts of consciences. Yet there must have been in Puritanism a spirit other and better than that of a peevish, perverse scrupulosity, which alienated from the Church as their heritage by birth and love the hundred scholars and divines from Oxford and Cambridge, and brought them with their flocks into these rude wilderness settlements to do patiently their severe life-work. Had the prompting come from mere contrariety of mind or temper, it would have driven them into eccentric individualities, with no accord in one earnest, consenting acceptance of doctrine, duty, institution, and discipline. That the distinctive principles for which the Nonconformists stood when the question of reform and reconstruction of the system of the Church — clearing it of many abominations — was first fully opened, were not prompted by caprice, by unworthy personal aims, or by any narrowness of spirit, has been abundantly assured by the persistency with which Puritan principles have been maintained in England from that time to this. They have not only survived, but have aggressively and yet peacefully continued their original protests and their consistent reforming work. What we in this land owe to the mastery secured by Puritan principles from their first full assertion, recognition, and prevalence here, needs no rehearsal on these pages. (These principles, as relating to religion, independently of politics, — save as they necessarily involved a radical influence in political affairs, — were thus set forth by the Puritans : The sole authority and the sufficiency of the Scriptures ; the parity of Christian ministers ; the independency of the churches in their institution and discipline ; the right of the laity to choose their own religious teachers, and freedom in worship and ritual.) Enough has been said upon the resolute and consistent persistency of the Puritans in refusing to be led outside of the Scriptures into the slough of tradition and patristic divinity. The parity of the ministry, with all the inferences and consequences following from it, was the most startling and revolutionary of all the principles of Puritanism, as it leaped back through all the towering assumptions and corruptions of the hierarchical centuries to the simplicity and equality of the first Christian brotherhood. Whatever of undue or harmful influence we may see occasion in the following pages for ascribing to the "elders" in the severity of the administration of the Massachusetts theocracy, we may rightfully claim for the Puritans the supreme achievement of prostrating, and for all time disabling, all that is fairly objectionable in what is conveyed by the phrase, "the power of the clergy," — the assumption and exercise by them of a ghostly, sacerdotal sway. Till within recent years one might read in the observations and criticisms of foreign visitors to this country remarks to the effect that under our voluntary system of religion, with no patronage from the State, there was no encouragement for devoting one's self to the clerical profession, as it offered no field for promotion, advancement, or ambition. That this is so, our tribute of award, of gratitude, and praise, in terms not easy of exaggeration, is due to our Puritan founders. What is there, or ought there to be, in the Christian ministry to provide a field for ambition, its favors, lures, and rewards? There may have been since the first Puritan age something more of decent regards for consistency and propriety in the conditions for advancement in the Church of England in the places for clerical ambition, and in the prizes of titles and honors. But no improvement in methods would have reconciled the Puritans to a system which under a reformation should have preserved even a semblance of the old Papal hierarchy, which tasked the powers of language to express the gradation of dignities in priestly offices. "His Holiness," "His Grace," "His Eminence," "Very Reverend," "Most Reverend," "Right Reverend," and the other variations for expressing successive superlatives of honor and dignity were as chaff to the Puritan, to whom the noblest of titles was that of "Minister of God's Word." Nor should we forget that as the direct result of this voluntary rejection by the Puritans of all these sacerdotal and hierarchical

pretensions, laymen for the first time reclaimed their full
equality in all the rights, functions, and methods of institution and discipline connected with religion. And it is of
the gravest import that our country — for at least this first
century of its life — has been saved from all complications
of its policy through ecclesiastical, hierarchical, and sacerdotal prerogatives, such as have contemporaneously distracted the administration of secular affairs in France,
Belgium, Italy, Germany, and Austria. There is, indeed,
a large variety of ecclesiastical titles strewn over our country among sectarian dignitaries, from cardinals downward.
But as these have no baronial, temporal jurisdiction, no
privileges or immunities above the humblest citizen, the
titles interest only those who bear or confer them, and are
as harmless as the grandiloquent epithets of Free Masonry,
Odd Fellowship, and of the knights, encampments, and
commanderies. Occasionally we may see some trivial and
ludicrous affectation in here and there a Bishop of the
Protestant Episcopal fold in our States, after the enjoyment
of the palatial hospitality of an English prelate, on returning home, using in his signature the name of the State in
which is his diocese, or donning the Episcopal apron, the
knee-gaiters, and the shovel hat. These are likely to suggest to the spectator a craving in the dignitary for other
prerogatives unattainable here. The mere profession and
office of a minister of religion are sure to draw to him
from the average class of sober-minded persons as much of
regard and influence as it is well for him to have, simply
on the ground — assumed or conceded — that his converse
is with interests above and beyond the secularities of
life. The spirit of Puritanism distrusts and rebukes all
sacerdotalism, and is even impatient of much clericalism. To the Puritans Christendom is indebted for first
giving bold and practical reassertion to the grand proclamation of an apostle, that every Christian is his own
" king and priest unto God," capable of discharging for

himself the two highest offices of the secular and the religious life.

The Massachusetts exiles, after a thirty years' trial of their own church institution, had learned to state with some precision the substance and extent of their nonconformity with their mother Church. The General Court in December, 1660, in an address to King Charles II., deprecating his possible interference with their religious liberties, wrote thus : —

"Wee could not live without the publicke worship of God. Wee were not permitted the use of publicke worship without such a yoake of subscription and conformity as wee could not consent unto without sinne. That wee might therefore enjoy divine worship without the humane mixtures, without offence either to God, man, or our owne consciences, wee, with leave, but not without teares, departed from our country, kindred, and fathers' houses, into this Pathmos. Ourselves, who came away in our strength, are, by reason of very long absence, many of us become greyheaded, and some of us stooping, for age. The omission of the pre-mentioned injunctions, together with the walking of our churches, as to the point of order, the congregationall way, is all wherein wee differ from our Orthodox brethren." [1]

This frank avowal of the degree of dissent or variance, and of the still surviving bond of accord in their relations to the mother Church, may stand as the explanation for which we are seeking, to reconcile an avowed attachment and gratitude to it, causing "teares" when they left their home, with the setting up of a "way" of their own. The explanation will pass for much or little, according to the view which may be taken as to what constituted the substance and identity of the English Church. Did this consist in the Church being the vehicle or channel for the transmission of the faith, with the Scriptures and ordinances, the institution of worship and Christian instruc-

[1] Records, vol. iv. pt. i. p. 452.

tion, — or in its remnant of hierarchical government, its forms, and ritual ? The Puritan believed that if the Church could preserve its identity and its divine character and office after being cleared of so many of the inventions and corruptions introduced into it under the Roman dominancy, it would be all the more a true Church if reconstructed after the primitive pattern. The passage of an ocean of space, with their savage surroundings, had not severed the dear ties of kinship with the English stock, nor could their preference of the congregational to the prelatical way deprive them of their church heritage. In this, as in so many other points of interest, we may safely study the course and example of Winthrop. He never in terms renounced communion with the Church of England, but at once adopted and was fully content with " the congregationall way."

As Puritanism, under its type of nonconformity, steadily developed its radical tendency, involving a complete revolution and reconstruction in the English Church, opposition to its whole spirit and work became naturally more decided and resolute. It could not have been otherwise. The very stones would have cried out against the substitution of a fully developed Puritanism, for that partial compromise with the old Church system, which the statesmanship and the ecclesiastical polity of the realm decided could alone be practicable and wise. The grand and solemn cathedrals, so majestic in their compass, so rich in their symbolism, with an altar for every Christian grace and virtue, with aisles once swept by gorgeous processions, with their shrines of saints and every emblem of sanctity within, and grinning devils and monsters put to service outside on the buttresses and water-gutters, — these proud temples of the " ages of faith" would have protested against being turned into Puritan meeting-houses. Little suited or serviceable as they are for the reduced solemnities of the English ritual, as they were designed for more elaborate

uses, the Established Church has with difficulty availed
itself of their empty and denuded walls; but a Puritan as-
semblage gathered in them, as open for only one day in a
week, with extempore prayer, vocal psalmody without organ
accompaniment, and led by the pitch-pipe, and long dis-
coursings measured by the hour-glass, would have been an incongruous spectacle.   The worshipper in some of the larger
ancient church edifices of Holland and Scotland has noticed,
not however with satisfaction to eye or thought, how parti-
tions dividing choir, nave, and transept afford accommoda-
tions to several companies of worshippers.   This is better,
however, than the yielding up of one portion of such an
edifice to the uses of a lumber-room.   The clergy of the
English Church have a plaintive reminder in their grand
minsters of what they had to leave behind them when
they parted with the " idolatries " of Rome.   The ridicule
and contempt which have been lavished upon the early
Puritan meeting-houses of Massachusetts have overshot the
mark.   The assumption has been that the bareness, grimness, and ugliness of these structures indicated the taste
and preferences of those who built them.   It was not so.
They did the best they could in their straits of necessity,
their lack of seemly materials, and dependence upon village
architects and carpenters.   Each renewal and substitution
of such edifices marked a steady improvement in the fitness of things.

It was certainly with no view to laxity or ease or deliverance from religious restraint and discipline that the responsible leaders of the exile to New England instituted
by preference their own way of " church estate."   With an
intense dread of the extravagant and fanatical sectaries
of that age, the Puritans were most exacting and orderly
in settling their church institutions, far exceeding in caution and discipline the methods of the English Church.
They demanded the highest standard of character, of abilities, and of learning in their ministers.   Their requisites

for church membership and communion were such as only absolute hypocrisy could trifle with. Accepting only the Scriptures as authoritative for them, we shall have occasion to note how absolute and implicit was their allegiance to the Bible.

Yet it must be frankly admitted, as already intimated, that the influences of exile, and of being left free to work out their own tendencies and preferences, soon completely alienated them from their mother Church; "the Lord Bishops" became the ogres of their visions. The Common Prayer was defamed as a "stinted and formal" service, repressive of devotion. Saints' days, inclusive of Christmas, became profane and idolatrous observances. The charter of the Bay Company assigns the times for holding courts, as "every last Wednesday in Hillary, Easter, Trinity, and Michaelmas Termes." But those ecclesiastical datings never appear on the court records, and Puritan children born here would have been wholly unable to define them, and probably never heard them spoken. Very significant is the quaint entry in the Journal of Judge Sewall: "The Governor committed Mr. Holyoke's Almanac to me. I blotted against Feb. 14, *Valentine;* March 25, *Annunciation of the B. Virgin;* April 24, Easter ; Sept. 29, *Michaelmass;* Dec. 25, *Christmas*, and no more. (*K. C. Mart.*) was lined out before I saw it. I touched it not." [1]

There is a remarkable entry in Governor Winthrop's Journal which may be cited as showing the difference of opinion entertained here in 1637 about Episcopal ordination : —

"April 6, 1637. The church of Concord kept a day of humiliation at Newtown for ordination of their elders, and they chose Mr. Buckly teacher, and Mr. Jones pastor. Upon a question, moved by one sent from the church of Salem, it was resolved by the ministers there present that such as had been ministers in England were lawful ministers by the call of the people there, notwithstanding their

[1] Sewall Papers, vol. ii. p. 230.

acceptance of the call of the bishops (for which they humbled themselves, acknowledging it their sin), but being come hither they accounted themselves no ministers until they were called to another church, and that, upon election, they were ministers before they were solemnly ordained." [1]

And so the breach widened till, through the action of single independent congregations, and the debates and plat-forms of synods summoned and ratified in their decisions by the General Court, there was perfected here a distinc-tive New England ecclesiastical polity. In this there was no trace of a hierarchy. There was no primate, no su-perior or inferior clergy. Laymen partook equally with ministers in everything appertaining to the institution and discipline of each single church. Except in cases of scan-dalous disorder there could be no interference, but only sisterly relations of advice and sympathy between the churches. The platform of doctrinal belief was adjusted by the Westminster formulas, and for a brief period se-cured a general accord. The services in public worship were as severely naked as were the edifices in which they were held. In the howlings of winter storms fervors of feeling were the substitute for artificial heat. A singular conviction, common alike to the Scotch Presbyterians and the Massachusetts Puritans, held it to be wrong to use in psalmody any more words than was unavoidable, besides those of the original, in metrifying the Psalms.

It was not till the lapse of a period which marks the term of a generation that that well-nigh forgotten manual, the Book of Common Prayer, was recalled to the notice of the Puritan churches in the Bay. This was by a peremp-tory order from the King in 1662, that full liberty should be granted to any persons in the Colony who wished to use that help and guide in their public worship. But it was not till nearly a quarter of a century after that, that an

1 Journal, i. 217.

assembly gathered in Boston, listened and responded to
those services, with a surpliced priest to lead them, though
as yet without the organ. The place reluctantly allowed by
the authorities for those unwelcome exercises was one of
the public halls. After that, an unsympathizing prerogative Governor, by his arbitrary encroachment upon the
proprietary rights, and his defiance of the earnest protests
of the owners of one of the three town meeting-houses,
took possession of it for the worship of the Church of
England. He even had the effrontery to suggest that the
public should furnish the funds to support his clergyman
and his rites. To this pass had it come between the officials of that mother Church from which the exiles had
parted with tears, and their children who were grieved by
its strange appearance among them.

Looking at the subject in all its points of full contrast,
one may well marvel that under the same profession of
discipleship in the Christian religion and of attachment
to it, two such diverse forms of opinion, character, and
conduct should present themselves as appeared respectively
in the English Church and in the fold of Puritanism. The
word "piety" surely carried with it quite different meanings for those who with equal sincerity sought to be guided
by its rule. But there were very different types of Puritanism. Milton, John Howe, and Bunyan were not of the
sort of men in opinion and temperament that served for the
caricatures of Ben Jonson in his "Bartholomew Fayre,
and of Butler in his "Hudibras." We may refer the un-
geniality and austerity of the Puritans of Massachusetts as
shown, for instance, in their aversion to and neglect of all
festival days bearing sacred names, to two effective influences which wrought upon them. The first of these was
that of their own sad and distressing creed, to be brought
to notice in the next chapter. In this, as they believed,
fallen and doomed world, with a race of beings upon it a
few of whom only were to escape perdition, all lightness of

heart, sportiveness, and revelry were unseemly and wicked. The other reason for their discountenance of church festivals might allege for itself some justification. They observed that sacred names for consecrating festive occasions were "prophanely" abused by license, wantonness, and coarse dissipation. The day after Christmas in England found the jails filled with rioters, wassailers, and brawlers. Within a score of years after the settlement of Boston, the quiet town with its staid and rigid ways was often scandalized by the follies and excesses of strangers and sailors brought here in the expanding commerce and traffic. This was the occasion of the following unamiable and repulsive enactment of the General Court in May, 1659 : —

"For preventing disorders arising in severall places within this jurisdiction, by reason of some still observing such festivals as were superstitiously kept in other countrys to the great dishonnor of God and offence of others, it is therefore ordered by this Court, and the authority thereof, that whosoever shall be found observing any such day as Christmas or the like, either by forbearing of labour, feasting, or any other way, upon any such accounts as aforesaid," shall be subjected to a fine of five shillings. The same enactment forbade "unlawful games, as cards, dice, etc." [1]

There is something alike pathetic and amusing in tracing through the Diary of good Chief-Justice Samuel Sewall the marks of his grief, chagrin, and, we may almost add, his spite, at the intrusion of "the Church" on the guarded domain of Puritanism. This, however, occurred only after the revocation of the Colony Charter, and the substitution of another which substantially put a period to the Puritan age and administration. There had come to be in the Colony many Englishmen, occasional visitors from the English West Indies, for purposes of trade, and soldiers and sailors of the British army and navy. In the tem-

[1] Records, vol. iv. pt. i. p. 366.

porary period of arbitrary government under Andros, aided by the persistent efforts of Randolph, worship by the English ritual was introduced in Boston, and a church was built in 1688. From that period on to the War of Independence a few missionaries of the Church were sent to Massachusetts, as to other of our Colonies, sustained by funds of a charitable organization in England, and a few of the natives of the Colonies went thither to obtain Episcopal ordination. By some of these, and by laymen preferring their ministry, the object of procuring from England one or more resident bishops was earnestly agitated. But the inherited and existing opposition to such temporal and spiritual ecclesiastics as those from whom the fathers had turned their faces, prevailed through our whole colonial period to effect the exclusion from our soil of English prelacy. After the Revolution the way was clear for the Episcopal, as for all other denominations of Christians, without favor or hindrance, to establish its own policy. Ten of the missionary clergy in Connecticut in 1783 chose another, Samuel Seabury, to go by their request to seek consecration in England. This was refused him, and as an alternative he sought it from the Non-juror bishops of Scotland, who were without standing and functions in England. Seabury received no official recognition there; and even here at home many Episcopal ministers and laymen hesitated to regard him as having the full Apostolic grace.[1] Three other ministers were afterward sent for consecration, which by negotiation, and the assent of Par-

---

[1] Seabury brought from England a "mitre," which is preserved under glass in the Library of Trinity College, Hartford. His return, with his dubious dignity, met with various greetings, from respectful courtesy to raillery and satire. He gathered under him fourteen "inferior clergy," resident missionaries then dropped from the pay of the Society. Though the State was plentifully strewn with religious societies and ministers not needing his supervision, he signed himself "Bishop of Connecticut." He so magnified his office that some of the people congratulated themselves that they had not had among them before the War a real "Lord Bishop."

liament, was granted to them ; a proviso, however, denied them any ecclesiastical standing in the realm. Thus by the regular methods of Episcopacy our country is well provided with its clergy, who are doing faithful and devoted service in its cause. So has the old breach with its animosities and its bitterness been healed.

IV.

THE PURITANS AND THE BIBLE.

THERE are cogent reasons for bringing into an emphatic relation of connection and union the Puritans and the Bible ; for that Book was to the Puritans what it had never been before to any class or communion of Christians, and what it has not been since the close of the Puritan age, even to those who in lineage and creed may be regarded as nearest in kin and sympathy with them. The leading aim and purpose which the writer of these pages has in view, and which have prompted the positive and unqualified statement just made, are to refer, to trace, and explain the spirit which moved the Puritan founders of Massachusetts, in their principles and legislation, to their own peculiar estimate of and way of using the Bible. Strong and resolute as were their own wills as men, sharing as they did all the passions, weaknesses, and limitations of human nature, they were held under the mastery of a religious belief, in stern loyalty to which they subjected themselves and attempted to subject others. All the noble qualities of the Puritans credited to them by candid judges least in sympathy with them, — their love of liberty, their fidelity to conscience, their stern and heroic constancy in self-sacrifice, the penetrating intelligence and good judgment shown in the institutions which they devised and fostered, and their generous thoughtfulness for the welfare of their posterity, — all found inspiration and guidance in their way of regarding and their way of using the Bible.

And to the same type or form of belief we are to refer all
the qualities of Massachusetts Puritanism which are un-
lovely, it may be even hateful, to us, the occasion of gibes
and satires, of contempt and invective, even from those
who have entered into the heritage of Puritanism. From
the same fountain flowed waters both sweet and bitter.
The bigotry, the austerity, the harsh and cruel rule of the
Puritans may be directly traced to the creed which they
firmly believed to be taught them by God in the Scriptures.
The Puritan estimate and use of the Bible will further
engage a somewhat detailed exposition when, in the following pages, we examine the scheme and method of their
Biblical commonwealth. We may here anticipate what is
to be more definitely studied there by some general remarks
illustrating the opening sentence of this division of our
subject.

There is no lack of grave themes, in open debate, on
which the minds alike of the common mass of men and of
those of the best training and enlightenment are divided
by the extremes of opinion and belief. But of such subjects that of the most transcendent and momentous interest
presents itself to us under terms which may be thus stated.
With the bold freedom of the speculative and scientific
processes of our own times, the profound and all-compre-
hensive question which engages our philosophy is this:
Whether the force which works through the Kosmos in
physical law can rightly be conceived of as directed by a
Person, a self-existent individual Being, a God manifested
in Nature, providence, and experience? While that question is debated on the high fields of philosophy, leaving in
suspense all the pregnant alternatives which wait on its
decision, another fact, of equal significance, is this: that
millions of our race have for many generations been reading reverently and with confident assurance, in their various
languages, a Book called "the Word of God." Leaping
over all the guesses, haltings, and doubts which result in

belief or denial to others, these millions of believers, through tradition, education, or individual conviction, rest in the assurance that in and by that Book they are in converse with God, who through it discloses to them his mind and will, his method of government, his decrees and purposes. As such a Book, the Bible was to the Puritans, in superlative regard, what it had not been to any generation or fellowship of Christians before them, and what in unimpaired, unreduced estimate it is not to any such fellowship now.

The great exigency of the Reformation substituted the Bible for the Church, for all the needs and uses of religion, as a rule of faith, for authority in the direction of conscience, in spiritual discipline, in the guidance of conduct, and through the whole course and experience of life. This substitution of the Bible for the Church was followed by the most serious and momentous consequences, of which even the most sagacious and prescient-minded men had at the time but vague apprehension and appreciation. The Church — and in what is now to be affirmed of it the Church signified the priesthood — stood for a supernatural society or ordering set up in this world, with divine authority and direction over the whole Christian fold. Its claim and functions, indeed, were asserted only for spiritual matters; but it reserved to itself the prerogative of defining the bounds between the sacred and the secular, and its sternest rule was often within the range of the latter. The source of its authority being divine, that authority was in its exercise absolute. It was not to be qualified or questioned at any point in which it might assert itself. The line between the priesthood and the laity was sharply drawn, and was complete and deep. Qualified theologians and ecclesiastics might discuss and pronounce upon matters of faith, but laymen had no privilege or share in such matters. They were to hear and obey.

The use of the Bible, which came in with the Reforma-

tion, broke the sway of the priesthood, and created what
have since been called *laymen* for full recognition in the
Christian Church. Through the whole dominancy of the
Roman or Papal system it is but half the truth to say that
the Bible held but a subordinate or secondary place in the
regard and service of Christians. The existence of such a
Book was absolutely unknown to the vast majority in succeeding generations, and only a very slender minority of
those who knew of it, wholly among the clerical order, put
it to any use. Even the monk Luther came to the knowledge of it by accident, when dusting a library. When the
authority of the Church for faith and discipline was renounced, the Book became the alternative. Never again
will the civilized world be witness to such an outburst of
fervor and enthusiasm in all classes of society as accompanied the free circulation of the Bible. The peasant and
the artisan took it in hand as if it were a direct gift to
them from the archives of the skies. The Book at once
rose to its august supremacy, not, as now so generally regarded, as a miscellaneous collection of the world's sacred
literature, but as an inspired, infallible, and complete disclosure to men of the mind and will of God. Its letter,
rather than what we call its spirit, had supreme regard.
We shall have abundant occasion to notice how the bondage to the letter of the single " texts," into which it was
divided, clouded the minds of its most devout readers from
the illumination of its divinest truths. The Westminster
Confession teaches that " the Holy Scriptures are to be
read with a high and reverend esteem of them : with a firm
persuasion that they are the very Word of God, and that
he only can enable us to understand them." What were
traditions, church councils, priestly teachings, in comparison with the direct, the original, the sole vehicle of communication between God and men ! To the supreme
estimate and the free use of that Book we are to trace
the source of democracy in Church and State ; for the

Bible, the greatest treasure which the world held, recognized no prerogative of rank or privilege in its use, save that it was to open itself most fully to the simple and humble. The learned, of course, soon discovered that they had an advantage over the illiterate in dealing with the Bible. But they were restricted in the use of this advantage by two limitations: first, the accepted belief that only God's illuminating Spirit, not human learning, could " open the Word " to the reader; and second, that anything like skill, ingenuity, or elaborateness in explanation would impair directness and simplicity.

Let us, by anticipation, here recognize some of the graver consequences which followed this substitution of the Bible for the Church, as if it were suited to serve all the uses of authority and guidance heretofore recognized as the functions of the priesthood. The first of these consequences was the assigning to the Bible a character, qualities, and authority, and a fitness for the uses made of it, which it does not claim for itself, which are brought under searching question when the Book is candidly and intelligently examined, and which have been discredited in part by positive knowledge obtained from other sources, and in part by the judgment of those best qualified to utter well-grounded opinions. There was assumed for the Book unity, homogeneity, and ultimate completeness in its contents ; but on the face of it it shows itself to be a miscellaneous collection of writings of vast diversity of tone, teaching, and value, by standards of truth and edification. With that easy credence often extended to objects and events invested with the glamour of the distant past and knit with fond and reverent associations passing down through generations, it came to be taught and believed that there was a time and occasion when certain qualified persons, divinely and infallibly directed, selected out of all the world's existing literature certain so-called " canonical writings," to which they assigned a divine authorship and sanction, inspired and

9

infallible in their teachings, designed and adapted for the use to be made of them. With the most profound sincerity and with the most devout gratitude was the Book taken to the hearts of men in this character. It could not be other or less to them than it was thus believed to be, if it was to serve as a substitute to them for all that the Church had been,—as the bridge between earth and heaven, the mediation between men and God. The Bible was to be the guide-book for every pilgrim who craved other guidance than that of cloud and star.

Another of the graver consequences of the substitution of the Bible for the teaching and guiding Church for all the needs and uses of faith and piety, for individuals, and in religious institutions and fellowships, was, that thenceforth all unity and accord in belief and observance became utterly impossible. If the Book itself were infallible, there was no longer an infallible interpreter of it. The right of private judgment was claimed for each individual reader of Scripture. It was for each to make what he could of it, as he did of the common free air of heaven. The ultimate issue, however denied or withstood, has been reached and stoutly maintained, never to be yielded, that no individual official, or institution, or representative body on the earth, is now interposed between God and man in eternal adjustments.

This is not the place for tracing the nemesis, or retributive penalties, which have been visited upon Christendom, of the fond belief and superstitious notions of so many forms and shades associated with the Bible, because, by constraint of circumstance and seeming necessity, it was received as a substitute for what the Church had been to Christians. They had been trained in the belief that there was on the earth an authoritative and sufficient mediation for them in all that constituted religion. The depository of that authority being discredited and renounced, where but in the Bible were they to find a substitute ? Painful and disheartening is it, to all who are not ruthlessly indifferent to the tender affiliations with which even fond superstitions connect themselves with all that is sincere and sustaining to human hearts amid the mysteries and burdens of life, to trace the long process of the assault and the defence involved in the conflict between the traditional view of the Bible and the discrediting and discomfiture of it. The old Church has been justly charged with discouraging and visiting with its penalties the utterance of views developed by intellectual progress, science, and positive knowledge, in opposition to its teachings. But the maintenance of the Puritan estimate of the Bible has required the same treatment of those whose candid inquiries, discriminating study, and intelligent criticism have exposed manifest tokens of human authorship, with consequent errors, in the Book. The favorite plea of the champions of the traditional view of the Bible is that the criticisms and objections raised against it, though constantly re-urged, have been over and over again met and confuted. This is not true. Dead soldiers do not reappear on the battle-field. Objections so often parried retain their vitality because they have not been confuted.

How vain is the attempt to give any intelligible definition of Inspiration as applicable to the whole Bible ! What ingenuities and sophistries, what playing upon the credulity of the ignorant and confiding, have been put to use in meeting the honest questionings of thoroughly earnest inquirers ! What freak of fancy in all the workings of human brains has equalled the inventiveness of the genius that first suggested that the amatory idyl called " Solomon's Song " is an allegorical illustration of the love between Jesus Christ and his Church ? Large portions of the Bible had no more need, or opportunity, for the intervention of " inspiration," than do those writings which engage the pen of the genealogist, the narrator, or the common clerk. In that sublime Scripture bearing the name of

" Job," the ablest discussion of the " Problem of Evil " to be
found in all the libraries of the world, his three " miserable
comforters " offer him solutions of the problem which he
confutes. How does the quality of Inspiration apply there ?
We might ask the same question about many of the sentences in the book called " Ecclesiastes," which holds the
same eminent place among the world's unnumbered essays
on the *Summum Bonum*, or the " Object of Living." The
book of " Proverbs " is a gathering up of all the floating
sententious wisdom of its age and place. Some of its sentences have a glow and pitch of supermundane wisdom in
them ; others are of the tone and earthliness of " Poor
Richard's Almanac." So we find through the Book utterances of lofty truth, as of the speech of angels, alternating
with such as lack the discretion and decency becoming an
ordinary standard of moral teaching. And what is to be
said of the discrepancies and the acknowledged errors of
statement in a book so rashly called in its whole contents
the " Word of God " ? And when that Book, set before
us as a substitute for the former offices and functions of
a Church, and left to be interpreted by the honest purpose
of every reader, is declared plainly to reveal the will of
God and the way of salvation, so that one who runs may
understand it, what shall we say of the enormous and un-
ceasing toils of scholars, critics, commentators, and apol-
ogists and defenders that have been spent upon it for
centuries to make it intelligible, acceptable, edifying, and
credible to its readers ? Why in all Protestant theological
seminaries should there be needed such able and learned
professors of dead languages, and such an apparatus of
erudite volumes piled in mountain heaps, with accessions
made to them every year, " so that the world can scarce
contain them " ? The time, expense, and toil that have
been spent by scholars and theologians in elucidating and
defending the Bible, if directed in other channels, would
long since have expelled illiteracy and ignorance from the

whole of Christendom. And all this in the service of the one single Book asserted to be inspired and supervised by God for the edification and salvation of the simplest in understanding!

How blind were those who, in their straits for an authority in religion, assigned to the Bible the estimate and use which it had for the Puritans, to the results which naturally and inevitably were to follow, when its devout and earnest readers should find in it such wholly inconsistent and contradictory systems and tenets for belief! While some have found in the Book a God who is a stern and dread Sovereign, bound by his relentless decrees, others are there won to love an indulgent and all-merciful Father. The hopeless doom of the vast majority of human beings to an eternity of suffering " in soul and body " is the doctrine yielded by the inspired and infallible Scriptures to one class of believers, — to another class beams forth the hope of salvation and bliss for every individual of the race. The four distinct conflicts in matters of opinion and belief, whose course we are to follow in these pages, as illustrating the intolerant rule of the Puritans, all found the whole material of variance and strife within the pages of the Bible. None of the disputants — save to some extent the Quakers — went outside of that Book for argument or belief, and all of them heartily and reverently accepted the Puritan estimate and use of it.

The legacy of rightful regard, or of fond superstition, which the Puritan belief of the Bible has left to us has within recent years had a striking illustration. Three well-known and assured facts have been recognized and admitted by all persons intelligently informed on the subject: (1) That materials exist for securing a better and more faithful original text of the Scriptures than were within the reach of those who translated the accepted English version; (2) That our living Biblical scholars are fully competent

to make the best use of those materials ; (3) That there
are acknowledged faults and errors, obscuring and miscon-
struing the sense and meaning in our version. Proceeding
upon these three undeniable facts, a body of scholars and
best-qualified men in England and America were announced
as set upon the sacred task of revision. At once most of
the " religious journals " sounded an " alarm," such as might
have been properly felt if a proposition had been made to
invalidate the title-deeds of their property. The intent
was that, accepting the traditional estimate of the Bible as
God's Book, a serious and faithful effort should be made
to clear it of all the faults and imperfections which could
be detected as having come into it through its human transmission. Of course any changes, even only of words, would
grieve the sensibilities and tender attachments of many of
the living generation. It was supposed that these would
be conciliated by the supreme purpose had in view, and by
the thought that the generations to follow them should have
a Book more worthy of the same attachments. The years
of conscientious and generous toil came to a close. The
results were given to English-speaking Christendom. The
ungracious reception of them need not here be discussed.
And even a graver theme would engage us, if we should
candidly recognize what is now freely described as " the
scandal of the clerical profession ; " namely, the reticence,
the insincerity, the duplicity even, of religious teachers who
withhold the frank avowal of their own qualified opinions
about the Bible, and leave those who confide in their teachings to infer that their traditional beliefs are unshaken. A
considerate allowance may suggest a partial palliation of
this compliance of religious teachers, in the extreme embarrassment they would find in reducing or qualifying,
while still seeking to retain, the old Puritan estimate of the
Bible as the veritable " Word of God."

The statement in my opening sentences affirmed that the
estimate and use of the Bible made by the Massachusetts

Puritans, as original in all the special and peculiar characteristics marking the Puritan age, were confined to that age. And by the Puritan age I mean the lifetime of the first two generations here. Those who come closest to the lineage and creed of the founders of New England do not really hold their estimate and make their use of the Bible. I know very well what strong or qualified protests may be made against this assertion; nor do I propose at any length to defend it. Those who are concerned are free to challenge it; but their chief contest must be with the air which we are all of us breathing. We may search our Puritan literature in vain for an apology for the Bible, while apology and defence are the chief services to it in our time. If one would attempt by a single word to describe the attitude of mind and thought in which the multitude of people of the average intelligence around us stand to the Bible, we might say that it is " a bewildering book." It puzzles and confounds them. We say and hear unchallenged, that the Bible is the best and most precious of books which the world contains, and that in it " holy men of God spake as moved by the Holy Spirit." But while we speak or assent to those words there is a baffled question in our minds, Why is it a book, one book, containing writings of every class and type which make up for us in these days the whole miscellany of literature ? And what a marvellous variety of contents and subjects does it present to us, — ranging over the whole scale between the extremes of heavenly purity, sublimity of heavenly counsels and revealings, and the grossest disclosures of human foulness and frailty. And to this Book was assigned the most august character and authorship. It was dictated and inspired by God, who informed the minds and guided the pens of those who wrote it. Filled with oracles and mysteries which our brooding thoughts ache in the effort to fathom, it was said to be so simple in its illuminating power that the sage had no advantage over the little child in the entering in of its light into his spirit. So keen and searching is its glance into the inmost being of man that it is " quick and powerful, sharper than any two-edged sword, piercing even to the dividing asunder of soul and spirit, and of the joints and marrow, and is a discerner of the thoughts and intents of the heart." It contains a whole armory of weapons and implements for offensive and defensive warfare for the pilgrimage through human life, — breastplate, shield, and helmet against all the fiery darts of the wicked, a girding of truth about the loins, and the sword of the Spirit.

It would not be in place here to trace by contrast with the Puritan view and use of the Bible the estimate of it held by those who read and study it with reverence and gratitude now, and try to deal with the doubts and perplexities which it opens for earnest minds. The full, confiding, unquestioning faith in it as held by the Puritans has yielded to cautious and discriminating rules for its use. Strangely inconsistent with the character for simplicity, authority, and divinity once ascribed to it, is the apparatus now provided for scholars and humble readers, of comment, explanation, and vindication.

One of the most striking characteristics of the use of the Bible by the Puritans was their rigid literalism, with such slight — if, indeed, any — allowance for what we call figures of speech, exaggerations, or orientalisms. If my memory serves me for the occasion, I am prompted to say that it is only or chiefly in some of the gushing and glowing pages of Roger Williams that we find the first allowances in all our early Puritan literature for the poetic personifications and rhetorical wealth of the language of the Bible. Neither can I recall a single instance in which preacher or reader in our Puritan age sought relief from any difficulty which the Scriptures presented to him in suggesting a possible mistranslation of the original. Wonderful, indeed, in its majesty, wealth, fulness, and variety of contents is that

volume for the uses made of it, in the aptness of its phrases
and " texts " for meeting and addressing all the experiences
and solemnities of human life. And will it not be a yet
more wonderful book to the world when we claim for men
their rightful share in the authorship of it ? While the
great illuminating Spirit has been seeking in it to come
into communication with humanity, men have responded
by trying in it their own flights and soarings above the
atmosphere of earth.

The fervent, intense, and confiding veneration of the
Puritans for " the Word," in the authority of its letter, its
divine fulness for precedent, usage, and guidance in all
things, was accompanied by as unswerving an allegiance to
a creed, believed to have been ably and faithfully digested
from the Scriptures, — one or more " texts " from which
accompanied and enforced each doctrinal statement. This
creed was the substance of catechisms for children, and
nutriment for the digesting and assimilating spiritual vigor
of strong men. Indeed, the most forcible illustration we
can give of the supreme reverence of the Puritans for the
Scriptures would be their constant, complete, and unswerving loyalty to the creed which they believed to be taught
and certified by those Scriptures. As one of the latest
students of Puritan history has written, " a living coal from
the altar of Calvin touched their lips. The gloom of Calvinistic theology, the atrocity of its logical conclusions,
went for nothing with men who were indifferent to abstract
speculations." [1]

Those among us of Puritan lineage who profess still to
hold and stoutly to defend the old creed, at least, as they
phrase it, " for substance of doctrine," — the very quality
in it which they appear to others not to accept, — are generally aggrieved at any summary statement of its terms
and contents made by one who rejects it and condemns it.
They charge that it is not understood, that it is misrepre-

[1] Doyle, The English in America, i. 132.

sented and even caricatured. It may be that in all such
cases candor should make allowance for the fact that only
a firm believer in any tenet apprehends fairly what it means
to him, as offered to, received, and interpreted by his own
mind ; and that it is only for him to state it with the qualifications, the tonings of light and shade which it has as he
receives it. One who rejects it misapprehends it. As a
matter of fact, we have become familiar with and must
reconcile ourselves to the claim of the privilege by many
around us to believe certain formulas and tenets which, as
stated in words, mean something quite different to them and
to ourselves. But we have need to make no such allowance for the Puritans' constancy to the Puritan creed. That
creed is the exponent of Puritanism. Literalism or looseness in adhesion to it measured the glow or the chill of
faith for them. They never apologized for their creed, or
mollified, reduced, or toned down its strong affirmations.
There is not now in Christendom a religious fellowship
which, assembling its divines in solemn convention, could
or would digest and send forth the Westminster Confession.
We have learned to make allowances for the different degrees of reality and intensity of conviction under which
belief is exercised. There is hardly a single religious truth
which men believe as they do the truth that they must partake of food in order that they may keep alive. The censorious contrast so often drawn between the earnestness of
men in the pursuit of secular interests and their lukewarmness in their religious interests, recognizes this difference in
the ways of believing. And here again we have to admit no
qualification for the fulness and intensity of the faith of the
Puritans in the Bible and their creed. In vain shall we
look in the records of what they sought for and did, for
any other key to their conduct — either in noble earnestness and constancy, or in bigotry, austerity, and severity of
rule — than their way of believing and finding their law
in the Scriptures. The God of the Old Testament rather

than of the New was the object of their supreme dread and
reverence. Their faith was stern, and only their strong
manhood made them able to accept it, — we cannot add
the words, love it. And this God presented himself to
them in the dreadness of his sovereignty with a spell that
enthralled them. He was absolute in his power, decrees,
and purposes. What he did was always and only " for
his own glory." Man was most filial and most obedient
when he magnified that idea of God. Do what God might,
it was enough that He had done it. It was in the constraint and completeness of an all-absorbing loyalty to
the sovereign will of the Supreme Ruler that we cannot
err in finding the main reason of the truth — so justly affirmed — that loyalty to an earthly, anointed king stood
for so little with the Puritans as distinguished from others
of their countrymen. They were poor courtiers. They
reserved all their gravest sentiments for the august Supreme. Without doubt it was the training in this direction
which the first Puritan generation born on this soil received from their parents, that made it so easy for those
who followed them to dispense with a king. Indeed, Puritanism involved in its first principles a latent and by no
means unconscious antipathy to kingly rule. The Puritans
read in " the Word " that God, after remonstrating with
the Jews for their demand of a king, in yielding to their
importunity gave them reason for regretting it. They so
loved to associate sovereignty and all its august prerogatives with the Supreme Majesty that they grudged granting
any portion of it to men. There is a chasm of difference
between the references and addresses of courtiers and of
Puritans to king and to God. The Puritans were equally
reconciled to both of the deprivations expressed in the
formula, " No bishop, no king." If the colonists of Massachusetts had been Episcopalians, under the royal head
of the English Church, there might have been no American Revolution. I have not found in the records of the

Puritan colony a single spontaneous prompting of "loyalty," nor an expression of it but what seems constrained. It is true that the monarchs on the throne of England in that period were unworthy of personal respect or homage, but this was not the sole nor even the chief reason for the weakness of the spirit of allegiance in the Puritan for the occupant of an earthly throne.

We cannot strain too hard the assertion that the sovereignty of God — absolute, unchallenged in will, power, and decree — was the root tenet of religion for the Puritans. Recognizing that, we can understand how they not only became reconciled but even found joy and comfort in assenting to, all the appalling doctrines of their creed as deduced from and consistent with it, including its "atrocious logical consequences." If in spite of what is to us the irrational, the shuddering substance and tone of that creed, they felt under a constraining obligation to believe it, and even found "a fearful joy" in accepting it, we can well understand what a reflex effect it would have on the fibres and nerves of their own being. Severity of bearing and of mien, austerity of discipline, and an awful discharge of their magistracy for God would mark their features and their rule.

We must have before us the leading propositions of the creed, as they concern the relations of human beings to the Creator, or, as we should express it, of the children of God to their Father, as follows: —

"After God had created all other creatures He created man, male and female; formed the body of the man of the dust of the ground and the woman of the rib of the man; endued them with living, reasonable, and immortal souls, and made them after His own image in knowledge, righteousness, and holiness; having the law of God written in their hearts, and power to fulfil it.

"God, placing man in Paradise, entered into a covenant of life with him upon condition of personal, perfect, and perpetual obedience, of which the Tree of Life was a pledge; and forbid-

ding to eat of the Tree of Knowledge of good and evil upon pain
of Death.

"Our first parents being left to the freedom of their own will,
through the temptation of Satan transgressed the commandment
of God in eating the forbidden fruit, and thereby fell from the
state of innocency wherein they were created.

"The covenant being made with Adam as a publick person,
not for himself only, but for his posterity, all mankind descending
from him by ordinary generation sinned in him and fell with him
in that first transgression.

"The Fall brought mankind into an estate of sin and misery.

"Sin is any want of conformity unto or transgression of any
law of God given as a rule to the reasonable creature.

"The sinfulness of that state whereinto man fell consisteth in
the guilt of Adam's first sin, the want of that righteousness wherein he was created, and the corruption of his nature whereby he is
utterly indisposed, disabled, and made opposite unto all that is
spiritually good and wholly inclined to all evil, and that continually, which is commonly called Original Sin, and from which proceed all actual transgressions.

"Original Sin is conveyed from our first parents unto their
posterity by natural generation, so as all that proceed from them
in that way are conceived and born in sin.

"The Fall brought upon mankind the loss of communion with
God, his displeasure and curse, so as we are by nature children of
wrath, bond-slaves to Satan, and justly liable to all punishments
in this world and that which is to come.

"The punishments of sin in the world to come are everlasting separation from the comfortable presence of God, and most
grievous torments in soul and body without intermission in hell-
fire forever."

The formula then proceeds to state that mankind being
thus wrecked by failure under a first covenant of works,
God, not leaving all to perish, of —

"His mere love and mercy delivereth His Elect out of it by the
covenant of grace made with Christ, as the second Adam, and in
him with all the Elect as his seed."

The three Divine Persons in the Godhead have each a part in this covenant. The Son, taking flesh upon him, is to satisfy the broken law of the Father, by a sacrificial offering for the Elect, whom the Holy Spirit is to sanctify so that they may avail themselves of the offering made in their behalf.

"They who having never heard the gospel know not Jesus Christ and believe not in him cannot be saved, be they never so diligent to frame their lives according to the light of Nature or the law of that religion which they profess.

"Effectual Calling is the work of God's almighty power and grace, whereby out of His free and especial love to His Elect and from nothing in them moving Him thereunto, he doth in His accepted time invite and draw them to Jesus Christ by His word and spirit.

"The souls of the wicked are at death cast into hell, where they remain in torments and utter darkness, and their bodies kept in their graves as in their prisons, till the resurrection and judgment of the Great Day.

"At the Day of Judgment the wicked shall be cast into hell to be punished with unspeakable torments, both of body and soul, with the Devil and his angels forever."

The Elect, including "their seed," baptized and dying in infancy, being thus saved, —

"the rest of mankind God was pleased — according to the unsearchable counsel of His own will whereby he extendeth or withholdeth mercy as He pleaseth for the glory of His sovereign power over His creatures — to pass by and to ordain them to dishonour and wrath for their sin, to the praise of His glorious justice."

That last reference to the sovereign will and glory of God stopped the mouth of the true Puritan believer, and answered what would have been his rebellious questions before he could ask them.

This "Confession of Faith" — the summary of the Puritan belief concerning the relations between God and the human race — derived its thrall of power over them from two sources: first, from the supreme sovereignty assigned to God by the fearful severity and the grim austerity of its tenets; and second, from the absolute and unshrinking loyalty with which it was held. The framers of it were content simply to state it, without analysis, explanation, or comment. Argument or reasoning in its advocacy would have been to them an impertinence; apology for it would have been cowardice. Put into the forms of our common speech, in equivalent terms, the creed may be set forth as follows : —

God "created" only a single pair of human beings. All the uncounted millions of our race, following on through the ages, are the product of natural generation by the same sexual method that propagates animals, birds, fishes, insects, reptiles, and plants. All these human generations existed " in the loins of Adam." God set him to be the " Federal Head " of the race, as its first representative, charged to act for his race, in responsibility and destiny. On his personal obedience or conformity to the divine command were staked the character and fortunes for this earthly life, and for an endless futurity of bliss or woe, of all of human birth. By disobedience the head of the race fell from innocence, and lost the fruition of blessing, bringing a curse upon the earth, the field of existence for his offspring blighted as the scene of sin and sorrow, and consigning all his posterity to guilt and condemnation. They are born with a nature utterly disabled, alienated from all that is good, and inclined to all evil. But this impaired natural ability carries with it no immunity, no privilege of reduced responsibility, as the divine law imposes its full exaction.

A method of redemption and salvation is provided, which, however, is in fact applicable not to the race as a whole, but to individuals called the " Elect." The Divine man, who comes to the earth to die as a sacrifice for sin in satisfaction for violated law, does not, by redeeming all, repair the whole catastrophe wrought by the human man. How easily Satan made the conquest of this once fair world, and of the destiny of those to whom was given its mastery! In view of the tragic failure of the first experiment of humanity in its opening stage on this earth, we are touched by the fitness of the pathetic lament which we read in Genesis vi. 6: "And it repented the Lord that he had made man on the earth, and it grieved him at his heart." We can but ask, however, whether by the theory of Inspiration we are to regard that sentence as an avowal of the Divine disappointment, or as a comment of the writer of it. The "Elect," whom alone Christ saves, the formulas of the creed leave us to conceive of as thus defined: In the archives of heaven there are, so to speak, record-books, on whose folios are the individual names in their generations of all who are to live and die on this earth. Of these, simply according to God's sovereign will, some are selected, with no reference to their own merits or efforts, to be the subjects of his saving grace. The rest, whatever be their proportion of the whole, are — momentous words! — "passed by," left as reprobates to an awful doom. These live their allotted time on the earth, whether only the days of infancy or the years of protracted age, and then at death, instead of being allowed to pass into nothingness, are kept in conscious existence forever to suffer the torments of hell.

It was never claimed that this creed was conformed to natural justice or to enlightened reason. Nor was it a valid objection to it that, instead of being so conformed, it outraged both justice and reason. It was therefore but futile for natural justice and enlightened reason to dispute the creed. This was accepted submissively and loyally, solely on the ground that it was the revealed will and decree of God. Only as coming from that Divine Source would it have been admitted as authoritative. And here we must recognize the sturdiness of temper, the front of courage, the heroism of spirit manifested by the Puritans in their attitude of docile and unquailing belief. And more than this; they were wont to glory in the crushing down of all their natural discomfiture and rebellings, in that the creed prostrated "the pride of human reason" and humiliated the creature, that honor and majesty might accrue to the Creator. Augustine's willingness to believe a thing because it was impossible was surpassed by the Puritan's humbled, but not bowed, loyalty to his creed.

What known form of heathenism presents to us more shuddering, hideous conceptions of the Divine rule, of the relations between the Father of men and his children, than the Westminster Confession? The curse of being born by the will of man, and the curse of dying by the decree of God, are equally darkened in woe. We know what penalties and agonies, by persecution and inquisitorial tortures, men have inflicted upon their fellows in the service of religion. Might they not plead that they learned their cruelty from God? Would those who held so cruel a creed shrink from any act of cruelty to their fellows? An Indian chief at Newport, so far as he could be made to understand that differences of religious opinions were the reasons for the gathering in his fair island of so many exiles from Massachusetts, exclaimed, in his bewilderment, "What a God have the English, who deal so with one another about their God!"

Whether it be offered in palliation or in condemnation of the severities of the Puritan rule, these must largely be charged upon their creed. An illustrative example may here be in place, allowing perhaps the sternest of the Massachusetts Puritans to speak for himself.

The materials are abundant for illustrating the harsh, vindictive, and cruel spirit quickened and intensified in men under the mastery of this assurance that as "God's people" they could interpret calamities to others as his direct personal judgments. Men otherwise of gentle spirit

10

in social and domestic relations, and of loving friendships, were signally enthralled by this spirit. Endicott's letters to Winthrop, especially when he was ill or under misfortune, are yearningly tender in their affection and sentiment. But let us see how he could write to his revered friend about others, not "godly," under the shock of a dire catastrophe. The ship "Mary Rose" "was blown in pieces with her own powder, being 21 barrels," in the harbor of Charlestown, July 27, 1640. On the next day Endicott writes : —

DEAREST SIR, — Hearing of the remarkable stroake of God's hand upon the shippe and shippes companie of Bristoll, as also of some Atheisticall passages and hellish profanations of the Sabbaths and deridings of the people and wayes of God, I thought good to desire a word or two of you of the trueth of what you have heard. Such an extraordinary judgement would be searched into, what Gods meaninge is in it, both in respect of those whom it concernes more especiallie in England, as also in regard of ourselves. God will be honred in all dealings. We have heard of several ungodlie carriadges in that ship, as, first, in their way overbound they would constantlie jeere at the holie brethren of New England, and some of the marriners would in a scoffe ask when they should come to the holie Land. 2. After they lay in the harbor Mr. Norrice sent to the shippe one of our brethren upon busines, and hee heard them say, This is one of the holie brethren, mockinglie and disdainefullie. 3. That when some have been with them aboard to buy necessaries, the shippe men would usuallie say to some of them that they could not want anything, they were full of the spiritt. 4. That the last Lord's Day, or the Lord's Day before, there were many drinkings aboard, with singings and musick in tymes of publique exercise. 5. That the last fast the master or captaine of the shippe, with most of the companie, would not go to the meetinge, but read the booke of common prayer so often over that some of the company said that he had worne that threedbare, with many such passages. Now if these or the like be true, as I am persuaded some of them are, I think the trueth heerof would be made knowen by some faithfull hand in Bristoll or else where, for it is a very remarkable and unusuall stroake. Pardon, I pray you, my boldness heerein. You shall command mee in any service I can doe. I write the rather because I have some relation that way, and shall therefore be glad to be throughlie informed of theise things. This bein all at present, I leave you with the Lord, desiring myne and my wief's heartie love and service to be remembered to yourself and your dearest yoakefellow, and rest

Yours ever assured,
Jo. Endecott.

Salem, the 28th of the 5th moneth, 1640.[1]

One may well marvel how the gentle and tender-hearted Samuel Sewall, as a judge of the victims of the stark delusion of witchcraft, could sit in condemnation of Rev. George Burrough, his contemporary in college, and the welcome guest of his home. But the spirit of a cruel and relentless creed had overmastered the amiability of its devout disciple.

In justice to the perspective of truth we should here remind ourselves that large allowance is to be made for the general inhumanities and the judicial severities of the Puritan age in all Christendom. Capital penalties, with extreme barbarities in inflicting them, were very numerous, and for trivial offences. Tortures, mutilations of the body, and disease, starvation, and death in loathsome dungeons were miseries endured by many of the selectest spirits of our race. It cannot, however, be doubted that some of the harshest severities of the Puritans here were stimulated, and in belief justified, by the spell wrought upon their spirits by their intense schooling in parts of the Old Testament Scriptures. They read there of direful deeds prompted, directed, and rejoiced over by God. Starting with the axiom that the heathen were to be exterminated, the wars of the Jews were favorite reading for the Puritans. The vindictive and relentless savagery which in-

<hr>

[1] 4 Mass. Hist. Coll., vi. 141, 142.

cluded women and children in slaughter, deeds of surprise and treachery referred to the Divine instigation and approval, fixed in the Puritan mind, as firmly as it was planted in the convictions of the Familiars of the Inquisition, the belief that the body should suffer any stretch of torture in the interest of the soul. The Book of " Judges " — a strange title for the military desperadoes who figure in it — was favorite reading for the Puritans ; it gives in round and large numbers the count of the slaughtered.

The facts that we have among us now, the friends and associates of our daily lives, those who profess reverently and devoutly the old standards of Puritan piety, that great religious fellowships are covenanted by them, and that theological seminaries are pledged to indoctrinate successive classes of candidates with them, to be prepared for the Christian ministry — are accepted by many of us with a mild acquiescence relieved by certain misgivings in our minds. We ask, Do they really believe so ? And we have a way of answering the question satisfactorily to ourselves. But this may lead to the further question, Did the Puritans, with whom we are dealing, verily, sincerely, and profoundly hold, without any reduction or hesitancy of faith, the tenets of their creed ? The answer must be that they did. We have all the evidence in the case that we could desire. We must remind ourselves, however, laying the greatest stress of emphasis upon the most significant fact, that the Puritan creed was constructed under vastly different views and beliefs about physical nature, human nature, and the Divine nature, from those which now guide and express the convictions and thoughts of intelligent persons. We must also bear in mind the fact already stated, that it would be utterly impossible for that creed to be formulated to-day in any Christian fellowship. We retain in use forms of speech founded on the Ptolemaic theory of heaven and earth, but we do not believe what the words assert.

As to the firm and sincere belief of the Puritans in the

very letter of their creed, the evidence, as I have said, is ample and cogent. I have tasked my memory in vain in the attempt to recall from all the pages of the real Puritan divinity which I have read, a single deprecatory or apologetic utterance indicating mental dissent from the professed creed. Calvin did indeed pronounce one of its tenets — that of the damnation of unbaptized infants — " a horrible decree." But this was simply the avowal of a strain upon his loyalty in bowing to it, not a hesitancy in accepting it. The Puritan creed was digested and formulated in terms as rigid and exact as the English language, when its words and forms of speech were more direct and concise than they are now in the expression of abstract statements, would allow. It was not intended that there should be any elasticity in the meaning of its words or in its propositions. This elasticity, however, has in our time been found by some who, while avowing an acceptance of the creed, do not believe it as did those who worded and phrased it. The Puritan did not set himself in judgment upon the creed. He opened the channel for receiving it as his life's food, and trusted to its own working for getting digested and assimilated.

The " burning question " which kindles the strife about the " Progressive Theology " of our day — as to any hope for those who have died in heathenism — was anticipated, with but one answer to it, among our Puritans. The noble, laborious, and patient John Eliot says that some of his Indian converts " had a gift in putting diverse, perplexing questions," as he tried to convey to them the tenets of Calvinism. Among them was a question as easy for him to answer as it was for them to ask, — " Where were their ancestors and deceased children ? " The good man unflinchingly wrote, " I could only answer that the promise was only for believers and their seed." He could not give them even the comfort of offering the petition which had found its way into the English Prayer Book, " Remember

not, Lord, our offences, neither the offences of our fore-
fathers." The creed was taught in the earliest years of
childhood, before any receptive or interpretative faculties
could connect with it intelligent ideas. The " atrocious
logical deductions " from the creed have not hindered but
that men of consummate intellectual powers have toughened
their mental sinews in grappling with it. Jonathan Edwards, intending prose, wrote its logic into poetry; and
Michael Wigglesworth, intending poetry in his doggerel
verses, gives us a prosaic conclusion in assigning to non-
elect infants " the coolest room in hell."

Another reason assuring us of the loyalty of the Puritans to their Creed is found in the suggestion that with no
less of appreciating love for the Scriptures, though with
less of indiscriminate bondage to the letter, they, as some
of their descendants have done, might have found in the
Bible the materials of quite a different creed. To many of
their lineage in blood and faith, to whom the Bible, instead
of being the absolute and final authority, is the most precious of all helps in religion, it opens by a more intelligent
and discriminating use the most illuminating and quickening truths for the guidance and sanctification of life. And
their reverence and love for it still exalt it above all other
books. But to say simply that the Puritan believed that
the Bible yielded to him the creed which he found in it
would be but a tame form in which to express his devout
trust in it, his entire submission to its doctrines. A matter of prime importance presents itself for our consideration here. When a creed or formula of doctrines has
passed by tradition and the succession of church-fellow-
ships, as an inheritance of several generations, while words,
phrases, and forms of speech, with the ideas and sentiments
intended to be expressed by them, are found to have a
range of meanings in the changes of their significance, there
may be fair occasion to concede, as we have abundant evidence in these our own days, that the creed may not signify

to their successors precisely what it did to the Puritans. It may then be a delicate matter to put to a test the sincerity of those who profess still to believe it. But we have to remind ourselves that the Puritans constructed that creed freely and deliberately, materials and opportunity being in their hands, and leaving them at full liberty to formulate what they believed to be the doctrinal teaching of the Bible. What they found there they set forth in literal terms and propositions. Of course, then, their assent, their hearty and full belief were spontaneous and thoroughly sincere. The substance and spirit of the doctrines which they thus received, and which to those who repudiate or would modify the creed are so hateful and incredible, were the very qualities which won to it their reverent belief. In the continuous discussions and controversies which that creed has opened among the descendants of the Puritans, those who have rejected it have been charged with doing so by the " conceit of human reason," and because of " its humbling of human pride." The Puritans, as has been already stated, loved to glory in their creed, because of those very offences in it. A portion of their descendants have frankly and deliberately renounced the creed, either as unscriptural or irrational, or both. Another portion, professing to adhere to it, allow themselves liberty to reconstruct it, as they say, by Scripture.

The full and intense sincerity of the Puritans in the belief of their creed is put beyond all question, and at the same time is most strikingly and instructively illustrated to us in a characteristic class of writings peculiarly Puritanic. One of the richest departments of our marvellously varied English literature is composed of diaries and journals. To them we are indebted for our most intimate knowledge of the characters of the writers and of some of their contemporaries, of the workings of human nature in individuals, of the secrecies and intrigues of domestic, social, and political life, and for the means of verifying and

reconstructing the past for comparison in an infinite number of details with the present. One special and distinct
class of these diaries, though not strictly confined to the
Puritans, was, in its most characteristic features, purpose,
method, and contents, peculiar to them. It was the class
of religious diaries. But they are to be defined more definitely than by that general epithet. The true Puritan
believed that he had entered individually into "a covenant
with God," the terms of which for both parties were distinctly known, understood, and solemnly binding on each
of them respectively. From time to time this covenant
was "renewed," on occasions of mental conflict, or under
the chills and fervors of pious self-consecration. Augustine
was the first of these Puritan diarists. If the expression
may be allowed, as conveying the literal truth in so many
cases, the Puritan opened "a debt and credit account" with
God. He had come under covenant by faith and profession and self-consecration. He had recognized the terms
which God required and accepted for the adoption of a
child of his grace and a subject of his mercy; and these
terms he had owned as the rule of a devout and obedient
life. In the mean while, holding himself to duty in fulfill-
ing his part of the covenant, he frankly and boldly required
of God to meet the terms of his own gracious promise.
Instances many, and of rich psychological interest, might
be quoted from old Puritan diaries, in which the writers, in
their own privacy with God, set down their accounts, and
then try to cast the balance. Nor are there lacking cases
in which the writers, under gloom or despair, while endeavoring to deal strictly and frankly with themselves,
dare to confront God with the question whether he has
been true to his own promise of grace and help. The histories of Governor Winthrop and Governor Bradford, though
in the main recording public matters for posterity, contain
many revelations of private religious experience, as of men
under covenant with God, owning a standard of duty, and

depending upon special Divine help. The diaries of Increase, and of his son, Cotton, Mather, have long served the historians, but have been for the most part put to use — whether fairly and profitably, or otherwise — by those who have tried to penetrate the secrets and infirmities of Puritan character in some of its most pronounced individualities. Both of those diarists, the son more than the father, often reveal themselves in their private records, as deliberately and with every effort of sincerity casting up their accounts of debt and credit with God, — with grim intimations, on some dark occasions, that the balance is on their side, that God had failed in some reasonable condition of the covenant. Cotton Mather's all too-communicative pen reveals him to us on his solemn days of fasting, self-reckoning, and intimate converse with God, as rolling and writhing on the floor of his locked and darkened library, moaning and weeping, pressing upon his present but unseen Companion his plans and labors of consecrated works, so ill-rewarded and appreciated that he himself was made the sport of detraction and contumely. The dismal impression made upon the reader of the record is that the human and the Divine parties in that interview are mutually teasing and fretting each other. There is one brief entry on that private record which draws to the sufferer the human heart's full sympathy. He had given the name of his honored father, the president of the college, to a son who grew to be wholly worthless and depraved, a disgrace and a poignant grief. When tidings came of the death of the outcast in a foreign land, the father writes in the record : " Increase ! my Son, my Son ! " [1]

Governor Winthrop does not appear to have kept one of these private religious diaries recording his personal inner experience. His refined delicacy of nature may have

[1] Only extracts of portions of the diaries of the two Mathers have been put into print. The originals, in manuscript, are preserved in the cabinets of the Massachusetts Historical Society and the American Antiquarian Society.

shrunk from the work. His expressions of individual piety, so simple and earnest, in his letters to his family, disclose the depth and fervor, the profound sincerity, the purity, and the tender affectionateness of his heart, free alike from despondency and elation of spirit. One can easily trace his own confidence in the obligations of " a covenant-keeping God " to meet the trusting expectations of those who had sought to bring heart and life into conformity with his will.[1]

John Cotton had before his death enjoined that his more private papers, especially those concerning his part in the Antinomian controversy, should be destroyed.

The very communicative and instructive journal of Judge Sewall divides its contents about equally between public affairs and his own private experiences. His pages abundantly inform us how precious and sufficient the Bible was to him on the estimate and use of it characteristic of the Puritans. His amiability and kindness of heart were turned to sternness only when " the Word" was slighted. He also boldly held God to conformity with covenanted obligations. Most touchingly in recording his trials and wearily taxed patience under the protracted sufferings of a daughter, does he add — and by no means as a commonplace utterance — that, after having called in the ministers one by one, he leaves the case with God.

These Puritan diaries, these reckonings of the devout in their covenant relations with God, were by no means confined to men in place and station. We have remnants and traces of them from many of both sexes in private relations. Their contents and spirit reveal to us the tone and method of Puritan piety, as derived wholly from, and in strict conformity with, the Puritan creed in all the sincerity and intensity of belief of which the human heart is capable. Sweet and gracious often are the religious communings of some of the finer spirits of the Puritan matrons

[1] See *ante*, p. 56.

and maids, like the "Meditations" and revealings of Anne
Bradstreet. But more often are we led to doubt and distrust these intended faithful records of the inner life,
reminders of solemn obligation, measurements of the
heights or depths, the elated or morbid exercises of the
spirit, and challengings of the Divine Comforter for a
promised help or assurance or peace.

To one who has turned the leaves and paused upon the
records of these Puritan diaries, the conviction will be
irresistible that they were prompted by and conformed to
an implicit and full belief of the doctrines of the Puritan
Creed concerning the relations of God and men. Of course
these private reckonings were written for the most part by
those who were both under individual covenant with God,
and in church covenant with brethren and sisters. The
standard of obligation and fidelity was all the more exacting to the thoroughly sincere, as, while left to apply it most
searchingly to themselves, they were held to critical and
inquisitorial observation by others. We may altogether
exclude from notice here the possible temptations of insincerity, partiality, and hypocrisy in facing self-revelations,
in favoring one's own case or interest, and in the judgment
of other persons of opposing views or interests. Hypocrisy,
selfish ends, and antagonisms are incalculable elements and
forces in all human relations. Our concern is only with
those who in their religious self-reckonings knew that they
were under the gaze of an All-seeing and an All-discerning
Eye. Experience and the judgments of the discreet in such
matters have for the main decided that religious diaries
of the Puritan kind are neither wise nor healthful exercises
either for conscience, cheerfulness of spirit, or charity for
others. Meteorological and physiological disturbances
creep into them. The tone of the nerves, the vapors of
ill-digestion, the depression and the excitement of momentary feelings and scruples, now keen and then relaxed, will
inevitably obtrude upon the calm and poise of the spirit of

the writer. The religious diary came into use with the Puritan type of piety, and has passed away with it. The changes of the weather and temperature, of the stocks and the markets are more likely now to fill the private records of our more practical times.

The Bible, the Creed, the personal Covenant with God, thus present themselves before us as the elements entering into the type and style of Puritan piety for belief and life, — a Book of literal inspiration and supreme authority, received as from the hand of God through a cloud ; a Creed which was to be devoutly and implicitly believed, by the subjecting and humiliating of the protests of natural justice and enlightened reason ; and a personal Covenant with God in terms of mutual obligation and promise. What outgrowth and form of character, what qualities of conscience, what standard of recognized duty for the individual, and what conceptions of rightful relations to others, would be the effects and results of this type of piety, we are relieved from the necessity of defining in terms, because we are to have before us practical illustrations of it in the legislation and administration of organized Puritanism.

One suggestion may be made here, in anticipation of facts to be more fully presented in dealing with the controversies between the Antinomians and Quakers, when the Puritan type of piety was brought under question and reproach. It was rightly charged by both these classes of reputed heretics that the Puritan rule and method of piety were, in the dialect of the time, " Legalism," a revival under the Gospel dispensation, of the Jewish "law of Works."

(The absorbing aim of the Puritan was to secure for himself " Sanctification," by obedience, compliance, and faithful observance of all the means and helps for training the will, directing the conscience, and conforming life and conduct to certain conditions required for salvation.) This object exacted scrupulosity, intense watchfulness, painful anxiety,

and stern self-reckoning to hold the believer to the terms
of " a Covenant of Works." The Antinomian and the
Quaker had found, if not an easier and laxer, certainly a
happier method, through " Justification," the attempt to
reach an internal peaceful assurance of the Divine favor
by a " Covenant of Grace or Faith." Reference to this
matter of deep and bitter conflict between the Puritans
and the heretics, is made here, that we may have before
us a contemporary view of the style and type of Puritan
piety as it was regarded by those who believed it to be
formal, mechanical, and superficial.

It is in place here to intimate the fact that, while the
Puritans made an estimate and use of the Bible, and accepted a creed peculiar to themselves and vitally distinctive
of their type of piety, so also was their view of the service
of prayer almost exclusively their own. One who has informed himself upon the inner exercises of the individual,
domestic, social, and civil life of a Puritan community, and
also of their method and conduct of worship in their
religious assemblies, will be at no loss to account for their
disapprobation and disuse, and soon their dislike and even
contempt, of all set forms of prayer, and especially for the
liturgy of the English Church. It had often been affirmed
by Church writers in their own time, as it is to this day,
that the apostles and first Christian disciples used a ritual
and a form of prayer, " Collects,'' etc., in their common
worship. The Puritan had but to refer to every place in
the Gospels, Acts, and Epistles of the New Testament
where reference is made to united prayer, to assure himself
that it was inconceivable that any collects or set forms
could have served on such occasions. The breathings and
petitions of devotion there referred to were as free and fervent, as unstudied and spontaneous, as was the spirit
which prompted them. From the beginning to the end of
the Bible they found no single recognition of a form for
common worship. " The Lord's Prayer," the only seeming

exception, was to them a guide for closet devotion, and the trivial and mechanical way in which in the penances of the Roman Church it had been employed in "vain repetitions," to be recited "twenty," "forty" times, had wellnigh alienated them from more than reading it in its place in the Gospel.

The distinctive peculiarity of the service of prayer in Puritan devotion was characteristic alike of what many of their lineage now approve and honor, and of what they regret and reject in their type of piety. Their ideas about their special covenant relations with God gave tone and form and substance and method to their prayers. Using the word freely, without stopping to limit or qualify it, we might say that *dictation* to the Deity, rather than petition or submission made them bold in prayer. They stated and defined in special terms, on occasion, in what form, direct and full, they would have their requests granted. The pledges, the promises, the assurances which they believed God to have ratified when they had put themselves in filial and sacramental relations with him, gave them claims and expectations of which at least they felt at liberty to remind God. Doubtless, the length of the Puritan devotions, as well as of their sermons, has been exaggerated. We know, however, that those most concerned as hearers did not complain of weariness, and that any " stinting " of religious exercises was a grievance to them. The distinctive peculiarities in the Puritan service of prayer are very significantly recognized when we trace and account for the changes and modifications in the tone, method, and usages of the public devotions in the worship of those in closest affinity with them in belief and observance in our own times.

It is within the recollection of some now living here that in the Sunday worship of congregations both in city and country towns, " Notes, requesting Prayers," in the name of individuals or families were read by the officiating minister before the principal devotional service. These Notes covered a large variety of experiences,—voyages, births, sorrows, afflictions, and bereavements. I recall an occasion in a country meeting-house when sixteen such notes were read,—more than one of them, perhaps, offered by different petitioners in different relationships referring to the same case. The birth of a child in a household prompted the parents —who rose in their pew at the reading of it — to send up an offering of "thanks for mercies received."[1] In the early New-England churches there was much that was befitting, edifying, and even beautiful, in thus engaging the devotions of a whole congregation in the deeper personal experiences and circumstances of individuals and families among them. Though there was a recognized distinction of degrees, dignities, and of social standing, — far beyond what there is now, — even in rural settlements, there were mutual interests which brought all into acquaintance and sympathy. Anything unusual, of a serious nature, in the experience of one was known to and appealed to all. Neighborly offices and ministries were lifted into public prayers. It was instructive to observe how, under changing circumstances of domestic and social life, when occupants of neighboring pews and houses might not know each other by names, the original, full-hearted wording of the Notes for Prayers yielded,—in its way to an entire disuse, — first, by a substitution of "A family in this congregation," etc., instead of the name, and then by silence on such subjects.

The "free prayers" in the Puritan assemblies took the widest possible range of tone, substance, detail, and, we must add, even of the temper of the spirit that breathed them. Not infrequently, as we may read in the Journals

---

[1] The Rev. Dr. Frothingham, minister of the First Church in Boston from 1815 to 1850, told me that after he had read many such "Notes" for his parishioners, he, in his own case, consigned the custom to desuetude by omitting the observance on the birth of his first child.

of Winthrop and Sewall, the private opinions, partialities, and grievances of a minister in his relations with others found utterance. On the occasions of the animosities and contentions which are to be rehearsed in the following pages, the public devotional exercises were made the medium of excited and even embittered feelings. No distractions or provocations of this nature appeared in the usual tone and method of the Puritan prayers, which, in the best sense of the phrase, became " Common Prayers" under the anxieties and straits of their wilderness beginnings, — dreads of Indian assaults, of foreign interference, of plagues, of murrain, of the failure of crops, of storms and earthquakes, and changes in the government at home, — which caused deep anxieties. Under those circumstances to have confined the devotional services of the Puritans to the forms, collects, and ritualisms of a parlor or a boudoir ceremonial would have deadened rather than calmed their spirits.

Several of the governors of Massachusetts now for many years, in regularly appointing the first Thursday of April and the last Thursday of November, respectively, as days of Fasting and Thanksgiving, have alleged the example of the Fathers in so doing. A careful examination of the Records will show under what important qualifications such a statement must be made. In no case was a day for either observance selected as a matter of routine, of course, with any reference to the season or calendar of the year. The occasions were indifferently assigned through all seasons, with this serious condition, — that a defined and emphatic reason, in opportunity or emergency, was given in each case in setting before the whole people of the Colony a matter which would be sure to engage their devotional sentiments. Without such a specific consecration, an official Fast Day cannot but be used as a holiday. There are instances on the Records in which the Court appointed at the same session both a Fast Day and

a Thanksgiving Day to be observed at a few days' interval,
— the reasons, occasions, and material for each being very
distinctly and cogently assigned.[1]

It is by the changes of time and circumstances, rather
than, as is often said, by changes in taste and regard for
the fitness of things, — except as these latter modifications
are the result of the former, — that the peculiar characteristics of the Puritan methods of public devotion have gradually yielded, occasionally giving place to book-services.
These, in their turn, have to be allowed some elasticity in
missionary wilderness work, and on emergent occasions
like those of the Puritans.

The subjects of the Creed, the Covenant, and the service
of Prayer, as deciding the tone and type of Puritan piety,
have thus presented themselves to our notice in connection
with their peculiar estimate and way of using the Bible.
All the modifications since traceable in matters of belief,
of religious fellowship, and forms of worship, have been
incident upon a changing regard for and a different estimate of the Book. If we have been digressing from the
main theme of this chapter we must return to a further
reference to the sacred volume. One other, and it may
be the supreme and crowning, reason for the exalted value
which the Puritans assigned to the Bible is yet to be mentioned. They held the Book to be not only a complete, but
also the final, communication of God to men. Their belief
is thus expressed in the Confession, of which we must
mark the emphasis : —

"The whole Council of God concerning all things necessary
for his own Glory, Man's Salvation, Faith, and Life, is either
expressly set down in Scripture, or by good and necessary Consequence may be deduced from Scripture. Unto which nothing
at any time is to be added, whether by new Revelations of the
Spirit or Traditions of Men."

[1] Records, vol. iv. part ii. pp. 280, 320, 346, 534.

The first impression made upon us by the last sentence is that of its presumption, the high and extreme assurance in its statement. It was well enough to exclude the expectation of any further religious help from the traditions of men; but to close the hope of any further communications from God to men, to put him to silence, seems incongruous with living faith, and certainly with anything consistent with humility and reverence in the Puritans. If it is to be pardoned, it is solely because it was a way of exalting the treasure in their possession. It seemed to say of the Bible, as we say of a critical opportunity, "Prize it, make the most of it, for you will never have another!" The Puritans applied to the whole Book, as if its contents were a unit, some of the closing sentences of the Revelation of Saint John, warning against taking from or adding to it. We can well understand how they would have grieved over a loss of anything in the Book, though we might well be reconciled to parting with some of its contents. But would they not have welcomed further communications from the Spirit? Two objections rise in our minds to their mode of silencing God. First, they rejoiced in believing that God had "at sundry times and in divers manners" spoken to the fathers. To assert that there had been, and was forever to be, a cessation of that mode of Divine intercourse was to prompt a spirit of scepticism and doubt — so effectively exercised in our time — as to whether God had ever "spoken," or whether imagination and credulity had not originated the belief. Second, continued revealings through the select spirits of saintly persons would have richly authenticated the earlier revelations, while the abrupt closing of the mute heavens would cover the earth with gloom. But this bold and positive assertion of the Puritan creed, stated as an article of faith, to exalt the estimate and value of the Bible, leads us to anticipate here a matter which we shall find to have had vast influence when, further on in these pages, we have to deal with the sad altercations and controversies of the authorities of Massachusetts with the Antinomians and the Quakers.

All the enthusiastic sects of the time claimed to have direct, private, personal illuminations and "revelations" independent of the Bible. The stress and importance which any of the wild sectaries of the period laid upon these divine motions and promptings marked the stage and degree of the fanaticism attributed to them. There was no standard or test to which these private revelations could be brought for a trial of their sanity, or even reasonableness. They might be alleged in justification of any form of eccentricity, fanaticism, and extravagance. Notoriously they were enlisted on the side of disorder, violence, indecency, and gross immorality. When a delicate and virtuous matron pleaded that she was compelled to divest herself of all womanly modesty by appearing unclothed in the public streets and in the public assembly, in order that she might comply with a Divine call upon her to do so, however clear and firm might be her own conviction in the case, the act itself would show it to be a delusion. The amazed spectators might or might not give her the benefit of a charitable construction, — that she was "distracted in her wits." It was enough, however, for the Puritans to abide by their accepted rule, that there were to be "no more revelations of the Spirit." All the illuminations and Divine promptings — and these were to them precious and inspiring — which they or others could enjoy must come through and from the Bible, but not outside or independent of the Bible. The edict which they announced in their Confession, of a final and closed communication from God, utterly precluded and interdicted all private revelations. We shall see what stress was laid upon this point in the trial of Mrs. Hutchinson, and in the judicial proceedings against the Quakers. To some critical readers of our time the question may present itself whether the Puritans in this matter did not act blindly and inconsistently. They read in the sacred volume of promptings and motions ascribed to God, under which his servants and prophets went from place to place, delivered messages, uttered their burdens and denunciations, and performed certain symbolic acts with garments, girdles, and bottles.[1] These narratives the Puritans found credible and edifying. The Quakers claimed the same divine promptings, and uttered similar warnings, with similar symbolic acts. The fatal difference, however, was that after the Bible was completed Divine revelations had ceased.

Most faithfully, with unwearied, patient application and constant study, — with the aid of learning, if they had it, otherwise with a simple craving for light and truth and guidance in the religious life, — did the Puritans use the Bible to serve for them directly in place of priestly teaching and to relieve the dumbness and silence of Nature. While they objected to the routine and formal way in which it was used in their old parish churches, their directory for worship provided that it should be read in course, always followed by exposition, not in the " dumb reading " of the Church. Though but few of the first comers here could have had the Book in the compact and convenient forms familiar to us, all who could do so, dispensing with a prayer-book, took the holy volume with them to their public worship, and diligently turned the leaves to follow the references and citations made by the minister. It can hardly have been but that some passages must have been omitted in the public reading as unedifying and even worse ; but not so in the private home. The family Bible in the Puritan household was the present angel of the dwelling, and the fire never went out on the altar. Happy were the families, especially the children in them, whose copies were enriched with the generously furnished and often beautiful engravings of the olden time. Besides the daily devotional services in each well-ordered home, there were special uses

[1] Isaiah xx.

of the Bible on the Sabbath which must have been irksome and weariful to youthful flesh and spirits. Both the sermons of the day were to be "repeated" and commented on with further explanations and applications. Portions or chapters of the Bible were to be "got by heart," as aids to the catechism. The bright child in the home who had attained to skill as a good reader had the privilege of serving as such, and many of the households furnished an imitative boy who could extemporize a sermon and occupy a chair as a pulpit. Very welcome was it to such children when in the course of the annual perusal of the Bible there came in turn the fascinating stories of Joseph, of Samson's foxes, of David and Goliath, and like narratives where the human transcended the divine. The perennial toy of childhood is a more or less artistically executed model of Noah's ark.[1] Many and richly suggestive have been the nursery discussions over that wonderful, sailless, rudderless vessel, with its three stories, each with its sealed door, and, heedless of ventilation, a window at the top which must needs have remained closed. Besides the eight full-grown persons that were to enter it for refuge, — the patriarch, Mrs. Noah, their three sons and their wives, — there were no infants or children to engage sympathy. Some perplexity attended the double narration, leaving it uncertain whether there were only a single or seven pairs of all the creatures to be preserved. There was no trouble about the larger of these creatures — the elephant, camel, rhinoceros, the horse, the horned cattle — as they marched with sober steps into the ark ; but where were two mice and two mosquitoes, with like small beings, stowed away ? And when the lonely dove went out not to return, what became of its mate ? We may be assured that many questions about the Bible were put to the elders in these

[1] It has been stated in public prints that three million models of this toy have been manufactured by a single firm in Germany.

households which it was necessary and wise to leave un-answered.

How the Bible, or " the Word," in its laws, examples, " instances," and precedents was put to use by the Puritans in their civil and religious policy, will appear as we next examine the Commonwealth which they attempted to fash-ion and administer by it.

Those who, deterred by its uninviting character and hav-ing no occasion to search it, are wholly unversed in our early Puritan literature cannot form any adequate concep-tion of the stores of instruction, illustration, and suggestion by incident and example which it yielded to its close and revering readers. In recalling the past we must be as faithful and lenient as is possible to its tone and spirit.

V.

THE BIBLICAL COMMONWEALTH.

In attempting to trace in the following pages the development of the aims of the founders of Massachusetts as set forth in the principles and measures of their rule in civil and religious affairs, the writer avails himself of a plain and positive statement to serve as did a text for a sermon by one of their divines. This statement must announce a matter of fact clearly assured and certified by satisfactory evidence. It may embrace a generalization of very many particulars which will serve as such evidence, and it must involve only such merely inferential and incidental elements as, without being strained or ingenious, shall be perfectly consistent with the facts which they are intended to explain or supplement. There is, however, but little occasion for relying on inferences rather than facts in defining the aims and principles of the founders of Massachusetts. These will be abundantly presented by themselves in their avowals and proceedings. The writer may be permitted, without personal obtrusiveness, to say that he has read and thought upon substantially all that is extant and accessible in print or in manuscript from the pens of those most concerned in the earliest years of our history. Mr. Doyle is not alone in suggesting that our early local writers were sufficiently impressed by a conceit or a conviction that their subject was to have interest for the world.

The statement advanced, to be followed up in narration, is this: The founders of Massachusetts — the prime movers in the enterprise, its responsible leaders, the proprietors of its franchise, charged with its government and welfare, and its watchful guardians against the many risks and catastrophes which might imperil the venture — held a deep and earnest conviction under the supreme inspiration of which they acted. It may be expressed as follows : they believed that they had the means of knowing the mind and will of the Supreme Being — the God whom they most reverently owned and worshipped — for the rule, government, and conduct of a community of human beings in a social, civilized state ; that this Divine will was communicated by revelation, transmitted through a Book. Those who accepted this rule put themselves under a covenant of obedience to it, and this secured to them the right and privilege, and held them to the obligation, of compelling at least a respectful regard for it from all who were under their government. The only alternative which they recognized for this divinely revealed rule was the being left to the insufficient light of Nature, as all other peoples of the earth had been except Jews and Christians, who were " covenant people."

It is a satisfaction to us that in the voluminous records of the Court of the Company of Massachusetts Bay we can find a full narration of its legislation and administration. These records are candid and communicative. They cover the proceedings of the corporation in England, presenting the reasons and method for its transfer with its charter to this country, and then give us a continuous account of legislative and executive government under it. We have already traced in the motives and avowals of the leaders of the enterprise of colonization before they left England, the religious spirit and prompting which moved them. Winthrop, in those touching and earnest expressions of his which we have read, may justly be regarded as representing his associates. And we have had before us that distinctively Puritan belief about the Bible and its use which would guide them in their government. The enterprise was prompted by a constraining sincerity and elevation of purpose. There can be no uncertainty or question about that. Such being the master motive, it should give tone to our judgment of it. That motive, though of course not exclusive of others of a secular character, was paramount to all others. It was not a mercenary prompting, nor self-seeking, nor with a view to license for themselves or dominancy over others. It was the inspiration of duty, not a grasping for power. The scheme would require self-subjection and sacrifice for themselves, and restraint and a very severe discipline to be exercised over others. But this was not all. Most certain it is that the leaders patiently and faithfully bore the burden which they had assumed for themselves. They were themselves subject to the stern and iron rule of their own principles. They were not restful, or, as we say, happy in themselves. They were perplexed and tormented by vexations of their own invention. Their rule over those on whom they imposed their discipline, including many who were in covenant with them, was harsh and cruel. And here we may present to ourselves what in our retrospect appears to us to have been the root and occasion of all their errors, of the infelicities of their own experience, and of the sufferings of others at their hands. We trace it in the assumption and conceit, the spiritual pride and intolerance involved in their persuasion that their religious covenant had secured for them the special favor of God, and qualified and empowered them to extend their religious rule as representing the will of God over others. Sincerity of the purest and most profound character in holding that conviction could not free it or guard it from an erroneous, a mischievous, and an unjust exercise of authority.

Let a suggestion be here interposed in which we may recognize and admit how reasonable and natural — we may even say how inevitable — it was that among the many and varied schemes, secular and religious in their aims, which have been devised in successive generations and under changing circumstances for the government of civilized men in their civil and social relations, trial in its turn should be made of a Biblical commonwealth. While the Republic of Plato and the Utopia of Sir Thomas More stand as expositions of the ideal of commonwealths, literal, practical, and experimental trials of such on various bases, and by ingenious schemes and organizations present themselves in long series in human history. Mennonites, Moravians, and Shakers have their historic and their living interest for those who study them in their substantial qualities or their eccentricities. Exactly two hundred years after the so-called Massachusetts Theocracy was established there appeared among us the phenomena of Mormonism, with its claim of religious sanctions and purposes. One may trace resemblances or utter contrasts between these schemes and those of the Puritan State. The Mormons professed to be directed by a Book of Revelation, with an interpreting prophet and inspired bishops. They planted themselves in remote regions with fresh, wild, but fertile territory, where they practised thrift and secured prosperity. Dark disclosures of acts of lawlessness and violence, massacres, and gross immoralities striking at the purity of domestic life, if they do not turn into contempt and scorn all the pretensions of Mormonism to be a divinely instituted and organized form for a commonwealth, put it wholly aside from the Puritan system as established here. Reasons quite in the order of nature and experience will suggest themselves to us, as we think upon the matter, why in due time, with fit and favoring conditions of human agents with motives and opportunities, a trial should be made of a Biblical commonwealth. It was for the founders of Massachusetts to make that trial. They not only believed that the conception admitted of being realized, but under the spirit and faith which guided them they were persuaded that a constraining obligation held them to place themselves under such a form of government, civil and religious, as became those who were in covenant with God. As before intimated, this experiment is not to be regarded as an invention of their own ingenuity, a conceit of their own fancies. It came to them and was listened to by them as a Divine call which they were constrained to obey.

If the fullest information which we can reach concerning the ruling motive and intent of the leaders in this scheme of a Biblical commonwealth warrants the view here taken of it, then we are at liberty to draw from it an inference which should come in to help us in pronouncing judgment upon the character of their administration. Had they been attempting to put on trial a scheme of their own devising, like a communistic or associative secular enterprise, or one which engaged more or less of a religious purpose, they would have been amenable to judgment not only for the practical working of their scheme, but also for the folly or the fancy manifested in conceiving it. But if the Fathers of the Massachusetts Commonwealth could speak to us it would be to tell us hardly more plainly than they do in their records, that the enterprise which they were putting on trial was not theirs; they did not devise it, and therefore, in trying to make it practicable, were not responsible for its working, nor for its incidental effects upon those who opposed it. It was not that they were forcing upon others their own principles, beliefs, and opinions. They had put themselves under a Divine rule which God had revealed as his holy will and law for all men. That rule was as authoritative and exacting for the unregenerate and the uncovenanted around them and among them as it was for themselves. The only difference between them and these others was that they had acknowledged their obligations to this Divine rule, had come under its directions, and intended that their whole policy in Church and State should be conformed to it. They had reconciled themselves to the self-subjection, self-denial, and sacrifice which it required of them. They had renounced all of their natural liberties and wilfulness and seeking of their own ends and pleasure which their covenant with God demanded of them, and had put themselves in his hands to obey his commands, and live and die for him.

As has been already avowed in these pages, the only motive which the writer recognizes as prompting an intelligent and candid study of this period of our history, with its stern legislators and the severities of their rule, is its significance and interest as presenting one phase in the working out of human progress for the enlightenment and enfranchisement of our race. The subject might claim an historical study if it merely concerned an outburst and spasm of religious fanaticism. But this Massachusetts episode was something other and better than that. Recognizing, as we have done, the purity, the prevailing sincerity, the earnestness, and elevation of purpose of the leaders of the enterprise, we acquit them of all hypocrisy and duplicity, and we accept their own avowal of the rule by which they were guided. Their self-defence, then, under any question or censure to which they were subjected, would consist in a plea that not they, but God, assumed the responsibility for all that followed in the sincere attempt to administer a commonwealth according to his revealed will.

This plea would have been a good one under certain essential conditions. It would have had force if all who were concerned in the Puritan Commonwealth — the leaders and the led, the governors and the governed, the magistrates and the people — had with one purpose and consent freely and heartily put themselves under that Biblical rule. Serious practical difficulties and perplexities, and enough of them, would even then have presented themselves; but they would have been different in form and in treatment from those which had to be dealt with here. Even in the Puritan churches where this covenant of a common belief and purpose was supposed to unite all the members, who also voluntarily pledged themselves to come under each other's "watch and ward," there was disorder with discord. But in the civil commonwealth this Divine rule, as interpreted and exercised by those only who had recognized its obligation, had not been accepted by all over whom it was extended. Those who represented God and who claimed to be acting for God in the commonwealth were from the first a minority of the people. They began by securing the civil franchise exclusively to themselves. Their struggles to retain it and their own way of exercising it involved them in all their austere and severe proceedings against disturbers and opponents. This claim to represent God, as his authorized agents in interpreting his laws and will for the administration of civil affairs, was constantly asserted by the magistrates of Massachusetts ; nor did they hesitate to affirm it in their intermeddling with the institution and discipline of their churches. In an appeal in behalf of the maintenance of ministers the Court speaks as " nursing fathers of the churches." [1] Nursing " fathers " may not be expected to be as tender and gentle as the more appropriate nurses ; and so we find that some of the most arbitrary proceedings of the Court were in the affairs of the religious fellowships, which in the institution of them were nominally intended and asserted to be independent and self-regulated.

(The most odious aspect and quality of Puritanism to those most repelled by antipathy to it, in its own age and in the judgment of our times, is the assumption and conceit connected with the belief of an elect and special favoritism with God secured by a personal covenant with him. Christendom in its average spirit will not allow that any one can hold that belief in humility and in generous sympathy with his race. The claiming a right to the " longboat " for escape from a wreck, leaving the whole ship's

[1] Records, iii. 424.

company to their fate, is not a manifestation of nobleness or generosity. The Puritan view of God as the pitying, merciful Father of all his children was wholly subordinate to their view of him as a stern sovereign, ruling by decrees which were as inexorable as those of Fate on its brazen throne of destiny. The familiar popular gibe which gained its currency in the Puritan age — " The world belongs to the saints, and we are the saints " — is not overstrained in its sarcasm against those who claim any measure of precedence or authority over others as themselves an elect and covenanted people.

We return from this digression to acquaint ourselves from their own records and proceedings with the form of rule in Church and State set up by the Massachusetts Puritans. It may fitly be described as a Biblical commonwealth. This was a form of government which should find its model in the whole Bible as the Jewish commonwealth was set forth in the Old Testament. And yet in tracing the working out of the Puritan form of government in Massachusetts, we are constantly reminded by many significant facts that the spirit and letter of the Jewish Scriptures had more weight with them — certainly were more frequently and constantly referred to for guidance and examples — than the Christian Scriptures. The Puritans, however, were undertaking to found and organize a state. The Christian Scriptures had nothing direct and specific for aiding this object. These rather assumed and took for granted the existence of civil and religious institutions, without designating or defining them. It was the Old Testament that furnished the Puritan pattern, " the statutes, laws, and ordinances of God." How they distinguished among these such as they should re-enact will by and by be stated. There was not a single professionally trained lawyer in their corporation, nor is there the slightest intimation in their records that they regretted or felt the deficiency. They believed they had a substitute in a Divine statute-book.

The politics of Puritanism were developed from its theology. Its legislation consisted in the re-enactment by men of the laws of God. The Puritans had satisfied themselves that they had means of knowing positively and fully what these laws of God were for the government of a civilized community. They did not feel the need of an earthly monarch, as the King of kings was enough for them. Hence their theology and their policy matured into democracy, though our early Puritans appear not to have apprehended that fruitage, and would have repudiated it. We have been accustomed in later times to the description of their Biblical commonwealth as a theocracy. Such in fact it was intended to be, and so far as their experiment succeeded, they thought it was. It is to be noted, however, that neither in their Court Records nor in their private papers do they adopt that term, though its intended equivalents appear. I can recall only one occurrence of the word " theocracy " in our earliest literature, and there its connection gives it interest. In 1636 Governor Winthrop received certain inquiries and propositions " from some persons of great quality and estate, and of special note for piety, whereby they discovered their intentions to join the Colony, if they might receive satisfaction therein."[1] The proposals contemplated two houses of government: the one of nobles and gentlemen, with hereditary rank and rights, from whom the Governor should be always chosen ; the other of freeholders of the commonalty. Each house should have a negative. In reply to these proposals Mr. Cotton, in a letter to Lord Saye and Sele, gives us the following very clear description of the form of government by the Bible model which was being set up here as " an administration of a civil state according to God : " —

" I am very apt to believe that the word and Scriptures of God doe conteyne a short *upoluposis,* or platforme, not onely of theology,

[1] Winthrop, i. 135.

but also of other sacred sciences, attendants, and hand maids thereunto, — ethicks, œconomics, polities, church-government, prophecy,
academy. It is very suitable to God's all-sufficient wisdom, and to
the fulness and perfection of Holy Scriptures, not only to prescribe
perfect rules for the right ordering of a private man's soule, but
also for the right ordering of a man's family, yea, of the commonwealth too. When a commonwealth hath liberty to mould his
owne frame, I conceyve the Scripture hath given full direction for
the right ordering of the same. Demoercracy I do not conceyve
that ever God did ordeyne as a fitt government eyther for church
or commonwealth. If the people be governors, who shall be governed? As for monarchy and aristocracy, they are both of them
clearly approved and directed in Scripture, yet so as referreth
the soveraigntie to himselfe and setteth up Theocracy in both
as the best forme of government in the commonwealth as well as
in the church." [1]

In "An Introductory Essay" to an edition of Wood's New
England's Prospect (Boston, 1764), the writer says: —

"The first plan of the government established a kind of Theocracy by making the Word of God the law. This gave the clergy
infinite weight in the constitution; they were naturally the expositors of the law, and in so young a country were almost the only
men of learning. From this circumstance the attachment and deference to their cloth was almost implicit; and for aught I know, to
this very cause may the greatest errors into which the country fell
in its first settlement be ascribed."

The qualification to which this intimation of the prevailing power of the clergy and of their main responsibility
for the errors of government must be subjected, will be
stated further on in these pages.

In a contention which arose in 1646 between the magistrates and the deputies, as to the powers of the former by
the Charter and by election to act in the vacancy of the
General Court, certain questions were submitted to the

---

[1] Hutchinson's History of Massachusetts, vol. i. Appendix iii.

elders as arbitrators. One of the questions was whether
the magistrates " in cases where there is noe particular expresse laws provided, were to be guided by the word of
God till the generall courte give particular rules in such
cases " ? To this the elders, with caution and yet decision,
made answer : —

" Wee do not find that by the pattent they are expressly directed
to proceed according to the word of God, but we understand that
by a law or libertie of the country they may act in cases wherein as yet there is no expresse law, soe that in such acts they
proceed according to the word of God." [1]

In this paper of the elders Scripture texts are quoted
to justify variable penalties for variable grades of guilt, as
in murder, and also to warrant magistrates in mitigating
the penalty to a delinquent who had previously done good
service to the State : " So Solomon mitigated the punishment of Abiathar for his service done to his father
formerly." [2]

More to the point of the purpose and intent of the government of Massachusetts to establish a theocracy than
would be distinct and repeated assertions of such a purpose, is the fact to be traced in their statutes and court
proceedings and in the penalties inflicted for various offences, that they invariably followed the rule and lead of
the Scriptures. Their delay in forming a code of their
own was submitted to by the assumption that the Bible
would serve them in all serious matters. How did they
fashion to themselves their idea of a theocracy ?

Those who believe in One Supreme Being as the Creator,
Disposer, and Ruler of all things, as a consequence believe
that the government of this and of all worlds is a theocracy. Its laws, physical and moral, its methods, operations, results, and destined issues are all under God's

[1] Hutchinson's Collection of Papers, pp. 179, 180.
[2] 1 Kings ii. 26, 27.

appointment and administration. So far as any faculties
which we possess qualify us for recognizing and understanding those laws and methods, they are to be inferred
by us from observation and experience. The character,
attributes, and purposes of God would then have to be
indicated and deduced from what that observation and
experience as the actual methods of his government assure to us. From what we could thus learn to be his will
we might infer our own duty, either as his subjects or his
children.

Here we have opened to us the vast theme of natural
religion, launching us upon the boundless ocean of all
perplexities and mysteries. The limitations of the subject
proposed for treatment in these pages preclude anything
beyond the mere statement of the two widely diverse directions into which natural religion has led the thoughts, the
imaginations, and the conclusions of men. One of these
is sufficiently defined under the general term of heathenism; the other has the nobler title of philosophy. Both
of them imply that man is left to himself in thought, inquiry, and search. He sees and he thinks, he imagines
and he reasons. He becomes abject or bold, in view of
his attitude before the Unknown, and according to the conclusions in which he rests. Of the follies and superstitions
of heathenism, the barbarities and atrocities which have
dehumanized its votaries, we need not simply to turn to
history for our knowledge, for the survivals of it are hideous. Philosophy has a brighter, if still an unsatisfactory
record; and of recent years science has come in as an aid
and guide in dealing with the vast problems which engage
men's minds. Cicero uttered the truth, which needs no
argument to support it, that if man is to receive any help
beyond his own observation and experience in interpreting
the ways of God, it must be furnished directly by God
himself.

The theocracy which is the subject of our present study

was one founded on the belief that God had disclosed himself, had put himself into direct communication with men,
prompting them and instructing them to set up a theocracy
among themselves, — a commonwealth to be administered
for and by God.

And what if man should not thus be left to his own
resources of experience and observation, of inquiry and
speculation as to a knowledge of God, his character, will,
and purposes ? It is supposable that, either according to
design in original purpose, as needful to complement the
resources of human nature, or in pity for its gropings and
failures, God may disclose himself, put himself into communication with men " at sundry times and in divers
manners." The proof, the assurance that he had done so
would be satisfactory if it secured thorough conviction of
its reality in the breasts of human beings, — prompting,
invigorating, and enlightening them. Two methods are
conceivable for this divine reinforcement, assurance, and
enlightenment of men. One is by some startling phenomena or marvels, out of the ordinary course of Nature,
engaging the senses and quickening the reverence of men,
bidding them heed, wonder, and respond. The other
method is by the illumination of man's inner powers by
motions and inspirations, impulses and assurances which
would leave the impress of divine messages. These, when
received by men, would bear repetition, — the transfer from
the mind and conscience of the receiver to other minds
and consciences. They might be written, and so stand for
revelations.

The self-disclosure of God to men by the method called
revelation offers themes for curious questioning and discussion, more direct and positive in their materials and
means, but not one whit less perplexing, than those of
natural religion. These, however, are not to our present
purpose ; for we are to deal with the form of government
of a commonwealth established and administered by those

who heartily and devoutly believed that God had revealed his counsels and will to them so as to furnish them statutes and ordinances enabling them to act in co-operation with him.

Revelation, as they accepted it, involved two processes: 1. The disclosure of himself by God to some chosen by him for such intercourse, in two ways, — one by startling phenomena through their senses, out of course with Nature, engaging their awe and reverence; the other by inward monitions and exercises, promptings and inspirations, impelling influences, which should be to them as voices, assurances, and messages. Men thus Divinely illuminated would need, first, to be self-convinced of the reality and Divine source of these communications, and then to be qualified to satisfy others that God had been in converse with them. 2. The record of these facts and communications would then constitute " a book revelation," inspired Scriptures, the Word of God.

The modern spirit of criticism, speculation, and rationalism comes into the sharpest collision with the faith which guided the convictions of the founders of the Massachusetts theocracy. In view of the tender and devout beliefs which have so long in tradition and enshrined affection accepted the Bible as revealing the Divine will and purposes to those favored with the knowledge of it, we may well recognize the fact that our object here is not to discuss the grounds of those beliefs, but simply to study the proceedings of a company of men who firmly held them and acted by them. We know with what a full, intense, and unquestioning confidence they held a " book revelation." In order that we may appreciate their belief, we may fairly ask what were the origin and grounds of it, — not, however, as we would follow the question if we were pursuing it for ourselves, but simply as tracing the attitude of their minds toward it. The religious literature of the Puritan age was in many of its distinctive qualities quite unlike that of our time, and in no one quality more than this, — that it did not deal with arguments, defences, and evidences addressed to unbelievers or rationalists, but took faith for granted, and sought for edification.

What were the methods and assurances by which God made these disclosures to men, as they were read and accepted by believers in a book revelation? How out of the silence and from behind the veils of Nature, from the mystery of the unseen and supernal, came intelligible revealings to sense and spirit to those whom God chose to receive his illuminations, his promptings, his messages, his defined and positive commands? We read of theophanies, — visible appearances or symbolisms of God. We read of signs, ordinary or startling, which waited for an interpretation. We read of actual tests to which God was subjected to confirm a halting belief. Some of these may appear to us trivial and puerile in the narration. Others of them are sublime and august in method and effect. In the affluence of Oriental idea and imagery they fix our deepest impressions. When men assume " to speak for God," the risks which they run must find a safeguard only in the fitness and adequacy of the utterance.

How do these revealings present themselves on the record? They are rich in variety, and winning in their simplicity. In recent years the ethnic religions have been the subjects of comparative study, with the materials for setting their divine elements by the side of those of the Bible. The Bible tells us that the first representative of our race had direct personal intercourse with God, which by disobedience he forfeited for himself and his posterity. The eleventh chapter of the Epistle to the Hebrews, which rehearses the champions of faith and the witnesses for God, may stand for all time and for all readers as the grandest of the roles of heroism. Noah was " warned of God," and the nature of the inward warning may be inferred from the course which he followed. Abram's call was certified in his self-exile and obedience. It would be difficult to match in any imagery of simplicity and beauty the dream of Jacob, when it was disclosed to him that God was in that place, and he had not known it, but had come to know it. Moses asked, first, for full assurance that God talked with him, and then for means of convincing his people of it. He became, save in moments of despondency, assured for himself, and he impressed the conviction — faltering and inconstant indeed — upon them. There is a charming and childlike simplicity in the tests or feats to which Gideon is represented as subjecting God to assure his own halting belief that he was chosen to wield "the sword of the Lord" against his enemies.[1] Gideon, first, proposed to leave his "fleece of wool" exposed, and if it should be moistened with dew while the earth around was dry, then he should know that God had made him his champion. The result was satisfactory. But to make assurance doubly sure, Gideon thought he should be safer in proposing a reversal of the experiment. He would again expose the fleece, asking that it should be kept dry while the dew moistened all the ground. In this also he was gratified. This is puerile; but offset it with a Scripture passage which we may challenge the whole literature of the world to match for august sublimity and the tenderest grace of simplicity. It is a passage which brings together the infinite remoteness of God and his intimate nearness. "Thus saith the high and lofty One that inhabiteth eternity, whose name is Holy: I dwell in the high and holy place, with him also that is of a contrite and humble spirit."[2] It is not in place here to present in further details examples of the two methods by which Divine communications were believed to be made and certified, — that is, by marvels, portents, visions, and miracles, and by inspirations and inner illuminations. The Puritans

[1] Judges vi. 37–40.　　　　[2] Isaiah lvii. 15.

received the sacred volume, as thus divinely attested to them, as revealing the will of God, — as the "Word of God." Why should it not furnish them not only the rule for their individual life, but also the statute-book for civil administration for themselves and for their rule to be exercised over others ?

We have here intimated the radical and fatal difficulty which the leaders in the planting of this State had prepared for themselves in the inception of a Biblical commonwealth. While their own recognition of it was sincere, and their loyalty to it was earnest, its authority over others was arbitrary, and required constraint to enforce it. It is a bold and hazardous assumption for a body of men, however noble, devout, and even wise they may be, to regard themselves as representing God to their fellow-men in magistracy and authority. In the class called by the inclusive title of " reformers," — the grander minds and the finer spirits, enlightened and quickened beyond all others of their age, protesters against error and wrong, seers of emancipating and liberalizing visions, martyrs in noble heroism, — latently, consciously, or avowedly lives the conviction that they represent God, his truth and will, to men, and that they are interpreting and applying them as his agents. There have been those — the elect of our race — whose visions were realities, and whose prophecies were fulfilled. But reformers, as a class, as viewed by conservatives, have been generally regarded as mingling their own inspirations with those from a higher source. Claiming to speak and work for God, they seem at times to be impatient of the slow processes and delays by which, as the seed grows to fruitage, what they regard as the purposes of God are matured. So to the patient conservative, who says that time will effect all wise and healthful changes gradually, the reformers seem, so to speak, as if they were hurrying God. Certainly the Magistrates of the Massachusetts theocracy presented themselves in that character

when they attempted to make for others a rule from what
by their own interpretation and faith they regarded as a
Divine method for administering a commonwealth. Not
all whom they governed held their belief about the Scriptures. Even writers of Scripture have said many things
for God which an intelligent reverence refuses to receive
as divine. Deeds have been charged to his prompting
which bear all the marks of having been instigated by the
malevolence, the passions, or the delusions of men. It is
to be noted that in no public or private records of the time
do we find a trace of any opening or discussion of the
question between the Puritan authorities and those who
smarted under their discipline, either of the rightfulness
and wisdom of the attempt to govern a commonwealth by
the Bible, or of the competency of the authorities to use
the Book discreetly in their legislation. We have to rest
in the admission that this ideal of a commonwealth was
entitled in its turn to have a trial, and then to study its
workings and results.

Let us select from the abounding variety of the matter
in our hands some illustrations of the use of Scripture
made by these Bible legislators. It being at once apprehended that the " Statutes and Ordinances of Israel " could
not be adopted in their completeness as a whole, the first
rule was to be found in distinguishing among them and
selecting such as were of general and permanent authority.
They were divided very readily into three classes, — judicial, moral, and ceremonial. The last was to be dispensed
with ; the former two were to be retained, with adaptations,
if such were needed. The " magistrate " in these matters,
rather than the elder, was the " minister of God," and it
was for him to assume authority as such. It was agreed
that the Ten Commandments were for perpetual and universal observance. But here was found the first rock on
which the State-Church struck. The Commandments were
divided into " Two Tables," — the first four covering one ;

the other six the other. The first table concerns the duties which man owes to God, as those of religion, — namely, reverence, worship, the use of oaths, and the observance of the Sabbath. The second table covers the duties which men owe to men. The magistrate, as the minister of God, claimed that his jurisdiction covered both tables. Roger Williams, as we shall see, took his firm stand, which he resolutely maintained, upon his bold denial of the jurisdiction of the magistrate — the civil power — over the matters of the first table. In plainer terms, that able and far-sighted prophet of soul-freedom forbade the State to assume any legislation or administration of religion. This was the first, indeed, the fatal blow dealt the Massachusetts theocracy. But the magistrates, with adroit ingenuity, had a way of parrying the blow. We shall note in the trial of Mrs. Hutchinson that Governor Winthrop charged her directly with a breach of the Fifth Commandment, — "Honour thy father and thy mother." She might well have been astounded by this charge had she not known what the Fifth Commandment covered for Puritan legislation. To the question in the Westminster standard, "Who are meant by father and mother?" we have the answer:

"By father and mother, in the Fifth Commandment, are meant not only natural parents, but all superiours in Age and Gifts, and especially such as by God's ordinance are over us in place of Authority, whether in Family, Church, or Commonwealth."

Nor were Scripture citations lacking to sustain this position. An effective argument was found in support of the authority of the civil magistrate in the province of religion, in the example of "Josiah the Supreme Governour of the true Church in Judah and Israel, who took away all the abominations out of all the Countries that appertained to the children of Israel, and compelled all that were found in Israel to serve the Lord their God."[1]

[1] 2 Chron. xxxiv. 33.

The Scripture called "Solomon's Song" or "the Canticles" is not in our times regarded as edifying, either in the pulpit or for private reading; but for the Puritans it was a deep and precious mine for devotion, as illustrating "the love of Christ for his bride, the Church." On the arrival of Mr. Cotton, Winthrop tells us there was a meeting of the congregation of Boston, Saturday evening, Sept. 4, 1633, in "their ordinary exercise:" —

"Mr. Cotton, being desired to speak to the question (which was of the church), he showed out of the Canticles, 6, that some churches were as queens, some as concubines, some as damsels, and some as doves," etc.[1]

When the planters at New Haven proceeded to organize, they met in a large barn on June 4, 1639. Mr. Davenport preached from Proverbs ix. 1: "Wisdom hath builded her house; she hath hewn out her seven pillars." His "improvement" was that in settling the foundations of Church and State seven approved brethren should be selected as pillars. His counsel was followed. He also taught "as fundamental orders," —

"1. That the Scriptures hold forth a perfect rule for men in their family, church, and commonwealth affairs. 2. That the rules of Scripture were to govern the gathering and ordering of the church, the choice of magistrates and officers, the making and repeal of laws, the dividing of allotments of inheritance, and all things of like nature. 3. That all 'free planters' were to become such with the resolution and intention to be admitted into church fellowship as soon as God should fit them thereunto. 4. That civil order was to be such as should conduce to securing the purity and peace of the ordinances to the free planters and their posterity."

Mr. Cotton, in answer to a letter of questions put to him by a friend, justified the praying for a person by name, from Ephesians vi. 19. He adds: —

[1] Winthrop, i. 110.

"Carding I take to be unlawful and containing in it a lottery, at least in the shuffling and cutting and dealing. A lottery also it is to choose valentines. Dancing (yea though mixt) I would not simply condemn ; for I see two sorts of mixt dancings in use with God's people in the Old Testament, — the one religious, Ex. xv. 20, 21 ; the other civil, tending to the praise of conquerors, as the former of God, 1 Sam. xviii. 6, 7. Only lascivious dancing to wanton ditties and in amorous gestures and wanton dalliances, especially after great feasts, I would bear witness against as a great *flabella libidinis.*" [1]

When that black sheep of the covenant, Captain Under-hill, — mildly dealt with for gross immorality by the out-raged Church because of his military prowess, — returned with his laurels from the Pequot war, he was " convented " for his Antinomianism and for having " set his hand " to a remonstrance offensive to the Court. He defended himself by quoting the case of Joab in his remonstrance, and insisting that military officers were by all states allowed free speech. He himself when in service in the Low Countries " had spoken his mind to Count Nassau." But his plea failed.[2] The Court carefully studied the Scripture citation, as lawyers now refer to decisions and precedents.

Mr. Cotton, expounding of the defection of the ten tribes from Rehoboam, and the prophet's prohibition of war, —

" Proved from that in Numbers xxvii. 21 that the rulers of the people should consult with the ministers of the churches upon occasion of any war to be undertaken, and any other weighty business, though the case should seem never so clear, as David in the case of Ziglag, and the Israelites in the case of Gibeah." [3]

The Bible having long been discredited for such uses as the Puritans made of it in finding parallelisms of occasion and rule for guiding their own course and administration,

---

[1] 2 Massachusetts Historical Collections, x. 183.

[2] Winthrop, i. 247.

[3] Winthrop, i. 237.

modern readers, not so familiar with the volume as they were, would be impatient of any extended illustrations of the matter now before us.

When a pressing need was felt for erecting a new hall for the College in 1677, the Court made an appeal for collections to the ministers and elders of several towns. The argument relied upon was by a citation of Scripture : —

"Wee shall only desire you to consider that Scripture, 1 Chron. xxix., especially from verses 10 to 17, wherein David and the people of Israell gave liberally unto a good worke, praysing God that he had given them hearts to offer so willingly, acknowledging that all their substance came from God, and that of his owne they had given him." [1]

These illustrations of the readiness and confidence with which Scripture precedents and examples were adduced, as well in the court-room as in the place of public worship, — indeed, one building served for many years for both uses, — are selected as they present themselves on incidental occasions. It will at once suggest itself to us that this ready and off-hand reference to the Holy Book assumes, as well it might, a perfect familiarity with its contents. The Scriptures were put to a very exacting test when incidents in far-off time in Oriental lands, and human personalities living under such different conditions and experiences, were used to furnish precedents and examples in a new world and in a modern century.

Many writers upon early Massachusetts history have — perhaps naturally, but none the less erroneously — assumed that as the government was theocratical, the influence of the clergy in its administration was supreme. So we have been made familiar with sharp and censorious accusations against "the elders" as really the prime movers and agents in bigoted legislation, the teachers of intolerance, and the instigators of persecution against those who challenged or

[1] Records, v. 144.

opposed their dictation and authority. These assumptions and charges are subject to very serious qualifications. In the sweep and positiveness of statement and censure with which they have often been uttered, they are simply untrue. A careful study of the Colony Records and other early original materials will rectify the errors in them. The elders and the civil magistrates were alike concerned in and responsible for, and were of one mind in administering, the theocratical government. Dudley, Endicott, and Bellingham needed no prompting in severity from the elders. What was peculiar, official, or personal in the influence of the elders will soon be set forth from the Records. What is to be said for the purpose of correcting over-statements on this point may well be introduced by a reference to a very significant fact, which those who have thus assigned to the early clergy of Massachusetts so supreme an influence appear to have overlooked.

The most potent and effective of all the changes wrought by the Reformation was in striking at and breaking the sway of the priesthood, and in securing for laymen a share in everything that concerned ecclesiastical affairs and religious institutions and discipline. The more radical and thorough the Reformation was, — the more the Protestant element prevailed at any time and in any place, — we find the assertion of the claims and influence of laymen against the clergy, or in connection with them, more and more resolute and secure. This characteristic feature of all Protestantism became most pronounced in that form of it called Puritanism. Under the Roman, or Papal, Church laymen were but ciphers or puppets in the hands of the priesthood. Substantially they are so still in that communion. They are not recognized in any council, they have no share in discipline, except to submit to it, no treasury reports of the Church are made to or audited by them, and they are simply the sheep of the fold of which the priests are the shepherds. The Reformation broke this

exclusive sway and prerogative of clericalism and brought
the laity forward. It was by the help of civil potentates
that Luther secured a hearing, and indeed his own life
and opportunity, and prepared the way for his supporters
and successors to grapple with the powers of the hierarchy. In the English Church, with a layman for its new
head and Parliament for its legislative court, the absolute
rule of sacerdotalism was crushed. And the Protestant
Episcopal communion in the United States carries the
agency of laymen one degree further than in the mother
Church by giving them a place on all committees, in all
conventions, and in all legislation.

It would have been a most extraordinary exception to
the working of this radical method of Protestantism if the
magistrates and freemen of early Massachusetts had put
themselves under the dictation and rule of their "elders."
The enterprise and scheme of colonization were inspired by
laymen, and their ministers were called in to be their advisers and helpers. From first to last this was the relation
here between those two classes of men. The ministers were
not functionaries, men "in orders," with an official character and sanctity, standing qualified to occupy and serve at
pulpit or altar as there might be a place for them. They
were chosen and put in office by the people of each congregation, and were dependent upon them for maintenance.
In every case their influence was graduated by weight of
character, by the qualities of their manhood, their learning
and abilities. It was a grave question among the Puritans
whether a minister could officiate in the ordinances to any
other congregation than the one he had been called to serve.
By the Congregational rule the teacher or pastor was simply one of the brethren in his own flock, and such only
there. In all church discipline he was subordinate to the
congregation. A lay brother or "messenger" was always
sent with an elder to a council.

When John Cotton arrived in 1633 and was instituted

as "teacher" in the church of Boston, he brought with
him a child born on the passage. Though Cotton, under
Episcopal ordination, had served as a vicar for a score
of years, he explained why his child had not as yet been
baptized : —

"It was not for want of fresh water ; for he held sea water
would have served, — but (1) because they had no settled congregation there ; (2) because a minister hath no power to give
the seals but in his own congregation." [1]

That the masters should have put themselves under the
dictation of their own servants, and that the Puritan laity
should have succumbed to the elders, would certainly have
been inexplicable had it been true. Those who have thus
apprehended and misrepresented the facts have been misled by not allowing for the perfect sympathy and accord in
spirit, judgment, and purpose between the magistrates and
the ministers. Elder Norton, who has suffered the severest
castigation for his harsh bigotry, had his full compeers in
Dudley, Endicott, and Bellingham. The two earliest sufferers by the discipline of the Court were themselves elders, — Roger Williams and John Wheelwright, — and no
prestige of office drew to them help from their brethren.

Even the revered Cotton but narrowly escaped that discipline. Hooker removed with his flock from Cambridge
to Connecticut because he felt himself overshadowed. We
find many entries on the Court records in which the authorities rallied respect and support for the clergy. Nor
are there lacking evidences on those records that the
elders were sometimes reminded that on some subjects
they should withhold the utterance of their opinions till
asked for them, and that while their advice was valued,
dictation did not become them. Cotton did not arrive till
two years after the franchise had been restricted to church
members ; so he was not responsible for that. Soon after

[1] Winthrop, i. 110.

he came he found some division and contention existing as to the powers of deputies and magistrates, and that the honored Winthrop was under a cloud as arbitrary in his government. Some of the people thought it was time for a change of governor. Cotton ventured to interfere with his advice in a sermon, teaching that only misconduct in office would justify dropping such a faithful Governor as Winthrop; but none the less he was displaced by Dudley. The Apostle Eliot complained in a sermon that the magistrates had made a peace with the Pequot Indians in 1634 without consulting the people. Three elders were sent to "deal" with him, to bring him "to acknowledge his error," which he did publicly.[1] Winthrop was challenged by the elders for having sent some papers concerning some action of the Court in a controversy, to be published in England. He reminded them that in its own province the Church was subordinate to the civil power.[2]

There is no denying the fact that the influence of the clergy was very great, though not supreme. This, however, did not constitute the theocratic character of the government which attached to it, as has been said, because its statutes were those of God, making the civil magistrate his minister. The elders had influence because of their accord with the magistrates. Had there been collision between them, the latter would have prevailed. The function of the elders, whether in civil or ecclesiastical affairs, was simply explanatory and advisory. They were consulted on slight as well as on serious questions. But their weight of consequence always depended on one condition, namely, their "opening the rule of God's Word" and sustaining advice or opinion by one or more "Scriptures;" that is, by a text. The magistrate, feeling himself charged "to take care for the things of God," had clerical functions of his own. Of course, he acknowledged himself as amenable to church discipline in his covenanted relations,

---

[1] Winthrop, i. 151.   [2] Ibid., i. 249.

but his oath of office as a magistrate conferred upon him his functions in the theocracy.

We may now trace briefly, from Winthrop and the Records, how the elders came to have influence in civil affairs, and the quality and effect of their influence.

Feb. 27, 1632, the Court having levied a tax on Watertown, the pastor and elder of the church advised the people to resist it; but their advice was overruled, and the tax was paid. In July, 1632, "the congregation at Boston" wrote to the elders and brethren of the churches of Plymouth, Salem, etc., for their advice, — "Whether one person might be a civil magistrate and a ruling elder at the same time?" It was unanimously decided in the negative.[1] In the autumn of that year a personal difference between the Governor and the Deputy, Dudley, was "ended" by the mediation of the elders.[2] February, 1633, three of the elders, with the Governor and four magistrates, went to Nantasket to confer as to the building of a fort.[3] Sept. 27, 1633, the Governor and assistants called all the elders to consider where John Cotton should settle.[4] Jan. 7, 1634, the Governor and magistrates asked for the views of the elders on the denial by Roger Williams of the validity of their Patent.[5] July 19, 1634, elders and magistrates of Massachusetts and Plymouth confer as to rights of trade at Kennebec.[6] The next month "diverse of the ministers" take part in the discussion about the fort on Castle Island.[7] In February, 1635, the elders were summoned to advise the magistrates as to what should be done under the apprehension lest a "General Governor" should be sent over to the Colonies. The advice, founded on their Patent, was that he should not be received.[8] In each and all of the successive cases that are to come before us, in which the Court inflicted its discipline and its penalties

[1] Winthrop, i. 81.   [2] Ibid., i. 89.   [3] Ibid., i. 99.
[4] Ibid., i. 112.   [5] Ibid., i. 122.   [6] Ibid., i. 136.
[7] Ibid., i. 137.   [8] Ibid., i. 154.

upon individuals or companies regarded as offenders, we shall meet with the elders in the same capacity, never as initiating measures, but simply as consulted for opinions or advice.

Special reference should be made to what the Records contain about the position of the elders in the preparation of the laws of the Colony. The Charter gave the Company authority —

"To make laws and ordinances for the good and welfare of the said Company, and for the government and ordering of the said lands and plantation, and the people inhabiting and to inhabit the same, as to them from time to time shall be thought meete. So as such lawes and ordinances be not contrary or repugnant to the laws and statutes of this our realme of England."

This exercise of legislative powers under novel and exigent circumstances proved to be a task which required the utmost abilities, judgment, and prescience of men none of whom had the special professional training for the work. Precedents in many important matters were wholly wanting. The composition of the constituency, intended to be homogeneous, became rapidly heterogeneous. The original membership of the Company was strictly of proprietors, stockholders, whose rights and interests were first to be protected. All others among them were their servants, subordinates, or dependents. All whom they should admit as new members, "freemen," holding the franchise, would have votes affecting the proprietary rights of the original stockholders, who had transferred their estates from the Old World to the wilderness. The risks of dissension would be imminent, and the consequences of it would be disastrous. Their code of laws, when perfected, always excepting those of a theocratical character, was substantially conformed to natural justice and humanity, with fewer capital offences than the code of England. Indeed, as a reader goes over their records he

will hardly fail to be impressed by the considerateness —
we may even say the tenderness — often apparent in the
treatment of the unfortunate, the infirm, the ignorant, the
penitent, the widow and the orphan, and the victims of
calamity. Severity there is, enough of it, but often tempered with mercy. Sedition and heresy were the especial
dread of the magistracy, and any contempt or defiance of
their authority was treated with a resoluteness which looks
like vengefulness; but there was a long delay and many
tentative efforts in this work of legislation. Nor was it
strange that this delay should have provoked restlessness
and discontent and murmuring among the people. It
seemed for a time as if the rule was to be arbitrary, depending upon the judgment and will, as each case arose,
of the magistrates. The first relief was found in a body
of deputies, having the negative power, made up of representatives of the freemen in the towns. We find under
date of March, 1634–5, intimations of discontent.[1] The
Governor, deputy, and two other magistrates, without any
elder, were charged as a committee with the consideration of the subject. In May, 1636,[2] the Governor (Vane),
the deputy, three magistrates, and now for the first time
three elders were intrusted with the work; but nothing
came of this. We learn from Winthrop[3] that Cotton, in
behalf of this committee, had prepared something called
" Moses his Judicials." Perhaps his friend Vane aided
him in this; but no notice is taken of it in the Court
Records. A manuscript, found in Cotton's study after his
death, was printed in London in 1641, and in a fuller form
in 1655. In the earlier form of them it is said, — " as they
are now established;" but they never were established.[4]
Each law is supported by texts from both Testaments, and
so not confined to Moses. There are eighteen capital

---

[1] Winthrop, i. 137, 160.   [2] Records, i. 174.
[3] Winthrop, i. 202.
[4] This code is reprinted in 1 Mass. Hist. Coll., v. 173.

offences, and six more which have an alternative of death or banishment; much fewer than by the English code at that time. The abstract is ratified by the Scripture quotation, " The Lord is our Judge, the Lord is our Lawgiver, the Lord is our King : he will save us." [1] Cotton's object was " to show the complete sufficiency of the Word of God alone to direct his people in judgment of all causes, both civil and criminal."

In two lines of his fine sonnet on Sir Henry Vane, Milton says : —

" Both spiritual power and civil, what each means,
     What severs each, thou hast learned, which few have done."

No other magistrate than Vane had then learned it. Cotton and the other elders certainly had not ; but this does not prove that the latter were the legislators of the Colony, or its ruling spirits in bigotry and severity.

A singular device toward legislation was proposed by the Court, March 12, 163⅞. The order recites : —

" For the well ordering of these plantations now in the beginning thereof, it having bene found by the little time of experience wee have heare had, that the want of written lawes have put the Court into many doubts and much trouble in many perticuler cases, this Court hath therefore ordered that the freemen of every towne (or some part thereof chosen by the rest) within this jurisdiction shall assemble together in their severall townes, and collect the heads of such necessary and fundamentall lawes as may bee sutable to the times and places whear God by his providence hath cast us," etc.[2]

These " heads " when collected were to be sent to the Governor, and were by him to be laid before the Council, attended by three elders of churches, to be digested into " a compendious abridgement," and to be laid before the next General Court for approbation or rejection. Winthrop

---

[1] Isaiah xxxiii. 22.   [2] Records, i. 222.

explains the delay in this matter by offering two reasons
for it, showing why "most of the magistrates and some of
the elders were not very forward" in it. One was a want
of sufficient experience of the nature and disposition of the
people, under the circumstances of the country, they
conceiving that the fittest laws would suggest themselves
as occasions arose *pro re nata*, as the laws of England and
other States had grown. The other reason was, that as by
their charter they could make no laws repugnant to those
of England, and nevertheless would be compelled by the
necessity of the case to do so, "to raise up laws by practice and custom had been no transgression, as in our
church discipline and in matters of marriage." So "two
models" were digested and sent to the several towns.[1]
The Court worked over the models in November, 1639;
and afterward four magistrates and two deputies were
directed to inspect them and send them to the towns for
the consideration of the elders and freemen. The result
was a "Breviate of the Liberties," etc., finally digested by
Nathaniel Ward, and voted by the Court in 1641 "to stand
in force." [2] Ward, minister of Ipswich, had been a minister in England, and previously a student and practitioner
of the common law. The "Breviate" contained a hundred
laws. After the original pamphlet had long been lost to
sight here, a copy of it accidentally came to light in the
Boston Athenæum.[3] The laws were first put in print in
the Colony in 1649. There are twelve capital offences
enforced by Old Testament texts.

From this brief review it appears that the elders
were not the prime legislators of the Colony. It would
have been strange if in the Biblical commonwealth, where
Scripture in precedent and authority was to be so closely
followed, they had not been called in as interpreters and

[1] Winthrop, i. 323.
[2] Records, i. 292, 320, 340, 344, 346, and Winthrop, ii. 55.
[3] It is reprinted in 3 Mass. Hist. Coll., vol. viii., 1843.

advisers. It was in their discourses and conferences that they were to win and exert their influence. As has been already shown, that influence was as little as possible official. They were but brethren. It would not be right to assign to them the chief responsibility for the ghostly rule of the Colony. Mr. Pynchon, magistrate of Springfield, a man of marked ability, had written and procured to be printed in England, a work on the "Atonement," esteemed heretical. On the arrival here of copies the Court took alarm, dealt by warning with the author, and committed the book to Mr. Norton, to be answered by him, also for printing in England. But Scripture texts were the weapons of that conflict. Pynchon consented to some concessions, not however satisfactory, and his book was burned in the market-place, as were many other heretical works. A further reference to this matter will be made in another connection.

We have thus before us the materials for an intelligent view of the sort of commonwealth which the founders of Massachusetts established after a Scriptural model, and which has received the title of a Theocracy. The term "Commonwealth," with its synonym of State, was a favorite one with them, boldly, even vauntingly, as well as tenderly, used here before it was freely current in England in Cromwell's time. The King's Commissioners sent here in 1665, to reckon with the Colonists, and Andros afterward, had a special spite to that word, and demanded its disuse and expurgation, making it all the more dear to its citizens here.

The one prime, all-essential, and sufficient quality of a theocracy, adopted as the form of an earthly government, was that the civil power should be guided in its exercise by religion and by religious ordinances. The magistrate came in with his efforts and help, to put into force what he regarded as the will and purpose of God. To effect this, not only the magistrate himself but those who put him in

office and gave him power must be in covenant with God
and have exclusive authority. How this critical condition
was sought to be insured we shall see in the next chapter.
The religious loyalty of the magistrates and their electors
being thus covenanted, there would remain the party outside to be governed, — those who were not freemen, who
could not hold nor elect to office. These, however, were
to be brought under the same theocratic rule with the covenanted. How was this to be secured ? It might be hoped
that when the magistrates and their way of rule were set
before the people as representing the sovereign law and
will of God, the people would even more willingly recognize
their obligations by loyal obedience than they would to
any human statutes of government. If it should be found,
as it was found, that numbers of the people would not accept the magistrates and their rule as representing God
to them, they were to be constrained, if not to obedience
then to compliance. While the covenanted willingly sustained a ministry and waited on worship and ordinances,
the uncovenanted must be compelled to do the same by
exactions and penalties for neglect. The rule found its
way into private homes, and even sought to intermeddle
with private hearts.

VI.

CHURCH MEMBERSHIP AND THE FRANCHISE.

A BIBLICAL commonwealth must needs have a Biblical rule and qualification for constituting and admitting membership or citizenship in it. How was this to be effected? While "the Governor and Company of Massachusetts Bay" was simply a corporation for trade, its members being joint-stock proprietors, partners in the ownership by shares, liable to assessments and entitled to dividends, the usual rules of all such secular and business enterprises were all that was needed in its administration. Selfish interests might be trusted, as they would be sure to have sway. The officers and existing members at any time might have regard for integrity of character and perhaps for desirable qualities of companionship in the admission of new associates, but would not necessarily or even naturally require anything of accordance in religious opinions and sympathies. But when that mercantile company was to be transformed to a body for legislating for and administering a government which was to plant a commonwealth in a wilderness across the seas, the qualifications of membership, of influence and authority in it, would at once become matters of supreme importance.

The Charter gave to the Company liberty to admit new members, called "freemen" of the Company. No method, conditions, or qualifications were prescribed for conferring this privilege. For all that appears, the proprietors then constituting the corporation might, had they chosen to do

so, have resolved not to enlarge their number, or have
made any secular conditions of a reasonable character
which they approved, requisite in the case.   But we have
seen that from the first suggestion in England of a purpose
for transferring the patent and government of the Company to be set up here, there came into its business meetings the minglings and influence of religious sentiment,
and a reference to religious objects.   The two London
ministers who were invited into the meetings to consecrate
them by prayer seem to have been made freemen of the
Company for that sole purpose, without possessing or pur-
chasing any shares in its property.   As soon as the Company after its arrival here set up the local government, it
imposed a condition of a very exacting and restrictive character for the enjoyment of its franchise by new members.
It was original too, it never, in its express terms, having
been before required in any civil State.   The condition
was in full organic consistency with the scheme of a
Biblical commonwealth, and indeed was vitally requisite
to it.   We are uninformed as to any discussions, conferences, or understandings between the leaders of the enterprise which would enlighten us as to their maturing
and privately agreeing upon the new condition to be imposed for the enjoyment of the franchise.   As we read it
in the record it comes upon us as a complete surprise;
and yet it was of so peculiar and novel a character that
we can hardly conceive of its adoption without some previous confidential concert among the leaders.

At the meeting of the General Court in Boston, May 18,
1631, several orders were passed, as is said, " with full
consent of all the commons then present."   If this covers
all the orders there set down, then all the freemen at that
Court agreed upon the following : " To the end the body of
the commons may be preserved of honest and good men, it
was likewise ordered and agreed that for time to come noe
man shalbe admitted to the freedome of this body polli-

ticke but such as are members of some of the churches within the limits of the same." [1] The operation of that order is prospective, for application in the future. We are not informed as to the number of those already freemen who voted upon it, nor whether all of them were at the time church members. If it is to be inferred that any of them at the time were not in church covenant, and as nothing is said of their being for that reason disfranchised, then it is possible that some of them might have retained their privilege without coming under the order. It is to be observed that though thenceforward no one could become free of the company without being a church member, it did not follow that every church member was a freeman. On the contrary, as we shall learn from a subsequent order of the Court, it undertook to deal with some church members who, for reasons assigned, refused to take their freedom. There were at the date of the order four organized churches in the jurisdiction ; namely, at Salem, Dorchester, Boston, and Watertown, the Boston church having been previously instituted in Charlestown. It may have been that some freemen considered their previous relation to the Church of England as constituting them church members; but henceforward membership of a church within the limits of this jurisdiction was imperative. At a previous Court, in October, 1630, one hundred and nine persons had sent in an application to be made freemen. This being before the order for church membership had been passed, such of them as had not been accepted at the time had to come under the new condition, and their names appear in subsequent years as obtaining the franchise. In May, 1634, it was agreed "that none but the General Court hath power to chuse and admitt freemen." [2] At that Court the terms of " the Oath of a Freeman," as previously written, were slightly modified. By this the freeman acknowledged himself a subject to the government, and swore " by the greate

---

[1] Records, i. 87.　　　　　[2] Ibid., i. 117.

and dreadfull name of the everlyveing God," to be true and faithful to it in obedience and support, with person and estate, to maintain its liberties and privileges, to plot or consent to no injuries against it, and to vote by conscience for the " publique weale of the body."

As no complete census of the inhabitants was taken in the Colony, we are at a loss for anything more than an approximate estimate of the proportion of numbers which those who were both freemen and church members bore to the adult males of the Colony. Up to June 2, 1641, the names of eleven hundred and ninety-two persons are given as having taken the freeman's oath. Four hundred and eighty-one more had done so up to May, 1649, and from that date to 1660, two hundred and one. Up to 1674, six hundred and fifty-three new freemen had been added to the list, some, however, coming in by a modification of the previous requisition, to be mentioned further on. The Court lists thus give to that last date the names of two thousand five hundred and twenty-seven men, sworn into citizenship. As has been intimated, the number of covenanted church members was larger. Steadily onward from the enactment of this covenant test for the franchise to the close of the rigid Puritan rule, the male citizens deprived of the full right of citizenship were increasing in the majority outnumbering those who enjoyed it. Probably the estimate was correct which gave the proportions between them as of five to one.

Thus was defined and enforced the fundamental, organic constitution of the Puritan State. The founders must be admitted to have exercised a keen discernment and a wise foresight in judging this condition for full citizenship to be a prime essential in the sort of commonwealth which they proposed to establish. They adopted it as an axiom that an orderly, peaceful, and secure government must be planted on the foundation of religion. Its laws and statutes were to be those of God, revealed and committed to

Christian magistrates for administration. These magistrates were to be put in office by electors from the people. Those electors must be under covenant in exercising their trust. We must now study the terms of the covenant which qualified them.

A formidable Remonstrance and Petition addressed to the General Court in 1646, by Robert Child and six others, complaining of their exclusion from church privileges, from the franchise, and other grievances, while still being taxed, drew forth a very elaborate Declaration from the Court. In this document a parallelism is instituted between Magna Charta and the common laws of England on the one side, and the " Fundamentalls of the Massachusetts " on the other. In the former it appeared that the people were represented in the Parliament by their deputies : " These deputies are chosen for all the people, but not by all the people ; but only by certain freehoulders and free burgers, in shires and corporations." In accord with this the Court pleads : " Our deputies are chosen for all the people, but not by all the people, but only by the companie of freemen, according to our charter." So the acts of Parliament " bind all the people, as well forraigne as free borne ; as well such as have no libertie in the election of the members of the Court as the freehoulders who choose them." Parallel with this : " The acts of this generall court do bind all within this jurisdiction, as well no-freemen who have no vote in election of the members of the court as the freemen who doe choose them. By the Charter." [1]

What might be the coveted, and what certainly was the responsible privilege of citizenship by the franchise, as the theocratical equivalent for being made a freeman of the Company, being thus conditioned on church membership, we must inform ourselves clearly upon the exactions and method by which that religious relation was obtained. What were the terms and requisitions of church member-

[1] Hutchinson's Collection of Papers, pp. 202-204.

ship, the process for securing it, the responsibilities attached to it, and the consequences involved in it ? It is in what relates to this matter that we have to recognize the fundamental, the vital, radical, and most distinguishing qualities and features of the Biblical commonwealth. Here it made its widest and deepest variance with the Roman and Anglican churches, through which it drew its lineage. Not even in its rejection of the theories of prelacy, ritualistic practices, and the ceremonials and observances of mediævalism, did English dissent alike in its forms of Puritanism and Nonconformity come so sharply into protest, and into an earnest and resolute course of its own, as in its views and methods of " church membership." In the English Church, as developed from the Reformation, as previously in the Roman Church, church membership was substantially the birthright to which the children of English parents acceded, by very simple processes, to be followed as a matter of course. Whatever might have been expected or desired in each case in which church membership was reached by these processes, they might or might not require or imply any profound heart experience of religion, as reaching the springs of character and consecrating life. Each child was to be baptized in its earliest infancy. And so exigent was the necessity for this, — considering what a peril for the immortal destiny of the child was suspended upon it, — that, in an emergency, the rite might be validly performed by anybody repeating the Scripture formula. Then, as the growing child was entering into the second decade of its years, after rudimentary instruction in the Creed, the Catechism, and the Commandments, the bishop, by the laying on of hands, and a blessing, made it a full member of the Church by " confirmation." Henceforward it was not only privileged but obliged to partake of the holiest of the sacraments. It was by these methods — the baptism of unconscious infants, and the qualification of those who were in the second

decade of their lives to partake of the Lord's Supper —
that the people of any country of Christendom were to
grow into and to perpetuate through their generations the
Christian Church. A nation became in this way entitled
to be called Christian, as distinct from heathen.

In sharpest variance with this usage, and in profound
disapproval of it, were the conscientious choice and the
searching tests of Puritanism. This easy, miscellaneous,
uncertified, and indiscriminating method of constituting a
member of the Church of Christ was to them without warrant, reason, or blessing ; indeed, it trespassed within the
borders of sacrilege and impiety. The risks to constancy
and fidelity in the Christian discipleship were many and
grievous enough for those who had assumed its obligations
after the best preliminary discipline of heart and conscience. Entered on without these, failure, reproach, and
condemnation were likely to follow. So the phrase fondly
used by the Puritans, that " the Church of Christ consisted
of Saints," elected, sealed, and covenanted, one by one, with
him, and with each other, expressed the stretch of their
divergence from the usage of the English Church. They
took nothing for granted as to the Christian standing even
of a child born of Christian parents, except in expecting
that such parents would give their child a Christian nurture. They would not baptize a child unless at least one
of its parents was in covenant with a church. The method
approved by them for admitting a new member of either
sex into their church fellowship was as follows : The pastor, conversant with his flock, was to maintain a faithful
oversight of it, as well of those who merely attended upon
exercises of worship, as of those who participated in the
" ordinances." This oversight was close and inquisitive
in their homes, and was followed with prayers and lessons
in the Catechism for children in the schools. The church
and pastor recognized a measure of responsibility to baptized children as having been already initiated or pledged

to a membership to be fully claimed or enjoyed when they should grow to mature years. Those for whom pastor, teacher, deacons, and the more zealous of the brethren and sisters were most concerned, were such as, not yet in covenant, gave evidence "in a godly walk," in conversation, habit, and tone of life, of being under sacred exercise of heart and spirit, with a measure of regenerated experience. New disciples, then, now, and always, were to offer themselves one by one, individually, under conviction of heart, as did the first disciples of Christ, Jew or Gentile. It was for each one under such conviction to make it known, or to avow it under appeal or question. Then followed a conference with an officer of the church, with an examination of heart, conscience, and experience at the stage which it had reached. If this was satisfactory, the candidate was " propounded " before the whole assembled congregation for admission into the select body, — " the Church." The ordeal at this stage of it was a severe one, for neighbors were free to raise objections, to ask questions looking back through the life of the candidate for whatever might need redress or repentance. Our older church records are very communicative about some subjects, the rehearsal of which is not now viewed as edifying. An interval, generally a month, was allowed to transpire for the full satisfaction of all parties. Then, again, in full congregation, the candidates at the call of the pastor, rising from their seats, gave an oral or written relation of their religious experience.[1] This might be brief and general, from the modest or the diffident; but fulness and detail were preferred by hearers till they had become wonted to such rehearsals. We can well appreciate the severity of this ordeal to those of a tender, delicate, and shrinking purity of spirit, as listeners

---

[1] This requisition from the candidate was made and justified by Scripture texts, as Matthew iii. 6, xvi. 16–18 ; Acts viii. 37 ; 1 Peter iii. 15. The French and the Dutch reformed churches, as also the English Presbyterians, required similar utterances from candidates for fellowship.

waited for the revealings of the holiest privacy. And in contrast with these were the volubility and confidence of some, who knew that they had the most, or seemed to feel that they had the least, for which to repent or be ashamed. It may be interposed here that the fourth Congregational Church gathered in Boston, the "Brattle Street," in 1700, which startled and shocked its elder sisters by its "innovations," that had to be justified and defended, made the most venturesome and revolutionary of them in dispensing with this public rehearsal of the private religious experience of candidates before the congregation.

The ordeal being passed, the new member was received into full covenant, henceforward, through conflicts, resolves, and helps of sympathy, to be one of the elect in privileges and responsibilities. Nor were the obligations of the member afterward merely individual and personal. He was under religious bonds to the brethren and sisters of the fold. He came, as the phrase was, under "the watch and ward of the church." Liable at any time to be challenged and rebuked for backsliding and lukewarmness, he must also take part in the frequent meetings for the discipline of others.

Of members thus covenanted and sealed, — the men among them, — the General Court of Massachusetts "by a general consent" of members covenanted and uncovenanted, present in 1631, decided that they alone henceforward should have the franchise for the administration of all civil affairs. Governor, magistrates, and the deputies or representatives of the people in all the towns were to be "in covenant with one of the churches." The intent was, "that the body of the commons may be preserved of honest and good men." The intent was fair, noble, and wise. No State could plant itself on a more righteous or hopeful basis. Had the churches really been composed of "saints," even though not including exhaustively all of that rare class in the community, the experiment might have triumphed. Fifty, forty, thirty, twenty, even ten righteous men might

save a city.[1] The difficulty was in finding them so gifted
in wisdom and policy that they could exercise mastery over
sinners, — which are really more proper, and certainly
more abundant material for a church than are " saints."
But the method which the Court of Massachusetts chose
for realizing its wise and noble intent was wrecked by two
fatal errors. It excluded from the franchise, as not in
covenant, some of the most righteous, exemplary, wise, and
serviceable men; and it let into the fold some of the unworthy, the unwise, and the hypocritical. The terms of the
covenant, the doctrinal system on which it was based, and
the character of the " religious experience " which it exacted, repelled many whose opinions, convictions, tone of
character, and real religious principles were not accordant
with it. Warnings against parting with one's private liberty of thinking, and the uttering of honest opinions, observances, and attendance upon religious meetings had
effect upon many who were half disposed and half in hesitancy as to entering into covenant obligations, when they
took note of the close espionage, the petty intermeddlings,
and the vexatious discipline to which church members subjected each other. The obligations of " watch and ward "
were by no means perfunctorily or slackly interpreted and
exercised. The church incurred a solemn responsibility
for each one of its members. Even after a sentence of excommunication had been passed against a member, the
duty of reclaiming him and restoring him by repentance
still held a suspended relation between the parties. When
we have to recognize further on the ecclesiastical as well
as the civil proceedings against such members of the Boston church as were banished with Mrs. Hutchinson, we
might suppose that the church having cast them out had
done with them. By no means. One might wish to regard
the act as a lingering tenderness of spirit in those who remained here ; but it was none the less the prompting of

[1] Gen. xviii. 26-32.

14

a covenant duty which moved the Boston church to send a committee to Aquidnec to such as were still held to it by a suspended tie. It does not appear from the records that any penalty from a civil court, other than the loss of the franchise, was at first inflicted upon an excommunicated person; but the fact that any one had been so dealt with would always be at his disadvantage when judicially proceeded against. As a rule, unless the offence committed by an excommunicated church member had been of so heinous a nature as to lead to his being utterly "cast out," as if henceforward to be "yielded over to Satan," it was expected that he would seek restoration by repentance and meek solicitation. The terms of forgiveness and renewed fellowship were often deeply humbling to self-respect and pride, but otherwise were not over-rigid. Yet only as it might deprive of citizenship, some excommunicated persons seem to have made light of the penalty, as if they were glad to be rid of fetters and annoyances. So we find this resolute order upon the Court records of September, 1638 : —

"Whereas it is found, by sad experience, that diverse persons who have bene justly cast out of some of the churches do prophanely contemne the same sacred and dreadfull ordinance, by presenting themselves overbouldly in other assemblies, and speaking lightly of their censures, to the great offence and greefe of God's people, and incuragement of evill minded persons to contemne the said ordinance, — it is therefore ordered, that whosoever shall stand excommunicate for the space of 6 months, without laboring what in him or her lyeth to bee restored, such person shalbe presented to the Court of Assistants, and there proceeded with by fine, imprisonment, banishment, or further for their good behaviour, as their contempt and obstinacy upon full hearing shall deserve."

But in September, 1639, the Court agreed that this order should be repealed.

It became a matter of necessity to define the relations to

the government and community of such persons as were residents and holders of property, but not freemen or members of churches. So the Court in April, 1634, ordered that every one above the age of twenty, after a residence of six months as a householder or sojourner, on the summons of the Governor, Deputy, or two Assistants, — for a first refusal to answer to which he should be bound over, and for a second refusal banished, unless further respited, — shall take an oath in substance as follows: promising to be subject in person, family, and estate to the authority, laws, orders, and sentences of the Government here established, to advance its peace and welfare, and to warn it of and help avert from it any peril or hurt with which it is threatened. The next month the former Freeman's Oath was slightly modified by another substituted for it, not altering its substance. And it was "further agreed that none but the General Court hath power to chuse and admitt freemen." In September, 1635, the exclusive privileges of freemen in the General Court were extended by the following: "It was ordered that none but Freemen shall have any vote in any town in any action of aucthoritie or necessity, or that which belongs to them by virtue of their freedome, as receaveing inhabitants and layeing out lands." It was by virtue of these exclusive rights of freemen as church members that these privileged persons acquired among other prerogatives one which long afterward caused much litigation in our successive legal tribunals. While the building and charges of the house of worship and the salary of the minister were laid as a tax upon all the inhabitants of a town, the body of covenanted church members claimed the right of selecting and instituting the minister. At least ten freemen were needed for choosing a deputy to the Court from any town.

The next step in this form of legislation was the assertion of the power of the magistrates over the formation and institution of churches. As follows: —

"In General Court, Mar. 1636. Forasmuch as it hath bene
found by sad experience that much trouble and disturbance hath
happened both to the church and civill state by the officers and
members of some churches which have bene gathered within the
limitts of this jurisdiction in an undue manner, and not with such
publique approbation as were meete, it is therefore ordered that
all persons are to take notice that this Court doth not, nor will
hereafter approve of any such companyes of men as shall hence-
forthe joyne in any pretended way of churcĥ fellowshipp, without
they shall first acquainte the magistrates and the elders of the
greater parte of the churches in this jurisdiction with their intentions, and have their approbation herein. And further, it is ordered that noe person, being a member of any church which shall
hereafter be gathered without the approbation of the magistrates
and the greater parte of the said churches, shalbe admitted to the
freedome of this commonwealthe."

Two very significant points are to be noted here. First
is the theocratic element. The franchise having been already limited to church members, it was evident that as
new towns and settlements were extended, new churches
formed in them might introduce some laxities, opening
membership on easy terms for securing the further coveted
right to the franchise. The magistrates and the existing
churches were to set up a guard against this risk, and to
be consulted in this case. The other point to be noticed is
that we have in this Court order the first intimation of a
restriction upon the perfect independency of each church.
The Scotch Presbyterian Bailey soon made 'it a reproach to
the New England churches that they were isolated and
discordant units, with no bond of union. So that henceforward we trace in our history the initiatory measures
which developed into the usage of councils of neighboring
churches, called at first for sympathetic and sisterly recognition, then for advice, then for degrees of dictation and
authority in the settlement or dismission of a minister, or
in a matter of variance.

It was not, however, only in holding the exclusive privileges of the franchise that church members were favored. It would have seemed but reasonable that they should have borne the whole charges of such provisions and institutions as existed for their special benefit. This, however, was far from being the case. In November, 1637, the attention of the Court was called to the fact that the churches had different methods for providing for the maintenance of ministers, and that " some ministers are not so comfortably provided as were fitting." The churches were to inquire into this matter and send some to advise with the Court at its next session " that some order may bee taken hearin according to the rule of the gosple." In immediate connection with this entry we find another which throws light upon it. The freemen of the town of Newbury had, in May, 1636, been mulcted with a fine of six pence apiece " for chuseing and sending to this Court a deputy which was noe freeman." Now we find that the inhabitants of the town are indebted to divers persons in the sum of sixty pounds —

" expended upon publike and needful occasions for the benefit of all such as do or shall inhabite there, as building of houses for their ministers ; and whereas such as are of the church there are not able to beare the whole charge, and the rest of the inhabitants there do or may enjoy equall benefit thereof with them, yet they do refuse, against all right and justice, to contribute with them, it is therefore ordered — "

that the major part of the freemen assembled in meeting shall have power to levy the amount due upon the estates of all the property holders, resident or non-resident. This precedent was well followed by an order of Court in September, 1638 : —

" This Court takeing into consideration the necessity of an equall contribution to all common charges in townes, and observing that the chiefe occation of the defect hearein ariseth from hence, that many of those who are not freemen, nor members of any church, do take advantage thereby to withdraw help in such voluntary contributions as are in use, [the Court declares] that every inhabitant in any towne is lyable to contribute to all charges, both in church and commonwelth, wherof hee doth or may receive benefit." All who will not voluntarily do this, "for all common charges, as well for upholding the ordinances in the churches as otherwise, shalbee compelled thereto by assessment or distress."

It was an ingenious suggestion in this general order, as in the special one for Newbury, that those who did not seek the help of church and ministry were free to do so if they would. Their not seeking that help for themselves, however, did not discharge them from the obligation to share in the expense of it to those who did. For reasons the whole force of which for that time we may not fully appreciate, there were some — enough of them to attract the jealousy of the Court — who, though having the quali- fication of church membership, did not avail themselves of their right to claim the franchise. May 10, 1643, in the Court, " It is ordered, concerning members that refuse to take their freedom, the churches should bee writ unto, to deale with them."[1] Here again we find the civil power interfering with the internal discipline of the churches. The justification which would probably have been offered for it was, that the State had the right to the aid in council of every good citizen, especially of those who as being under covenant might be expected to sympathize with its religious administration. The Court declared itself more fully on this subject in November, 1647, thus : —

"There being within this jurisdiction many members of churches who, to exempt themselves from all publike service in the common- wealth, will not come in to be made freemen, it is therefore ordered by this Courte, and the authority thereof, that all such

---

[1] Records, ii, 38.

members of churches in the severall townes within this jurisdiction shall not be exempted from such publike service as they are chosen to by the freemen of the severall townes, as cunstables, jurers, selectmen, and surveyors of high wayes; and if any person shall refuse to serve such office, he shall pay for every such refusall, being legally chosen thereunto, such fine as the towne shall impose, not exceeding twenty shillings, as freemen are liable unto in such cases." [1]

Compulsory attendance upon religious services next engaged the attention of the Court in the exercise of its Bible authority. In November, 1646, we find the following: —

"Forasmuch as in these countryes, where the churches of Christ are seated, the prosperity of the civill state is much advanced and blessed of God when the ordinances of true religion and publike worship of God do find free passage in purity and peace, therefore, though we do not judge it meete to compel any to enter into the fellowship of the church, nor force them to partake in the ordinances peculiar to the church [as was then compulsory in England] which do require volentary subjection thereunto, yet, seeing the Word is of general and common behoofe to all sorts of people, as being the ordinary meanes to subdue the harts of hearers not onely to the faith, and obedience to the Lord Jesus, but also to civill obedience, and allegiance unto magistracy, and to just and honest conversation towards all men — "

therefore, attendance upon worship on the Lord's Day, and on days of fasting and thanksgiving, is required of every one not incapacitated, on a penalty of a fine of five shillings for each case of absence.[2] The penalty exacted in England at that time for that offence was twelve pence.

The dignity and authority of the ministry were to be maintained by an order of the same Court. Any one contemptuously behaving himself toward the Word preached, or to the preacher, interrupting, disputing, or denying, causing reproach or ridicule for the service or ordinances,

---

[1] Records, ii. 208.   [2] Ibid., ii. 177.

shall for the first offence be rebuked by a magistrate at
a lecture, and bound to good behavior, —

"and if a second time they breake forth into the like contemptuous carriages, either to pay five pounds to the publike treasury,
or to stand two houres openly upon a block 4 foote high, on a
lecture day, with a paper fixed on his breast, with this, A Wanton
Gospeller, written in capitall letters."[1]

It was but natural — indeed, how could it have been
otherwise? — that the Court, composed exclusively of members of churches, and chosen to their civil offices by the
same class of electors, should have assumed the oversight
of the religious interests and order of the jurisdiction with
the same sense of responsibility and the same exercise of
authority as in secular affairs. The elders may have interposed more or less in prompting the magistrates and
deputies; but the clerical and the civil leaders were of
the same mind and spirit. The Court on many occasions
must have been very much like a church meeting, with its
prayers, its Scripture citations, its phraseology in speeches,
and its subjects of debate. We may trace continuously
through the Records the persuasion on the part of the
Court that it should take the lead in advising and directing all measures successively found to be essential for a
religious commonwealth. Even the original independency
of the churches must yield to such a degree of imposed
uniformity as was needed to secure the strength of union.
So, as early as March, 163$\frac{4}{5}$, —

"This Court doeth intreate of the elders and brethren of every
church within this jurisdiction that they will consult and advise of
one uniforme order of discipline in the churches agreeable to the
Scriptures, and then to consider howe farr the magistrates are
bound to interpose for the preservation of that uniformity and
peace of the churches."[2] June 2, 1641. "It is desired that the

---

[1] Records, ii. 179.   [2] Ibid., i. 142.

elders would make a catachisme for the instruction of youth in the grounds of religion."

Cotton's "Milk for Babes" was a response.

It is without surprise that we meet the first recognition by Winthrop of the presence and expression of a feeling among those deprived of the civic franchise that the time had come for a hearing upon their disabilities.   Winthrop writes in March, 1644 : —

"A proposition was made this Court for all the English within the united colonies to enter into a civil agreement for the maintenance of religion and our civil liberties, and for yielding some more of the freeman's privileges to such as were no church members that should join in this government.   But nothing was concluded, but referred to next Court." [1]

Those who had — not always patiently — waited to put in their grievances on this score, had yet to wait much longer before the full rights of citizens were secured to them, — not then by the free concession of the Court, but from royal dictation ; and even this mandate was at first so grudgingly yielded to, that for a time it was ingeniously circumvented.

It was with very great deliberation, and with a formal detail of grounds and reasons, that the Court, pursuing its assumed task of supervising the churches and providing for the interests of uniformity as overriding their independency, initiated the proposition of a synod of the elders and messengers, not only of the churches in its own jurisdiction, but of the other three confederated colonies. May 6, 1646, we find the record of the first action of the Court on this subject.   A long and carefully-drawn preamble opens it : —

"The right forme of church government and discipline being a good parte of the kingdome of Christ upon earth, the settling and

[1] Records, ii. 160.

establishing thereof by the joynt and publicke agreement and consent of churches, and by the sanction of civill authority, must needs greatly conduce to the honor and glory of our Lord Jesus Christ, and to the settling and safety of church and commonwealth, where such a duty is dewly attended and performed."

Reference is then made to the quiet state of the plantations here at the time, as favorable to such an object, in contrast with the distractions then convulsing the mother country. Friends at home had written lamenting the variances which had arisen in our churches, and counselling more uniformity. The differences principally concerned the proper subjects of baptism. The New England churches baptize only a child one or both of whose parents is under covenant. Some are claiming the ordinance for children whose grandparents only were church members. There are persons resident here " who have binn members of the congregations in England, but are not found fitt to be receaved at the Lord's table here," while they and some sympathizers with them think their children entitled to baptism. More than all, the Baptists are asserting their conviction that no child is a proper subject of the rite. The preamble proceeds : —

" Therefore, for the further healing and preventing of the further groweth of the said differences, and upon the other grounds, and for the other ends afore-mentioned, and although this Courte make no quaestion of their lawfull power by the word of God to assemble the churches, or their messengers, upon occasion of councell for anything which may concerne the practize of the churches,[1] yet because all members of the churches, though godly and faithfull, are not yett clearely satisfyed, itt is therefore thought expedient for the present occasion not to makè use of that power, but rather hereby declare it to be the desire of this present Generall Courte that there be a publicke assembly of the elders and other messengers of the severall churches within this jurisdiction, who may come together and meete at Cambridge upon the first day of

---

[1] The Court here assumes the prerogative of Parliament.

September now next ensewing, there to discusse, dispute, and cleare up, by the word of God, such questions of church government and discipline."

The assembly is to continue indefinitely till the major part at least shall have come to some substantial agreement on the matters proposed. If necessary, there may be two or more sessions. The result is to be presented to the General Court for examination and, if possible, approbation. The churches are to meet severally their own charges. Inasmuch as Massachusetts had three years previously brought about a civil confederation with its sister colonies of Plymouth, Connecticut, and New Haven, their churches were to be invited to take equal part in the assembly.[1]

One can but pause here to recognize the introduction for the first time on this continent of one of those church councils which, in long succession, have proved the bane and scourge of Christendom. Called to promote harmony and uniformity, they have invariably resulted in variance, discord, and a widening of previous breaches. They proceed upon the assumption that those who are supposed to share common beliefs and purposes may be moved by coming together in free discussion to come into accord on matters upon which they differ. It is further assumed that these matters of difference are of secondary import, and that the strength of the bond which holds all to " fundamentals " and essentials will prevail in reconciling them to yield up or subordinate their individualities of divergence; but these assumptions or expectations have always been baffled. Essentials and non-essentials, fundamentals and specialties, common beliefs and individualisms, invariably change places on such occasions. The points on which a man differs in his belief from his brethren are to him the matters of primary importance. The things which are not to be left undone come to signify far more than the things

[1] Records, iii. 70–73.

that are to be done. The degree of unity which existed
among the members before they met in Council is always
diminished rather than increased by their debates, in which
their differences come to mean even more to themselves,
and are found to be more disagreeable to one another. The
special element in each man's creed is to him the life of it.
The product of the common peaceful labors of bees is
honey; but the individuality of each bee is protected by
his sting.

Among many of the elders and messengers of the New
England churches there was a dread of Presbyterianism,
then rife in England; but a few were supposed to favor it.
It was well understood before the meeting of the synod
how its work, or results, or advice would be limited by
the principles of Independency and Congregationalism.
There had been, as Winthrop tells us,[1] a serious difference
of opinion between the magistrates and the deputies as to
the rightful province of the Court in proposing a synod, as
the Court might be made responsible for giving force to
its results and conclusions. The magistrates, however,
asserted their responsibility in the case, as coming to them
by "the word of God;" yet they consented that the synod
should be convened "by way of motion only to the churches,
and not by any words of command." We look to Winthrop still for information. But few of the elders of the
other colonies came to the appointed gathering at Cambridge, and the session, which lasted only fourteen days,
as the winter was coming on, was unsatisfactory. The
elder from Concord was unable, though willing, to attend.
The church at Hingham held back. Boston and Salem
churches had objections to being present. About thirty or
forty Boston members — some of whom "had come lately
from England, where such a vast liberty was allowed " —
excepted that the churches had a right to meet in synod
without the intervention of the magistrates: that the call

[1] Winthrop, ii. 264.

was really prompted by the elders, and not by the Court, and that the Court might enforce the results upon the churches. The elders of Boston were moved to attend for courtesy's sake, though not sent by the church. Norton, preaching a Thursday lecture, tried to reconcile the relations of Church and State in the matter by discoursing upon " Moses and Aaron meeting in the mount and kissing each other."

The synod assembled again at Cambridge, June 8, 1647, but a prevalent epidemic caused its adjournment in a fortnight. It reassembled in August, 1648. The childlike faith of Winthrop found a propitious omen in an incident of the occasion. Midway in the sermon a snake, creeping in at the door, crawled into the seat occupied by the elders. An elder of Braintree, " a man of much faith," while " divers of the others shifted from it," crushed it with his foot and staff. Winthrop wrote : " This being so remarkable, and nothing falling out but by Divine providence, it is out of doubt the Lord discovered somewhat of his mind in it. The serpent is the devil ; the synod, the representative of the churches of Christ in New England." [1] The synod ended its work in fourteen days, contenting itself with adopting the Westminster Assembly's Confession of Faith, and by drawing a form of discipline, according to the practice of their churches. This latter was to be " presented to the Churches and General Court for their consideration and acceptance in the Lord." In October, 1649, the Court submitted these results to the churches for their consideration, and in October, 1651, after this deliberate examination, it received a substantial approval.

An interesting matter appearing in several entries on the Court records illustrates both the assumed responsibility of the civil government in the internal affairs of the churches, and its jealous care to preserve the high standard

[1] Winthrop, ii. 330.

of the ministry for ability and training in professional learning. The rude structure for the worshippers in the First Church, after it had been enlarged, had in ten years become decayed, and no longer serviceable nor spacious enough for its general uses for various purposes as a meeting-house. In 1640 a new and larger edifice, on another site, was substituted. In ten years more, so rapid was the growth of the town that a second church was gathered, the thirtieth in the jurisdiction, and seven brethren entered into covenant to constitute it. It was not, however, until four years after its house of worship had been built that it succeeded in securing a pastor. Several acceptable preachers had transiently served it, but declined the permanent office. The first of the signers of its covenant was Michael Powell. He had been licensed by the Court in May, 1646, " to keepe an ordinary and sell wyne," in Dedham, where he lived. He was a deputy from that town to the Court in 1648, and took up his residence in Boston. He had "a gift in prayer and exhortation," and the church, wearied with waiting, invited him to become its teacher, and he assented. The Court interposed its prohibition. In answer to a petition from the church, the Court, in October, 1652, in considerate and courteous terms, in the way of " loving advice," gave its reasons to both parties. It was at a time when in England Cromwell's troopers and a most miscellaneous company of men, from camp, fields, and workshops, rude and illiterate, exhorted in pulpits, to the scandal of the scholarly Puritans, bringing the ministry into contempt. The Court, recognizing the dignity of Boston in its ministry, makes a reference to " the humour of the times in England inclineing to discourage learning, against which we have born testimony, this Court in our petition to the Parliament, which we should contradict if we should approve of such proceedings amongst ourselves." The Court was willing that Mr. Powell should serve the church as " ruling elder," but not as pastor or teacher, for which it considers him unfit, as lacking in "such abilities, learning, and qualifications as are requisite and necessary for an able ministery of the gosple." Mr. Powell might edify by exhortation, but he might not be able to convince "gayne sayers." The church may enjoy him as a ruling elder, but they must wait for "the ordinances till they can secure a fitt pastor or teacher." The Court even ventures to propose such an one by name, but in vain. Both parties acquiesced in the advice, Mr. Powell in a very modest letter.[1]

On another special occasion the Court intervened, as if in discharge of its trust in "the care of all the Churches." The death of Mr. Cotton in 1652 was a grievous blow to his flock, and Boston must do what it could to supply his place. John Norton, at that time minister of Ipswich, had then the highest reputation in scholarly and ministerial qualities, which had already been frequently put to trial in Boston. His own church seems at first to have loaned him, as if liable to recall, to the bereaved town, and it was not till 1656 that he was instituted there as teacher. Previous to this the divisions and contentions between his church and that in Boston about his removal, became so aggravated that the Court itself summoned and constituted a council of elders, and two messengers from each of twelve towns, to meet with the two conflicting churches, at Ipswich, to compose the differences. The expenses, paid from the public treasury, amounted to about twenty-five pounds.[2]

The Court appears again in a very curious exercise of its ecclesiastical functions, in addressing a letter in October, 1663, to the famous dissenting divine, Dr. John Owen, of London. The Court thought the best supply none too good for the service of its leading church. After the death of Mr. Norton his flock had sent an invitation to

---

[1] Records, iii. 293, 331, 359, and Records of Second Church.
[2] Records, iii. 378, 387.

Dr. Owen to come and fill the vacancy. The Court's letter was to second and advance this appeal. It is really a
graceful and charming epistle, modest and earnest, recognizing the sacrifice to be made if the invitation should
be accepted, but pressing upon him the sacredness and
urgency of the need of the wilderness work. He is reminded " that Abraham and Moses at the call of God for-
sooke theire country and the pleasures thereof." Governor
Endicott signs the letter in behalf of the Court.[1]

While the Court thus steadily extended its interference
in the affairs of each and all the churches, in carrying
into effect its theocratical principles, it kept a watchful eye
upon all heretical utterances that might bring its doctrinal
system under question. They had had many warnings
from religionists in England who were in general sympathy
with them, that their administration of affairs in Church
and State was sharply scrutinized, and that much anxiety
was there felt lest the activity and perversity of some restless minds among the colonists might bring upon them the
scandal of heresies. The Court meeting in October, 1650,
found occasion to take measures " for the clearinge of ourselves to our Christian brethren and others in England."
The occasion was that the Court " had had the sight of a
booke," copies of which had been printed and dispersed in
England, " containing many errors and heresies generally
condemned by all orthodox writers." Unfortunately the
book had been written in New England by one of the most
honored gentlemen and magistrates of the Colony, William
Pynchon. Its heresies concerned the received view of the
doctrine of the Atonement. The Court was at pains first
to prepare and transmit to England " A Declaration and
Protestation " asserting vehemently their " innocency, as
being neither partyes nor privy to the writinge, composing,
printinge, nor divulginge thereof ; but that, on the contrary,
we detest and abhorre many of the opinions and assertions

[1] Records, iv. pt. ii. p. 98.

therein as false, eronyous, and hereticall." Second, " that it be suffycyently answered by one of the reverend elders." Third, " that Mr. Pinchon be summoned before the next Generall Court, to answer for the same." Fourth, " that the book be burned by the executioner in the market-place in Boston after the Thursday lecture." The affair occupied the protracted attention and action of the Court.[1] Mr. Norton was appointed to answer the book " with all convenient speed." After a conference with three of the elders, Mr. Pynchon so far explained and qualified some of his expressed views that the magistrates in May, 1651, having hopes of his convincement of his errors, and on account of troubles in his family, allowed him to return to his home in Springfield, he taking with him Mr. Norton's answer to his book " to consider thereof." He was enjoined to appear at the October session to give satisfaction. Mr. Norton received twenty pounds " for his paynes," and the Court sent a copy of his writing to England for the press. At the October session the patience of the Court was greatly exercised at not getting satisfaction from the heretic. The grave censure hanging over him was suspended, that he might further weigh the " judicious answer " of Mr. Norton, and he was put under bonds of £100 to appear the next May. Worried by these proceedings Mr. Pynchon returned to England in 1652, and soon published there a new edition of his book.

The austerities of the Puritan Sabbath are familiarly known among us both by tradition, with some faint relics of them, and by the frequent references to them in our modern literature. The compulsory attendance upon public worship has already been noticed. Historic fidelity requires that the most exacting law upon our old statute-books concerning the Sabbath should appear at length here:

" At a Generall Court at Boston, Aug. 6, 1653: Upon information of sundry abuses and misdemeanors committed by several per-

[1] Records, iii. 215.

15

sons on the Lord's day, not only by children playing in the streetes
and other places, but by youthes, maydes, and other persons, both
straungers and others, uncivilly walkinge the streetes and feilds,
travilling from towne to towne, goeing on ship-board, frequentinge
common howses and other places to drinke, sport, and otherwise
to mispend that precious time, which thinges tend much to the
dishonor of God, the reproach of religion, and the prophanation of
his holy Saboath, the sanctification whereof is somtime put for all
dutyes immediately respectinge the service of God conteined in
the first table; it is therefore ordered by this Court and the
authoritie, that no children, youths, mayds, or other persons shall
transgress in the like kind on penalty of beinge reputed great pro-
vokers of the high displeasure off Allmighty God, and further incur-
ringe the pœnaltyes hereafter expressed; namely, that the parents
and governors of all children above seven yeares old (not that we
approve of younger children in evill), for the first offence in that
kind, upon due profe before any magistrate, towne commissioner,
or select man of the towne where such offence shalbe committed
shalbe admonished; for a second offence, upon due profe as aforesaid, shall pay as a fine five shillings ; and for a third offence, upon
due profe as aforesaid, ten shillings; and if they shall agayne
offend in this kind they shalbe presented to the County Court, who
shall augment punishment according to the meritt of the fact; and
for all youths and maydes above foorteen yeares of age, and all
elder persons whatsoever that shall offend and be convict as aforesaid, either for playing, uncivilly walking, drinkinge, travillinge
from towne to towne, goeing on ship-board, sportinge, or any way
mispending that precious time," shall for successive offences meet
the same graded punishments of fines, — " and if any be unable or
unwillinge to pay the aforesaid fines, they shalbe whipped by the
constable, not exceeding five stripes for ten shillings fine ; and this
to be understood of such offences as shalbe committed during the
day light of the Lord's day." [1]

The Court made this the subject of renewed and constant
legislation. All servile labor, and all passing from place
to place save for necessity, mercy, or attendance on worship

[1] Records, iii. 316.

were prohibited on penalties.   The Sabbath laws were to be publicly read by the ministers in March and September. Constables and tithing-men were to apprehend all Sabbath breakers, and to search tippling houses for them.   Noisy offenders were to be put into a public " cage."   A man was to be appointed to look after each ten of the houses of neighbors in a town, to see if the law was observed.   Officers were stationed on the Neck to prevent horses and carts from passing through or out of Boston after sunset on Saturday.   In 1679 ministers were relieved of the public reading of the Sabbath laws, and the duty was committed to the constable at some public meeting.

The aims and the general and special measures of this theocratic legislation will further appear as we proceed to examine the Puritan administration.

VII.

ADMINISTRATION UNDER THE CHARTER.

THE turning-point for a judicial decision on the course pursued by the founders of Massachusetts in their civil and ecclesiastical administration, is the question as to their legal or inferential territorial rights under their charter, whether positive, exclusive, or in any way qualified or limited. The alternative of these rights, as strictly legal or inferential and constructive, is thus presented for a reason here to be stated. The two directly antagonistic positions have been affirmed and argued, that the founders of Massachusetts on the one hand could, and on the other that they could not, legally claim under their charter the exclusive rights which they exercised. Postponing this issue for the present because of the antagonistic positions taken concerning it, and because of the novel elements and the lack of precedents which enter into it, we may ask if other than strictly legal considerations may not properly be had in view. One fact stands out before us which we cannot fairly set aside, as recognizing inferential as distinct from strictly legal rights. It is that the magistrates and Court of Massachusetts when initiating and administering their government, from the very first, always, persistently, and consistently, proceeded on the assumption — was it not also their honest belief? — that they had here exclusive territorial rights for admission of other persons within their jurisdiction and rejection from it. Of course they maintained, as some of their champions have argued, that they had these

rights by the terms of their charter; but whether they regarded these as sufficiently definite and positive or not,
they planted themselves also on their inferential rights.
They were, at their own joint cost and peril, to subdue
and occupy a portion of a waste wilderness, as individuals
and parties have ever since been doing — with recognized
pre-emptory and exclusive right all over this continent — in
securing homesteads and settlements. The circumstances
and exigencies of their position; their putting their all at
stake; the perils of catastrophe; the liberty which was
open to others to occupy other sections of a boundless wilderness, and their joint obligations to each other to protect
their mutual interests; their readiness to welcome congenial new-comers, and their dread of mischief from unfriendly intruders, — these, if not standing for strictly legal
rights, were to their minds equivalents of or substitutes for
them. The terms of a written charter, however free or
restricted, would not suggest or furnish the motives and
means by which the founders of Massachusetts could plant
their commonwealth.

If their prevailing motive and intent, as profoundly religious, has been thus far defined and certified as engaging
the leading parties in the Massachusetts Bay in their enterprise, — those most heartily committed to it through
their consciences and hearts, and the investment of their
means, — then it follows that as men thoughtful, prudent,
and practically sagacious, they would recognize the necessity of a plan and a method. Two conditions would present
themselves as of supreme importance : (1) They must be
pledged and covenanted with each other for union, harmony, and concert of action in a way to make their religious
purpose prominent and paramount; (2) While inviting and
welcoming to their fellowship such as would co-operate and
sympathize with them, they must rigidly " repulse and exclude " — as the charter worded it — all those who would
cause strife, variance, feuds, and endanger sedition and the

failure of an enterprise in itself hazardous and much imperilled through its own inevitable risks. It will be well,
for obvious reasons, to deal first with this second condition. Both these conditions were had in view, indeed,
in the method by which they limited the franchise, and in
their treatment of dissenters and intruders. But as the
latter condition more directly involved the matter of their
legal rights under their charter, we may here give it the
precedence.

As a most pertinent illustration of what these chartered
English colonists either assumed or believed to be their
territorial rights as soon as they initiated their authority,
let us take from their records some of the series of measures by which they stoutly proceeded to clear the domain
of all unwelcome occupants here.

Sept. 7, 1630, "It is ordered that noe person shall plant
in any place within the lymitts of this patent, without
leave from the Governor and Assistants or the major parte
of them." [1]

Previous to this order "Morton of Mount Woolison"
had on the 23d of August been "sent for by processe,"
"sett into the bilbowes, and after sent prisoner into England." But this measure may be regarded as a judicial
proceeding against him for offences. Similar charges having been made against Thomas Gray, he was, on Sept. 28,
1630, "injoyned to remove himself out of the lymetts of
this pattent before the end of March nexte."

March 1, 163$\frac{0}{1}$, eight persons, who are named, are ordered to be sent to England, as persons "unmeete to
inhabit here," with two more, as prisoners.

May 3, 1631, "Tho. Walford of Charlestown," after
being fined "for contempt of authoritie and confronting
officers, etc.," is ordered, with his wife, "to departe out of
the lymits of this pattent before the 20th day of October
nexte."

1 The Records give these proceedings under their dates.

June 14, 1631, "It is ordered that noe person whatsoever shall travel out of this pattent, either by sea or land, without leave from the Governour, Deputy, or some other Assistant, under such penalty as the Court shall," etc. It might seem as if Mr. Blackstone, who had been a solitary resident here since 1624 or 1625, needed from the Court no allowance of a homestead on the peninsula. But we read, April 1, 1633, "It is agreed that Mr. William Blackestone shall have 50 acres of ground sett out for him neere to his howse in Boston, to injoy for ever." This he sold to the town when he removed. When at a later period we shall have occasion to note that a sentence to banishment was so little regarded by some of the Quakers, we may recall that the Court had generally found this process to be effective. But here is an exception. Oct. 3, 1632, Nicholas Frost having been convicted of theft, drunkenness, and fornication, was sentenced, after whipping and branding on the hand, to be " banished out of this pattent, with penalty that if ever hee be found within the lymitts of the said pattent, hee shalbe putt to death." He returned in 1635, and gave the Court much trouble, and finally disappears unaccounted for.

As the Court thus claimed in all cases rights of exclusion, so it bestowed privileges of residence under its sanction. Thus, Sept. 25, 1634, "It is ordered that the Scottishe and Irishe gentlemen which intends to come hither shall have liberty to sitt downe in any place upp Merimacke Ryver, not prepossessed by any."

Sept. 3, 1635, "Ordered, that John Smyth shalbe sent within theis six weekes out of this jurisdiction, for dyvers dangerous opinions which hee holdeth and hath dyvulged, if in the mean tyme he removes not himselfe out of this plantation."

Sept. 6, 1638, " Mr. Willi: Foster, appearing, was informed that wee conceive him not fit to live with us; therefore he was wished to depart before the Generall Court

in March." March 13, 163⅔. " Mr. Ambros Marten, for
calling the church covenant a stinking carryon and a
humane invention, and saying hee wondered at God's patience, feared it would end in the sharpe, and said the
ministers did dethrone Christ and set up themselves. He
was fined ten pounds, and counselled to go to Mr. Mather
to bee instructed by him."

Sept. 7, 1641, " Francis Hutchinson, for calling the
church of Boston a whoare, a strumpet, and other corrupt
tenets, hee is fined fifty pounds, and to bee kept close
prisoner till it bee paid, and then hee is banished upon
paine of death."

So far as these sentences of banishment were for offences
or crimes of lawlessness they would not enter into our
questioning as to whether or not the proceedings were legal
or arbitrary. But in those cases already presented, and
those yet to come before us, in which opinions, or simply a
restless or " unconforming disposition " made individuals
" unmeet to inhabit here," the question becomes more
complicated. It may be well at this point to define what
was signified by the term " banishment." The Court
makes use of the word in the sentences which it inflicted,
but we must recognize a limitation of the full significance
of the penalty as a legal one, and of its effects upon its
victim. The full meaning of " banishment " was the exclusion of a subject from the realm. The King of England
could not pass that sentence. Both Magna Charta and
the Act of Habeas Corpus denied him that prerogative as
attaching only to Parliament. The legal rights of a subject " banished " from this colony were not impaired in
England, nor in any other part of the realm save that he
was excluded from the limits of this jurisdiction held by
patent. The severity of the infliction would depend upon
many circumstances and conditions, and would not necessarily involve barbarity or inhumanity. Substantially the
whole continent here was to Englishmen a wilderness. In

the sharp controversy on the " Bloody Tenent" between
John Cotton and Roger Williams, the former, evidently
thinking that Williams had rather whined over his banishment and wilderness hardships, yields to a somewhat grim
humor in referring to it.   He queried whether such banishment as Williams had suffered —

" be in proper speech a punishment at all, in such a Countrey as
this is, where the Jurisdiction (whence a man is banished) is but
small, and the Countrey round about it large and fruitfull; where
a man may make his choice of variety of more pleasant and profitable seats than he leaveth behinde him.   In which respect, Banishment in this Countrey is not counted so much a confinement
as an enlargement; where a man does not so much loose civill
comforts, as change them.[1] "

Yet in spite of this pleasantry the magistrates did not
concern themselves with any view of the after experiences
of a banished person.   Their sole object was to be rid of
him.   And, still leaving for the present the question of
their legal right thus to exclude from their jurisdiction,
we are dealing with the subject from that point of view
in which they assumed the right as an inferential one on
grounds of necessity and exigency.

We may well give a thought here to the responsibilities
of the leaders of this enterprise, and to the personal risks
and charges which it involved for themselves.   It was not
strange that they should read, as if seeking special lessons
for their own guidance, the straits and buffetings of Moses,
as, himself directed from on high, he led his hosts into
the wilderness.   Every association which we connect with
mere adventurers, or with those seeking for fortune and
gain, must be wholly set aside as we contemplate those
leaders, their inspirations and resolutions.   Winthrop, Saltonstall, Humphrey, Johnson, and Dudley, had no need to
seek any bettering of their fortunes.   Winthrop had his

---

[1] Reply to Mr. Williams.

manor and freehold, and his right of Church presentation
in the parish of his ancestors; Humphrey and Johnson were
the husbands of daughters of the Earl of Lincoln; and
Dudley held the responsible office of his steward. When
they landed upon this soil the noble Commonwealth of
Massachusetts had its birth. As we trace back our developed history to its first pages and to deeds written and
acted by them and their immediate associates, we shall
have to note on the record much that we might wish were
otherwise. Common human weaknesses intensified by narrow and rigid principles, by harsh and unyielding religious
tenets, gave to their proceedings an aggravation of severity. This is largely to be referred to the then universal
spirit in Christendom which allowed inhumanity and barbarity a very free indulgence in connection with the infliction of legal penalties. ⸤The fact that this severity of
discipline was by no means peculiar to the Puritan rule in
Massachusetts may to a degree relieve their fault in this
respect. ⸥In tracing the course of that rule here we have
found that a tax for the support of religious institutions
was exacted from all the inhabitants, and that attendance
upon worship was compulsory on the penalty of a fine.
Such was the law in force in the mother country. In the
colony of Virginia, in 1610, attendance on church services
twice every Sunday was enjoined " upon pain, for the first
fault, to lose their provision and allowance for the whole
week following; for the second, to lose said allowance,
and also to be whipped; and for the third, to suffer death."
Subsequent modifications of the law in Virginia were as
follows: " The Governor published several edicts, — That
every person should go to church Sundays and holidays,
or lie Neck and Heels that night, and be a slave to the
colony the following week; for the second offence he
should be a slave for a month; for the third, a year and
a day." In Virginia Assembly, Aug. 4, 1619, a penalty
of three shillings a time was exacted for non-attendance,

and in case of a servant bodily punishment was to be inflicted.[1]

The fact of the transfer of the Patent and the administration of the Company under it from England hither would have but a qualified relation to the legality of the proceedings here ; for all the rights and prerogatives claimed or exercised by those bringing that Patent with them would have been enforced on this soil by resident officials and subordinates of the Company through directions from home. The two chief matters of legislation which bring the legality of the administration by the Charter under question are, the restriction of the franchise to church members, and the exclusion of all unwelcome intruders or offensive persons presenting themselves here. The writer will not venture beyond his depth in discussing the principles of law and equity as bearing upon these matters. It may be difficult to define rights and immunities, incidental and constructive, as conferred by the Charter ; but it is not at all difficult to say how the proprietors of that Charter regarded, interpreted, vindicated, and applied their rights. They did not lay claim to a continent, but to a patch of wilderness lying between two out of a thousand of its rivers. The whole remainder of that wilderness was open and free for occupancy by other persons who wished to try other experiments under other charters. The Records of the Court show in their pages how earnest it was to fix the bounds and follow the lines of its covenanted territory. The skill of the earliest surveyors of the Colony, of master-navigators, and of students in Harvard College, who for the occasion are called " artists," was put to well-appreciated service for that object. This indicated the consciousness of a valued possession, and a jealousy in protecting it. In the discussion by papers between Winthrop and Vane, which will be in place in the matter of the Antinomian controversy, the point at

[1] Force's Tracts, iii. (ii.) 11, and Stith's Virginia, p. 147. 1618.

issue was whether the proprietors of the chartered territory had a right by it to exclude from it strangers and all unwelcome persons, or whether all Englishmen could enter and reside here. Mr. Doyle, the latest English writer on our early history, has some forcible remarks on this subject. He says : —

"Winthrop sets forth effectively enough the abstract right of the community to keep out those whose presence might bring danger. He shows that the whole fabric of political society in New England rested on the assumption that the State was a self-electing body, requiring from its members certain religious qualifications. Where he fails is in proving that the infliction of suffering and the interference with individual liberty were in the present instance necessary."

The instance referred to was the banishment of the Antinomians, the reason for which, as laid down by the Court, was that their principles were such as made it impossible for them to live here peacefully and harmoniously. Mr. Doyle adds : —

"If Winthrop's apology for the order shows an inadequate appreciation of the principles of religious freedom, Vane's answer to it did so equally. He neither takes the broad line of general toleration, nor the equally tenable line that toleration was in the present instance consistent with the safety of the State. He showed, too, how little he understood the community which he had joined, by putting forward the argument that the Patent gave a right of settlement in New England to all persons whatsoever. Such a contention was wholly needless for controversial purposes, while the practical acceptance of it would have been fatal in the long run to the objects which Vane had in common with Winthrop."[1]

But none the less, whatever were the limitations of Vane's argument, he and Winthrop represented, respectively, the two opposing sides on the vital question. Did

[1] The English in America, i. 178.

the Charter give paramount and exclusive rights to the patentees of this territory to possess it and rule it, and to exclude from it all undesirable strangers, — English as well as Dutch or French,—or did that Charter leave the territory free to the entrance and residence of any Englishman who might choose to come? Lawyers may decide; indeed, lawyers have decided this — as also so many other questions — on its different sides. But one thing is certain; namely, that if Winthrop and his Company, before their emigration, had even conceived that such a plea to warrant the coming into their domain freely of any persons unwelcome to them could have been asserted and maintained, the territory, so far as they were concerned, would have been a wilderness to-day.

Whenever occasion called for it, the assertion of the exclusive rights of the Company was made in the plainest and most unqualified terms, — not with the tone of special pleading, as an afterthought, a device, strategetically, or as if to rally failing courage. The territory was worthless till toil and money had been spent upon it, and then its value accrued to those by whose pains and charges it had been secured. What were even the King's rights compared with theirs? A technical usage and a winking understanding between foreign sovereigns had brought it about, that newly-discovered territory, sighted from the ocean, should come under the sway of the monarch whose mariners first reported it. It was a very easy process for securing possession and dominion of vast expanses of a continent. One may well pause upon the question, What was the relative rightfulness of a claim like this compared with that of a subsequent actual possession secured by private cost, and turned from worthlessness to intrinsic value by the removal of forests, the subjection of wild beasts and wild men, and the planting in it of homes and civilized communities? In the reading of our annals from the first settlement down to the Revolution we are often

tempted to pause upon the question, What after all were
the grounds of natural right which tied this and the other
colonies to subjection to the mother country ?

On the arrival of the Company with the Patent it is
estimated that there may have been some three hundred
persons already here within the limits of the jurisdiction.
All but a few scattered individuals, or groups, were at
Salem, previously sent over by the Company as its employees. Winthrop's first company was a round thousand,
and a second thousand at once followed. During the first
twenty years after the arrival at Plymouth more than
twenty thousand persons from the Old World had found
homes in New England. Parchment charters were the
only contribution made by the monarch to this vast enterprise. No patronage or help of any kind, no treasury
grant, no supplies of army or navy or muniments of war
were furnished to aid the work of colonization. It seems
to have been by a sort of premonition with the founders of
Massachusetts that the time would come when their posterity would find an argument for independence in claiming that they had never incurred any debt or obligation to
the mother country, that they themselves were so jealously
on their guard neither to ask nor receive any government
favors, even when their own resources seemed to be
exhausted.

The Hudson Bay Company, incorporated twenty years
after that of Massachusetts, neither in its charter, in the
avowed purposes of its stockholders, nor in its conduct or
management, made the slightest recognition of any ends
of religion. But in its rights of monopoly it practised a
most rigid exclusion of all outside of its membership. It
allowed no one to enter its patented domain but its own
employees. More than this : it was covenanted to make
and to advance explorations. It not only wholly failed on
its own part to meet this obligation, but it forcibly resisted
all attempts or designs of others in such enterprises. Its

resolve from the first was to continue its vast territory —
rivalling the whole European continent — in its original
wilderness condition, as a preserve for fur-bearing animals.
Its administration was carefully guarded in secrecy. Its
annual profits were enormous. By ingenuity and intrigue,
by high patronage and presents, and by pointing to the
astounding powers conferred on it by its Charter, the Company maintained its monopoly for exactly two centuries.
When compelled by royal and parliamentary action to re-
lax its control, in the interests of colonization in some
part of its territory, it succeeded in driving a bargain
which continued largely its profits by trade, and for the
rest converted it into a most thrifty land company. If
any one should attempt a comparison of the rights conferred respectively by the charters of the two Bay companies, and of the administrations under them, Massachusetts
would not be found to have been the more exclusive or
intolerant.

We have seen that in the protracted and tentative efforts
of the colonists to frame and digest a body of laws suited
to the novel circumstances of their condition and needs,
they admitted that they might be compelled to deviate
from English statutes, or at least to supply their defects
in application here. Winthrop states the case frankly and
with force, the Bible coming in the parenthesis : —

" Our Government is framed according to our Charter and the
fundamental and common laws of England, and carried on according to the same (taking the words of eternal truth and righteousness along with them), with such allowance for the difference
between an ancient, populous, and wealthy kingdom and an infant, thin colony, as common reason suggests and requires."

Even the Episcopal lawyer, Lechford, unwelcome and
obnoxious as he was to the fathers of the Colony, and
retiring disaffected from their discipline, wrote of them
in 1642 : —

"I think that wiser men than they, going into a wilderness to
set up another strange government differing from the settled government in England, might have fallen into greater errors than
they have done." [1]

We are still keeping ourselves outside of the province
and judgment of jurists, as to the legal rights of administration conferred by the Charter, and confining ourselves
to those which the magistrates, in apparent sincerity of
conviction, regarded as constructively and inferentially belonging to them as of necessity and emergency. Mr. Doyle
justly affirms that "the legislation of New England did but
approve and confirm those modes of life the adoption of
which had been the chief motive for colonization." [2]

Let us suggest, for help in following up our present line
of comment, a supposition, not forced, but simple in its use.
Suppose that as Winthrop's fleet was weighing anchor in
the Downs, a ship not belonging to the Company had sailed
in among them, and that the captain on being hailed had
announced that he had with him a considerable number of
passengers who proposed to join the Bay Company in its
enterprise, to share their rights, privileges, and fortunes,
saying nothing about their own schemes, or proffering any
stock or aid. Will any one maintain that the responsible
leaders of the Company had no alternative but to accept
these volunteers, and allow them, on their own terms, to
join the fleet, to land with them on the chartered territory,
and at once to take part with them in the administration
of it? If this case supposed had really occurred, the party
in the strange ship would doubtless have been told that till
fuller information could be had concerning their intent and
means, their company was not desirable. Further than
this, they would have been forbidden all share and participation in the territorial rights and administration of the

---

[1] Plain Dealing. (To the Reader.)
[2] The English in America, ii. 84.

Company. Now, if the Company could rightfully exercise this authority of exclusion at the beginning of their enterprise, by forbidding strangers and unwelcome persons to join it, when and how could they be subsequently divested of that right? When and how could their own proprietary claims be so qualified that every Englishman would have an unchallenged liberty to enter and abide here?

What, we may ask, were the rights of the colonists as Englishmen on their purchased and patented territory? What privileges and immunities did these rights secure, and how were they to be maintained, not only against those who might intrude upon or trespass against them, but also against any mischievous or arbitrary interference with them by the Government at home? We shall have answers to these questions, most resolute and emphatic, given by the magistrates in their dealings with troublesome persons, and in their vindication of their proceedings, and also in their stout remonstrances and pleas even against royal instructions.

If they were so bold as directly to challenge and defy the measures of the King and Council in interfering with their jurisdiction and administration, and yielded only through compulsion and hopelessness of resistance, and not by free-will, to the vacating of their Charter, they made the strongest possible assertion of what they believed to be their rights. Their challenge to the King was ineffectual when finally made by the first Colonists of Massachusetts, but it proved successful and effective when made on precisely the same grounds by a later generation of the original stock. At the time of the threatened vacating of the Colony Charter Andros had exasperated the Colonists by taunting them with the insult that they could not expect the liberties of Englishmen would follow them to the ends of the earth. Very well. Assuming this to be true, what followed? If shorn of any of the liberties attaching to residents in England, then, of course, their only resource

16

was to find an equivalent for what they had lost, in falling
back upon their liberties as men, and claiming and exercising these. This was precisely the proposition advanced by
John Adams at the outbreak of the Revolution. By just
so much as the Colonists lacked of the rights and immunities of Englishmen they were to find a substitute in their
rights as men, for self-protection and self-government.

If this were true of those who were living here at the
era of the Revolution, there was all the more of right and
reason in it for the exiles of the first generation. There
were reasons making it necessary and imperative for them
to claim and exercise these natural rights here in a wilderness, expatriated, at their own charges, without government protection or patronage, amid rude and rough beginnings, surrounded with perils. They had successfully
withstood the first demand of the home authorities in 1635
to return and surrender their charter. Soon after this the
civil war and the upturning of the royal government in
England, put into power in the administration of public
affairs principles and men in sympathy with the republican
and religious proclivities of the Colonists. This gave them
a breathing, an opportunity for stiffening grit and muscle,
and for familiarizing themselves with their own experiment
of government. All the positions and principles which
came into assertion in the opening measures of the Revolutionary War, may be found in something more than their
germ in the early Court Records.

So far the strict legality by the terms, privileges, and
limitations of the Charter, of the rights claimed and exercised by the General Court of Massachusetts, has been
deferred for consideration. And here I may say with
frankness that I do not feel competent or qualified to deal
with the strictly legal bearings of this question ; nor should
I care even to discuss it. The fact that eminent jurists
as well as other able but non-professional men have pronounced directly opposite decisions upon it, might well

dissuade a layman from intermeddling with it. The last discussion of the subject, which has claimed the attention of the readers of our earliest history, is that which came from the pen of that able and acute jurist, the Hon. Joel Parker, Chief Justice of the Supreme Court of New Hampshire, and Royall Professor in the Dane Law School of Harvard University.[1] Judge Parker treats the topic of the " Religious Legislation of Massachusetts under the First Charter." This involves the questions " how far any such legislation was lawful; and to what extent the grantees had any right of legislation, properly so called, by the provisions of that instrument." The variances of judgment which have been expressed on these questions, he says, have turned upon the alternative " whether the Charter was regarded as instituting a corporation for trading purposes, or as the constitution and foundation of a government." The grantees, he believes, " regarded it as the latter, and acted upon that construction." Looking at " the terms of the Charter, and to a sound construction of its provisions to ascertain what rights of legislation, religious or otherwise, were possessed by the grantees," the Judge confidently maintains the following propositions : —

1. " The Charter is not, and was not intended to be, an act for the incorporation of a trading or merchants' company merely. But it was a grant which contemplated the settlement of a Colony, with power in the incorporated company to govern that Colony."

2. " The Charter authorized the establishment of the government of the Colony within the limits of the territory to be governed, as was done by the vote to transfer the Charter and government."

3. " The Charter gave ample powers of legislation and of government for the Plantation or Colony, including power to legis-

---

[1] See, in "Lectures on the Early History of Massachusetts, by Members of the Massachusetts Historical Society, before the Lowell Institute," Lecture XI. on the First Charter of Massachusetts. By Joel Parker, LL.D. 1869.

late on religious subjects, in the manner in which the grantees and their associates claimed and exercised the legislative power."

4. " The Charter authorized the exclusion of all persons whom the grantees and their associates should see fit to exclude from settlement in the Colony; and the exclusion of those already settled, by banishment as a punishment for offences."

The reader will notice the sweep and comprehensiveness as well as the positiveness and the unqualified character of the terms here set forth. And if their justice and force are admitted, the reader can also judge how far they go to relieve and even justify those measures and proceedings of the Colony, which besides being condemned as arbitrary, tyrannical, and cruel, have also been adjudged illegal. But the reader must turn to the lecture of the Judge, covering more than fourscore pages, with its citations and arguments, its elaborate and learned pleadings, its luminous statements, and its frank and candid recognition of all the evidence and considerations that have been advanced by those who have maintained directly opposite views on the great subject of debate, if he would fairly apprehend the alternative views on the lawfulness of the legislation of Massachusetts under the Charter.

The writer need not here repeat what he has already affirmed in the plainest possible terms, that these pages are not written in championship or vindication of the views and proceedings of the legislators of the Colony. It is not for him, therefore, to offer pleas or arguments on any disputed matters, nor to pronounce upon the strict legality or illegality of their construction of their Charter. This question of legality is indeed a most vital one, in view of the whole legislation and administration of the government. But it is especially pertinent, as it bears upon the four episodes in our early history to be rehearsed in the latter half of these pages, in which, independently of what may be charged as persecution, there was also a rightful or an usurped exercise of sovereign powers. The writer still confines himself to an historic statement of the doings of the colonial authorities as set forth under the circumstances and conditions, with their reasonings, and constructions of their rights and duties. These constructions are to be regarded at first sight either as presumptuous and high-handed assumptions of illegal authority, or as honest interpretations of privileges and obligations under the stress of exigency and necessity. It is to be granted that to some extent the authorities brought their embarrass-ments and exigencies on themselves, if in an illegal and presumptuous way, as by artifice or trick, in the removal and transfer of their government from Old to New Eng-land they had perverted the original intent of a home ad-ministration into a foreign one. Judge Parker's argument is to be studied on this point. All that the writer of these pages has been concerned with is the views and opinions, whether assumptions or convictions, of the authorities, about their own rights and privileges under their Charter. On grounds already set forth, the writer, upon the closest and most candid study of all that has come within his reach, has assured himself that the authorities of Massa-chusetts not only assumed, but were honestly and thor-oughly convinced that they rightfully possessed, the powers which they exercised. They had not cajoled themselves into this belief, nor were they driven into it as a covert, in attempting to turn their position of aggression into one of defence. And I have chosen to present their views of their own legal rights as inferential or constructive. Very likely some of the magistrates, when challenged for their course, would have stoutly pleaded that if they had not legally the authority they exercised, they ought to have it. It was essential, indispensable to them. As proprietors of terri-tory, and magistrates under a charter, they certainly were empowered to keep out interlopers and prevent sedition. The Charter empowered them to choose new associates, joint proprietors, " freemen " on their own terms, and all

who were not members of the Company were to be restrained from doing it any mischief. If anything further
were needed to prove what they believed their Charter
assured and covenanted to them of valued and exclusive
rights, this would be found abundantly in the tenacity with
which they held it, and those rights under it when challenged by the royal commissioners in 1665, as will further
on appear. Under the screws of those commissioners they
contested each demand for concession. If they yielded at
any point, they would have it appear that it was not from
pressure, but as an " enlargement " on motives of friendship. And when they consented, with seeming helpless-
ness, to give up the church membership restriction of the
franchise, they got round it by requiring as a substitute a
full equivalent as an assurance of orthodoxy. Indeed, the
last assertion of their covenanted Charter rights, just as
they were to be deprived of them, was the most resolute in
its obstinacy. They use the strongest language, and that
most emphatically. One reads in it now how the vigor
of an independent spirit had been nourished in the wilderness till they had well-nigh forgotten that they had a
King.

Some stress may justly be laid on the fact that those who,
as original proprietors and members of the Company, and
their subsequent representatives, maintained their rights
and claims under the Charter, were all in accord in so
doing. It was as partners and proprietors, and not as individually interested, proceeding on the belief that their
privileges were guaranteed to them, that they sought a
foundation for their legislation, and unitedly opposed those
who questioned or resisted their administration. If they
could assure and preserve accord among themselves, retaining the rule by a firm hand, they felt that they should
succeed in maintaining their rights and in resisting opposition from the unsympathizing and the disaffected among
them. The failure of some previous attempts at coloniza-

tion on this continent, they ascribed, as we have seen, to the wholly worldly, secular aims had in view, while they exalted and thought to secure prosperity for their own by making religion its master motive.   Before the coming hither of Winthrop's company there had been many publications and reports of the distractions among the successive companies and adventurers in Virginia.   A civil community, especially one gathered of materials in a raw and uncontrolled medley of fortune-seekers in a colony, would be sure to become a pandemonium, save as a strong moral and religious restraint could be brought to bear upon them by men in authority, themselves sincerely and thoroughly under the sway of such motives.   The preceding pages have shown us that the responsible authorities in the administration of affairs in Massachusetts had sought, consistently with their avowed purpose, to make not only religion in the abstract, but the literal commandments and statutes of it as given in the Bible, the basis of government for the community.   However we may judge or censure the severity of their rule, we owe even to the sternest of the magistrates and elders the generous recognition of the fact that they did not lay upon others burdens which they themselves shrank from bearing.   For reasons which then had weight, and the force of which seems to have been unchallenged, the estates of magistrates and ministers were exempted from the colony rates, or public taxes.   The charges to which their position and duties exposed them, and their generosity of spirit shown in free contributions to all good objects, were considered an offset to such exemption.   But the magistrates were in no sense a favored or indulged class of men like the privileged orders and the sharers of social distinctions in the Old World.   They were held to a more exemplary " walk and carriage," and had observant eyes upon them.

Whatever else may be said of Puritan legislation, we must admit its rigid and scrupulous impartiality.   Winthrop tells us [1] under date of Sept. 1, 1635 : " At this General Court was the first grand jury, who presented above one hundred offences, and among others some of the Magistrates." Indeed, Winthrop, Dudley, Endicott, Sir Richard Saltonstall, and Humphrey were in turn subject to court processes. In May, 1644, " Mr. Robert Saltonstall is fined five shillings for presenting his petition in so small and bad a peece of paper." [2]

In following out the spirit and method of the administration of the Colony through the general and county and magistratical courts, we have to make large account of the rapid and extraordinary increase of the population from the swarming in of immigrants during its first twelve years. It is safe to say that the original promoters of the enterprise had had no previous anticipation of the increased responsibilities and perplexities which would come upon them from this source. Happily for them, a large proportion of the elements of this rapid addition to their numbers were in sympathy and in general harmony with them in their religious and republican sentiments and principles. The distraction and ferment working in the mother country, before it resulted in civil war, in the prostration of kingly rule, and the temporary humiliation of the Church of England, had led many timid or peace-loving persons, of strong religious principles, not in all cases however Puritanical, to seek here if only a temporary refuge for themselves and their families. It was thus that the Colonists were enabled to welcome here, just where they were most needed in the rapidly settled towns and plantations of New England, those scholarly men who " as ministers and teachers " proved to be the best guides and fosterers of the institutions which alike in Church and State have directed the development of this section of our country, and have had a paramount influence for good over its most extended sections through pioneers trained here. After those dozen years of the

[1] Winthrop, i. 166.   [2] Records, ii. 76.

earliest rapid immigration, the process was suddenly arrested, and the concourse ceased, because men of New England principles found congenial occupation for themselves in the stirring scenes of revolution in the mother country. Indeed, there was a considerable return flood of active and fervent spirits setting thither. Names found in the catalogue of the graduates of the first years of Harvard College are conspicuous on the public stage of affairs in England ; and other names familiar here of those who roamed these wilderness pathways are connected with the tragedies of the times. Venner, the wild leader of the Fifth Monarchy rising, had been a cooper in Salem. We are to meet in these pages with the prominent influence in our earliest years of Sir Henry Vane and Hugh Peter, who suffered in England as traitors. Sir George Downing, of Harvard's first class, won distinctions rather than honors.

But going back to the twelve of our first years when the immigration was so rapid and numerous, and in general so welcome, we take the count of Johnson, in his " Wonder-Working Providence," as trustworthy, for he had the means and purpose of accuracy. He writes of —

" The transportation of these Armies of the great Jehova, for fifteen years' space to the year 1643, about which time *England* began to endeavour after Reformation, and the Souldiers of Christ were set at liberty to bide his battels at home, for whose assistance some of the chiefe worthies of Christ returned back; the number of Ships that transported passengers in this space of time, as is supposed, is 298. Men, women, and children passing over this wide Ocean, as near as at present can be gathered, is also supposed to be 21,200, or thereabout." [1]

For these multitudes, composed of strongly-marked individualities, groups, and companies, whether strangers to each other previously, or bound in fellowship, the General Court, representing the governing board of an original

[1] Wonder-Working Providence, p. 31.

trading company, was to assume the office of legislation and administration. That the trust was discharged so wisely and so well, demands our grateful recognition. We are soon to deal successively with four episodes in that administration which are at least exceptional as to our commendation of it. Yet it is but fair to regard them as exceptional incidents in the matter and course of legislation, though the spirit of severity and bigotry which prompted them was the ruling element of the whole of it. The Court had much more to do than to deal with heretics, dissentients, and disturbers of its peace. For one who would instruct himself upon the responsibilities and trusts committed to the magistrates — advised on emergency by the elders — there are two chief sources of information now provided. The one is the Records of the General Court, by no means repelling even an ordinary literary interest by their mustiness, but with many matters suggestive of some romantic elements of the time, and provocative of humor. The other source of information is found in the numerous histories of the old towns of the State generously published by those satisfied with if not even proud of their contents. The earliest pages of these annals of our original municipalities show about an equal division between matters of local concern managed wholly by the inhabitants, and those which indicate the agency and authority of the General Court, either necessary, or interposed, or solicited in the oversight of their affairs. From these two sources one may easily learn how multifarious were the interests of infant and growing civil communities, of neighborhoods and of scattered settlements committed to the Court for direction and disposal. There are pages of the Records referring to matters to us so petty and trivial as to cause us to marvel how men who really had serious and profitable subjects to engage their time and thought could for a moment entertain them. But the most trivial of these matters had some relation to great concerns of right between man and man, and the equities of justice. A smile is often provoked from us when we read of the recourse for relief which the Court found in committing to two or three most trustworthy men in a settlement the authority " to end small causes," — that is, to dispose of variances involving a specified amount of money. The Court set itself first scrupulously to deal with the rights of the Indians, to protect them from extortion and oppression, and, always excepting the wars which it honestly believed were thrust upon them by the savages, it contributed often and largely by its enactments for the general benefit of these forlorn and intractable children of the forest. The Court assumed for many years the office of guardianship for widows and orphans, the settlement of estates, the jealous watch over the interests of the unfortunate and the insane, and in many cases the difficult work of arbitration in personal and local disputes. Indeed, one may gather from the miscellaneous and comprehensive materials of the Records, that the Court, though of course on a much reduced and provincial scale, had items of business, of debate, and legislation before it comparable with the responsibility and routine which engage a modern legislature of a State, and even the Parliament of a nation. Selecting from those Records and gathering together all the references to fortifications, and an elaborate military organization, local and central, with orderly drill and trainings, provisions for subsistence, arms, ordinance, and ammunition, with rules for inspection, a board and articles of war, we obtain a formidable view of all the essentials involved in the system of a militia and a standing army. Competent, brave, and faithful officers were never lacking, and the trained bands of every town were ever ready for regular and emergent service. An apt method was found for exciting alarms and for spreading intelligence. Drafts were readily responded to. Surgeons and chaplains were provided on all needful occasions, and the pay-roll was honored.

The Court early and continuously gave its attention, and, when needful, its patronage, to the development of mining wealth, to promoting manufactures, iron-works, and the making of salt; and there were instances in which it anticipated patent and royalty laws by protecting ingenuities, devices, and inventions. Though one might naturally suppose that the straits and necessities of early colonial life on rough soil and with raw materials would have compelled the exercise of all human energies for self-support, yet, as one of the chief dreads of the authorities was that of unthriftiness in any part of the community, its rule was severe in exacting industry and punishing idleness. A vagrant, a spendthrift, a loiterer, " an unprofitable fowler," an habitual drunkard, — of which last there were very few, — had before him as warnings the bilboes, the stocks, the cage, the stool of humility, or the lettered badge of disgrace. The Court also learned by practice some skill in the arts of diplomacy. It had often delicate relations with the other colonies, with French and Dutch, as neighbors or enemies, with formidable Indian sachems. And this diplomatic skill, lacking nothing in intrigue, pleading, self-justification, and remonstrance, of its practice among nations and princes, was brought into full exercise, in the relations of the Colony to the mother country. Indeed, it was with full reason that Charles II. was prompted to object, when messengers of Massachusetts as its agents at his court hedged and dickered about their instructions, that he could not deal with them on the footing which they assumed as ambassadors of a foreign and independent power, but simply as subjects held to obedience.

Following the legislation of the Colony Court into its workings and effects in the towns where it directed, supplemented, or enforced the powers of self-government left to them severally, the town histories, to which reference has been made, give us much interesting and instructive information. Though many of the pages of those histories are similar in their contents and tenor, covering the same struggles and incidents of the settlements, yet they have several special points in recording conditions and experiences. As the population of the Colony increased, two principal conditions would regulate their dispersion. Straggling and camping in the wilderness at each man's pleasure were neither allowable nor safe. The Colonists did not expect to obtain much of their subsistence by hunting, but relied upon the savages to gather peltry for them. One condition for a new settlement was, that families should be near enough in their dwellings to a common centre to attend on Sabbath worship, and to be rallied in case of an alarm. The other condition was, that each townsman might have, not too distant for oversight, his acres of meadow, upland, tillage, and woodland. It was soon discovered that the soil of the Colony was neither rich nor easily tilled, nor favorable to raising stock in the places first occupied. So bottom lands, with meadow and stream, with falling waters to be dammed for sawmills and grist-mills, were at once desirable. The grant of bounds for a township was made by the Court to petitioners, the prime and invariable condition being that the settlers should have and support a competent and able minister. Then, partly by statute and partly by usage and precedent, a partition was established between the matters of business and management in which the inhabitants of each town should be left to their own liberty and discretion, and those which the General Court still held under its control. These beginnings were in all cases severe, yet were met with firm courage, with patience and general cheerfulness. The meeting-house and the school-house were soon raised. The poorest piece of land — generally a sand-hill, for easy digging — was set apart for a burial-place, and before a generation rested in it the homes of the living had been made comfortable.

There was one subject of Puritan legislation which, for

the intelligent, generous, and far-looking spirit of the highest public interest which prompted it, has ever since been regarded as largely redeeming their administration from the burden of reproach for its narrowness and austerity. It is the order of the General Court of November, 1647, providing for what has since been known as the system of common schools, to be supported by public charges in every municipality. This single provision, however, is but suggestive of a general and comprehensive characteristic and distinction of the Puritan polity and principles. He has been but a superficial reader of the form and development of Massachusetts Puritanism who has not penetrated to the evidence of the fact that that Puritanism, both in its secular and its religious principles, provided some self-restraining, self-corrective agencies and influences which were constantly reducing its bigotry and harshness. Puritanism provoked and engaged a vigorous activity of the intellect, a constant, teasing, restless inquisitiveness of the spirit, sure to result in variances, protests, and even eccentricities of individualism in opinion. There was no torpidity of conscience or of mind possible under it. It followed as a matter of course that even those of ordinary mental vigor and of average ability who were constantly taught and exhorted by the pulpit, and in private conference, on subjects which engaged their best thoughts and feelings, should occasionally find questioning, doubt, dissent, arising within them in their efforts to digest and assimilate the instruction offered to them. Those of a bolder or more acute activity of the reasoning faculties would venture into the regions of speculation, and often bring themselves dangerously within the borders of heresy. So we find by careful search that the so-called Liberalism, or Rationalism, which is generally represented as coming to its full and bold development in Massachusetts only near the opening of the nineteenth century, had been working in preparatory phases and stages of individual freedom and enlargement of opinion from the first age. The dissenting or heretical subjects of Puritan discipline, with whom the future pages of this volume are so largely to deal, will abundantly illustrate this assertion. The honored and able magistrate, Mr. Pynchon, was the first in the unbroken line of heretics here on the Calvinistic doctrine of the Atonement. Had the Puritans sought only to secure uniformity of opinion, they would have favored sluggishness rather than a restless activity of mind. In all that they did for the promotion of common schools and for the higher stages of education they were offering not only the means, but the temptation for the vigorous testing of their own principles.

More than thirty years after the College and the common schools of Massachusetts, with the printing-press at Cambridge, had begun their enlightening work, Sir William Berkeley, the Governor of Virginia, with different subjects, materials, and objects in view than those which engaged the Puritan legislators, had written to the Commissioners of Foreign Plantations in London : —

"I thank God there are no free schools nor printing, and I hope we shall not have these hundred years; for learning has brought disobedience into the world, and printing has divulged them and libels against the best governments. God keep us from both ! "

But the founders of Massachusetts did not wait till the date of the order of 1647 to show their zeal for the interests of education. What that order was designed to effect had been substantially long before anticipated. Besides the College, dating from 1636, the Boston Latin School, from 1635, and the Roxbury Latin School, from 1645, there had been more or less care taken in most of the towns, either by "dames'" schools, or by "grammar" teachers, and in every home, for the elementary training of children. One year before the order of 1647, — namely, in November, 1646, — we find on the Records the following entry : —

"This Courte, being sensible of the necessity and singuler use of good literature in managing the things of greatest concernment in the commonwealth, as also perceiving the fewness of persons accomplished to such imployments, especially for future times, have thought meete to propose to all and every of our reverend elders and brethren that due care be had from time to time to improve and exercise such students, especially in divinity, as through the good hand of God may issue forth of the colledges, that so, for want of imployment or maintenance, they be not forced from us, and we left destitute of help that way : to all which intents and purposes every church which hath but one officer, and can conveniently bear the charge of such scholler (which we hope most may do), is hereby desired to request a pore scholler to be helpful to their officer, that so they may improve their gifts, and the church have some proof of them against times of neede."[1]

But College and Latin schools, with their special purposes of providing for the succession of the ministry, would have had but unrewarding subjects of their care among an ignorant stock of common people; therefore provision of the broadest and most comprehensive character must be made for the education of every child growing up in the jurisdiction.

The preamble of the order now to be copied arrests our attention by its quaintness and point, as follows : —

"It being one chiefe project of that ould deluder, Satan, to keepe men from the knowledge of the Scriptures, as in former times by keeping them in an unknowne tongue, so in these latter times by perswading from the use of tongues, that so at least the true sence and meaning of the originall might be clouded by false glosses of Saint-seeming deceivers, that learning may not be buried in the grave of our fathers in the church and commonwealth, the Lord assisting our endeavors!"

[1] Records, ii. 167.

The Court does not cite any "Scripture" as a warrant for attributing to "that ould deluder" the particular form of malignity here ascribed to him. He certainly has found no difficulty in communicating with men in all known languages, and this may be an illustration of the truth that when any one has acquired a bad reputation he may be charged with mischief which he never did. But in its touch of satire the Court struck at the "deluder" through the Roman Church as an *alias*. The order proceeds : —

"It is therefore ordered, that every towneship in this jurisdiction, after the Lord hath increased them to the number of fifty householders, shall then forthwith appoint one within their towne to teach all such children as shall resort to him to write and reade, whose wages shall be paid either by the parents or masters of such children, or by the inhabitants in generall, by way of supply, as the major part of those that order the prudentials of the towne shall appoint; provided those that send their children be not oppressed by paying much more than they can have them taught for in other townes : and it is further ordered, that where any towne shall increase to the number of one hundred families or householders, they shall set up a grammer schoole, the master thereof being able to instruct youth so farr as they may be fited for the university, provided that if any towne neglect the performance hereof above one yeare, that every such towne shall pay five pounds to the next schoole till they shall performe this order." [1]

This order was followed by others from time to time, making it compulsory upon all parents and masters to send their children to school, and investing town officers with authority to enter houses to see that the requisition was complied with. The records of many towns in the early years of poverty and hardship show how faithfully this order was obeyed. And there are cases of the interposition of the authorities when it failed of its purpose, under peculiarly difficult circumstances. Yet compliance was always insisted upon, with penalty for neglect.

[1] Records, ii. 203.

17

We might almost condone the ungenial and melancholy act of Puritan legislation in forbidding the observance of Christmas, by offsetting it with the occasion for fun, raillery, and satire which the act has furnished for so many of later generations, including some of the descendants of the Puritans. Of course their antipathy to the observance of that and of like Church days had been formed in England,[1] and concerned wholly the extra Scriptural and ecclesiastical usage which had devised them, and the excesses of jollity, revelry, and wild indulgence, which, as we read, caused all the jails of the kingdom to be more full on the day following Christmas than on any other day of the year. In the view of the Puritans the mission of the Saviour, to rescue the elect few out of a doomed and dying race, was too grave a one to be in any way associated with mirthful observances, and a serious celebration of it would not have attractions for those not in sympathy with them. Before quoting from the Records the order about Christmas, our attention may be drawn to the date of it, which was in May, 1659. This being nearly thirty years after the first settlement of the Colony, we might wonder why they had so long delayed to bring their legislation to bear on a matter about which Puritan antipathy was so strong. The explanation may be found in reminding ourselves that the space of time which had elapsed since the settlement, and the coming in of new elements of population, — sailors, transient residents, and others with strong attachments to the ways of their old home, — had introduced practices which had begun to occasion alarm. The order already partially copied is as follows: —

" For preventing disorders arising in severall places within this jurisdiction, by reason of some still observing such festivalls as were superstitiously kept in other countrys, to the great dishonnor of God and offence of others, it is therefore ordered by this Court

[1] See *ante*, p. 109.

and the authority thereof, that whosoever shall be found observing any such day as Christmas or the like, either by forbearing of labour, feasting, or any other way, upon any such accounts as aforesaid, every such person so offending shall pay for every such offence five shillings, as a fine to the country. And whereas, not only at such times, but at severall other times also, it is a custome too frequent in many places to expend time in unlawfull games, as cards, dice, etc., it is therefore further ordered, and by this Court declared, that after publication hereof whosoever shall be found in any place within this jurisdiction, playing either at cards or at dice, contrary to this order, shall pay as a fine to the country the some of five shillings for every such offence." [1]

Among the demands made upon the Court by the Commissioners of Charles II. sent over here in 1665, to be noticed later in another connection, was one requiring " that the poenalty for keeping Christmas, being directly against the lawe of England, may be repealed." [2] The Court, however, took time for acting deliberately on this injunction; for it was not till after further pressing, and in May, 1681, that it consented that " the law against keeping Christmas be left out." At the same time the law for putting to death Quakers returning from banishment was repealed.[3]

A subject for legislation which presents itself on the pages of the first volume of our statute-books, and has never since failed to find a place on them, is that relating to the sale and use of intoxicating drinks. A candid reader is forced to admit that there has been no advance in any wise and practical measures for dealing with the evil. The fathers anticipated every device and scheme and safeguard and penalty that has since been put on trial by their posterity, — with one signal exception. The method of legal prohibition of the sale of intoxicating liquors throughout the jurisdiction was never attempted, or even suggested. On the contrary, it is very plain from many sig-

[1] Records, vol. iv. pt. i. p. 366.   [2] Ibid., ii. 212.   [3] Ibid., v. 322.

nificant intimations that the fathers considered such beverages as not only innocent but essential things, for which gratitude should be offered to the Great Provider. They took care that facilities should be offered for the abundant provision of them in all fit times, occasions, and places, under due oversight and control, always, however, under allowance from the Court for sale at ordinaries, trucking-houses, etc. More than this, the Court took order that the price of beer, etc., should be regulated by its proper strength of materials used in the brewing of it. We might even be surprised to notice from multiplied tokens how abundant and freely distributed in all places were these spirituous beverages, from our earliest days. One must have been in straits in hard and lonely scenes to have lacked them. In accounting for this fact we have to remind ourselves how soon a brisk commerce was established with the Canaries and the West Indies, and how well the skill of English brewers and distillers was appreciated here. It has often been asserted, that, although liquors were used so freely in our old times, the deleterious effects of them were not so severe or so common as now. And this has been explained by the suggestion that the elders were favored by pure and unsophisticated liquors, in place of the poisoned compounds of our time. While the cases on our records of punishment inflicted for drunkenness are not as numerous as we might have expected to find them, we meet with enough of them, — of persons "distempered with drink," "disguised by liquor," etc., — to show that the offence was a grievous one and a reproach, so that the penalty often, besides a mulct, drew some form of humiliation and disgrace.

At first there was a positive prohibition under a heavy fine for the sale or gift of intoxicants to an Indian. The temptation to offend in this particular grew steadily stronger and stronger as the craving and passion for the stimulant exhibited itself uncontrollably in the savages from the very first indulgence, till they would run any venture, or make any sacrifice, to gratify it. Step by step the rigidness of the prohibition was relaxed by allowing individual white men, under restrictions of place and amount, to use the article with the Indians in barter, or pay for labor or hunting. There is something like a generous gush of feeling in an order of the Court passed in November, 1644, as follows : —

" The Court, apprehending that it is not fit to deprive the Indians of any lawfull comfort which God aloweth to all men by the use of wine, do order that it shalbe lawfull for all such as are or shalbe alowed license to retaile wines, to sell also to the Indians so much as may be fit for their needfull use or refreshing." [1]

There was, however, one usage of good fellowship connected with this " lawful comfort," against which Puritan legislation set itself, as follows : —

" Sept. 1639.   Forasmuch as it is evident unto this Court that the common custom of drinking one to another is a meere uselesse ceremony, and draweth on that abominable practice of drinking healths, and is also an occation of much wast of the good creatures, and of many other sinns, as drunkenness, quarlling, bloudshed, uncleannes, mispence of precious time, etc., which as they ought in all times and places to bee prevented carefully, so especially in plantations of churches and common weales, wherein the least knowne evills are not to bee tollerated by such as are bound by soleme covenant to walke by the rule of God's word in all their conversation, —

" It is therefore ordered, that no resident or comer into the jurisdiction, after a week's residence, shall directly or indirectly, by any color or circumstance, drink to any other, contrary to the intent of this order, upon paine of twelve pence for every offence." [2]

Whether the Court came to realize the unreasonableness of this rule, or the impossibility of enforcing it, we read

[1] Records, ii. 85.   [2] Ibid., i. 271.

upon its Records of May, 1645, " The order against drinking one to another is hereby repealed." [1]

It is possible that Winthrop may have prompted the Court to the enactment against " health-drinking; " for he enters in his Journal as early as October, 1630, " The governour, upon consideration of the inconveniences which had grown in England by drinking one to another, restrained it at his own table, and wished others to do the like, so as it grew, by little and little, to disuse." Among his papers was found one in which he sets down two reasons for the passage of a law against "drinking healths," — first, because it is " an empty and ineffectual representation of serious things in a way of vanity; second, because it is a frequent and needless temptation to dissemble love." It is hardly necessary to remind ourselves that this discrediting a mere form associated with hospitality was not intended to reduce the generosity or cordiality of that virtue as duly honored among the Puritans.

Much of the attention of the Court was given to a jealous oversight of the " ordinaries," which became numerous, and required watchfulness as to what might be done in them. In May, 1651, we find the following order : —

" Whereas, it is observed that there are many abuses and disorders by dauncinge in ordinaryes, whether mixt or unmixt, upon mariage of some persons, this Court doth order that hence forward there shalbe no dauncinge uppon such occasion, or at other times in ordinaryes, upon the paine of five shilling for every person that shall so daunce in ordinaryes." [2]

Allowance is to be made for what has been before referred to, in our reading in the Records of the espionage practised by the authorities in checking irregularities and

---

[1] Even the scruples of Quakers to like practices were soon found to yield. They had a Quakers' "Coffee House" in London, where the formula between two friends seated at table, with the appliances, was, " Friend, let us wish each other well, and take another glass."

[2] Records, iii. 224.

indulgences, that these came into a threatening presence in the community chiefly by the visits and transient residence of strangers. The letter of Governor Endicott, on a previous page,[1] is a very suggestive reminder of what were regarded the free loose speech and the contumacious behavior of seamen, when brought into intercourse with "the saints." All the sources of our information go to prove that among the homes and families of the fixed population decorum and serious ways and habits were almost universally spontaneous, or enforced by the best examples.

The Court had made several attempts by statutes and penalties to forbid extravagance and "bravery" in apparel. It found an embarrassment in dealing with the subject in its own necessary admission and allowance that there were gentlemen and gentlewomen — not to say an element of "aristocracy" — in the Colony, with whose class prerogatives· it could not interfere, but in fact would rather protect. We may copy at some length a law passed in October, 1651: —

"Although severall declarations and orders have bin made by this Court agaynst excesse in apparill, both of men and woemen, which hath not yet taken that efect which were to be desired, but on the contrary we cannot but to our greife take notice that intolerable excesse and bravery have crept in uppon us, and especially amongst people of meane condition, to the dishonor of God, the scandall of our profession, the consumption of estates, and altogether unsuteable to our povertie; and although we acknowledge it to be a matter of much difficultie, in regard of the blindnes of men's mindes and the stubbornnes of theire wills, to set down exact rules to confine all sorts of persons, yet we cannot but accoumpt it our duty to commend unto all sorts of persons a sober and moderate use of those blessings which beyond our expectation the Lord hath been pleased to afford us in this wilderness, and also to declare our utter detestation and dislike that men or women of meane condition, educations, and callinges should take uppon them

[1] See *ante*, p. 146.

the garbe of gentlemen, by the wearinge of gold or silver lace or buttons, or points at theire knees, to walk in greate bootes; or women of the same rank to weare silke or tiffany hoodes or scarfes, which though allowable to persons of greater estates, or more liberall education, yet we cannot but judge it intollerable in persons of such like condition: its therefore ordered by this Court and the authoritie therof, that no person within this jurisdiction, or any of their relations depending uppon them, whose visible estates, reall and personall, shall not exceede the true and indeferent value of two hundred poundes, shall weare any gold or silver lace, or gold or silver buttons, or any bone lace above two shillings per yard, or silke hoodes or scarfes, uppon the penalty of ten shillings for every such offence; and every such delinquent to be presented by the graund jury."

Still recognizing the difficulty of defining particular rules applicable to persons of different qualities and estates, the selectmen of the towns are required to be observant of the apparel of persons who exceed their rank or ability in this matter, and to assess them at the same rate as those to whom such luxury is suitable and allowed.

" Provided that this law shall not extend to the restraynt of any magistrate, or any public officer of this jurisdiction, their wives and children, who are left to their discretion in wearinge of apparill, or any settled military, or souldier in the time of military servise, or any other whose education and imployment have been above the ordinary degree, or whose estates have been considerable, though now decayed." [1]

One can scarcely fail to see in this wholly impracticable piece of legislation a prudent and strong desire on the part of the Court to check and interdict those manifestations of folly, improvidence, and wastefulness which struck at the security and prosperity of the still struggling Colony. The effective way of dealing with the excess aimed at would have been for those who were exempted from the

[1] Records, iii. 243, 244.

restraint of the law to have set a better example. The incipient democracy of the Colony would not brook the class favoritism allowed by the law. Indeed, in this exemption and immunity granted to a privileged class there was a marked relaxing of one of the former orders of the Court on this matter of apparel. In 1639 the Court had given ear to complaints against " lace and points," against short sleeves, " whereby the nakedness of the arm may be discovered," and against "immoderate great sleeves, immoderate great breches, knots of ryban, broad shoulder bands and rayles, silk races, double ruffes and cuffes," etc. Tailors and seamstresses were forbidden to make such articles, and all who had them were ordered to alter them.[1]

The Scripture warrant for this prohibition, so far at least as it concerned women, was Ezekiel xiii. 18.

As late as 1675, amid the distresses of the Indian war, the Court, in seeking to learn why the hand of God was laid so heavily upon them, finds this as one cause: —

" Whereas, there is manifest pride openly appearing amongst us in that long haire, like weomen's haire, is worne by some men, either their owne or others haire made into perewiggs, and by some weomen wearing borders of hayre, and their cutting, curling, and immodest laying out theire haire, especcially amongst the younger sort, this Court doeth declare this ill custome as offensive to them, etc. The evill of pride in apparrell, both for costliness in the poorer sort, and vayne, new, strange fashions, both in poore and rich, with naked breasts and armes, or, as it were, pinioned with the addition of superstitious ribbons," etc., the County Courts are charged to attend to this grievance.[2]

In reading this specimen of curious intermeddling with matters of female apparel and array, frettings about which have always been proved utterly powerless, one might be inclined to forget that more than two hundred years have passed since the enactment. Many of the articles, atti-

---

[1] Records, i. 273, 274.   [2] Records, v. 59.

tudes, gestures, and adornments described are by no means antiquated, but seem to be before us even in exaggerated forms.

We have now had presented, generally in the words of those who prompted and guided the scheme for the planting of a Commonwealth in the Bay of Massachusetts, the principles which they adopted for its religious administration according to the Biblical model. Our pages will close with a review of the protracted and sturdy struggle which the authorities maintained against the King of England in their baffled effort to uphold their Charter, in which they had found a basis for their theocracy. But before that catastrophe came, the authorities had to contend with a series of four successive conflicts, which in fact proved to be warnings and preparatory occasions of that catastrophe. These conflicts covered all the subjects, claims, interests, and matters of legislation and administration which entered into the life of their theocracy. The validity of their Charter and their mode of construing it were brought under question; the right of the magistrates to deal in the province of religion was denied; heresies threatening alarming immoralities were broached among them; fundamental principles in their church institution were set at nought; and last of all, their exclusive dependence upon the Bible for light and guidance, and for the formalities of observance, was greatly discredited.

VIII.

THE BANISHMENT OF ROGER WILLIAMS.

ROGER WILLIAMS was the first, and, through the whole period of the theocracy, the most conspicuous person to come under the discipline of both the civil and ecclesiastical powers of Massachusetts. Whether that discipline was, under the circumstances, harsh or unjust, or whether a candid review of the facts of the case will show that he unwisely or pertinaciously brought its severity upon himself, is a question about which the means of forming a fair and impartial judgment are more complete than in most similar cases that have been confused in their historic narration. Certainly a full compensation has accrued to him for all that he may have suffered from court and church penalties, and from exile, in gathering to the honor of his name the rich laurels of being virtually, though not by the tenure of a legal office, the founder of the State of Rhode Island, and the great apostle of "soul-freedom," or of unlimited toleration for conscience and religious opinions. As to the fulness of the historic material relating to the subject, it may be said here that, while we find much less of information and of references in detail to his case in the Records of the Court than we might naturally expect, we have sidelights from other sources furnishing us exhaustive and even wearisome reiterations of every particular and incident in the controversy to which he was a party. His own letters, the pages of Winthrop's Journal, and the admirably edited and annotated volumes issued by the Narra-

gansett Club,[1] especially those which contain the tracts of
Williams and Cotton on the "Bloody Tenent of Persecution," enable us to stand and listen as contemporaries to
the rehearsal of the whole story. And having this privilege of historic retrospect, we may find a fit and pleasant
preparation for re-reading that story in anticipating it by
a summary statement of the aspect and character in which
Williams presents himself to us.

Alike for the noble qualities and for the petty infirmities
singularly blended with them, he is to us an admirable and
a picturesquely engaging person. He was wholly free of
guile, open, sincere, and of a most generous disposition,
with traits of a childlike simplicity and tenderness. The
resolute front which he presented to those who opposed
him in his opinions or his actions had in it nothing of
ugliness or perversity. He was forbearing and magnanimous. Stoutly asserting and holding to convictions honestly and independently formed and resolutely maintained,
his weakness showed itself only in an occasional outflow
of sentiment over his privations, not in any shrinking from
the inflictions they brought upon him. It seemed to be a
joy to him to speak with a yearning affection of those who
he believed had misjudged or wronged him, and he sought
opportunities to do them kindly and very valuable service.
With him, contention was a strange blending of duty and
satisfaction. Though all the powers of State and Church
were engaged against him in Massachusetts, with many
fretting altercations and the final infliction, — yet not without forbearance on the part of the authorities, — Williams
never had there a single personal enemy. His spirit was
provocative, and his pertinacity could exasperate, but his
opponents commended his patience and availed themselves of
his generosity. What strange contrasts of scenes and com-
panionships his experience and career present to us ! How

[1] These constitute six quarto volumes prepared by the members of the
Club, and published in sumptuous form in Providence, 1866–74.

keenly must he have enjoyed, in his visits to England, his free and congenial intercourse with such friends as Cromwell, Sir Henry Vane, and Milton! How cheerfully, from the comforts of English homes, chambers, and food, did he return to his wilderness haunts, the guest of the savages in " their filthy, smoky holes," sharing with them the scant and miscellaneous diet of the woods! How diligently, while tossing on the waves of the Atlantic, did he occupy his long voyage in writing and preparing for the English press his " Key into the Language of America," being his Indian Grammar and Vocabulary! How laboriously, and with but a haphazard help from the books of reference which he abundantly cites, did he catch and use the moments out of public business, a scattering hospitality in chamber lodgings, in travel, and by the roadside, to pen his sharp and often stinging tractates in his controversy with " Master Cotton "! Of one commodity when in England we may be sure the voyager took care to provide himself with a full supply, that is, writing paper; for he used very much of it.

His biographers have been numerous and zealous. Each of them in succession has introduced some fresh errors or misreadings of the truth, and has added some valuable helps to our knowledge of facts. His opinions and his career have been very variously set forth with comments, with a singular tendency to confuse and subordinate the most important to the less essential matters of the controversy. His great doctrine of " soul-freedom " appears indeed in his contention here with court and church, but quite in a secondary relation to other grounds of variance. Many have supposed him to have been banished for avowing the tenets of the Baptists, and to have been the founder here of that denomination. But when he left Massachusetts he was still, as he had been, a Congregationalist minister, in full accord with his brethren in matters of doctrine. His views about baptism were especially erratic, and the

Baptist denomination would have but slight satisfaction in claiming his membership, much less his leadership. Some two years after his removal to Rhode Island, becoming distrustful about his baptism in infancy, he subjected himself to the ordinance as administered by one Ezekiel Hollyman, after which he rebaptized Hollyman and some ten others. Within a few months Williams had " scruples" about the matter, as Hollyman had not been himself baptized when he administered the rite to Williams. So this conscientious man renounced his rebaptism, and remained through his life, free of all fellowships, a " seeker " for the truth. Winthrop, who kept anxious watch upon the doings of the unsettled free-thinkers gathering at Providence, says [1] that " a sister of Mrs. Hutchinson, the wife of one Scott, being infected with Anabaptistry, and going last year to live at Providence," induced Williams to rebaptism by Hollyman, who had gone from Salem. Williams came to believe that there was no one on the earth qualified to administer the rite. No one can be surprised that the now numerous and respected fellowship of the Baptists crave the honor of so noble a founder on this continent. But if they accept his own statement of his views he would seem rather to have discredited the denomination than to have assumed its leadership.

The birthplace, parentage, and age of Roger Williams have as yet remained in obscurity, and according to such particulars and inferences as have been available to his biographers, his age when he appears in Boston has been variously taken to range between twenty-five and thirty years. He proceeded from Pembroke College, Cambridge, January, 1627, as Bachelor of Arts, was ordained and beneficed, but driven from England and his ministry, as he says, by dread of Archbishop Laud. He had known some of the New England people, but seems to have come hither by his own prompting. He arrived at Boston with

[1] Winthrop, i. 293.

his wife Feb. 15, 1631, with the repute of being "godly." Wilson, the teacher of the First Church, having gone to England to bring his wife, Williams says that he was invited with unanimity to fill his place. There is no record of this invitation other than that made by Williams himself, and the inference naturally is that he was informally conferred with on the subject. In a letter written by him to Rev. John Cotton, Jr., in 1671,[1] after referring "to gains and preferments refused in universities, city, country, and court, in Old England" because his "conscience was persuaded against the national church," he adds that he made a similar sacrifice in not accepting the proffer of the Boston church. The reason which he gives for his refusal is, "because I durst not officiate to an unseparated people, as upon examination and conference I found them to be." Here we have distinctly brought before us the position assumed by the Boston church toward the Church of England, as one of Non-conformity, not of Separation. Williams was a positive and pronounced Separatist. He wished the Boston church to renounce all communion with the English Church, to humble itself penitently for ever having held such communion, and to forbid her members, on occasional visits to their native land, to join in the old worship and ordinances. Williams never yielded, but stood stoutly by his principle in this, and when he had a church of his own in Salem, he rigidly exacted a compliance with it from all whom he admitted to membership. It was in this antagonistic attitude that Williams introduced himself to his friendly countrymen in Boston, and it certainly was an unpromising beginning here of the career of one who was to win the honor of an apostle of "soul-liberty" and unlimited toleration. The impressions at once formed of him, alike of certain winning and lovable personal qualities and of his rigid individuality and pertinacity of opinion, continued unchanged through his whole life. He never

[1] Mass. Hist. Soc. Proc., March, 1871.

came into genial relations with his associates anywhere.
He never really identified himself with their general aims
and interests. As the name " Roger Williams" appears
on the list of those who took the freeman's oath, some
of the biographers of the founder of Rhode Island have
affirmed that he was thus sworn into allegiance; but that
was another person of the same name, and of quite a
different career, who had taken the oath some months
before the arrival of his ministerial namesake. In his
interview with members of the Boston church, Williams
must have disclosed some other of his opinions; for
Winthrop makes the following entry in his Journal,
April 12, 1631 : [1] —

" At a court holden at Boston upon information to the governour that they of Salem had called Mr. Williams to the office of a
teacher, a letter was written from the court to Mr. Endecott to
this effect : That whereas Mr. Williams had refused to join with
the congregation at Boston, because they would not make a public declaration of their repentance for having communion with the
churches of England while they lived there, and, besides, had
declared his opinion that the magistrate might not punish the
breach of the Sabbath, nor any other offence, as it was a breach
of the first table, therefore they marvelled they would choose him
without advising with the council, and withal desiring him that
they would forbear to proceed till they had conferred about it."

This was a court of the magistrates or assistants, at
which were present Winthrop, Dudley, Ludlow, Nowell,
Pynchon, and Bradstreet. Two different views may be and
have been taken of this proceeding. One is, that it was a
high-handed and unwarranted intermeddling of the magistratical authority with the rights of an independent church.
The other view is — and this finds support in the fact that
there is no entry of the proceeding on the records of the
Court — that it was simply intended as an unofficial remon-

[1] Winthrop, i. 52.

strance and expostulation with some who were endangering amicable relations and the public interests. There is also a difference of opinion as to the effect of this interference. It has been affirmed that Williams was instituted in the office of teacher, as successor to Higginson, on the same day on which the letter was written, and also that the letter stopped the proceedings. However this may have been, Williams left Salem in season to present himself in Plymouth, in August, 1631, where he was received into the church, and assisted its teacher, Ralph Smith. Williams says that while in Plymouth he labored with his hands, engaged in trade, and companied much with the Indians, " to gain their tongue," and engage their friendship, which he always and everywhere most happily secured.

The same conflict of opinions and sentiments about himself which Williams had excited in Boston followed him in Plymouth. His guileless and affectionate nature, his sincerity and good purposes, were appreciated, and so were his " headiness," his singularity and eccentricity, and his obstinacy in notions and judgments. He was found to hold " diverse singular opinions which he sought to impose on others." Patient Governor Bradford and gentle Elder Brewster speak of him kindly and hopefully, but intimate some abatements of their sympathy and confidence. Bradford pronounced him " godly and zealous, having many precious parts, but very unsettled in judgment." When Williams, at his own request, was dismissed from the Plymouth to the Salem church, the letter contained a " caution." Some of the members being unwilling to dismiss him, Brewster persuaded them to do so, as he feared strife from elements of mischief already working from Williams's strange opinions. Winthrop says that Williams was in Salem by November, 1633, helping Mr. Skilton " by way of prophecy," but " not in any office." This, however, he acceded to in a year, when Skilton died. He had united with Skilton in November, 1633, in objecting to a friendly semi-monthly meeting at each other's homes, of the "ministers of the Bay," lest it should grow "to a presbytery, or superintendency, to the prejudice of the churches' liberties."

It was probably while he was at Plymouth, where his eldest child was born, that Williams had written, and shown to some friends who were alarmed by the strange opinions expressed in it, "a large Book in Quarto." This was undoubtedly his treatise questioning, or rather directly denying, the validity of the King's Patent, under which the Company held and could maintain its territorial rights. As Williams's expressed opinions on this highly critical matter — asserted, apologized for, yielded up, and then re-asserted — were substantially the chief grounds of the Court's dealings with him, resulting in his banishment, we must have the bearings of the case intelligently before us. The "treatise" itself is not extant, as it was probably burned, either by Williams himself, or with his consent, by the Court. We know its spirit and purport by the references to it, and by quotations from it. Williams would himself be very ready to show and discuss with others any product of his busy brain, and would be sturdy in defending it, however erratic they might regard it. After he had returned to Salem it became noised abroad that he had written such an alarming treatise, and it was at an anxious crisis for the colony, as then dreading interference with its affairs from abroad, when every scruple was a bombshell, and every breeze was a gale. Winthrop, hearing of the "treatise," sent to Williams for a copy. The Governor and Assistants at a meeting, Jan. 6, 1634, — not an official one, as it is not entered on the records, — perused and criticised it. The Governor reports it to us, for its matter and tenor. He says the treatise was "formerly written to the governor and council of Plymouth:"[1] —

[1] Winthrop, i. 122.

" Wherein, among other things, he disputes their right to the lands they possessed here, and concluded that, claiming by the King's grant, they could have no title, nor otherwise, except they compounded with the natives. For this, taking advice with some of the most judicious ministers (who much condemned Mr. Williams' errour and presumption), they gave order that he should be convented at the next court, to be censured, etc. There were three passages chiefly whereat they were much offended : 1. for that he chargeth King James to have told a solemn publick lye, because in his patent he blessed God that he was the first Christian prince that had discovered this land; 2. for that he chargeth him and others with blasphemye for calling Europe Christendom, or the Christian world; 3. for that he did personally apply to our present king, Charles, these three places in the Revelations, viz — "

We are able to supply the blank which follows the abrupt close of the Governor. Endicott, one of the Assistants, a member of Mr. Williams's church, not being present at this meeting of magistrates, the Governor, a week after the meeting, wrote him a letter, which has come to light.[1] This letter adds a fourth grievance against Williams : " 4. for concluding us all heere to lye under a sinne of unjust usurpation upon others' possessions." The references to the Revelations are also supplied as follows : Chaps. xvi. 13, 14; xvii. 12, 13; and xviii. 9. These passages have no significance here except as admirably illustrating that Puritan usage in quoting Scriptures which have no conceivable connection with the matter in hand.

A doubt might reasonably be raised whether Roger Williams had ever read with intelligent study and careful reflection the original Charter of James I., so impertinent appear his strictures upon those terms of it of which he complains. We have only by anticipation to look forward to his maturer life of experience, and converse with men of pronounced wills and individuality like his own, to find

[1] Mass. Hist. Soc. Proc., February, 1873.

him, thirty years later, petitioning for, welcoming, and
holding several offices under a royal charter for Rhode
Island, granted under precisely the same terms and conditions as those of the Bay Charter. The King of England
did not claim an absolute, but only a relative, ownership
and power of disposal of the territory granted here. His
gift to those who received it was limited by the conditions
under which he claimed to bestow it. By the law of nations as then recognized, the fact that English navigators
had first sighted the coast of newly-discovered land gave
to the monarch whose subjects they were a right to it
above that of other sovereigns. His grant of a portion of
it to an incorporated company of his subjects was good
against the trespassing of any other Englishmen upon it,
and against the inimical intrusion of the subjects of any
other European monarchs. Any usufructuary rights of a
people actually resident upon or claiming the territory,
even though they were heathen, were to be recognized and
fairly adjusted. The most grievous charges of Williams
are that against James I. of telling " a solemn publick lye "
in his Patent, and that against James I. and Charles I. of
" blasphemye," for calling Europe " Christendom, or the
Christian world." Winthrop writes respecting "the grande
Patent," that it might contain the ground for such charges,
but " for my parte I never sawe it, and I doubt whether he
[Williams] did or not." [1] That Winthrop had reasons for
doubting whether Williams had ever seen James's Patent,
appears from the fact that his charge of a " lye " against
the monarch is based upon his assuming " to have been the
first Christian prince that discovered New England." But
the Patent makes no reference whatever to this discovery;
and in neither of the patents is Europe spoken of as
" Christendom."

All that is pertinent to the matter at issue is found in
the following extract from the Patent of James I. : —

[1] Mass. Hist. Soc. Proc., February, 1873.

" Forasmuch as We have been certainly given to understand by divers of our good Subjects that have for these many Yeares past frequented those Coasts and Territoryes between the Degrees of Fourty and Fourty-eight, that there is noe other the Subjects of any Christian King or State, by any authoritie from their Soveraignes, Lords, or Princes, actually in Possession of any of the said Lands or Precincts, whereby any Right, Claim, Interest, or Title may, might, or ought by that means accrue, belong, or appertaine unto them, or any of them. [The Patent then mentions the recent devastations by war and pestilence, which have left the territory for many leagues together without inhabitant or claimant, thus marking the fit time for improving land so depopulated.]   In Contemplacion and serious Consideracion whereof Wee have thought it fitt, according to our Kingly Duty, soe much as in Us lyeth, to second and followe God's sacred Will, rendering reverend Thanks to his Divine Majestie for His gracious favour in laying open and revealing the same unto us, before any other Christian Prince or State, by which Meanes without Offence, and as We trust to his Glory, Wee may with Boldness goe on to the settling of soe hopefull a Work," etc.

The proviso, recognizing any rightful claims of other nationalities, is thus stated : —

" Provided always that any of the Premises herein before mentioned, and by these Presents intended and meant to be granted, be not actually possessed or inhabited by any other Christian Prince or Estate." [1]

Williams went to the whole length of affirming that the King's Patent gave the colonists no right to their territory, " but that the Natives are the true owners of it," so that the colonists had committed the " sinne of unjust usurpation upon others' possessions." The right course, therefore, for the trespassers to pursue was to repent of having acted under the Patent, to restore it to the King, to abandon the territory, and to return to England. What con-

[1] Hazard's Hist. Coll., i. 103–118.

sequences would have ensued on the adoption of these notions of Mr. Williams we may take note of in a moment, after a reference to the course pursued as to any rightful claims of the savages that might be found here. It is to be frankly admitted that none of the European colonists to America — Spanish, French, or English — had any generous allowance for the rights of the aborigines whom they found either residing upon or roaming over parts of this continent, or any delicate scruples about crowding or displacing them. Their aimless and wasteful lives, their roaming over and transient occupancy of vast spaces of fruitful territory, — which they skimmed for a subsistence without enriching by labor, — their cruel wars with one another in their tribes, and their general state of barbarism, were regarded as good reasons for their giving place to a superior race. But the kings in their patents by no means assumed, nor did the colonists settling under them act on the assumption, that these barbarians had no natural rights. It was not long before the English colonists came to understand what estimate the Indians themselves had of those rights as implied in the deeds and covenants which they made with the whites. We learn what it was which they considered as belonging to them, and the value which they set upon it, when we know what they supposed they were deeding to the whites for a consideration. In general, the savages in these transactions appear to have supposed that they were granting to the whites a privilege of joint occupancy of a territory with themselves, for the various uses of tillage and hunting. They had no idea that they themselves were to move off at a distance without any reserved rights. The complaint of King Philip against the people of Plymouth was, that by building fences, dams, etc., the whites made the land deeded to them unavailable for equal privileges to the Indians. Indeed, instances were not infrequent in which a sachem in behalf of his tribe deeded the same portions of territory to more than one party, as if he thought that they might all put it peacefully to the same uses which had served him. As to the relations between the Indian proprietors and the English colonists whom Williams charged with an usurpation of their rights, the facts of the case did not at all trouble the consciences of the latter. It is true that we find them laying much stress upon the opportunity of entering here upon a *vacuum domicilium*, — a large territory wasted and cleared by pestilence. And their faith was cheered by the belief that Providence had so disposed the matter for their benefit; yet they by no means were indifferent to the rights of the few scattered and humbled natives in their neighborhood, but sought in every case to satisfy them. Before the transfer of the government here, the Governor of the Company, writing from London to Endicott, their agent in Salem, instructed him thus: " If any of the salvages pretend right of inheritance to all or any part of the lands granted in our pattent, we pray you endeavour to purchase their tityle that we may avoyde the least scruple of intrusion." [1] The instruction was strictly followed.

Mr. Williams was not a man to be deterred or appalled by a view of the consequences which would follow from any course of action which his conscience set before him as right. But one may doubt whether he had deliberately recognized the inevitable results which would ensue here if his views as to the iniquity and worthlessness of the Patent, and the obligation to surrender it, recommended themselves to the authorities for adoption. Desolation, ruin, and anarchy, with spoliation and free plunder, the prostration of all proprietary rights and of all securities for life, would be the inevitable issues of the baffled efforts and sacrifices for planting a colony on the edge of a wilderness. There were enemies and mischievous plotters near the Court at home, and a threatened revocation of the

[1] Court Records, i. 394.

Charter. The crude and speculative fancies and impulses
of this visionary young divine might insure for the colony
the ruin which imperilled it. Nor does it seem to have
occurred to Williams that he was a consenting party to,
and a profiter by, the wrong and outrage which he charged;
for he himself owned a house and ten acres of land in
Salem, which he mortgaged on leaving there for Rhode
Island. By a touch of humor rare in the pages of Winthrop, it appears that the Governor took note of this fact.
In his letter to Endicott he writes, " But if our title be not
good, neither by patent, nor possession of these parts as
vacuum domicilium, nor by good liking of the natives, I
mervayle by what title Mr. Williams himselfe holds."

After the Court of Assistants, as above related, had had
the conference with Williams about the contents of his
" treatise," and Endicott, at the request of Winthrop, had
" dealt with" him, in confuting his errors and inducing
him " to retract the same," Winthrop writes : —

" Mr. Williams also wrote to the governour, and also to him
and the rest of the council, very submissively, professing his intent to have been only to have written for the private satisfaction
of the governour, etc., of Plymouth, without any purpose to have
stirred any further in it, if the governour here had not required a
copy of him ; withal offering his book, or any part of it, to be
burnt. At the next court he appeared penitently, and gave satisfaction of his intention and loyalty. So it was left, and nothing
done in it." [1]

It is evident that Winthrop thought this a final and amicable disposal of an alarming matter.

We must pause a moment here upon a point raised by
more than one of the friendly biographers of Williams.
They charge it as an intrusive and inquisitorial proceeding
on the part of the magistrates in summoning Williams to
produce before them, as from his private desk, an unpub-

[1] Winthrop, i. 122.

lished manuscript which he had penned for the satisfaction of a few friends, and had not intended to send abroad. In the pages of some writers, who in reviewing the conflict of the authorities of Massachusetts with Roger Williams have shown their favor toward him by attempting to put those authorities in the wrong, appear aspersions or charges in substance as follows: The assumption is taken that the paper which he had written invalidating the patent, with its alarming notions, had never really been made public by him. It was not much more than a speculative, tentative essay on the subject, written by him for self-satisfaction, and still kept in the privacy of his own repository, except so far as he had shown it confidentially to a few friends in the same privacy of intercourse. The implication therefore has been drawn, that there was something underhand, something of artifice in the ingenuity used in rifling and forcing that private paper into the light and making it the subject of public excitement and remonstrance. From the facts of the case which have been presented, the reader must judge whether there are grounds for that imputation. He must remind himself, however, that at that time important papers, whether expository or controversial, were often copied — in lack of the press — and privately handed from one to another interested party. And he must also remind himself that if Williams by confidentially submitting his paper to a few chosen men had thus exposed his sense of its inflammatory character, the authorities on their side would have been all the more alarmed by the secrecy under which the mischief might work, compared with the effect of its open and stout avowal. To them the difference would have been that between the sinuosity of a snake and the ferocity of the wolf. All that can be said in answer to this charge is that Williams had furnished Winthrop at his own request a copy of the "treatise," and that the common bruit of its tenor must have originated in the shock which it had given to those of Plymouth who had seen it and been greatly troubled by it. The fact that Williams had thus guardedly passed the "treatise" only through private hands, might be alleged as proving that he was himself aware of its inflammatory character.

It was plain that the Court had not come to a full knowledge of the spirit of the man with whom they had to deal, when they supposed the matter disposed of. Williams was a man of that self-assertive and antagonistic frame of spirit, that a nursing and brooding over any unfair restraint imposed upon his mental freedom would stir him to a fresh assertion of it.

The Court of Assistants met again in Boston, Jan. 24, 1634, to consider Mr. Williams's letter to them above mentioned —

"when, with the advice of Mr. Cotton and Mr. Wilson, and weighing his letter, and further considering of the aforesaid offensive passages in his book (which being written in very obscure and implicative phrases, might well admit of doubtful interpretation) they found the matters not to be so evil as at first they seemed. Whereupon they agreed, that upon his retractation, etc., or taking an oath of allegiance to the king, etc., it should be passed over." [1]

We are not informed whether or not Williams wrote any further "retractation," or took the oath of allegiance.

Before his case was resumed, two pleasant little incidents interpose themselves in our grave annals, which must have engaged some lively interest. The first was about "a question raised on Lecture-day at Boston," as to whether it was the duty of women to veil themselves on going abroad. Cotton thought it was. Endicott, backed by Williams, thought it was not. The other incident, a more lively one, was the mutilation of the King's colors by cutting out the cross, as "idolatrous." The deed was done by Endicott, at the supposed instigation of Williams.

As a sign of the watchfulness of the magistrates against

[1] Winthrop, i. 123.

any challenge of what they held to be their rightful authority, mention should here be made of their grievance with
another of the elders.   Mr. Eliot, teacher of the Roxbury church, had blamed the magistrates in a sermon for
concluding a peace with the Pequot Indians without consent of the people, through their deputies, and, as Winthrop
writes,[1] —

"for other failings (as he conceived).   We took order that he
should be dealt with by Mr. Cotton, Mr. Hooker, and Mr. Welde,
to be brought to see his errour, and to heal it by some public explanation of his meaning: for the people began to take occasion
to murmur against us for it."   He was brought "to acknowledge
his errour — and so promised to express himself in public next
Lord's day."

But Williams was not so pliant in the fibres of his conscience.   Winthrop writes, Dec. 7, 1634,[2] —

"The Court was likewise informed that Mr. Williams of Salem
had broken his promise to us, in teaching publicly against the
king's patent, and our great sin in claiming right thereby to the
country, etc., and for usual terming the churches of England antichristian.   We granted summons to him for his appearance at the
next court."

Our confidence in the rigid truthfulness of Winthrop
can alone assure us as to any breach of his plighted word
by Williams, for we have no other information as to the
terms of his promise made in February preceding.   But
when the Court met in March following, 1635, there is no
record referring to his case, nor in the Governor's Journal.
We learn, however, from another source[3] that Mr. Cotton,
with the consent of his fellow-elders and brethren —

"presented a serious Request to the Magistrates, that they would
be pleased to forbeare all civill prosecution against him, till our-

---

[1] Winthrop, i. 151.   [2] Ibid.

[3] Cotton's Reply to Mr. Williams his Examination, p. 38.

selves (with our Churches) had dealt with him in a Church way, to convince him of sinne: alledging that my selfe and brethren hoped his violent course did rather spring from scruple of conscience (though carried with an inordinate zeale) than from a seditious principle."

An earnest effort was made by the elders, with the approval of the magistrates, in this pacificatory direction, but not with the desired result.

A new difficulty now arose from the teaching of Mr. Williams, which caused the Court of Assistants to summon him May 10, 1635. The freeman's oath was effective for securing the allegiance only of that portion of the male inhabitants of the jurisdiction who enjoyed the civil franchise. What authority or restraint could the Court exercise over those not enfranchised? It appears that the Court was at this time alarmed by the influx of some restless strangers from other parts of the continent and islands. It provided a "resident's oath" to secure the obedience to the laws, and the loyalty and peaceful conduct of all above the age of twenty years who intended to reside here for six months or more, and to pledge them to reveal any mischievous plottings. All who should refuse after being twice called upon to take this oath were to be banished. A slight change was made in the wording of the freeman's oath. But Mr. Williams had "scruples" which impelled him publicly to preach and to protest against the resident's oath. "Swearing" was in his view an act of worship. A magistrate, he maintained, might not tender an oath to an unregenerate person, for this was to "have communion with a wicked man in the worship of God, and cause him to take the name of God in vain." This was the occasion of a fresh and intense excitement. It appears that the exaction of the resident's oath was not rigidly pressed. May 30, 1635, the Governor (then Dudley, who the next month gave place to Haynes) and Assistants sent for Mr. Williams and charged him with

errors in his public preaching. Winthrop says: " He was
heard before all the ministers, and very clearly confuted.
Mr. Endicott was at first of the same opinion, but he gave
place to the truth." [1] Williams, however, did not regard
himself as confuted. He was then strong in the affections and confidence of the church at Salem, which had
invited him to office in it while he was under the censure
of the Court, and while it was being dealt with by the
elders. There was a great " apprehension of his godliness," and women were warmly on his side. Summoned
and appearing before the General Court May 10, 1635,
we read in Winthrop: —

" It was laid to his charge that, being under question before
the magistracy and churches for divers dangerous opinions, viz.,
1. that the magistrate ought not to punish the breach of the first
table, otherwise than in such cases as did disturb the civil peace ;
2. that he ought not to tender an oath to an unregenerate man;
3. that a man ought not to pray with such, though wife, child,
etc.; 4. that a man ought not to give thanks after the sacrament nor after meat, etc.; and that the other churches were
about to write to the church of Salem to admonish him of these
errours, notwithstanding the church had since called him to the
office of a teacher. Much debate was about these things. The
said opinions were adjudged by all, magistrates and ministers
(who were desired to be present), to be erroneous and very
dangerous, and the calling of him to office at that time was
judged a great contempt of authority. So, in fine, time was given
to him and the church of Salem to consider of these things till
the next general court, and then either to give satisfaction to the
court, or else to expect the sentence; it being professedly declared by the ministers (at the request of the court to give their
advice) that he who should obstinately maintain such opinions
(whereby a church might run into heresy, apostasy, or tyranny,
and yet the civil magistrate could not intermeddle) were to be
removed, and that the other churches ought to request the magistrates so to do." [2]

[1] Winthrop, i. 158.   [2] Ibid., i. 162.

The reader of our time will not fail to note the perplexities and encroachments into which the fathers were led by their tentative and experimental practical efforts in theocratic government. Here were elders consulted indeed, but in effect deciding the action of a civil court; magistrates intermeddling with church affairs; and besides this, other churches, each of them asserting its own independency, — for as yet no common platform for union, council, or discipline had been recognized, — intruding their advice and threatenings upon a sister fellowship.

But something more questionable and more mischievous was yet to follow at the same Court. We read it in Winthrop, as follows: —

"Salem men had preferred a petition at the last general court for some land in Marblehead Neck, which they did challenge as belonging to their town; but because they had chosen Mr. Williams their teacher, while he stood under question of authority, and so offered contempt to the magistrates, etc.,[1] their petition was refused till, etc.[1] Upon this the church of Salem write to other churches to admonish the magistrates of this as a heinous sin, and likewise the deputies; for which at the next general court their deputies were not received until they should give satisfaction about the letter."[2]

Here were indeed new elements of confusion and acrimony stirred into a strife already sufficiently alienating and threatening. In its own view this action of the Court was in part retaliatory, and in part an exaction from the Salem people of a *quid pro quo*, as the Court, having bestowed the civil franchise upon the church members who sent to it their deputies, felt justified in exacting from them an equivalent respect. But neither our sympathy nor our approval can go with the Court in this proceeding, which

[1] These "etc., etc.," indicate a method of Winthrop in an incomplete sentence.
[2] Winthrop, i. 164.

has a look of spite and vengefulness, and which prepared for it further trouble. Up to this point, for anything which appears to the contrary, all the variances which Williams had created might have been in part harmonized, and for the rest tolerated or condoned as eccentricities in a thoroughly sincere and well-reputed man. But not so after this action of the Court. It is clear upon the record that this action justly excited and exasperated Williams, if it did not also embitter him, driving him into rash or ill-considered measures for putting himself in the right by putting others in the wrong. The Court attempted to punish the town of Salem for an act of such of its inhabitants as belonged to the church of Salem. If the town had a rightful claim on the piece of territory for which it petitioned, the affair should have been left, conciliatorily to a decision on its own merits, not mixed with an entirely independent issue. Resenting the doings of the Court in deferring action upon the Salem petition, Williams, with the approval of his church, and in its name, proceeded to address very sharp and stinging "letters of Admonition" to all the churches of the Bay to which the members of the Court belonged, and enjoined that they be dealt with for an act of "injustice," and for "heinous sin." These epistles we shall find described in the sentence of the Court soon to be passed upon Williams, as "letters of defamation." Here was material for the most intense excitement and strife, with agitation and threatened debate in the separate and the united elements of Church and State throughout the whole jurisdiction. It subjected the theocracy to a most severe strain. Only reflection, with the help of imagination, if we care to exercise them on so unattractive a subject, can bring before us the consternation and the minglings of the passions of zeal and resentment with which in the circles alike of the "godly" and the "profane," these proceedings were accompanied.

The busy occupations, distractions, and amusements of life, with the newspapers and the world-wide intelligence which fills them, however unwholesome may be some of their influences upon us, afford security against, or relief from, those morbid and teasing exercises of conference and discipline which trespassed upon the active duties and tormented the leisure hours of this Puritan community. The English population in the Bay may then have been about five thousand, of which one tenth were freemen and church members. There were twelve organized and a few incipient churches, and about a score of ministers. Probably the threatened conflagration was dealt with as judiciously as the case admitted. Instead of engaging the direct action of each of the churches challenged in Williams's letters of admonition, some of the elders individually and jointly took the matter in hand, and addressed themselves, by remonstrance, intercession, or appeal, to members of the Salem church. They succeeded in drawing away a majority of them from any further countenance of their teacher in the course he had adopted, though some of them remained steadfast to him. If Williams had been prompted by the sturdiness of his conscience, and not by temper, in his comprehensive exercise of a method of ecclesiastical discipline, one can hardly wonder that the falling away from him of a majority of his church should have infused into his subsequent course toward them something that seems to have been anger and alienation. There had been an intermission in the session of the Court while the elders had been privately doing the work just referred to. A terrific gale and tempest had been raging in the Bay on the 25th of August, and the day following the devastation was Sunday. It was said that Williams was ill. He had officiated in his place for the last time; for, instead of appearing for the service, he sent to his church a letter to be read by his ruling elder, Sharpe. Winthrop thus refers to it: —

" Mr. Williams, pastor of Salem, being sick and not able to speak, wrote to his church a protestation, that he could not communicate with the churches in the bay, neither would he communicate with them, except they would refuse communion with the rest; but the whole church was grieved herewith." [1]

The letter itself is not extant, and we know its spirit and tenor only fragmentarily, leading us to infer that it was scorching in its severity. He was thus left what in modern phrase is called a " come-outer ; " and as the majority of his church expressed penitence for their course to the other churches, they may be held to have repudiated him. For two weeks — on Sundays and week days — he held meetings at his own house, with a group of ardent followers. In these meetings he insisted upon his renunciation of communion with his own or any other church, and extended his individualism even to a refusal to pray with his wife, or join in grace with her at the table, because she still attended the public assembly.

The General Court met at Cambridge in September, 1635; and now we find upon its records the first and the only reference to these doings of the man whose course for more than four years had caused so many vexations. It is in these words : —

" Whereas, Mr. Roger Williams, one of the elders of the church of Salem, hath broached and divulged dyvers newe and dangerous opinions against the auchthoritie of magistrates, as also writ letters of defamacion, both of the magistrates and churches here, and that before any conviction, and yet mainetaineth the same without retracion, it is therefore ordered, that the said Mr. Williams shall departe out of this jurisdiction within six weekes nowe next ensueing, which if hee neglect to performe, it shalbe lawfull for the Governor and two of the magistrates to send him to some place out of this jurisdiction, not to returne any more without licence from the Court." [2]

---

[1] Winthrop, i. 166. [2] Records, i. 160, 161.

19

He was thus free in his choice of any other place of habitation. He might go to Plymouth, to the Piscataqua, or elsewhere on this continent, or return to England; though a frank avowal of his opinions there might have brought upon him harder measure than he received here.

At this same Court, Endicott, who had been under suspension of office for mutilating the King's colors, after making a stout show of opposition, was ordered to committal, but "upon his submission and full acknowledgement of his offence he was dismissed." The Court seems to have resolved to act decidedly in the whole matter before it, for it —

"ordered that if the major parte of the freemen of Salem shall disclame the letters sent lately from the church of Salem to severall churches, it shall then be lawfull for them to send deputyes to the Generall Court." [1]

They did so. Neither in the interval of eight weeks between the courts in which Williams had been summoned, and the meeting of that in which he was sentenced, nor in the five weeks following, did Mr. Williams at all meet the expectations of the authorities by silence or caution in his speech. We learn from Winthrop that at the Court what seemed like gentle and patient efforts of appeal and remonstrance were made with Williams. His two letters — the one "to the churches complaining of the magistrates for injustice, extreme oppression," etc., and the other to his own church to persuade them to renounce communion with all the churches in the Bay, "as full of antichristian pollution," etc. — were brought before him. "He justified both these letters, and maintained all his opinions." On being offered a month's delay for further conference or disputation, he preferred present decision. Mr. Hooker, who was appointed to dispute with him, "could

[1] Records, i. 158.

not reduce him from any of his errours." So he was sentenced on the next day.[1] Williams afterward wrote of his resolve at this time,[2] that he was ready for his opinions "not only to be bound and banished, but to die also in New England, as for most holy truths of God in Christ Jesus." The date limiting Mr. Williams's departure expired on the end of November; but as he was reported to be ill, and on consideration of the season, he was informed that he might delay till the spring, on condition that he should not "go about to draw others to his opinions." Again we turn to Winthrop, who writes that in January, 1636 —

" The governor and assistants met at Boston to consider about Mr. Williams, for that they were credibly informed that, notwithstanding the injunction laid upon him (upon the liberty granted him to stay till the spring) not to go about to draw others to his opinions, he did use to entertain company in his house, and to preach to them, even of such points as he had been censured for; and it was agreed to send him into England by a ship then ready to depart. The reason was, because he had drawn above twenty persons to his opinion, and they were intended to erect a plantation about the Narragansett Bay, from whence the infection would easily spread into these churches (the people being, many of them, much taken with the apprehension of his godliness). Whereupon a warrant was sent to him to come presently to Boston, to be shipped, etc. He returned answer (and divers of Salem came with it) that he could not come without hazard of his life, etc. Whereupon a pinnace was sent with commission to Capt. Underhill, etc., to apprehend him and carry him aboard the ship (which then rode at Natascutt [Nantasket]); but when they came at his house, they found he had been gone three days before; but whither, they could not learn." [3]

We must infer that there was some interval of time between Williams's sending word of his illness and the

---

[1] Records, i. 171.

[2] Mr. Cotton's Letter Examined, etc., p. 5.

[3] Winthrop, i. 175, 176.

date of his departure. It is one of the quaint and charming illustrations of the kindly personal relations which existed between Winthrop and Williams, who appear here before us as magistrate and offender, that they must have had private friendly converse together as to what the banished man might most wisely do for the future. Williams wrote of this time, from Providence, to Major Mason, in 1670 : —

> " That ever honored Governour, Mr. Winthrop, privately wrote to me to steer my course to the Nahigonset Bay, and Indians, for many high and heavenly and publicke ends, incouraging me from the freeness of the place from any English claims or pattents." [1]

Reminiscences of our childhood's sympathy with " the Babes in the Wood " come up to us as we read the pathetic touches with which Williams refers to his wilderness experiences before his final comfortable rest at Providence. In the letter just quoted he writes Major Mason, " I was sorely tossed for one fourteen weekes, not knowing what bread or bed did meane." In his letter to Cotton he says he was " exposed to winter miseries in a howling wilderness." Again, he speaks of " the miserie of a Winter's Banishment amongst the Barbarians." Perhaps a recent writer, sympathizing with the exile in other of his experiences, is too keen on this point when he speaks of Williams on his course as " enduring hardships by the way with which we might perhaps sympathise more if we heard less of them from the sufferer himself." [2] Williams left Salem about the middle of January, with at least four companions; and there are intimations that some of his friends had preceded him to make preparations for him. They received the hospitalities of the natives at Sowam's (now Warren), Rhode Island, under the protection of Massasoit. Their experiences, probably, were not much unlike

[1] 1 Mass. Hist. Coll., ii. 276.
[2] The English in America (The Puritan Colonies), by J. A. Doyle, i. 166.

those of very many wayfarers then in these regions. The excitement at Salem continued after Mr. Williams's departure. Three men and eight women stood tenaciously for his opinions. Winthrop tells us that the Salem church sought advice of some of the other churches whether these dissentients should be encouraged to form a church by themselves. But this was disapproved.[1]

It is not to our purpose to follow the career of this firmly independent man in his experiences outside of Massachusetts. Being kindly reminded that at Sowam's he was within the then limits of Plymouth patent, he moved to the fair ·region on a finer bay, and received a present of land from a friendly sachem. There gathered around him, soon and afterward, a strange company representing " all sorts of consciences," men and women of strongly marked individualities and eccentricities emphasized and pertinaciously asserted. Lechford, in 1642, describes them as " a company of divers opinions ; most are Anabaptists ; they hold there is no visible church in the Bay, nor any true Ministerie." [2] The Scotch Presbyterian Bailey writes: " Sundry of the Independents are stepped out of the church, and follow my good acquaintance Mr. Roger Williams, who says there is no church, no sacraments, no pastors, no church officers or ordinances in the world, nor has been since a few years after the Apostles. " [3] True to covenanted obligations, Williams's deserted Salem church brought its admonitions and discipline to bear upon him by letters and committees in his exile, and finding him incorrigible, passed upon him, through his successor in office, the famous Hugh Peter, a sentence of excommunication.

Williams in his responsibilities in civil affairs with his new fellow-citizens was loyal to his principles of untrammelled freedom in " soul matters." He was, however, in

---

[1] Winthrop, i. 186. [2] Plain Dealing, p. 42.
[3] Letters and Journals, ii. 43.

continual broils and vexations with the independent minds and eccentric opinions and fancies of the strange variety among those more or less intimately associated with him in matters of fellowship, religion, or administration. Dr. Palfrey, in closing his judicial review of Williams's character and career, puts much of wisdom in the following sentence: "Roger Williams was not the first man, nor the last, to discover that it is one thing to conduct an opposition, and another thing to carry on a government." [1]

There has been much controversial discussion and comment, not wholly free of asperity of judgment, of the rightfulness, wisdom, and humanity of the dealing of the Massachusetts authorities with Roger Williams. No judicial review or opinion concerning it is called for, or would be in place here, as the single aim of the writer is to present each of the leading incidents in early Massachusetts as exhibiting the fruits and workings of the theocratic theory of government. For this purpose the reader asks, not for a plea, nor an arbitration, but the facts, as they have in this case been laid before him. It appears that the authorities, after the lapse of eight years had calmed the more excited passions of the quarrel, saw no reason to regret or blame, or reverse their action in the case. Mr. Williams made a voyage to England in 1643, where he obtained from the Commissioners of Plantations what is called the First Charter of Rhode Island. This did not convey a grant of land, but only powers for governing settlers according to the laws of England. On his outward passage, not having liberty to come to Boston, he embarked at New York. On his return he came to Boston provided with a letter from the Duke of Northumberland and others, seeking for him a passage through this jurisdiction. Of this, an early historian writes: —

"Upon the receipt of the said letter the Governour and magistrates of the Massachusetts found, upon examination of their

[1] History of New England, i. 423.

hearts, they saw no reason to condemn themselves for any former proceedings against Mr. Williams ; but for any offices of Christian love, and duties of humanity, they were very willing to maintain a mutual correspondency with him. But as to his dangerous principles of Separation, unless he can be brought to lay them down, they see no reason why to concede to him, or any so persuaded, free liberty of ingress and egress, lest any of their people should be drawn away with his erroneous opinions." [1]

It is pertinent to mention distinctly here two facts setting forth how Mr. Williams, in the exigencies and perplexities encountered in his new home with his unmanageable or intractable associates, was induced to commit himself to proceedings very strangely like to those his protesting against which had caused him and others such trouble in Massachusetts. Mention has already been made of the fact that in 1663, after the restoration of the Monarchy, Williams, with others, was a petitioner for, accepted, and held many offices under, a charter procured from Charles II., the terms of which, in its grant of land and powers of government, were substantially the same as those which he thought it so wicked in the Governor and Company of the Massachusetts to accept from a former English monarch. The other fact leads us to recall Mr. Williams's course in reference to the freeman's oath, to be taken by those who had the franchise, and the resident's oath, required of inhabitants not freemen. Within two years after his exile his restless companions at Providence, having as yet no patent, led Williams to realize the necessity that they should "be compact in a civill way and power." He wrote to Winthrop asking advice on a scheme which he suggested of providing " a double subscription," — otherwise, two forms of obligation. The one was to bind all householders, and others who should become such, in active and passive obedience to the orders and agreements made by the majority. The other subscription was to bind

---

[1] Hubbard's History of New England, p. 349.

young men and others, not householders, to a like obedience.[1] With the omission of the oath in each case, these subscriptions correspond to the two Massachusetts covenants. In the draft of the obligations as proposed by Mr. Williams, the restriction to "only in civill things" does not appear. It is introduced afterward. Historians of Massachusetts and historians of Rhode Island will probably for all time to come, as heretofore, have two ways of telling the life story in the former State of the founder of the latter; but they will alike honor and love the man.

Roger Williams, as the agent of the towns of Providence and Warwick for obtaining a charter, went to England in 1651. Wishing to embark from Boston, he addressed "a Humble Petition" to the General Court for liberty to come into the jurisdiction for that purpose. He refers to his banishment, and "the consequences (bitter Afflictions and miseries, Losses, Sorrowes, and Hardships)." Yet all through his "Exile" he had been "a professed and known servant" to this and all the Colonies, "in peace and war," averting troubles and mediating with the Indians. He owns that he is to go as a public agent to the High Court of the Parliament of England. He asks for civility and courtesy from the authorities, and promises to conduct inoffensively. He is ready, however, — as he always was, — to pause on his way and hold a debate with any two or three of the Court deputed for the purpose. His petition was granted, "provided he carry himself inoffencively, according to his promise." [2]

The wording of this petition and of the answer to it, fifteen years after the disputations and the sentence of banishment in the case of Williams, show us that while time enough had passed for the cooling of the passions of the hour, the opportunity for matured reflections had left both parties in the same mood of mind concerning

[1] 4 Mass. Hist. Soc. Coll., vi. 186.
[2] Ibid., iv. 471.

the original elements of the strife. This might serve as assurance to us that neither of the parties suffered from reproach of conscience.

How the people of Rhode Island rejoiced in their immunities may be inferred from the nervously worded terms in which they expressed themselves in a letter to their noble and steadfast friend Sir Henry Vane, in 1654. "We have not felt the iron yoke of wolvish bishops, or the new chains of the Presbyterian tyrants, nor in this colony have we been consumed by the over-zealous fire of the (so-called) godly Christian magistrates."

John Quincy Adams, in his admirable Address on the commemoration of the second century after the formation of the New England Confederacy, pronounced Roger Williams a "conscientiously contentious man." As I heard the grand ex-President speak those words, I remember being impressed by their peculiar felicity. More than that; as the speaker, then hardly mellowed, though in old age, had had full opportunity of knowing what his own temper had been in public life, I thought there was a rich candor in the description, as it applied as well to himself as to Williams. Far less fitting was Cotton Mather's description of Williams as "having a windmill in his head." A windmill must be adjusted by breezes and points of the compass, as Williams never was. He never turned on axis or spindle, though he created a stiff breeze when it was not furnished for his use. Within, he was tempered for the south wind. The air in which he most thrived was not from the sour east, but from the wholesome and bracing northwest.

In closing this episode in the theocratical history of Massachusetts, it is grateful to recur to the generous and lovable qualities, the friendliness and magnanimity of spirit of this signal sufferer, alike for his own conscience' sake, and from the workings of other people's consciences. Opinionative, obstinate, mischievous, and truculent as he showed himself to the authorities, he never indulged in his actions a single prompting of spite or malice. The tone of his correspondence, especially with the Winthrops, father and son, is respectful, courteous, and tenderly affectionate. We have farther on to note how the Quakers vexed his spirit and set him alike with tongue and pen upon a fair match in the free use of the epithetical adjectives and the hard names richly furnished in the English language. But in his personal argumentative and Scriptural trials of skill, logic, and rhetoric with others, we meet with no acid or bitter utterances. Even in his elaborate and most vigorous controversy with Cotton he seems sometimes to bring his antagonist into the mood of " lovers' quarrels," and to alternate between pats and spats. Noblest of all was he in his friendly services for Massachusetts in the quarrels and wars with the natives, as arbiter and peacemaker when this was possible, or otherwise as watchful to ferret out stratagems and treacheries, and to give wise warning to the people of the Bay.

In the year 1875 a petition bearing several names — which perhaps the bearers might not wish to be here copied — was presented to, and advocated before, the Legislature of Massachusetts, by a member of it, asking the revocation of " the sentence of banishment against Roger Williams," passed by the General Court in 1635. In this petition the cause of his sentence was said to be his championship of " perfect religious liberty." The reader of the preceding pages must decide for himself how truly that one definite and concentrated statement applies to all the subjects in controversy with Williams. Winthrop would have laid more stress upon the seditious tendency of Williams's utterances than even upon his schismatic opinions. The critical aggravation of his offences, which inflamed the whole community, was in writing in many directions his " letters of defamation " of the churches and their members. But however this may have been, the petitioners before the Legislature, and the member just referred to might, if better informed, have read in the State House, both in the original manuscript and in print, published by the Legislature, that their wish had been anticipated.

The words which are the most agreeable for a historian in these days to copy as a close for this subject, are the words of an Act passed by the Council of Massachusetts March 31, 1676 : —

"Whereas Mr. Roger Williams stands at present under a sentence of Restraint from coming into this Colony, yet considering how readyly and freely at all tymes he hath served the English Interest in this tyme of warre with the Indians and manifested his particular respects to the Authority of this colony in several services desired of him, and further, understanding how by the last assault of the Indians upon Providence his House is burned and himself in his old age reduced to an uncomfortable and disabled state, out of Compassion to him in this condition The Council doe Order and Declare that if the sayd Mr. Williams shall see cause and desire it, he shall have liberty to repayre into any of our Towns for his security and comfortable abode during these Public Troubles, he behaving himself peaceably and inoffensively, and not disseminating and venting any of his different opinions in matters of religion to the dissatisfaction of any." [1]

Roger Williams died in Providence in April, 1683, probably at the age of eighty-four, showing the robustness of a wilderness life, active, rough, and full of exposure. He is represented by living descendants. His memory is honored in many institutions, — as by a beautiful park and an ideal statue in Providence.

[1] Mass. Archives, x. 233.

MRS. HUTCHINSON AND THE ANTINOMIAN
CONTROVERSY.

AMONG the many reasons we have for satisfaction in the fading away into the troubled past of the old polemical and sectarian bitterness of religious controversy, we may welcome the disuse of many once familiar terms freely, but perhaps not even then intelligently, used as the symbols and technicalities of strife. The pulpit and the theological tractate made these terms vernacular to classes of persons in various grades of life. Recourse must now be had to an unabridged dictionary to learn their meaning. True, the tricks and mysteries of the stock-exchange and the political campaign have brought into use catchwords and vulgarisms by no means self-interpretative, and which may in some future age require a glossary to explain them ; but these popular catchwords are short, generally of a single syllable, though intimidating, as "bears" and "bulls." The technicalities of the old polemics ran into words of six and even seven syllables. Predestinarianism, Solifidianism, Supralapsarianism, and Antinomianism, and how many more like terms, representing the mastodons and megatheriums of a fossilized past in polemics, when brought under exhibition or study need to have labels in current speech to explain them. It might even be that some haphazard reader, catching under his eye this formidable word "Antinomianism," may have supposed that it had something to do with the drug called antimony.

As a fierce and bitter controversy, defined under that hard word, came very near to wrecking into total ruin with shame and passion the infant colony of Massachusetts, we must put the word into a modern interpretation. The frights which it caused were in part bugbears, but in part, too, actual moral and social perils. It is only by translating the jargon of polemics into plain ethical terms that we can reach the vital centre of that bitter strife.

To the stern and earnest Christian of the Puritan age, the most solemn and momentous question for his brooding thoughts, to be asked of any one who could help to answer it, was this: "How shall a man be justified with God," — put into right relations with God, acquitted by discharged and balanced obligations? It was admitted that the Bible alone could answer it with authority. But what answer did the Bible give to it? One called the great Apostle, Paul, taught them in many scattered sentences, called "texts," — as Romans iii. 28, v. 1 ; Galatians ii. 16, iii. 24, — that "justification" was to be obtained by faith, not by works, and that perfect obedience to the "law" was impossible for sinful men. Another Apostle, James, affirming that "faith without works is dead," taught them "that by works a man is justified, and not by faith only."[1] Here then were two covenants, the one of "works," the other of "faith." To the Puritan, the truth suspended between these two covenants was infinitely more momentous than the issue in his day between the Ptolemaic and the Copernican theory of the universe. Seeking still to modernize the terms and bearings of the controversy, let us use an illustration.

A debtor is hopelessly overwhelmed by the burden of pecuniary obligations. Whether crushed by misfortune, or through his own fault, he cannot discharge his debts, but is firmly held by them. If he is a man of an honest conscience and sound principle his burden is two-fold. In one form it is subjection to the rightful claims of others, pressed demandingly upon him and holding him to their exactions ;

[1] James ii. 24.

in the other form it is a painful, crushing self-infliction,
with a sense of failure and dismay. In the human and
business relations of such a hopeless debtor there is a
method of relief found in the processes of insolvency and
bankruptcy. The creditors, when having reason to believe
that there is no holding back, no fraudulent concealment,
consent to release the debtor once for all on a fragmentary
payment, leaving him free from the obligations of the past,
to try the future. But how of the other part of his burden,
the inner consciousness, with its pangs of undischarged
and undischargeable obligations, — what of that? Is there
any way of relief from it consistent with conscience and
integrity? There is one, for a truly upright and pure
man. If he feels sincerely and heartily assured within his
breast of a manly integrity of purpose, and can ascribe his
misfortune to causes other than wilful depraved self-seeking, he can look up to the light serenely, and feel released
from his inward burden. Of the sincerity of this inward
process the creditors cannot judge; they can have no certain knowledge of it. The debtor alone is his acquitter or
condemner.

We have in this illustration the elements of the religious
problem with which we are now concerned, — the obligations of a debtor no longer to his fellow-men, but to his
God. Accepted doctrine, certified by experience, had assured religious believers that it was practically impossible
for sinful men to be brought into right relations of approval and acquittal with God, — that is, to be "justified"
by strictly and fully meeting the exactions of His law.
But an alternative of leniency and mercy was provided
here. This was in a state of heart profoundly and humbly
conscious of undischarged duty, yet willing and longing to
meet such obligations, and giving a contrite and trusting
spirit as an equivalent. A perfect obedience and full discharge of debts would secure "justification" by "a covenant of works." The alternative of this would be a release

by "a covenant of grace." The latter, if honestly and sincerely assured, would bring perfect peace, as to a debtor not only released by his creditors, but quieted by the conscience within.

Here were two forms and methods of "justification." Incident to a belief in, a reliance upon either of them, and the availing one's self of the relief afforded, were risks, possible errors, and perils. One who should try, even proximately, to meet the exactions of the law, as under a covenant of works, would find life a constant and unending struggle, through vexations, scruples, and compunctions,—watchful at every point, lest in observing one injunction he should fail of another ; balancing punctilios ; mechanically faithful even in trifling matters ; "praying without ceasing ;" asking a blessing upon and giving thanks for every morsel of his food, that it might not be his bane ; keeping in close converse with God, lest he be unguardedly left to himself ; seeking his rule in everything in the Scriptures ; practising a constant introspection and reckoning with his heart ; noting its meteorology in heights and falls of devotion ; confusing sometimes the protests of a dyspeptic or bilious stomach with the pangs of conscience ; and attempting to meet the terms of a covenant of works by " sanctification," — by becoming holy.

The other covenant, that of " grace," was beset by many perplexities and dangers. It is difficult to put into concise and simple terms the significance of the word " antinomianism," as commonly used. Etymologically, it would signify antagonism, opposition, to the law ; but by usage it meant, without the help of the law, independence of it, and elevation above it. Instead of a relief from obligation by a compliance with a covenant of works, it trusted to an inward assurance of having been brought into right relations with God, accepted and forgiven, by a gracious influence of his Spirit. The process and work were wholly internal, known and experienced and witnessed only by the individual himself. The creditors of an insolvent debtor could not possibly have any positive knowledge of his integrity of purpose. But God, " reading the heart," could judge of its sincerity, its penitence, its supreme longing to be at peace with him. But the risks of delusion, of enthusiasm, of self-deception, and of applying flattering unction to the heart and conscience, were the besetting perils of the Antinomian. He might be tempted to compound for a class of sins and infirmities, and trust more to the "peace" which he enjoyed in spite of them than to the fidelity of his struggles against them. All the abounding and extraordinary forms of sectarism among the fanatics and enthusiasts that swarmed in the Puritan age were affiliated with Antinomianism. As they boasted of intimate private relations and intercourse with God, they claimed to have individual revealings from him, — promptings of what they should do or leave undone. Some of them even frankly and boldly claimed immunity for serious breaches of the laws of morality. None of them indeed could profess to claim a warrant of Scripture for an actual contempt of the methods of "sanctification;" but it seems to have been an open question with the zealots of Antinomianism how closely they must keep themselves to the law of " works," though repudiating its covenant as a whole. They could not fail to note that some of their neighbors, who sought to make sanctification their rule, attained only to what is known as *sanctimony*. Opposition to " Legalism" was only the negative side of Antinomianism. Deep spiritual exercises and experience made its positive side. " Good works " were the fruits of piety, not proofs of it. A changed heart would insure holiness; a form of life might only assume the show of it.

It is grateful to every one who reviews historically the ensuing controversy about Antinomianism in Massachusetts, that with the exception of a single case there was no charge or proof of immoral behavior, of looseness, or license brought against any reputed disciple of the heresy. This exceptional case was a very marked one. It was that of the redoubtable military officer, Capt. John Underhill, who having served valorously in the wars of the Low Countries and in Cadiz, coming to Boston with Winthrop in 1630, became a member of the church, and Court Deputy. He was a man of prowess and a sturdy Indian-fighter, and as such was to the Bay Colony much what Miles Standish was to Plymouth. Standish's infirmities were those of a hot temper, and of using strong vernacular language. Moreover, he was never "under covenant;" but Underhill was. His gross sensuality — the relation of which by Winthrop illustrates his own guilelessness — brought him under the severest church penalties, from which he secured relief and restoration by protestations and hypocritical tears. He was a unique and a pictur-esque offender. Avowing Antinomian principles, he had the front to give the Church this account of his inward justification: "He had been under a spirit of bondage and a legal way five years, and could get no assurance; till at length, as he was taking a pipe of tobacco, the Spirit sent home an absolute promise of free grace, with such assur-ance and joy as he never since doubted of his good estate, neither should he, though he should fall into sin." [1]

Mrs. Anne Hutchinson, with her husband, William, and their family, arrived in Boston, Sept. 18, 1634, and her brother-in-law, Rev. John Wheelwright, and family, arrived May 26, 1636. The mention of the name of the wife before her husband's by Winthrop is a recognition of her more prominent position, though her husband was in sympathy with her opinions and shared her experiences. Winthrop, with a possible bias of judgment, wrote of him as "a man of a very mild temper and weak parts, and wholly guided by his wife." [2] He was a "merchant." Wheelwright, who had been a contemporary with Cromwell

[1] Winthrop, i. 270. [2] Ibid., i. 295.

at Cambridge, and vicar of a church near Alford, was displaced by Laud for nonconformity. The avowed purpose of Mrs. Hutchinson and of some others who came with her was to renew the satisfaction of enjoying "Mr. Cotton's ministry." We are reminded here, in view of the large immigration and the influx of persons of consequence at that period, that the colony must have witnessed here the meeting of many parted friends who had been in close relations of friendship and religious sympathy in England. Possibly, too, in some cases the seeds of earlier alienations may have been transplanted here. But strong and tender ties bound many of them together, especially those who had shared in common misfortunes. The young exiled scholar John Harvard, for instance, whose benedictive generosity has been fruitful here for more centuries than he lived years upon this soil, renewed during his brief sojourn the fondest associations of his academic life. The records of the first church show that Mrs. Hutchinson was admitted to membership in November, 1634. This was a month after her husband's admission. The delay in her case is explained by what gives us a forecast of the agitation of which she was to be the cause. Her fellow-passenger, Symmes, afterward minister of Charlestown, communicated to the church the uneasiness he had felt as to her opinions and elations of spirit, and the " venting of her revelations," on the passage. Her husband became a freeman March 4, 1635, and was at once sent by Boston as a deputy to the Court.

Mrs. Hutchinson immediately made herself known, confided in, and loved, by a steadily increasing number of intimates, by her kindly services to those of her own sex, in the privacies of their own homes, in their special needs. It seems as if she limited this most intimate friendliness to the women of her little neighborhoods of Boston; for while her influence prevailed here on the opening of the conflict, it does not appear to have extended outside. She

possessed marvellously that gift, from her time onward
of high esteem in New England, known as "capacity."
She could minister to body, mind, and spirit, and had skill
in a comprehensive pathology. Welde, of Roxbury, ever
unfriendly to her, describes her as "a woman of a haughty
and fierce carriage, of a nimble wit and active spirit, and
a very voluble tongue, more bold than a man, though in understanding and judgement inferior to many women.", He
also calls her "the American Jezabel." Though he should
have known her, as before he wrote she was an inmate of
his brother's home, we cannot accept this sharp judgment
of her. More true and appreciative are other words of
his: "A woman very helpful in the time of childbirth, and
other occasions of bodily disease, and well furnished with
means for those purposes."[1] Her services were those of
a friend, not of a hireling. The women revealed to her
their experiences and burdens. As these were matters of
comparison in confidence, it was inevitable that she should
be at the risk of gossip, actively and passively. Maladies
of mind and spirit were more prevalent and severe than
those of the body, under the morbid conditions of life and
thought given to religious questioning and brooding. The
transition was easy, in these confidences, to free converse
on the help to be derived from the teachings of the differ
ent ministers in sermons, conferences, and lectures. These
soon reached down to matters concerning the deepest secrets of one's being. There was a spirit of cheerfulness,
and an evident relief from the sternness of the prevailing
teaching, in the views of Mrs. Hutchinson. She was assured that the consciousness of a Heaven-directed heart,
and a prevailing purpose of rectitude, would secure to the
spirit a serenity not to be attained by the formalisms of
piety. She drew a broad distinction between an external
devoutness in deportment, tone, speech, and method of life,
with rigidity and austerity of aspect, and that penetrating

[1] Welde, Short Story, p. 31.

peace of heart which confided itself to divine grace working within. Many of the incessant religious meetings were of men only. But in those of both the sexes, silence was the attitude of women, except when relating their religious experience. Mrs. Hutchinson soon gathered around her, first in her own home, and occasionally in the homes of others, groups and companies of women, ranging from fifty to near a hundred, who seem first to have occupied themselves with doing only more freely and searchingly what was done in every Puritan household, — repeating and discussing the last delivered sermon. As she herself had come over to New England again to enjoy the ministrations of Mr. Cotton, her preference and strong approval of him were very manifest. This proved in the event to be prejudicial to the general esteem for a time of that honored teacher. When the conflict arose, he was claimed to favor and side with certain opinions, and when he afterward complained of misjudgment, and alleged that he had been made a covert and ensnared, his exceptions and rectifications exposed him to suspicions of inconsistency, if not even of duplicity. As a member of the Boston church, Mrs. Hutchinson could not enjoy his ministrations as teacher without listening also to those of the pastor Wilson. Her manifest and freely expressed preference of the preaching of the former, and her depreciation of that of the latter, was the entering wedge of the parting controversy which was to convulse the colony. To the keen and watchful discernment of this gifted woman the two elders had adopted and presented two widely contrasted schemes for the nurture of the religious life. The teaching of Wilson covered external observance, deportment, and sanctifying methods severely exacting; the teaching of Cotton aimed to kindle a deep heart-piety, calm, serene, and self-assuring. The reports of her critical judgments expressed with force and frankness went forth from her meetings through the tongues of her hearers, with a more or less adequate comprehension of their full significance, to be received and repeated under the same condition of risks as to their intelligent apprehension by those who caught the echoes of them. Comparisons and personalities were the raw material of strife; and some persons other than the wholly illiterate began to hear and use words new to them.

At this point, in preparing to follow out the occasion for the intense excitement and even passionate altercations leading to severe judicial proceedings which were to follow, it may be well to remind ourselves to what an extent personal relations of friendship or alienation entered into it. This was especially one of that class of controversies which engage feelings and sentiments more strongly than opinions and convictions. The discussions and altercations provoked by the original points of variance soon ran into abstruse metaphysical and technical forms of expression, in which it was utterly impossible that the mass of those involved in them should follow them with any clear mental apprehension. Of course, therefore, many were parted by prejudgments and personal preferences between the parties, and these were respectively led by the most honored and influential alike of the magistrates, the citizens, and the ministers. The town of Boston, with nearly all the members of its church, came to pronounce their adherence to Mrs. Hutchinson; while the country towns and churches, with their elders, were almost without exception from first to last out of sympathy with her.

The public agitation, however, independently of what came from rumor as to the teachings of Mrs. Hutchinson in her women's meetings, was opened by other parties, whose appearance and agency we must now notice. Winthrop[1] notes the arrival here on Oct. 6, 1635, of "two great ships," with a notable company. The two of these most distinguished in historic fame for strong traits of character, for strange careers, and for their tragic fates,

[1] Winthrop, i. 169.

were Henry Vane and Hugh Peter, as he himself wrote his
name. It was just at the time when the Court had sentenced Williams to banishment. Winthrop thus writes of
Vane : —

" Here came also one Mr. Henry Vane, son and heir to Sir
Henry Vane, comptroller of the king's house, who being a young
gentleman of excellent parts, and had been employed by his father
(when he was ambassadour) in foreign affairs, yet, being called to
the obedience of the gospel, forsook the honours and preferments
of the court to enjoy the ordinances of Christ in their purity here.
His father being very averse to this way (as no way savouring the
power of religion) would hardly have consented to his coming
hither, but that, acquainting the king with his son's disposition
and desire, he commanded him to send him hither, and gave him
license for three years' stay here."

Of the other noted passenger Winthrop writes : —

" Mr. Peter, pastor of the English church in Rotterdam, who,
being persecuted by the English ambassadour, — who would have
brought his and other churches to the English discipline, — and
not having had his health these many years, intended to advise
with the ministers here about his removal."

He succeeded Williams at Salem. Mr. Vane was admitted a member of the Boston church Nov. 1, 1635,
within a month after his arrival. It may well excite our
surprise to note how these two strangers at once made
themselves prominent, by appearing and taking part in a
very delicate matter of variance between the two most influential magistrates of the Colony. John Haynes was
then Governor, but was soon to remove to Connecticut.
There had always been a lack of perfect cordiality in the
relations between Winthrop and Dudley, but mediation
had to a degree harmonized them. At this critical time
the variance was again opened. It touched the point that
when in office Winthrop had " carried matters with more

lenity and Dudley with more severity."[1] Factions had
thus been raised among the people, each of the two having
his adherents. Some of the magistrates and elders were
prompted by Vane and Peter to hold a meeting in Boston
for disposing of the matter, "where, after the Lord had
been sought, Mr. Vane declared the occasion of the meeting, and the fruit aimed at, a more firm and friendly
uniting of minds." Vane informed Winthrop of the censures he had heard of his leniency, which had not come
to Winthrop's knowledge, and with some tender pathos
pleaded for full accord between him and Dudley. Governor Haynes, apologetically, and yet frankly, unbosomed
himself in referring "to one or two passages wherein he
conceived that Winthrop dealt too remissly in point of
justice." The ever gentle and magnanimous Winthrop replied that he might in some matters have been misunder-
stood. But he advanced as his judgment in general, —

"that, in the infancy of plantations, justice should be administered with more lenity than in a settled state, because people were
then more apt to transgress, partly of ignorance of new laws and
orders, partly through oppression of business and other straits;
but, if it might be made clear to him that it was an errour, he
would be ready to take up a stricter course."

The matter was referred to the ministers to consider
and report a rule on the next day. The conclusion and
advice were —

"that strict discipline, both in criminal offences and in martial
matters, was more needful in plantations than in a settled state,
as tending to the honour and safety of the gospel."

Winthrop said —

"he was convinced that he had failed in over-much lenity and
remissness, and would endeavour (by God's assistance) to take a
more strict course hereafter."

[1] Winthrop, i. 177.

He was soon to have occasion for the exercise of an austerity and severity not natural to him. We mark at this point the strengthening in the Colony of a harsh spirit already sufficiently strong. The meeting broke up with "a renewal of love," and an agreement upon ten articles, covering strictness, courtesy, and formal observances in Court. The last of these had significance for men in a wilderness who had seen pageantry, robes, liveries, and processions: "The magistrates shall appear more solemnly in publick, with attendance, apparel, and open notice of their entrance into the court." Vane and Peter were thus put on a footing with the first comers, and initiated into contentions in which they were to take a full part. The war against the Pequot Indians was now in preparation, amid many distractions and perplexities. The readiness and heartiness with which Vane threw himself into the service of the Colony at this juncture may relieve his officious engagement in what was to be a perilous contest.

It was not till the end of October, 1636, when she had been two years in Boston, doing her works of love and exercising her gifts, that Winthrop mentions Mrs. Hutchinson, and as follows: —

"One Mrs. Hutchinson, a member of the church of Boston, a woman of a ready wit and bold spirit, brought over with her two dangerous errours: 1. That the person of the Holy Ghost dwells in a justified person; 2. That no sanctification can help to evidence to us our justification. From these two grew many branches, as (1) Our union with the Holy Ghost, so as a Christian remains dead to every spiritual action, and hath no gifts nor graces other than such as are in hypocrites, nor any other sanctification but the Holy Ghost himself." [1]

A pause must be allowed here to recognize an element which worked effectively and mischievously in the coming strife. The reader may have noticed that many of the

[1] Winthrop, i. 200.

quotations already made from Winthrop in these pages end with an "etc." In some cases this sign probably indicates a lack of time for the writer to complete an intended fuller statement. In others, it evidently represents an unfinished action of his own mind, and intimates to the reader the opinions or conclusions which the writer would have reached or expressed. Nor is this all Winthrop, all through this controversy especially, and in other cases, was in the habit of drawing "inferences" or deductions of his own from the avowed opinions of others. There was enough even in the most clearly stated propositions of Mrs. Hutchinson and her friends to try the faculties and to startle the apprehensions of those not in sympathy with her. But when her opponents proceeded to infer other propositions which they thought must naturally and consistently follow from her premises, they introduced many new complications and perplexities in the controversy. Winthrop, as just quoted, draws one of his own inferences from Mrs. Hutchinson's expressed opinions, evidently intending to have drawn more which he had in mind as objectionable. Cotton (foremost among Mrs. Hutchinson's earlier friends), Wheelwright, and others complained that they were thus made answerable for opinions and notions not really chargeable upon them. Winthrop adds to the above, — "There joined with her in these opinions a brother of hers, one Mr. Wheelwright, a silenced minister, sometimes in England." It was with him, not with her, that the strife was to be opened, as Winthrop dates it, Oct. 30, 1636. The church of Boston was already furnished with a pastor and a teacher, well-trained and able men, by the standard of their time, and up to the opening trouble equally confided in and beloved.

It now transpired that many members of the church, having come under the influence of Mrs. Hutchinson and her brother-in-law, had "propounded" that the latter be called to office as an additional teacher, Oct. 30, 1636.

" One of the church stood up and said he could not consent, etc." This was undoubtedly Winthrop. After his " etc." he gives his reasons. They were reasons of force and persuasion. The church was well furnished —

" with able ministers, whose spirits they knew, and whose labours God had blessed in much love and sweet peace, he thought it not fit (no necessity urging) to put the welfare of the church to the least hazard, as he feared they should do, by calling in one whose spirit they knew not, and one who seemed to dissent in judgement, and instanced in two points, which he delivered in a late exercise there: 1. That a believer was more than a creature; 2. That the person of the Holy Ghost and a believer were united. Hereupon the governour [Vane] spake, that he marvelled at this, seeing that Mr. Cotton had lately approved his doctrine. To this Mr. Cotton answered, that he did not remember the first, and desired Mr. Wheelwright to explain his meaning. He denied not the points, but showed upon what occasion he delivered them." [1]

Here we have the elements of the strife, the chief parties in moving it, with an earnest listening group, silent, or if speaking, not reported to us. An attempt was made at reconciliation. Winthrop said that though he might possibly agree with Mr. Wheelwright, and —

" thought so reverendly of his godliness and abilities, so as he could be content to live under such a ministry, yet, seeing he was apt to raise doubtful disputations, he could not consent to choose him to that place."

The church yielded, that Wheelwright might be called to another at Mount Wollaston.

The breach was to be widened, not closed. Winthrop had given offence to some of the brethren by what he had said against Wheelwright. He should have charged him privately, not publicly. " In his speech appeared some bitterness." By his " inferences " he had ascribed to

1 Winthrop, i. 202.

Wheelwright some opinions which he did not hold. Partly by apology and partly by explanation Winthrop vindicated himself, but he stood stoutly by his "inferences" as following from Wheelwright's avowed opinions. We may believe that Vane took part in the dispute. In conclusion, Mr. Winthrop besought of Wheelwright —

"seriously and affectionately, that seeing these variances grew (and some estrangement withal) from some words and phrases [as "the person of the Holy Ghost and real union"] which were of human invention, and tended to doubtful disputation rather than to edification, and had no footing in Scripture, nor had been in use in the purest churches for three hundred years after Christ, that for the peace of the church, etc., they might be forborn."

The noble magistrate added, that it was not his call or place publicly to dispute these matters; but if any brother privately "desired to see what light he walked by, he would be ready to impart it to him." No one of the church replied. Soon after Winthrop "wrote his mind fully, with such scriptures and arguments as came to hand, and sent it to Mr. Cotton." [1]

At the General Court, May 25, 1636, the members in their pride and hope in having among them the son and heir of a privy-counsellor, had assigned the sage and moderate Winthrop to the second place in the government, and put over him the young and inexperienced enthusiast Vane, of the age of twenty-four, who had been in the country not yet eight months. "Fifteen great ships" in the harbor gave him "a volley of shot," and the Governor invited the masters to dinner.

The next phase of the contention is thus presented by Winthrop, under date of Nov. 17, 1636: —

"The governour, Mr. Vane, a wise and godly gentleman, held with Mr. Cotton and many others the indwelling of the person of

[1] Winthrop, i. 203, 204.

the Holy Ghost in a believer, and went so far beyond the rest as to maintain a personal union with the Holy Ghost; but the deputy, with the pastor and divers others, denied both; and the question proceeded so far by disputation (in writing, for the peace' sake of the church, which all were tender of) as at length they could not find the person of the Holy Ghost in Scripture, nor in the primitive churches three hundred years after Christ. So that all agreeing in the chief matter of substance, viz., that the Holy Ghost is God, and that he doth dwell in the believers (as the Father and Son both are said also to do), but whether by his gifts and power only, or by any other manner of presence, seeing the Scripture doth not declare it — it was earnestly desired that the word ' person ' might be forborn, being a term of human invention, and tending to doubtful disputation in this case." [1]

Now we are presented with a scene and occasion which, with its mingling of sentiment, pathos, tears, and a seeming vacillation of purpose on the part of Vane, offers to the reader matter for his own interpretation.

Governor Vane, in previous conference with the Council and some others, had procured a meeting of the General Court to be called, out of course, for Dec. 7, 1636, on a representation which he had made to the magistrates that letters received from friends recalled him home on matters of urgency in his private affairs. The Court records do not describe what followed as fully as does Winthrop. Vane made known the case; then writes Winthrop: —

"One of the assistants using some patheticall passages of the loss of such a governour in a time of such danger as did hang over us from the Indians and French, the governour brake forth into tears, and professed that howsoever the causes propounded for his departure were such as did concern the utter ruin of his outward estate, yet he would rather have hazarded all, than have gone from them at this time, if something else had not pressed him more, viz., the inevitable danger he saw of God's judgements to come upon us for these differences and dissensions

[1] Winthrop, i. 206.

which he saw amongst us, and the scandalous imputations brought upon himself, as if he should be the cause of all; and therefore he thought it best for him to give place for a time, etc. Upon this the court concluded that it would not be fit to give way to his departure upon these grounds. Whereupon he recalled himself, and professed that the reasons concerning his own estate were sufficient to his own satisfaction for his departure, and therefore he desired the court he might have leave to go; as for the other passage, it slipped him out of his passion, and not out of judgement." [1]

The Court then consented to his departure, assured, as the record says, " of his serious resolution to return to us again." [2] Though the Court took measures for a special meeting, — it not being thought discreet to risk the government on the life of the deputy, — there proved to be no occasion for it; for in the mean while some of the Boston church, after consultation, sent to the Court a protest against Vane's leaving for the reason assigned. On this he, professing himself " an obedient child of the church," added that " without its leave he durst not go away."

The end was not yet. The court of deputies proceeded to call in the elders, to advise about pacifying the differences of opinion so heated among them. Some of the elders had " drawn into heads all the points wherein they suspected Mr. Cotton did differ from them, and presented them to him." Vane took great offence at this preliminary action of the ministers. The sturdy and plain speaking Hugh Peter confronted Vane, as if he had been the spring of all the troubles, telling him —

" how it had sadded the ministers' spirits that he should be jealous of their meetings, or seem to restrain their liberty, etc. The Governour excused his speech as sudden and upon a mistake. Mr. Peter told him also that before he came, within less than two years since, the churches were in peace, etc. The governour answered that the light of the Gospel brings a sword, and the

[1] Winthrop, i. 207-208. [2] Records, i. 185.

children of the bondwoman would persecute those of the free
woman. Mr. Peter also besought him humbly to consider his
youth, and short experience in the things of God, and to beware
of peremptory conclusions, which he perceived him to be very
apt unto." [1]

The reader may well infer that such altercation and
bickering as this, between two such spirits as were represented by Vane and Peter, would not help to harmonize
the relations between those so scripturally classed by the
Governor as respectively under "a covenant of grace"
and " a covenant of works." Winthrop adds that Mr. Wilson, with evident reflections on a somewhat ambiguous
sermon preached on the same day by Cotton, —

"made a very sad speech of the condition of our churches, and the
inevitable danger of separation if these differences and alienations among brethren were not speedily remedied; and laid the
blame upon these new opinions risen up amongst us, which all the
magistrates except the governour and two others did confirm, and
all the ministers but two."

Out of the jargon of the discussion which followed, the
least unintelligible sentence is the question whether "evident sanctification could be evidence to a man without a
concurrent sight of his justification?" Vane and Cotton
answered "no." Of course Mr. Cotton took Mr. Wilson's
speech "very ill," and with "divers others" went to admonish him. But Wilson stood for the right of a free utterance of opinion which had been asked of them all by the
Court. He was reproached with bitterness on all sides in
the congregation, whereas that under the strong urgency
of Vane, Winthrop had but one or two supporters. But
Wilson firmly sustained his own warm friend, and "answered them all with words of truth and soberness, and
with marvellous wisdom." Well might Winthrop add,
" It was strange to see how the common people were led,

[1] Records, i. 209.

by example, to condemn him [Mr. Wilson] in that which (it was very probable) divers of them did not understand." It would be wearisome and profitless to follow into further details this phase of the controversy. With alternate attempts, as it advanced, to use "love and gentleness," and with manifest interminglings of very bitter feelings, the strife increased till it was evident that it could find its close only in some civil action or in a catastrophe. Fortunately there was then no printing-press in the country, and when there was a brief intermission in the oral disputations in the meeting-house, many of the contestants had recourse to written papers which were copied and passed around. These, not to our loss, are not extant. Cotton wisely took care that all his own papers on the quarrel should be burned before his death.

Simply as another illustration of the leading aim under which this volume is written, — namely, to trace the perplexities and vexations, as well as the nobleness and virtues of these Puritan people to their way of receiving and using the Scriptures, — one further quotation from Winthrop will be helpful : —

"Other opinions brake out publicly in the church of Boston, — as that the Holy Ghost dwelt in a believer as he is in heaven ; that a man is justified before he believes ; and that faith is no cause of justification. And others spread more secretly, as that the letter of the Scripture holds forth nothing but a covenant of works; and that the covenant of grace was the spirit of the Scripture, which was known only to believers ; and that this covenant of works was given by Moses in the ten commandments; that there was a seed (viz., Abraham's carnal seed) went along in this, and there was a spirit and life in it, by virtue of which a man might attain to any sanctification in gifts and graces, and might have spiritual communion with Jesus Christ, and yet be damned.[1] . . . All the congregation of Boston, except four or five, closed with these opinions, or the most of them; but one of the brethren [Win-

[1] Winthrop, i. 211.

throp] wrote against them, and bore witness to the truth, together
with the pastor, and very few others joined with them.[1] The rest
of the ministers" taking offence at Cotton's doctrines and sympathy
with the obnoxious party, "drew out sixteen points," some of
which "he cleared," but on others "he gave not satisfaction."

The reader is advised not to attempt to work his brain
upon these propositions with an effort to understand what
they mean, or to explain how human beings, with the
ordinary cares of life to engage them, could possibly stir
themselves into an excitement concerning them. Their
remoteness of meaning and of intelligibleness to us will
have their due effect, if they help us to realize that we
are not to judge by our own standards men and women
of a long past, who could not only listen intently to the
discussion of such matters, but could also quarrel bitterly
about them.

Replies were made to Cotton, but only to the further
vexing of the strife. He seems to have been the only one
who tried to be an umpire, moderating between the two parties, and leaving himself open to misunderstanding by both
of them. The ministers agreed to give up all their week-
day lectures for three weeks, "that they might bring
things to some issue." A Fast was kept in all the churches
on Jan. 20, 163$\frac{6}{7}$, for sundry reasons, among them "the
dissensions in our churches." A ship being about to sail
for England, there was reasonable anxiety and alarm as
to the reports she would carry of the prevailing distractions, to the grievous injury of the troubled Colony. So
sermons and letters were written to relieve the aspect of
things and to put the best face on them, as aiming only
in various ways "to advance the grace of God." Winthrop writes : —

"Every occasion increased the contention, and caused great
alienation of minds; and the members of Boston (frequenting the

[1] Winthrop, i. 212.

lectures of other ministers) did make much disturbance by public questions, and objections to their doctrines; and it began to be as common here to distinguish between men, by being under a covenant of grace or a covenant of works, as in other countries between Protestants and Papists." [1]

The next General Court furnished occasion for new excitement. The speech of Wilson at the previous Court was brought under question, but the majority passed upon it an approval. The ministers were called upon for advice as to the authority of the Court in things concerning the churches. They agreed in two things: (1) That without the license of the Court a church could not call any man in question for what he had said there; (2) That all heresies or errors of a church member, as are manifestly dangerous to the State, may be dealt with by the Court, without waiting for the church; but that doubtful opinions are first to be dealt with by the church. As Mr. Wheelwright was to be proceeded with for a sermon he had preached on the Fast Day, "which seemed to tend to sedition," nearly all the members of the Boston church petitioned the Court that as freemen they might attend the proceedings as a case of judicature, and that the Court would declare its right to deal with cases of conscience before the church. The petition was pronounced to be a groundless and presumptuous act, and it was answered " that the Court was always open in judicial cases, but chose to proceed privately in matters of consultation and preparation of causes." One Stephen Greensmith, " for saying that all the ministers except A. B. C. [Cotton, Wheelwright, and Hooker] did teach a covenant of works, was censured to acknowledge his fault in every church, and fined £40." [2] Cotton, having preached in the Boston church on the morning of the Fast Day, Wheelwright preached in the afternoon. His sermon, which was the occasion for his subsequent banishment, is charac-

---

[1] Winthrop, i. 124.   [2] Records, i. 214.

terized by Winthrop, with great severity and sharp censure, as offensive, vehement, and bitter against all described as " walking in a covenant of works," and as designed to stir up the people against them. And it was the more to be complained of because the occasion of the Fast was to promote reconciliation, and was used by Wheelwright to kindle and increase differences. In no one of the documents bearing upon this controversy will impartial and discerning readers see more clearly than in this, tested by Winthrop's judgment of it, the evidence of the morbid, high-wrought and inflammable state into which the feelings of men and women had been stirred by this distracting strife, largely on unintelligible matters. Those who listened so testily to the preacher must have heard between the lines and sentences, interpolating from their own suspicions and fancies what he neither uttered nor suggested. The sermon seems to us earnest, but wholly peaceful, kindly, and harmless.[1]

It is to be noted that neither Mrs. Hutchinson nor her brother-in-law Wheelwright ever assumed to be Antinomians. On the contrary, he, in the sermon for which he was dealt with, expressly repudiated the name. But the magistrates and Court interpreted their expressed opinions as involving what they held in dread as such. In Europe the sect known as Antinomians were the disciples of John Agricola, a tailor, born at Eisleben in 1492, afterward a university scholar, rector, and preacher, and in 1526 chaplain of the Elector of Saxony, at the diet of Spire. As a disciple and worker with, and afterward an opponent of, Luther and Melanchthon, he carried to extreme the doctrine of the former of justification by faith, in opposition to the Roman Church doctrine of good works. He afterward renounced his errors. Both his disciples and his enemies

---

[1] From a copy found in manuscript in the State House it has been thrice put into print. See a volume of the Prince Society's Publications, Boston, 1876. The sermon expressly warned the hearers "to have care that we give not others to say we are libertines or Antinomians."

perverted doctrines which he had carefully and guardedly defined. So Antinomianism came to stand for — what the authorities of Massachusetts held it to be — a grossly immoral doctrine; superseding the need of good works, and reaching the monstrous conclusion that nothing which a believer might do could be sin.

After much debate with elders and others, the Court judged Wheelwright guilty of sedition and contempt. Vane and a few others, dissenting, tendered a protestation, which the Court rejected. The Boston church sent in a petition justifying the sermon. Sentence was deferred to the next Court, and the ministers were consulted as to whether Wheelwright could be enjoined to silence in the interval. As they were in doubt on this point, he was commended to the care of the Boston church.

Though the first Court held in Boston had pronounced it "the fittest place in the Bay for publique meetings," an exception was now to be made. The town and its church were strongly and almost unanimously on the side of the man who was to undergo sentence. So, after much contention, the Court was appointed to be held at Newtown (Cambridge). Vane refused to put the motion for this to vote; Winthrop, "because he dwelt in Boston," hesitated to do so, except required by the Court; so Endicott put it. One of those manifestations of feeling, petulant, or conscientious, as we may regard them — to which reference has been made, occurred at this time. Vane, Cotton, Wheelwright, "and the rest of the Boston church that were of any note," refused to attend an ordination at Concord, because they accounted the candidates for office to be "legal preachers."

Things were in a state of ferment, of jealousy, passion, and struggling partisanship, at the meeting of the Court of Elections, at Newtown, May 17, 1637. Vane tried to anticipate the regular course of business by reading a petition from many of the town of Boston. This, Winthrop,

as Deputy Governor, opposed, as clearly out of order and
obstructive. After protracted contention and uproar, only
stopping short of personal violence, a division was effected.
The meeting was on a warm day, held out of doors. Mr.
Wilson then inaugurated "stump speaking" at an election
on this continent. Seated on the bough of a tree, he ha-
rangued the people on the proper business of the day as
provided by the Charter. The majority carried it for the
old order of things, electing Winthrop Governor, Dudley
Deputy, with their former associates as Assistants, in place
of Vane and his friends, Dummer, Haugh, and Coddington.
Boston delayed the choice of its deputies till this result
as to the magistrates was reached, and the next morning
elected Vane, Coddington, and Haugh, to the inferior office.
The Court rejected them on a technicality, but they were
re-elected and then received. Some piques and slights
followed this upturning in official places. The sergeants
" being all Boston men," who with their halberds had been
wont, with a form of state, to attend Vane to and from
public meetings, "never less than four of them," in respect
to his being " a person of quality," refused to perform the
same service for Winthrop. He declined the proffer of the
Court to furnish others, and set to that use two of his own
servants. Both he and Vane were put thus into relations
very exacting upon their courtesy and magnanimity. The
elder of the rivals sustained well his self-respect and dignity. Vane, with those who had been left out with him,
abandoned their wonted seats with the magistrates in the
meeting-house, and sat with the deacons; nor when solicited by Winthrop to do so would Vane resume his former
seat. A flood of papers now came forth : from the magistrates, to justify their course against Wheelwright ; from
him, qualifying or explaining passages in his sermon; and
from the ministers, on all the tangled threads of the controversy. Winthrop says that " Mr. Cotton reduced matters to a very narrow scantling," and that had it not been

for the heat of former alienations, there might have been reconciliation, as " only the few who knew the bottom of the tenents of those of the other party, could see where the difference was."[1] The Court deferred sentence against Wheelwright till its next session in August, hoping that the effect of a general Fast Day, and further conferences with the ministers, would help to reduce the alarming excitement of the community, and also exhibit the moderation of the Court when so provoked, and reconcile matters.

The only relieving motive which, amid the abounding stores of interesting and instructive matter for his perusal, can sustain the patience of the reader of our time in following the details of this to him petty, often unintelligible and wholly profitless dispute, is that by it he is helped to put himself into more or less sympathetic relations with those who, in the seclusion and limitations of their situation and experience, could thus exalt such matters of contention into themes of supreme and transcendent importance. One of the results and fruits of the steady progress made by generations in advanced and liberalized views is, that the themes opened for debate and discordance of opinion become larger and of more serious import. And the larger the theme, the more serious and momentous its import, the nobler is the range of human faculties engaged upon it, while the vexing and inflammatory passions which stir a petty strife are kept in check. The opponents of Vane, Mrs. Hutchinson, and Wheelwright in this heated altercation sought to conserve their fundamental covenant in the terms of it drawn from the Bible. But the perplexity was that the so-called Antinomians raised perfectly fair questions as to the interpretation of the Biblical terms of that covenant. The Quakers by and by were to raise an issue which subordinated that covenant. The Antinomians took one step toward liberalizing it.

But a fresh matter of contention now came in to engage the

[1] Winthrop. i. 221.

zeal and pen of Vane during the short remaining period of his stay in the country. It was an act passed by the Court for the protection of the country against an apprehended trouble from the expected coming here of persons of weight who might favor the obnoxious opinions. This act forbade, by a heavy pecuniary penalty, the entertainment by any resident of any stranger for more than three months, or the sale of land to such, without permission of one or more magistrates. This order, which Winthrop says was designed to keep out persons " who might be dangerous to the Commonwealth," proved very obnoxious to most of the people of Boston, who treated Winthrop with slights on his return to the town. Mr. Cotton was so aggrieved by the order as to meditate a removal to New Haven. Winthrop wrote an earnest argumentative " Defence " of this order, which presents a point of great interest to us. With evident sincerity and earnestness of conviction, and with much weight as coming from the foremost promoter of the Colony, Winthrop maintains that the Charter conferred exclusive right of territory on the patentees, and a power such as a householder has, of restraining from entrance in his domicile of any unwelcome visitor. Vane wrote an " Answer " to this " Defence," and Winthrop followed with a " Replication." [1]

A Thanksgiving Day was observed for a victory over the Pequots. Winthrop, making a visit to Ipswich, received guards and great respect, beyond his wishes, through all the towns, as an offset to the slights of Boston. Private alienations were very much embittered. There was then in Boston Lord Leigh, son of the Earl of Marlborough, a youth who had come to see the country. Winthrop invited him and Vane to dine with him ; but Vane declined, " alleging by letter that his conscience withheld him." [2]

Vane, accompanied by Lord Leigh, sailed for England on the 3d of August. His friends, many of them in arms,

[1] The three papers are in Hutchinson's Collection of Papers, pp. 67–100.
[2] Winthrop, i. 232.

honored him with volleys of shot and salutes from the vessel and from the fort. Winthrop could not leave the Court, but had given orders for this honorable dismission.

The historian Hubbard, who should have known, says that the Court had passed an order that henceforward no man should be qualified for the place of governor until he had been at least one year in the country. No such entry appears on the records. Whether or not this stinging arrow was shot at the young nobleman, it is certain that his rejection, even as a magistrate, must have satisfied him that while he had a large circle of the most attached friends, including those of prominence in Boston, the ministers and the majority of the people regarded him with great disfavor, and held him chargeable with the fierce dissensions, the estrangement and acrimony of feeling, and more than all for the threatenings of sedition and alarming outbreaks which they apprehended. He left matters in a state of fearful distraction. The two ministers of his church were made to lead two angry factions. The honored and ever true-hearted Winthrop, now dependent upon his own calm of spirit in meeting the coldness and misrepresentations of those to whose welfare he had devoted his life, was so sorely buffeted that his equanimity was shaken, to the extent of a possible failure of judgment. The strife was yet to rage, with new elements of variance and bitterness. In dismissing Vane from any further direct agency in it, it is most just to him, and most grateful to one reviewing this dissension, to be able to add that he took home with him no grudges, no personal smarts. He had done good service while here, in aiding the younger Winthrop's business for the settlement of Connecticut, as agent for Lord Say and Sele and Lord Brooke. He had also been in warm sympathy with Roger Williams in his views of what ought to be the relations between the whites and the Indians. He performed many kindly offices, and was ever ready to render helpful service to Massachusetts and New England when he had influence with those who held the helm of State. Two widely different estimates of his character and career, with its tragic close, have come down to us from those writing in the interest of parties. To some he represents all that is impracticable, visionary, and revolutionizing in the wild idealism and theorism of a zealot and enthusiast in religious mysticism, brought to bear upon affairs of State. To others he presents himself as one of the noblest, wisest, and best of English worthies, in the purity of his purposes and the consecration of his wisdom and virtue to the highest human services. It is by that estimate of him that Milton immortalized him in his grand sonnet. Vane distrusted Cromwell, and openly rebuked him for his ambition for the kingship. Cromwell, in return, called Vane a " juggler," and Carlyle adopts the epithet. Clarendon regarded him as " a man of extraordinary parts ; a pleasant wit, a great understanding, which pierced into and discerned the purpose of other men with wonderful sagacity, whilst he had himself *vultum clausum.*" Dean Swift, in terms characteristic of his own personality, wrote to Burnet, " Vane was a dangerous enthusiastic beast." Sir James Mackintosh says, " Vane was probably the first who laid down with perfect precision the inviolable rights of conscience, and the exemption of religion from all civil authority." Hallam says, " The royalists have spoken of Vane with extreme dislike ; yet it should be remembered that he was not only incorrupt but disinterested, inflexible in conforming his public conduct to his principles, and averse to every sanguinary and oppressive measure." Richard Baxter was perplexed and offended by the element of mysticism in Vane, and coupling him with Sterry, another with whom he was at variance, cast a gibe at both of them, in writing of their principles as " Vanity and Sterility." The King was faithless in his royal promise to save Vane from execution, as his father had been to Strafford. The sentence that Vane should " be hanged, drawn, and quartered at Tyburn," was " mitigated " to beheading on Tower Hill. He refused the proffer to petition for his life. Vane's wife was allowed to pass the night with him in the Tower before his execution. With a view to possible results, he required that an attested record of the fact should be made by the lieutenant of the Tower. His posthumous son, Sir Christopher Vane, was sworn of the Privy Council, under James II., Aug. 12, 1688. There is a tinge of romance in the connection of such a man as Vane, the friend of Milton and Roger Williams, and once of Cromwell, with our early days of Indian warfare and religious contention. His portrait should hang in our State House.

We return to the scene and actors of the strife in Boston. Mrs. Hutchinson was continuing her women's meetings, gathering toward her jealousies which were to manifest themselves after the case of her brother-in-law had been disposed of. Though he was under censure of the Court, sentence had been deferred pending the attempts at conciliating at least some of the differences by the circulation of papers. But as if in unconsciousness of the fact that the ingredients already mingled in the strife were sufficient to overtask the shrewdest and most practical skill brought to deal with them, the leaders of the parties rallied new contributors to it. Hooker and Davenport came from Connecticut and had many meetings with the elders, and it was agreed, that with the consent of the magistrates there should be a conference of a most comprehensive kind on the 30th of August. This was preceded by a day of humiliation on the 24th. Mr. Davenport, from a text [1] rebuking those who cause divisions, after the ingenious fashion of so many of the clergy in all time, preached a sermon most adroitly adjusted to promote the mischief designed to be averted. So in the Boston church " he clearly discovered his judgement against the new opinions and bitter practices which were sprung up here." [2]

[1] 1 Corinthians, i. 10. [2] Winthrop, i. 236.

Cotton then took his turn, expounding the occasions on which civil rulers might consult with the ministers of the churches.

The New Town (Cambridge), where the earliest measures were then in inception for the planting of the wilderness college, has been the witness in the lapse of years of many occasions engaging thought and speech upon all subjects concerning the highest interests of humanity. But we may feel assured that none of these occasions has enlisted a profounder earnestness of expectation, a more intensified spirit of fervor and zeal, nor more acute and stimulating exercises of mind and soul, than that of which we are now to write. Not convinced, as so many of us in these times are, that clerical synods have been among the worst pests and perils of Christendom, through all the ages, the Court had provided that the first of them in the long list of those that have since been held on this continent should be convened at Newtown, Aug. 30, 1637. Stimulated to fever heat were all the passions and sentiments that were to be engaged in it,—in ministers, delegates, or "messingers" from the churches, and magistrates. The synod was to be composed of all the contestants and parties to the strife, instead of having any of the character of an external or independent tribunal which might be looked to as an impartial arbitrator. The diet of those in attendance, and the travelling expenses of those coming from outside the Colony, were to be paid from the public treasury. "There were all the teaching elders through the country, and some new come out of England, not yet called to any place here, as Mr. Davenport, etc."[1] Cotton, as the head of the ministers, had he not been so prominent a party, would naturally have been the moderator. But Bulkeley of Concord and Hooker of Connecticut shared that honor. After prayer by the pastor of Cambridge, Shepard, the assembly listened to the reading of a most

[1] Winthrop, i. 237.

extraordinary paper, signed by all the ministers except
Cotton. This was a gathering up and an attempted classification of all the "erroneous opinions spread in the country," including "unwholesome expressions," "unsavory
speeches," and "abused Scriptures," or texts falsely or
wrongly turned to arguments. There were exactly eighty-
two erroneous opinions. They were largely "inferences"
again, constructions, deductions, glosses, tasking the ingenuities and technicalities of speech to give them intelligible expression, and often failing of that. Well is it
written, "with the heart man believeth." There could have
been but very little of mind in most of those propositions.
That noble, but much abused word, "opinions," signifies the
fruits of thought, the results of thinking. And this meaning the word ought always to carry with it, if we are to
listen otherwise than contemptuously to the common plea
that "every man's opinions are entitled to respect." We
cannot yield that respect to notions and fancies when we
know that they involve no real thought, that nothing from
the working brain or the brooding mind has gone into
them. Opinions are to be formed, not taught or adopted.
The startling inventory read before the synod would be
as unintelligible to-day, save to experts, as would be the
formulation of a process in modern chemistry. The intent
was to impute the responsibility for all these erroneous
opinions, unwholesome expressions, and unsavory speeches,
to the party of Cotton, Wheelwright, and Mrs. Hutchinson.
Cotton was willing to bear testimony against most of them
as heretical and absurd, while some of them were blasphemous; but he would not condemn them all. Every one
in the synod, lay or clerical, had free speech in debating
the propositions through three weeks. This statement,
however, must be qualified. Some in attendance from the
Boston church were irritated and scandalized at having
such a travesty of heresies, crotchets, and absurdities ascribed to them, and protested that the publication of them

would bring a reproach on the whole country. They insisted therefore that the names of persons chargeable with such notions should be given. This the synod would not consent to, alleging that it was dealing with "heresies," not with persons. To their over-urgency with protests they received a hint that they would be withheld by the magistrate, lest they should provoke a civil disturbance. Some of these Boston protesters then left the synod and never returned to it.

The opinions, so called, were discussed, then papers and arguments were prepared on both sides, with attempts to simplify and clear up. This met with partial success. The result, approved by a large majority, to which some assented, without subscribing, was a condemnation of the new "opinions." The last day of the three weeks' session was given to some other debating. With an eye to what was going on vigorously in Boston, under the lead of Mrs. Hutchinson, the following proposition was agreed upon:

"That though women might meet (some few together) to pray and edify one another, yet such a set assembly (as was then in practise at Boston) where sixty or more did meet every week, and one woman (in a prophetical way, by resolving questions of doctrine, and expounding Scripture) took upon her the whole exercise, was agreed to be disorderly and without rule." [1]

Restraint was also put upon the freedom of speech and questioning by persons after sermon. The magistrates' help might be engaged to compel the attendance of one under church censure who would not present himself to meet it, — another illustration of the steady advance in identifying civil and religious administration. A fourth conclusion was, that a member differing from the rest of the church on "an opinion not fundamental," ought not for that reason to forsake the ordinances there; "and if such did desire dismission to any other church, which was of his

[1] Winthrop, i. 240.

opinion, and did it for that end, the church whereof he was ought to deny it for the same end." The increasing individuality and eccentricity of opinion was not, however, to be withstood by thus restraining the liberty of choice in seeking more congenial fellowship and ministrations. The individual would be likely to regard his special opinion as "fundamental" to him. These multiplying annoyances and variances incident to the attempt to bring into forced accord those whose "tender consciences" and busy wits were inventing scruples and notions, were sure to increase under the activity of church discipline. It is, however, to be kept in mind that each member when entering into fellowship pledged himself to come under "the watch and ward" of the church. This obligation was indefinable as to its extent and range.[1]

Governor Winthrop was so relieved and gratified by the general temper and conclusion of this assembly, "all in love," that he yielded to one of those occasional failures of discretion, — not frequent with him, — and " propounded if it were not fit to have the like meeting once a year, or at least the next year, to settle what yet remained to be agreed, or if but to nourish love." He adds, " This motion was well liked of all, but it was not thought fit to conclude it." A fortunate decision. To the credit of the ministers it is to be noted that they objected to any measures being adopted by the assembly for providing a method for their maintenance "agreeable to the rule of the Gospel." They would avoid the imputation of using the assembly for their own advantage. Mr. Davenport closed the synod with a discourse in which he prepared the way for more divisions by preaching against them. A Thanksgiving Day was kept on the 12th of October for victories over the Pequots, and " for the success of the assembly; but by reason of this latter some of Boston would not be present at the publick exercises." [2]

---

[1] Winthrop, i. 243.   [2] Ibid.

We are well prepared to find Winthrop acknowledging his disappointment when it proved that the action of the assembly, so far from pacifying the strife, was followed by further contention. He had thought that Wheelwright and his party had been clearly confuted and confounded; but they were by no means of that mind themselves, and showed their discontent by renewed activity. The General Court, meeting on the 2d of November, 1637, availed itself of what Winthrop calls an " opportunity." Whether the device adopted ought not to be defined by a very different term, let the reader judge. It will be remembered that at a Court held on the 9th of March, eight months previous, a remonstrance or petition had been offered by some of Boston, in earnest behalf of Wheelwright and in indirect censure of the Court. No notice was at the time taken of this remonstrance, and it was passed over in subsequent sessions in May and August. But this Court determined, on consultation, to make it available for a purpose which Winthrop thus states: —

"The Court finding that two so opposite parties could not contain in the same body, without apparent hazard of ruin to the whole, agreed to send away some of the principal." [1]

There were more than sixty signers to the remonstrance. One of these, William Aspinwall, was a deputy to the Court from Boston. On suspicion — which proved to have reason — that he had drawn the paper, he was dismissed from the Court, then called again to be disfranchised and banished. The same disposal was made of John Coggeshall, another Boston deputy, who, though he had not signed, yet said he approved the petition. The indignant constituency of Boston proposed to send them back to the Court again, but Cotton dissuaded them. Yet the town found such difficulty in selecting such deputies as it approved, while unacceptable to the Court, as to leave the places vacant during the session. Wheelwright was then summoned. He refused to yield either "his opinions, his place, or his public exercisings." He was disfranchised and banished, his appeal to the King being denied. He was allowed to go to his house on his promise that if he were not gone out of the jurisdiction in fourteen days he would yield himself to one of the magistrates.[1]

The terms of the sentence are as follows : —

"Mr. John Wheelwright, being formerly convicted of contempt and sedition, and now justifying himselfe and his former practice, being to the disturbance of the civill peace, hee is by the Court disfranchised and banished, having 14 days to settle his affairs; and if within that time hee depart not the patent, he promiseth to render himself to Mr. Stoughton, at his house to bee kept till hee bee disposed of." [2]

Before quoting from the Records the disposal made of Mrs. Hutchinson, we may read Winthrop's account of her arraignment : —

"The Court also sent for Mrs. Hutchinson, and charged her with divers matters, as her keeping two public lectures every week in her house, whereto sixty or eighty persons did usually resort, and for reproaching most of the ministers (viz., all except Mr. Cotton) for not preaching a covenant of free grace, and that they had not the seal of the Spirit, nor were able ministers of the New Testament: which were clearly proven against her, though she sought to shift it off. And after many speeches to and fro, at last she

---

[1] Winthrop, i. 246.

[2] Records, i. 207. Mr. Doyle — "The English in America" (Puritan Colonies), i. 180 — pertinently remarks upon the new elements which excitement and agitation had introduced in the original matter of the controversy, "that the attitude of Wheelwright and his associates was not precisely what it had been at the outset. It is clear that both he and his sister were among those to whom strife was a delight. A combative temper, the need for satisfying that love of novelty which they had themselves done so much to create, and that spirit of aggressive opposition which even the semblance of persecution begets in original and self-reliant minds, all prompted them to extend their differences from the established creed."

was so full as she could not contain, but vented her revelations: amongst which this was one, — that she had it revealed to her that she should come into New England, and should here be persecuted, and that God would ruin us and our posterity, and the whole State, for the same. So the Court proceeded and banished her; but, because it was winter, they committed her to a private house, where she was well provided, and her own friends and the elders permitted to go to her, but none else." [1]

This private house was that of Mr. Joseph Welde in Roxbury, brother of the elder, one of the bitterest opponents of Mrs. Hutchinson. Her "revelations," private special illuminations, which she claimed were made to her by the Spirit, were the dynamite missiles of those times which struck shocks of indignation and dread in those who restricted all communications between God and men to the Bible. But it needed no special revelations to forebode the ruin likely to befall the wilderness colony in its first score of years if these distractions were not quieted.

A report of this trial, covering forty pages, from an unknown hand, enables us to follow its course, and to catch its salient points. [2] Winthrop presided, and put most of the questions and charges. His position, office, and duty were most trying to him. We have to fall back upon our profound impressions of the deep sincerity and integrity of his character, his singleness and devotion of purpose, and the consecration of his fortune and life to a beloved work which he saw threatened with a dire and humiliating catastrophe, to read without some faltering or misgiving of approval, not to say with regret and reproach, the method with which he conducted the examination of this gifted and troublesome woman. Her weapon was a censorious tongue; her defensive armor was a consciousness of a pure and sanctified heart. Impartiality, if it involved any degree of tolerance and sympathy, was, under the circumstances,

---

[1] Winthrop, i. 247.

[2] Hutchinson's History of Massachusetts, ii. Appendix.

impossible. For three years Winthrop had seen his social and church fellowship with once loving and trusting friends riven by alienation, by asperity, and by uncharitableness of judgment. His official duties had been embarrassed by hostile partisanship. A youthful rival for the confidence and honors of the people, after a short residence here, had left open many bleeding wounds and inflamed much angry passion. And, above all, the strife which was raging was mainly concerned with unintelligible propositions, used to furnish catchwords of jealousy, disparagement, and offensive comparisons utterly unedifying as concerning their religious guides. Winthrop seriously and earnestly, but without heat, charged Mrs. Hutchinson with the matters of offence already stated, as promoting strife and factions, and as being the prime cause and agent in their grievous troubles. To her request for some specific accusation, Winthrop reiterated his charges. After the Puritan fashion in quoting Scripture, he used her transgression against the civil law in entertaining strangers, as a breach of the commandment to honor parents. She had also countenanced Wheelwright for his sermon, and the signers of the remonstrance. Winthrop, abashed in his dignity, or parting with his courtesy, said, " We do not mean to discourse with those of your sex." To the complaint against her for holding women's meetings, she quoted " a clear rule in Titus, that the elder women should instruct the younger." To the question of the Governor, whether if a hundred men should come to her for instruction she should impart it, she said she should not; and when the question was varied, she said she would instruct any one man coming for the purpose. She naïvely asked, " Do you think it not lawful for me to teach women, and why do you call me to teach the Court?" The Governor told her that her rule from Titus meant that " elder women should instruct the younger about their business, and to love their husbands." She thought the duty included

22

more; and then the Governor reminded her of the divisions, dissensions, and distraction caused by her meetings. She still insisted to know what " rule from God's word " forbade her. Winthrop replied, " We are your judges, and not you ours, and we must compel you to it." The Deputy Governor, Dudley, here interposed, reviewing the dissensions of the last three years, all of which he charged upon her and Vane; also that she had implicated Mr. Cotton, " who hath cleared himself that he was not of that mind." Bradstreet and Endicott put in questions, but Mrs. Hutchinson kept her self-command and answered with discretion. Hugh Peter then spoke at length, stating that Mrs. Hutchinson's fellow-passengers had suspicions of her opinions, and that when it was bruited that she drew invidious comparisons between ministers, he with some others who felt aggrieved called her to account; and after some debate, " tender at the first," had drawn from her the plain avowal of " a broad difference between our brother Mr. Cotton and ourselves." The " inferences " they forced upon her were that the others were not able ministers, and " had not the seal of the Spirit."

Six other ministers testified plainly that in interviews with them she had drawn the same invidious distinction between them and Cotton. She replied that they had got this frank opinion from her " in a way of friendship," which was afterward, not with her intent, used in reproach publicly. Some discussion followed about Scriptural texts. On the next day Winthrop began by reviewing the yesterday's proceedings. The Court declined Mrs. Hutchinson's request that the witnesses be put under oath, and there was much debating upon it. Mr. Cotton was called in and put in a very embarrassing position by having to admit that, to his own regret, she had drawn the unfavorable distinction between himself and the other ministers. The discussion soon reached the matter of " revelations," and Mrs. Hutchinson was understood as saying that she had assurance that God would relieve her of all trouble. Winthrop caught at this as proving her "desperate enthusiasm." Cotton was drawn into sharp altercation by endeavoring to define two kinds of "revelations." Winthrop in his impatience parted with judicial impartiality, and pressed for sentence. Two of the Court opposed it, and one more refused to vote. Winthrop put the question "whether it was the mind of the Court that, for the troublesomeness of her spirit, and the danger of her course," she should be banished, and until she could be sent away, be imprisoned? Mr. Jennison, deputy from Ipswich, declined to vote either way, offering to give his reasons if desired. Mr. Coddington, magistrate, and Mr. Colburn, deputy of Boston, opposed the motion. All the other members of the Court approved.

The sentence is recorded as follows: —

"Mrs. Hutchinson (the wife of Mr. William Hutchinson), being convented for traduceing the ministers and their ministery in this country, shee declared volentarily her revelations for her ground, and that shee should bee delivred and the Court ruined, with their posterity, and thereupon was banished, and the meane while was committed to Mr. Joseph Weld untill the Court shall dispose of her." [1]

Those who had shown their approval of this prime offender, and were more or less in sympathy with her as manifested by having their names on the Remonstrance, were visited with various penalties. Ten of the signers apologized for the act, and wished to have their names erased. There must have been lively work in the Court, as the resolute or the timid one by one were called for judgment.

There have been differences of opinion expressed upon the manifesto issued by the Court in justification of these and of its subsequent proceedings. The issue is whether

[1] Records, i. 207.

the apprehension it avowed of a threatened insurrection and resistance of the government was sincere, with reasons that operated as warnings, or a mere pretence to avert charges of tyrannical severity.

The substance of the manifesto and order is as follows:

"Whereas the opinions and revelations of Mr. Wheelwright and Mrs. Hutchinson have seduced and led into dangerous errors many of the people heare in New England, insomuch as there is just cause of suspition that they, as others in Germany, in former times, may, upon some revelation, make some suddaine irruption upon those that differ from them in judgement — "

the Court proceeded to add an order that certain persons named, should on penalties for delay or refusal, before the 30th of the month (November, 1637), give up all their arms and ammunition of every kind, to those designated for receiving them. Of those named, fifty-eight were of Boston, including some of its best and most trusted citizens. This is true also of citizens of other towns, — five of Salem, three of Newbury, five of Roxbury, two of Ipswich, and two of Charlestown, — who were to be disarmed. Such of these as would " acknowledge their sinn in subscribing ' the seditious libel,' or do not justify it," were to be exempt from the order. Mrs. Hutchinson was to be kept in charge at Roxbury, at the expense of her husband.

Winthrop makes note of an incident occurring at this time to which reference is to be made as illustrating the fact that he, as a magistrate, chose to remind the church that he was not amenable to its discipline for some things done by him in that capacity. He had prepared and sent to England for publication an account of the proceedings in the Court with observations upon them, "to the end that our godly friends might not be discouraged from coming to us."[1] Many of the Boston church took offence

[1] Winthrop, i. 249.

at this, and prompted the elders to call him to account
for it. Coming to the knowledge of this, and wishing to
avert the disorder that might follow by addressing it to
the congregation, he anticipated it and prevented it. His
plea was a Scriptural one, and he quoted the authority
of Christ for the independence of the civil power. The
examples of Uzziah, Asa, Salam, Abiathar, Lot, Hagar,
and Ishmael come in to illustrate parts of his argument.
None the less the churches had their duties yet to perform
to those who as under their " watch and ward " had been
proceeded against by the civil power. After " admonitions " pronounced in vain, the Roxbury church cast out
diverse of its members. " In their dealing with them,
they took some of them in plain lies and other foul
distempers." [1]

The whole community had been wrought up into a fever
of restlessness, anxiety, murmuring, readiness to listen to
all idle rumors and suspicions, which court and church
tried in various ways to restrain and quiet. The Court
passed an order for severe penalties against all who should
question or contemn any of its proceedings or sentences:
it attempted to secure dignity and accountability in the
behavior and speech of the magistrates, and saved the
privilege of petition as of free use " in any way of God."
In the Boston church some wasted their time and zeal
in ferreting out from the by-currents of privacy all secret
opinions and extravagances, and magistrates and elders
spent two days over these trivialities. The only one
among them intelligible to us is " that there is no resurrection of the body." From Mrs. Hutchinson's denial of
a corporeal resurrection it seems to have been inferred that
this supreme idealist was a materialist. Her real opinion
was " that the souls of men are mortal by generation, but
are afterwards made immortal by Christ's purchase." Mr.
Cotton availed himself of the opportunity to affirm that he

[1] Winthrop, i. 250.

had been abused and made a "stalking horse" by the heretics, in being quoted as holding some of their notions which he abhorred. Meanwhile Mrs. Hutchinson at Roxbury was daily beset by elders and others in efforts to convince or to convict her. It is a marvel that she retained her reason under these rasping afflictions. They found her still to hold some thirty "gross errours." Fifteen of these were put into shape and sent to Boston church, as matter for dealing with her after a lecture in March, 163$\frac{7}{8}$.

The governor and treasurer, being members, were allowed to leave the Court at Newtown, that they might attend the church meeting. The "errours" being read to her, after standing for them a while, Mrs. Hutchinson appeared to yield, as if "convinced by reason and scripture." She was then plied with three more errors, but she would not admit the opinions to be such. With but two dissidents, and these her own sons, the church voted that she should be admonished, "and because her sons would not agree to it, they were admonished also." This distressing church session was prolonged till eight at night, when "Mr. Cotton pronounced the sentence of admonition with great solemnity, and with much zeal and detestation of her errours and pride of spirit." "The special presence of God's spirit" was felt in the assembly, and the harassed woman had a respite till "the next lecture day." [4] Some "chief military officers, who had declared themselves favorers of the familistical persons and opinions," being sent for, acknowledged that "the opinions and practice tended to disturbance and delusions," and thanked God for their deliverance. In the interval before her second appearance before the church, Mrs. Hutchinson, having "given hope of her repentance," had been permitted by the Court to make her home with Mr. Cotton, in order that he and his guest, Mr. Davenport, "might have the

[1] Winthrop, i. 256.

more opportunity to deal with her." It is to be hoped that thus among personal friends, perhaps partial sympathizers, sharing kindly hospitality, and in incessant talking upon subjects made of lively interest to all parties, the troubled spirit of the woman found some repose. At the meeting of the church, March 22, 163$\frac{7}{8}$, —

" the articles being again read to her, and her answer required, she delivered it in writing, wherein she made a retractation of near all, but with such explanations and circumstances as gave no satisfaction to the church; so as she was required to speak further to them. Then she declared that it was just with God to leave her to herself as he had done, for her slighting his ordinances, both magistracy and ministry; and confessed that what she had spoken against the magistrates at the court (by way of revelation) was rash and ungrounded, and desired the church to pray for her. This gave the church good hope of her repentance; but when she was examined about some particulars, as that she had denied inherent righteousness, etc., she affirmed that it was never her judgement; and though it was proved by many testimonies that she had been of that judgement, and so had persisted, and maintained it by arguments against divers, yet she impudently persisted in her affirmation, to the astonishment of all the assembly. So that after much time and many arguments had been spent, to bring her to see her sin, but all in vain, the church, with one consent, cast her out. Some moved to have her admonished once more; but it being for manifest evil in matter of conversation, it was agreed otherwise; and for that reason also the sentence was denounced by the pastor [Wilson], matter of manners belonging properly to his place." [1]

I have copied the foregoing paragraph from the Journal of the Governor, who was present at both the examinations of Mrs. Hutchinson before the church after the Thursday Lecture. His record prompts many suggestions. It closes his account of a controversy which had been in progress for three years, steadily becoming more embarrassed and

[1] Winthrop, i. 257, 258.

obscure in the propositions of opinion and doctrine which
it involved, and with increasing bitterness in its alienations
and heats of spirit. We must take in connection with
Winthrop's statement the following entry on the ancient
records of the First (then the only) Church of Boston:

"The 22d of the 1st Month [March], 1638, Anne, the wife of
our brother, William Hutchinson, having on the 15th of this
month been openly, in the public congregation, admonished of
sundry errors held by her, was on the same 22d day cast out of
the church for impenitently persisting in a manifest lie then expressed by her in open congregation."

I cannot believe either that Mrs. Hutchinson was guilty
of "a manifest lie," or that Winthrop and the church
would have attributed to her the heinous offence because
of prejudice or opposing judgment. Nor need one look
beyond the obscurity and intricacy of the terms used in
the statement of equally obscure and intricate propositions
of doctrinal beliefs, to find a reconciling medium for the
integrity of both parties. Undoubtedly Mrs. Hutchinson
became inextricably involved in the maze and labyrinth
of the utterly unprofitable strife, and was open to misapprehension and misrepresentation by others who could
not follow her abstractions and qualifications. She had
made courteous and womanly apologies for any failures
of social etiquette or respect for magistrates. But she
had persuasions, deeply cherished sentiments, opinions,
and beliefs which, though they might not signify the same
to her and to others, whose interpretation and inferences
from them as false or mischievous she could not accept,
she could not and would not renounce.

But how, we may ask, had it come about that, while
three years, and even less than two years before, she had
carried with her in sympathy and support all but half-a-
dozen members of the Boston church, its sentence now
should be a unanimous one against her? Three reasons

for this offer themselves. The firmest, warmest, and most influential of her friends had no part in these proceedings, and were not present at them. Some had been banished, or had gone away, or yielded to their feelings and would not attend. Again, some really stood in fear of the penalties of the Court, — of banishment and separation from their families, which their friends had already suffered. And once more, a real alarm was working in the panic-stricken community, of a complete disruption of all peace and order as likely to result from some of the " inferences," which they had come to understand as rightfully drawn from Antinomian doctrines and practices. A further word from Winthrop adds an explanation : —

" After she was excommunicated, her spirits, which seemed before to be somewhat dejected, revived again, and she gloried in her sufferings, saying that it was the greatest happiness, next to Christ, that ever befel her. Indeed, it was a happy day to the churches of Christ here, and to many poor souls who had been seduced by her, who, by what they heard and saw that day, were (through the grace of God) brought off quite from her errours, and settled again in the truth." [1]

Cotton had been put to a severe trial in pronouncing the first church censure upon Mrs. Hutchinson. He has been called " a trimmer " and " a coward," " a false friend " and a mean time-server, for the course which he pursued. Of the justice of these personal constructions and judgments, a candid and considerate reader must decide for himself. Of all the persons concerned in these painfully distracting proceedings, Cotton had been the most privileged for knowing and comprehending the sentiments and principles, the Christian graces and virtues, and the unselfish services to others of this highly-endowed woman. Her regard, confidence, and affection toward him were very strong. It was to renew and continue the satisfaction she had found in his

[1] Winthrop, ii. 256.

ministry that she had left her English home and joined
the exiles here. But the wholly spontaneous and un-
guarded way in which she manifested her partiality for
him became at once embarrassing to him. To be singled
out by her, as he was, emphatically, and soon offensively,
as "the only one of the ministers in the Bay" whose
preaching was pitched in the tone of vital truth for edification, and to have this preference impressed and reiterated to the groups of admiring women who listened to
her words with respect for her character and gratitude for
loving and skilful service, would act as effectively upon
his repute as upon her own. The caprices as well as the
convictions of her female followers would lead to words,
acts, tokens of like and dislike, of sympathy and of antipathy, in the presence both of men and women. The toss of
the head, the look of aversion, the thronging upon the dis-
coursings of Mr. Cotton, and the pressing out from the
assemblies when other elders were to preach, were aggravations not to be unheeded. The fact that the young and
interesting nobleman Henry Vane, after having been only
seven months in the Colony, with which he had no intent
to cast in his lot, and who had been enthusiastically caught
up to displace the faithful and experienced Winthrop, was
one of the few men privileged to attend the women's
meetings, sharing with their leader the partiality for Mr.
Cotton, was another embarrassment to that elder. It is
certain, also, that Cotton sympathized with and approved
some of her first utterances, as he understood them. Indeed, she may have adopted her distinctive views, or the
mode of expressing them, from him. Apart from all the
subsequent developments and aggravations of the contention, it would have been perfectly natural and accordant
with the religious fervors and engrossing theological interest of the community, that there should have been from
time to time, agitating it, a brisk and vigorous polemical
excitement. This would have been as much in keeping

with the fitness of things as are drill-parades and sham-fights for exercising regiments in camp. But it was those developments and aggravations of the original elements of the contention, the "inferences" and deductions of opinion, the "exorbitant doctrines" and "unsavory speeches," that might well prompt Cotton, as we have seen, to plead that he had been wrongfully claimed as in sympathy with the extremes to which the controversy had been carried.

When a real or only a panic-like alarm struck through the community of coming disasters forenounced by "Revelations," and memories were recalled of the Antinomian and the Anabaptist abominations and prostrations of civil order and decency in the Low Countries, in Munster, and under John of Leyden, Cotton might well enter his protest against being charged with overt sympathy with the revolutionists. When he saw more than fifty of his own flock — some the most honored and foremost citizens of Boston — deprived of their arms, disfranchised, and some banished, he might shrink from being regarded as the chaplain of sedition. But Cotton shifted the sentencing upon Wilson as the pastor in the final scene.

Before pronouncing the first church censure of admonition upon Mrs. Hutchinson, Cotton recognized with warmth and tenderness the deep and high esteem in which she had been held in the community for her generous and valued services; but he added that her recent course and heresies had caused more harm by exciting such distraction and apprehensions of dread, even among her friends. "He laid her sin to her conscience with much zeal and solemnity; he admonished her also of the height of her spirit: then he spake to the sisters of the church, and advised them to take heed of her opinions, and to withhold all countenance and respect from her, lest they should harden her in her sin." [1] These were sad if not harsh and cruel words to

---

[1] Welde's Short Story, etc., p. 62. Cotton says only one of her sons dissented from her sentence of admonition. Welde says two.

be spoken officially by a revered teacher to one of the most worthy and confiding of his flock. I have found no trace of any resentment, or even of grief or disappointment, as coming from Mrs. Hutchinson in return for them.

Mr. John Clarke, one of the most prominent and honored of the fifty-eight members of the Boston church who had been disarmed, had already proposed to some of his censured brethren a removal from the jurisdiction to some fit place for habitation. By advice of Roger Williams and other friends they settled at Pocasset, now Newport, R. I. They were soon followed by others of the banished or disarmed, who made another settlement, at Portsmouth, the head of the island. Eighteen of these exiles entered into a civil compact, March 7, 1638, a fortnight preceding the excommunication of Mrs. Hutchinson. Twelve of these were members of the Boston church, which afterward sent messengers to deal with them as still under its " watch and ward." [1]

Two or three days after her excommunication, Winthrop sent to Mrs. Hutchinson warning her to comply with the sentence of the Court, and to leave the jurisdiction by the end of March. She had intended to accompany Wheelwright and his family to Exeter, on the Piscataqua; but her husband having joined in the purchase of Rhode Island, she went with him by land first to Providence. Vigorous measures were taken by the Court to rid the jurisdiction as soon as possible of all who were under its sentence of banishment, if they would not retract and apologize. There was in consequence a considerable emigration to the Island in the summer of the year. The effects and consequences were in every view lamentable, especially in domestic, social, and religious relations. The disruptions between members of families, and in private friendships, the aban-

---

[1] Callender's Century Sermon, R. I. Hist. Coll., iv. 84. The island was ceded by the Indians. Manuscript of Capt. Robert Keayne, in Cabinet of Massachusetts Historical Society.

donment of cherished homes, and the sacrifices of property were grievously submitted to. The Boston church seemed to be threatened with absolute ruin by dissolution before its first decade of life had closed. The loss of so many of its best esteemed members, and the rancors and alienations among the remnant, must have tasked all the best efforts of those who sought for or offered edification in its ministrations, or tried to heal the wounds of the aggrieved. A period of many months, and even the slow process of years, was necessary for restoring peace. This was greatly helped by the voluntary confessions or concessions, and the return to its fold, one by one, of several who had been inflamed by the passions of the time, and who were ready to admit more or less of wrong done by them and repented of, the church gladly restoring them.

But the most resolute and fully assured of the banished offenders stood for the views and the course which they had espoused. Their sufferings for a few distinctive opinions, which need not have severed them from a general attachment to the fellowship, creed, and discipline of the Puritan Church, very naturally led them on to more expansion of thought and to freedom of speculation, resulting in wide ranges and variances of opinions on religious subjects, and compelled them to recognize, if it did not persuade them to approve, the full principles of toleration. Individualism running often into eccentricities and impracticabilities for anything like accord and joint activity, was the natural result. We may trace to this settlement in Rhode Island of so many banished Antinomians and their sympathizers, rather than to the perhaps exaggerated leadership of Roger Williams, the really most effective first step in the introduction of liberalism into the theocratic commonwealth. Massachusetts, indeed, for a long time was made to realize, and mournfully to regret, and try to nullify or control, the results of her impolicy, — to look at it only in that light, — of having prompted the vigorous planting of a neighbor and rival colony, with antagonistic principles, which she regarded as the hot-bed of all sorts of wild and alarming fancies, follies, and mischievous notions. Cotton Mather was prompted to say that if any man or woman had lost a conscience, or wished to find one of a special sort or license, he could be accommodated in Rhode Island. Nor was it strange that Massachusetts should put to service all the ingenuities of its policy, with some ventures in the arts of intrigue and adroitness, in a series of intermeddlings with the affairs of Rhode Island. That island for a while had a separate charter and administration of its own, but afterward came into junction with Providence Plantations, the two forming the present State.

There was, however, one unruptured tie which still held the banished and exiled members of the Boston church to the once endeared fold, and that was the covenant of " watch and ward." Dec. 13, 1638, was observed in the Bay as a solemn Fast, on account of prevailing sickness and heresies, " and the general declining of professors to the world." Cotton in his sermon, lugubrious and saddened in heart, reviewed the melancholy contention through which they had been passing. He enlarged upon and sought to explain and rectify the charges against himself, as already stated, his name and alleged countenance of opinions which he did not hold and had never expressed having been used as a cloak or subterfuge. While approving the banishment of the leaders in the strife, he recommended that others under censure, instead of being sent out of the jurisdiction, which would sever them from religious oversight or drive them into heresies, should be dealt with by the church, or fined or imprisoned.[1] Mrs. Hutchinson anticipated further action by the church, considering that she and it had reciprocal rights and duties. She therefore addressed to it a letter of " admonition," which was not read because

[1] Winthrop, i. 280.

she was under sentence of excommunication.[1] Reports came to Massachusetts that she continued to exercise her gifts; and also one of doubtful truth, that she had denied the necessity and lawfulness of magistracy.[2] Another report was that admonished and excommunicated members from Boston, and some " new professors," had joined with others on the island in " gathering a church in a disordered way." Some of these venturing to visit Boston, when they could be caught, were " dealt with; " among these was the head of the Island Colony, Mr. Coddington. Misfortunes in maternity by deformity of nature, which befell both Mrs. Hutchinson and her friend Mary Dyer, were made the subjects of distressing discussion as Divine judgments, and much strengthened the popular feeling now increasing against them among the superstitious.

The Boston church concluded to send a deputation — Welde says, " four men of a lovely and winning spirit; " there were, however, only three — to the island on an effort to reclaim Mrs. Hutchinson and others. Their report was made to the church, March, 1640. This was an interesting rehearsal of the incidents of their journey, and of their unsuccessful efforts in the purpose of their errand. The church decided not to enforce a final severance of its hold upon the recusants.[3]

One of Mrs. Hutchinson's sons had remained in Boston and with the church. At this meeting he contented him-

---

[1] Winthrop, i. 293.

[2] See Letter of Chief-Justice Eddy, note to Savage's Winthrop, i. 296, and Baylie's " Dissuasive from the Errors of the Time," p. 150. Baylie says that Roger Williams told him that Mrs. Hutchinson held this opinion.

[3] This report, which is the only detailed account of such method in discipline in the Boston church known to me as extant, has a peculiar interest, but is too long to be copied here. It is given in a thick manuscript from the pen of Captain Keane, of the Ancient and Honorable Artillery, in the Cabinet of the Massachusetts Historical Society. I have heretofore printed much of it from the original in my Life of Mrs. Hutchinson in Sparks's American Biography. Keane was strictly orthodox. Those who had been disarmed had been compelled to deposit their weapons with him.

self with expressing a general disapproval of what had been done, declining to open an argument. For this the pastor reprimanded him. Another of her sons, Francis, who would not vote for the "admonition" of his mother, and so had been admonished himself, while with his parents at the Island, in a letter of July 20, 1640, asked dismission from the church, which he could not now attend, that he might join another communion. This was refused, because that other communion, by Puritan usage, was not recognized as a church at all. "They could only recommend him to God, and to the word of his grace, when there was any such word for him to hear."[1] The church felt kindly to him, and addressed him as "our beloved brother." He was not in full sympathy with his mother. Mr. William Collins, a minister and schoolmaster in Gloucester, England, and afterward in Hartford, becoming interested in Mrs. Hutchinson's case, had visited her in Newport and had warmly espoused her cause, expressing himself in very sharp reproaches which reached Massachusetts. He married a daughter of Mrs. Hutchinson. Venturing to come to Boston in the summer of 1641, with his brother-in-law, Francis, who was charged with calling the Boston church "a strumpet," the treatment to which they were subjected indicates a sharp resentment and vengefulness. Their reproaches of Court and Church must have been extremely aggravating. They were imprisoned till a fine of a hundred pounds should be paid by Collins, and one of fifty pounds by his companion. One might prefer to regard Winthrop in the following entry in his Journal as rather the recorder than the prompter of this vengefulness : —

"We assessed the fines the higher, partly that by occasion thereof they might be the longer kept in from doing harm (for they were kept close prisoners), and also because that family had put the country to so much charge in the Synod, and other occasions, to the value of five hundred pounds at least. But after, because the winter drew on, and the prison was inconvenient, we abated them to forty pounds and twenty pounds. But they seemed not willing to pay anything. They refused to come to the church assemblies except they were led, and so they came duly. At last we took their own bonds for their fine, and so dismissed them." [1]

The charges on the records against these offenders are worded thus : " Mr. William Collens being found to be a seducer, and his practices proved such," etc. " Francis Hutchinson, for calling the church of Boston a whoare, a strumpet, and other corrupt tenents," etc. Having given their personal bonds for their reduced fines, " when it shalbee called for, if they bee able," they were free to leave the jurisdiction, " not to return but at their utmost perill." [2]

Sorrows and tragic experiences gathered around the closing years of the life of Mrs. Hutchinson and of most of the members of her very large family. The treatment of her son and son-in-law in Boston, and the annoying messages constantly coming from the Boston church and others, kept open many wounds. But surrounded as she was by eccentric and self-willed opinionists of all discordant notions, she endeavored with a group of friends to maintain an orderly religious assembly. There was no lack of the means of subsistence on her beautiful island. Her husband, though he may have been, as Winthrop says, " a man of weak parts," and never appears to have stood manfully in her support or defence, nevertheless followed her fortunes, and called her a " dear saint and servant of God." He died in 1642. Sad it was for him, after having crossed the ocean with friends of his youth, for sympathy in faith, to be restrained from intercourse with them, though so near. After his death Mrs. Hutchinson, then probably fifty years of age, with all her family except a daughter and a son, to be soon referred to, moved from the island to the Dutch settlements

---

[1] Journal, ii. 38–40.   [2] Records, i. 336, 340, 344.

near Astoria, or Hell Gate. Many others moved with her, apprehending that Massachusetts, on some arbitrary pretences, might attempt jurisdiction over the island. The Indians were then in open hostility with the Dutch, in pillage, burning, and massacre. In one of their raids, in August, 1643, Mrs. Hutchinson, Mr. Collins and wife, grandchildren, and all the rest of the family save one child, with neighbors, in all being sixteen persons, perished by a lamentable fate. In conformity with the grim and unforgiving spirit of her opponents this fate was by many regarded as the special judgment of an angry Providence, which had already visited her pride, contumacy, and delusions with " a curse upon the fruit of her womb." The child of eight years of age which was spared and taken away by the Indians was, four years afterward, restored through the Dutch governor to her friends, at the conclusion of a peace. Winthrop says she " had forgot her own language, and all her friends, and was loath to have come from the Indians." [1]

It is grateful now to gather some of the tokens and incidents of reconciliation, and effective though slow and cautious recuperation from the rents and passions of this convulsing strife, which nearly wrecked the fortunes of the Bay Colony. However some of the most exasperated enemies of Mrs. Hutchinson may have viewed the tragic method of her death, we may trace from its occurrence the rise and increase of regretful and forgiving feelings. With the single exception of William Coddington, all who had been most devoted to the cause of Mrs. Hutchinson shared in these reconcilements. He was a thriving Boston merchant and the owner of much property. He had built the first brick house in Boston. Becoming after his banishment chief ruler, and dying as Governor, of Rhode Island, under the charter he had secured for it, he continued steadfast to his protest against Massachusetts, "that his dissent might appear to succeeding times." William Aspinwall, hon-

[1] Winthrop, ii. 267.

ored as deacon and deputy of Boston, after having served as secretary of Rhode Island Colony, regretted his course of opposition to court and church. Applying, as one banished, for liberty to visit Boston, he there, March 27, 1642, tendered his submission, and was reconciled to the church. Winthrop says " he made a very free and full acknowledgement of his error and seducement, and that with much detestation of his sin." [1] He did the same before the magistrates, and was reinstated by the Court. He afterward manifested his enthusiasm of spirit by countenancing the ideas of the Fifth Monarchy men. In November, 1639, the Court ordered " that all that were disarmed, remaining amongst us, carrying themselves peaceably, shall have their armes restored to them." [2]

It must have been with calm satisfaction and the approval of his own conscience for the course which he had pursued, assured by the sympathy of those around him, that Governor Winthrop made the following entry in his History, in the autumn of 1639 : —

" By this time there appeared a great change in the church of Boston ; for whereas the year before they were all (save five or six) so affected to Mr. Wheelwright and Mrs. Hutchinson, and those new opinions, as they slighted the present governour and the pastor [Wilson], looking at them as men under a covenant of works, and as their greatest enemies ; but they bearing all patiently, and not withdrawing themselves (as they were strongly solicited to have done), but carrying themselves lovingly and helpfully upon all occasions, the Lord brought about the hearts of all the people to love and esteem them more than ever before, and all breaches were made up, and the church was saved from ruin beyond all expectation ; which could hardly have been (in human reason) if those two had not been guided by the Lord to that moderation, etc. And the church (to manifest their hearty affection to the governour, upon occasion of some strait he was brought into through his bailiff's unfaithfulness) sent him £200." [3]

---

[1] Winthrop, ii. 62.   [2] Records, i. 278.   [3] Winthrop, i. 323.

Here certainly was a peaceful triumph modestly appreciated, and a grateful tribute touchingly rendered. The gift to Winthrop, when his private estate was impaired by the fraud of a servant, was not from the Colony treasury, but from the private purses of those who shortly before had regarded and treated him with strong aversion. I am well aware that some will judge me partial to Winthrop. But it is from this and many like incidental marks to be traced through the course of the breach opened by Vane and Wheelwright that I have been led to allow less of censure than some of his critics have expressed upon some objectionable attitudes and utterances of his, which certainly were not judicial, in the trial of Mrs. Hutchinson. Incidentally the paragraph which has just been quoted brings us very close to the critical risks, the intensity of a popular animosity, happily but of brief continuance, and the method of a genial conciliation, marking the ripening and then the cooling of the Antinomian schism. It seems that Winthrop and Wilson, having at one time but five or six of the whole church membership on their side, had been advised to withdraw themselves. Cotton, though sustained by all the rest, had in his distraction or disgust for a while entertained the purpose of abandoning his charge and going to Connecticut. Under these circumstances I cannot but infer that it was the constancy and solid wisdom of Winthrop, the founder, the statesman, the pure and devoted servant of the Colony, that saved it, in the dismay of an internal convulsion, from absolute anarchy.

More grateful still is it to mention the valuable services rendered to the Commonwealth by the forgiving descendants of Mrs. Hutchinson. Her son Samuel, who had remained in Boston under a cloud, was submitted for examination by the elders Wilson and Eliot, and if found "sound in judgment" was to be free to dwell here.[1] He proved a useful citizen. One of Mrs. Hutchinson's daugh-

[1] Records, i. 338.

ters was the wife of Major Thomas Savage, afterward a distinguished captain of the Ancient and Honorable Artillery Company. Though one of the "disarmed" sympathizers, he remained in Boston, was made commander-in-chief of the forces of Massachusetts in the Indian war, and was a member of the Council. His descendant, the Hon. James Savage, the incomparable editor of Winthrop's Journal, in his annotations on the Governor's text, treats with great skill and naïveté the case of his ancestress, and introduces some pleasant banter into the narrative of the tempestuous contest. By a curious coincidence, Major Savage, on the death of his Hutchinson wife, married a daughter of Elder Symmes, of Charlestown, a fellow-passenger and resolute opponent of Mrs. Hutchinson, and an effective witness against her on her trial. A grandson of Elder Welde, whose enmity stopped little short of calumny upon her, became the husband of one of her great-granddaughters. Another of her sons, Edward, who, though disarmed for a time, remained in Boston, did good military service, and as a captain in Philip's War was fatally wounded in the Quaboag fight. He was the great-grandfather of Thomas Hutchinson, unfortunate in his career as a Royal Governor of Massachusetts, but highly honored in many preceding offices and services, not the least of which is his able and faithful work as historian of the Colony. He also, in his impartial and judicious account of the Antinomian controversy, is far from espousing any ardent championship of his famous ancestress.

To this list of the reconciled and the restored, though after a longer interval, must be added the name of the prime heresiarch and offender, Wheelwright. He had a long and varied career, attracting and repelling friends and enemies, earnest in work, stirring contentions, standing stiffly for his opinions and rights, but with a prevailing purpose of fidelity in all things. He was minister successively to flocks in Exeter, Wells, and Hampton. By the following entry on the Court Records, Sept. 27, 1642, it would seem that there had been an intervention on his behalf. "The petition for Mr. Wheelwright, if hee himself petition the Court at Boston, they shall have power to grant him safe conduct." Another record, under May, 1643, is as follows : " Mr. Wheelright had a safe conduct granted, and liberty to stay 14 days, so it bee within three months next ensuing." Prompted by friends, he addressed a letter unnecessarily humiliating in its tone to the Massachusetts Court, in September, 1643. This was ungraciously, not to say meanly, misconstrued. He wrote another, of a more guarded character, in March, 1644, in which he refused to admit the " inferences " which had been drawn from his avowed opinions. Winthrop wished him to appear in person. To this, however, he was not inclined, though the relenting Governor thought that " a wise and modest apology " by mouth would help his cause.[1] But " the next Court released his banishment without his appearance." The record is as follows :

" It is ordered that Mr. Wheelwright (upon a particuler, solemne, and serious acknowledgment and confession by letters, of his evill carriages, and of the Court's justice upon him for them) hath his banishment taken of, and is received in as a member of the commonwealth." [2]

This record is certainly not worded with any magnanimity of tone, indicating that his old associates were pleased to meet him half-way. I cannot find whether he ever visited Boston again. In 1655 or 1656 he made a voyage to England, and had converse with his old college friend the Protector. They must have compared their opinions as to the character and spirit of Vane. On the Restoration, Wheelwright returned here, in the summer of 1662. He aided, and succeeded in the ministry at Salisbury, the unfortunate George Burrough, afterward executed in the

[1] The interesting correspondence is in the Journal, ii. 162–164.
[2] Records, ii. 67, May, 1644.

witchcraft panic, and died suddenly of apoplexy, Nov. 15, 1679, aged eighty-seven years. His last feud was with Robert Pike, known as the " New Puritan."

There is hardly occasion to review with many comments the distracting and tragic narrative which has been given at sufficient length. The struggle was one of the series of strifes and assaults which aimed at the very life of the Biblical commonwealth. Roger Williams had stood almost alone, without a party, and with but few sympathizers in his bold radicalism. There had been no prompting or desire to secure a reconciliation with him; and as for any wish that may have been cherished that he might meet with due retribution, this must have been fully met, by learning with what an intractable and harassing fellowship of come-outers, seekers, and disorganizers he had to deal. He must often have felt as does a traveller treading his difficult way through swamps and thickets, beating off a swarm of buzzing and stinging insects. But he was admirably furnished for such exposures, and always had a serene refuge within himself amid all externals and buffetings. He did no permanent harm to Massachusetts. He was its protector and benefactor.

But the Antinomian controversy was most threatening of convulsion, disaster, and of a final overwhelming catastrophe. Its unintelligible elements, its obscure and mystifying oracles, made a penumbra of dread shadows around an almost equally undefinable nucleus that might be falsehood or truth. The conflict was thoroughly Puritanic in all its features and materials. The Covenant covered and held both parties to it, though it forked into a dilemma of Faith and Works. Of the many points which the matter of the contention and the method of dealing with it offer for remark there are two which may briefly engage us.

The first of these is that the contention found its occasion and the mode in which it would be pursued and aggravated in the theocratic form of the colonial administration. The controversy was in its substance purely a doctrinal one. As such it might properly have been confined within the terms of church discipline and disposed of by church members. And as it began and for the most part was confined within the covenanted fold of the Boston church, two very mischievous and seemingly needless agencies came in to extend and complicate the controversy. One of these was the intermeddling of other churches in it through the interposition of a synod. But the synod was invited and empowered for this intermeddling by the advice of that other agent of mischief, the General Court. The civil arm of the Biblical commonwealth was engaged to dispose of a doctrinal variance between church members. The reason given for this civil interposition, though consistent with the theocratic principle, was that Antinomian doctrines threatened civil order and pure morals. This justification was not wholly unsupported by thoroughly sincere reasons and apprehensions incident to the time and circumstances of the strife. The difference between living under a " covenant of faith " and a " covenant of works," as distinguished literally by persons of ordinary intelligence, would be the difference between being rigidly restrained in conduct by external commands, rules, and practical scruples, and the more or less of laxity, as one or another might apply the rule to himself, in life and behavior, of a private internal guide. The immoralities and abominations of fanatical Antinomians in Germany in the previous century had not passed from memory, nor from living reference to them. It would be the grossest injustice to ascribe to one like Winthrop a reliance upon poor credulity in his apprehension of some fanatical outburst here. The disarming of citizens was not the impulse of any bugbear conceit. The controversy had reached a really alarming stage. So the Court, acting for the theocracy, with an unquailing front, and daring the risk of the most decisive measures if it should be overmastered or thwarted, brought either its vengefulness or its discretion, as we may decide the alternative, to crush the threatening anarchy.

The other point of importance to which we must allow a very serious concern on the part of the constituted authorities of the Colony, looked beyond their own immediate surroundings and constituency. There are many extant and very emphatic evidences of the anxiety felt by the authorities here, — those most vitally interested in the security and good repute of the Colony, — to guard it from reproach and slander in England. Vane had carried home with him the account of the sad dissensions; but he was of too generous a nature to mingle any malignity in his report, or to aggravate them. Massachusetts through its whole colonial period, and indeed for some time afterward, till its era of Independence, always was anxious and careful to have warm friends, even strong partisans and pleaders, in both religious and political groups, near to the government. It depended upon these to explain its course of action and to stand for it against its impugners and enemies. And there is one point bearing upon this matter on which it would be impossible to lay undue stress. Massachusetts was jealous of its good repute for an orderly, sober, dignified, and serious form of citizenship, grave and watchful maintenance of moral rectitude, and freedom from every form of the fanaticism and license and discord of sectarism. It intended that in all the interests of private, domestic, social, and civil life its standard should be even above that which was recognized under the discipline of the Church of England. How lamentable, then, the apprehension of the effect on their friends or their enemies at home of the reports of the distractions in the Colony. They took all the care they could to correct or nullify this effect. Passengers for England at this crisis were instructed to put the best construction possible on the contention, by explaining that the two parties to the strife differed only "as to how they might most magnify the grace of God *in* them or *to* them." Doubtless the stiff and severe measures of the Court were relied upon as showing to friends abroad the intention and ability to crush down the threatening mischief and its abettors. In concluding this review, it should perhaps be intimated that as the authorities on their Records give no intimation that they ever repented of, regretted, apologized for, or retracted any of their penalties, except to suppliants, and that all the concessions, retractations, and petitions came from the discomfited party, this result may be taken as vindicating the justice and policy of the Court. But this conclusion might be gravely questioned.

X.

A JESUIT ENJOYS PURITAN HOSPITALITY.

IT is a relief to turn awhile from the sombreness of the matter of some of the preceding pages, and before dealing with the yet more painful matter of pages that are to follow, to entertain for the moment a more genial theme. This presents to us a charming view of some social amenities extended to a Jesuit visitor in the Puritan Colony, who, in his character of an envoy from the Governor of the French Colonists in Canada, circulated here freely as a welcome guest in private homes and at public tables. Had he ventured here in any private capacity, his reception would have been an ungracious one, and his lodging would have been in the jail. Dreaded as were Antinomians, Baptists, and Quakers by the magistrates and Court of the Bay, a Jesuit priest concentrated upon himself their sternest antipathies and their hate. Indeed, one of the fancies passing into dark rumors connected with the coming of the first Quakers here was that they were Franciscan friars in disguise, on some errand of mischief. The Court of the Bay, in attempting afterward to vindicate its capital law against the Quakers, ventured to plead that it had dealt with them as English law, then inquisitorial and relentless, with tortures and the block, dealt with Papal intriguers. So we find a law on our court records anticipating a possible occasion for its use.

There is an historic interest in the wording of this law in which the Colony Court followed the lead of the mother country. It is as follows : —

May 26, 1647. "This Courte taking into consideration the great warrs, combustions, and divisions which are this day in Europe, and that the same are observed to be chiefly raised and fomented by the secret underminings and solicitations of those of the Jesuiticall order, men brought up and devoted to the relig- ion and courte of Rome, which hath occasioned diverse states to expell them their territories, for prevention of like evils among ourselves, it is therefore ordered and enacted by authority of this Courte, that no Jesuit or spirituall or ecclesiasticall person (as they are tearmed) ordained by the authority of the pope or sea of Rome, shall henceforth at any time repair to or come within this jurisdic- tion; and if any person shall give just cause of suspition, that he is one of such society or order, he shalbe brought before some of the magistrates, and if he cannot free himselfe of such suspition, he shalbe committed or bound over to the next Courte of Assistants, to be tried and proceeded with by banishment or otherwise, as the Courte shall see cause; and if any such person so banished shalbe taken the second time within this jurisdiction, he shall upon lawfull triall and conviction be put to death." [1]

Exceptions are made for the shipwrecked, public messen- gers, and seamen, coming peacefully, behaving inoffen- sively, and departing.

The jealousies leading to actual hostilities, with their chronic rivalries and contentions between the English and the French colonists for mastery on this continent, which extended over a century and a half, were preceded by some desultory intercourse through messengers. It is amusing to read in Winthrop the gingerly and cautious recognition of the visits to Boston of these "Papistical" personages. In 1643 the Court had been greatly exercised by the call for its mediation or hostile action in the quarrel between D'Aulnay and La Tour. The Scriptures were searched from beginning to end by the magistrates and elders in their disputations, for warnings, prohibitions, or sanctions in emergent cases, as to entering into dealings or alliances

[1] Records, ii. 193.

with "idolaters;" Papists being allowed by all to be such.
Jehoshaphat, Ahab, Josias, Amaziah, Pharaoh Necho, and
others are put to service.   Reference is made to this matter
here only to note the mention by Winthrop that in the
retinue of La Tour, when he arrived in Boston, March 4,
1643, were "two friars and two women sent to wait upon
La Tour his lady." These "friars" seem for the most
part to have considerately remained on shipboard.   But
Winthrop tells us : —

> " Of the two friars which came in this ship, the one was a very
> learned acute man.   Divers of our elders who had conference with
> him reported so of him.   They came not into the town, lest they
> should give offence, but once, being brought by some to see Mr.
> Cotton and confer with him ; and when they came to depart, the
> chief came to take leave of the governour and two elders of Bos-
> ton, and showed himself very thankful for the courtesy they found
> among us." [1]

Again, in September, 1646, Monsieur d'Aulnay, with two
more of these Papists, arrived in Boston on the Lord's Day.
After the exercises of public worship, with scrupulous consideration courteous hospitalities were extended to the
visitors by the Governor.   Lingering in their visit, Winthrop tells us : —

> " The Lord's day they were here, the governour, acquainting
> them with our manner, that all men either come to our public
> meetings, or keep themselves quiet in their houses, and finding
> that the place where they lodged would not be convenient for
> them that day, invited them home to his house, where they con-
> tinued private all that day until sunset, and made use of such
> books, Latin and French, as he had, and the liberty of a private
> walk in his garden, and so gave no offence," etc. [2]

There is a charming naïveté in this relation.   No doubt
the urbane Governor used the most delicate terms for

---

[1] Winthrop, ii. 127.   [2] Ibid., ii. 275.

informing the Papists that if they would not go to " meeting," no strolling about the streets was allowed in Boston on the Sabbath. But what constrained relations were thus exhibited between Christian disciples !

As reference is soon to be made to the fishing and trucking place of the Plymouth people near the Kennebec, another matter may have an incidental interest.

Our historians have long recognized something unexplained in the relations between the famous peppery-tempered — but for his prowess invaluable — military captain, Miles Standish, and the Pilgrims at Plymouth. He had followed their fortunes from his service in the Low Countries, and was constant to and fully trusted by them. But he was not under their church covenant, though not shocking them otherwise than by free speech. It has been suggested that the explanation may be that Standish, loyal to the faith of his ancestry and family, may have been an adherent of the old Church, being quietly reticent on the matter. He was always ready to go in his pinnace for trucking with the Indians at the Kennebec. Here on his visits he might easily have had the services of a priest for adjusting his conscience.

The French in Canada had received several tenders for negotiations from the Massachusetts Colonists, for the peaceful conduct of trade, and for amity, even if their monarchs should be at war at home. In 1650, Father Gabriel Druillette, of the Company of Jesus, a man of a gentle and devout spirit, and one of the most heroic of missionaries, was faithfully pursuing his toilsome work for the Abenaquis in parts of the region disputed between the two crowns as Acadie in 1646. He had, as he believed, by a miracle, recovered his sight wholly lost in the smoke of Indian cabins. His red catechumens were warmly attached to him for his zeal and kindness. The French in their alliance with the Hurons and Algonquins had of course been compelled to espouse their enmity with the

Five Nations of New York, the ferocious Iroquois. The English had had no trouble with these warlike tribes, and one of them, the Mohawks, had always been in friendly relations with the Dutch, up the Hudson. With a view to engage the English Colonies in alliance with the French against the Iroquois, as well as to promote a league for trade, D'Ailleboust, the Governor of Canada, sent Druillette in 1650 with the credentials of an ambassador on that errand. He hoped that the bribe of trade would secure the alliance of arms by drawing from the English military aid. We have the good Father's Journal of his mission; and it is because of his genial narration of the kindness which he received, not only from Englishmen, but from grim Puritans, that full particulars from it are given here.[1]

The Father left Quebec on the first of September with one of his Indian converts, a chief. Passing through Narautsonat (Norridgewook), the highest settlement of the Indians on the Kennebec, he met at the present Augusta the "Commissioner Jehan Winslau." This was John Winslow, the agent of Plymouth at its factory, or trucking-house, on the Kennebec. The Father took most fondly to Winslow, who, he says, treated him with much kindness, and they lodged together. He believed Winslow to be warmly interested in the conversion of the savages, as was his brother Edward, then the agent of the Colonies to Parliament. Druillette says that he wrote of these matters to his Governor and Superior at Quebec. Winslow, at his own inconvenience, made the difficult foot-journey with the priest to Maremiten (Merry-Meeting Bay). On the 25th of September the latter embarked on an English vessel, seeing the English fishermen at Temeriscau

---

[1] Narré du Voyage faict pour la Mission des Abnaquiois, et des Connaissances tirez de la Nouvelle Angleterre et des dispositions des Magistrats de cette République pour le secours contre les Iroquois, ès années 1650 and 1651. Par Le R. Père Gabriel Druillette, de la Compagnie de Jesus. Quebec.

(Damaris-Cove). Contrary winds delayed his reaching Kepane (Cape Ann) till December 5. Thence by foot-travel and boat he came to Charlestown, where, his mission being recognized, he was directed to cross the river to Boston, to the house of "Maj. Gen. Gebin," to whose affection he had been commended by his friend Winslow.

The Father could not have fallen into better hands than those of Maj.-Gen. Edward Gibbons, a man of elastic conscience, and of worse than dubious habits, though in covenant a church member, and at times before the courts. He was one of that not small class of picturesque and loose men, Captain Underhill being the most conspicuous specimen, who were somewhat leniently tolerated in our early days for their needful military service. This "Sieur Gebin," as the priest writes, invited him to his hospitalities and charged him to make no other house his home while he remained here. The following sentence is suggestive: "Sieur Gebin me donna un clef d'un departement en sa maison où je pouvais avec toute liberté faire ma prière et les exercices de ma religion." In thus furnishing the priest with a key and a private chamber where he might say his prayers and perform the exercises of his religion, the Puritan church member — it would have been to the scandal of his more rigid brethren had they known it — connived at the performance of probably the first Mass in Boston. On the 8th of December Gibbons accompanied the priest to a village distant from Boston which he calls "Rogsbray," — known to us as Roxbury, — where he was to present himself with his credentials to that austerest of Puritans, Governor Dudley. The Governor having opened the papers and listened to a translation of them by an interpreter,[1] courteously promised to lay them before the magistrates in Boston, before whom the priest was to present himself on the 13th of the month. On that day the

[1] Dudley ought to have kept his French, as Endicott did, for he had served in the Huguenot army under Henry IV.

Governor, magistrates, secretary, and one deputy received him at dinner, after which they listened to his message. Then he was asked to retire for a while that they might confer together. Being summoned again to supper, he received their answer. The priest does not tell us what it was, but we are informed about it. The four Colonies, Massachusetts, Plymouth, Connecticut, and New Haven, having formed a union for certain general interests, neither of them could enter into such measures as the Governor of Canada desired, without consultation and accord. So the priest would be informed that his mission must come before the commissioners, two from each Colony, at their next meeting. He had pleaded before the magistrates, he says, in behalf of his Abenaquis catechumens against the murderous Iroquois. It was intimated to him that as the catechumens whom he represented at Kennebec were under the jurisdiction of Plymouth, his application might well be made to the authorities of that Colony. Spending the interval doubtless with his friend Gibbons, he started on the 21st for Plymouth, arriving the next day, where he lodged with " one of the five farmers at Kennebec named padis " [Paddy]. He was received with courtesy by the Governor " Je-Brentford," — whose name, however, was William Bradford, — and an audience was appointed for the next day. He was also invited to a repast of fish which the Governor fitted to his " occasion," knowing the day to be Friday. The priest found favor among the people of the town, and Capt. Thomas Willets supported his application to the Governor, and no doubt he felt encouraged. Though he does not mention the result, we learn from the Plymouth court records of June, 1651, that the Court did not favor the design of allowing the French to pass through their jurisdiction for purposes of war.

On the 24th of December the priest started by land for Boston, with the son and nephew of his friend Gibbons, who, he says, paid his charges on the route.

24

And now we have to present to ourselves a notable scene. The priest writes: "On my way I arrived at Rogsbray, where the minister, named Master heliot, who was instructing some savages, received me to lodge with him, as the night had overtaken me. He treated me with respect and affection, and prayed me to pass the winter with him." Here is a scene that might well engage the pencil of an artist whose sympathies responded to the subject. Two men, then in the vigor of life, who were yet to pass their fourscore years in their loved but poorly rewarding labors for the savages, separated as the poles in their religious convictions, principles, and methods, trained in antipathies and zealous hostility to each other, are seen in simple, human, loving converse as kind host and responsive stranger guest. The humble sitting and working room of the Apostle Eliot, in his modest cottage, has the essentials of comfort, and there is a guest-chamber. Around the hearthstone are two or three Indian children, which Eliot always had near him as pupils, while he himself was a learner from some docile elders of the race whose " barbarous tongue" he was seeking to acquire through grunts and gutturals, that he might set forth in it " the whole oracles of God." His hopeful experiment in the Indian village at Natick had recently been put on trial. The priest was, after his own different fashion, spending himself in his own work. The aims of both were the same; their methods widely unlike: Eliot's most severe in its exactions, the priest's lenient and indulgent in its conditions. Eliot insisted that the savages " should be brought to civility," abandoning all wildwood roaming, be humanized, cleanly, clothed, and trained in home and field industries. They should be taught to pray, be put through a course of Calvinistic divinity, and have the Scriptures " opened" to them in their own tongue. The priest pestered his catechumens as little as possible by crossing their native instincts for a free life in the wilderness. The rosary, the crucifix, and the sacraments, with repeated prayer and creed, and the procession following the arbored cross, were his agencies for salvation.

It was the Christmas season when the Puritan minister and the Jesuit priest thus blended their alienating antipathies into reconciling sympathies in consecrated work. Perhaps their conversation was in Latin, though Eliot was an accomplished scholar, and might have the mastery of the French. The two might have spent the winter profitably together. They certainly would have passed it amicably. The evening and morning devotions of the Puritan household, with grace and blessing at each meal, must have kept their wonted course; while the faithful priest had his oratory, his orisons, and his matin Mass before breaking his fast.

Druillette returned to Boston on the 29th of December, and reported himself to " Major Gen. guebin." The next day he had speech with " Sieur Ebens [Hibbins] one of the magistrates, who encouraged him with the hope that the Governor of Plymouth would afford him help against the Iroquois, saying " that it was reasonable to aid brother Christians, though of another religion, especially against a Pagan persecution of Christians." He received through Hibbins the answer of the Governor and magistrates of Boston, not telling us what it was, though probably as before stated. The last of the month he went to Roxbury to take leave of Dudley. The Governor assured him that the way through Boston should be open for any of the French who wished to go against the Iroquois, and wished him to inform his own Governor of the desire of Massachusetts to be at amity with him, even though war should spring up between the two crowns. Dudley also expressed his belief that the Governor of Plymouth would comply with the wishes of the French for help against the Iroquois, and promised all in his power in aid of the measure. The priest the next day, being January 1, wrote a letter to his brother Jesuit, Le Jeune, to be franked by an English vessel to sail on the 8th, asking a reply to be sent to Boston on some matters concerning the fisheries at Gaspee. He also wrote to Edward Winslow, by suggestion of his brother, soliciting him to address the commissioners of the four Colonies in favor of his cause. He made a similar appeal to John Winthrop, Jr., Governor of "Kenitigout," — "a very good friend of the French and the savages." His friend Gibbons promised his co-operation, but frankly told him that he thought the people of Boston would not aid him, as it would alienate the Iroquois, and thus interfere with a design for a new project of a settlement in the interest of New Sweden. January 5, Gibbon conducted the priest to the harbor and commended him strongly to "Thomas Yau," master of a bark about sailing for Kennebec. The 9th of the month bad weather stopped him at Morbletz (Marblehead), where, among many persons, the minister, William Walter, "received me with great affection, and I went in his company to Salem to have speech with Sieur Indicott, who understands and speaks French well, is a good friend of that nation, and very earnest that his children should retain that affection. Seeing that I had no money he supplied me, and treated at his table for eight days the magistrates who gave audience to everybody. I left with him a letter to advance my object with the General Court to be held in Boston on the thirteenth of May. He assured me that he would do his utmost to influence the Boston Colony, which served as a lead for the others, saying that the Governor of Plymouth had a good cause for asking aid from the other colonies. At my departure he said he was much pleased that I had left a writing on the part of my Governor and my catechumens, which he thoroughly approved, and that he would despatch a man to take a letter for me to the Kennebec that would inform me of what had been done."

This is certainly a very graceful and genial narrative. The French Governor had a faithful and accomplished

diplomatic servant on his errand, coming out of the woods
and his rude companionship, to pass freely and without offence among those who in person, speech, manners, and the
ways of their homes, were the representatives of a Puritanism as yet unreduced in its austerity. They must all have
known that the priest carried with him the " idolatrous "
furnishings for his devotions, and observed the sanctities
of his profession. But no slight, no challenge was inflicted
on him. His visit was at midwinter, with its snow and
tempests on land and sea. He seems to have been wholly
penniless, but lacked for nothing. His host, Gibbons, was
not a man likely to practise a lean hospitality in larder or
good liquors. Most happy was the luck by which the
priest, who had started on his home voyage, was compelled
by stress of weather to delay so that he was favored by a
visit to Endicott, so charmingly described. That grim old
European soldier had preserved his French, and was doubtless pleased to give it an airing. Under other circumstances he would without shrinking have swung the priest
from the ladder with a halter about his neck. But he had
in him warm human sympathies. There may have been
subdued mutterings among the common people at this prolonged circulation of a Jesuit among the homes and official
halls of the colony, but no record remains of any disaffection or complaint. Nor does the priest intimate anything
of a religious discussion. He and Eliot would have found
enough in their general interests to engage them. If he
had accepted Eliot's invitation to pass the winter with
him, avoiding his homeward journey, they might have
opened their polemics.

The following April the priest met John Winslow at
the Kennebec, on his arrival from Plymouth and Boston,
who assured him that the magistrates and the two commissioners of Plymouth had pledged themselves, on account of
the interest of that Colony in the Kennebec, to press the
other Colonies in the favor of the Abnaquis against the

Iroquois. Encouragement and hope came to the priest from many sources, and he diligently used all appliances for his cause. But he was doomed to disappointment. Finding that the matter would be disposed of by the commissioners of the four Colonies then to meet at New Haven, Druillette was despatched again from Quebec, with one of the Governor's Council in company. In September, 1651, the emissaries were most courteously received, and presented their case forcibly and adroitly. But the commissioners, while pliant in behalf of the interests of trade, had no inclination to open hostilities with the Mohawks, who were neither in subjection to, nor at war with, the English. The ambassadors had this to carry back in a dignified Latin letter to the French Governor. The reader may have noticed in Druillette's Journal how freely he deals with English names of persons and places. His own name fares no better in the records of the commissioners, — which appears under the aliases of Mr. Derwellets, Mr. Derwelletes, Mr. Drwellets, and Mr. Drovillety.

This Narration of Druillette was found in a bureau containing some of the effects of the Jesuits, in Quebec, and was published at the charge of Mr. James Lenox, of New York, in 1855.

XI.

THE BAPTISTS UNDER PURITAN DISCIPLINE.

THE difference of meaning and use between the two words Baptists and Anabaptists gives us the occasion and the matter of one of the largest sectarian divisions among Protestants, consequent upon the rupture of unity in the Church at the Reformation. It was in Germany, about a century before the settlement of Massachusetts, that the most formidable and deplorable social convulsions, with wild excesses of fanaticism, made those then first known as Anabaptists to be regarded as the most dreaded class of opinionists. The representatives of the sect in England, while having to bear the odium of its earlier representatives in Germany, gave the earnestness of their zeal rather to fidelity to conscience than to offensiveness of conduct. A very interesting episode in early Massachusetts history is connected with the first introduction of the controversy here, as the stern discipline of authority was brought to bear severely upon a much beloved and honored man, the first President of Harvard College. He may well stand as the central figure among the sufferers by the theocratic administration, in the narration now to be traced. This controversy, like the Antinomian, was within the limits of Puritanism, its weapons being Scripture texts.

Up to the time of the Reformation we may assume as substantially true the general statement, that every human being in Christendom had been baptized in infancy, — the rite being performed by pouring or sprinkling. The supreme importance of the rite attached to it because of the belief in its absolute necessity and its sovereign efficacy. The teaching of the Roman Church about it is, that "Baptism washes away original sin, in which we were all born by reason of the sin of our first father, Adam; it infuses the habit of divine grace into our souls, and makes us the adopted children of God; it imprints a character or spiritual mark in the soul; it lets us into the Church of God."[1] The Church of England and the Puritans equally maintained the importance and necessity of the rite, and assigned to it these high uses. But the Roman Church had one supreme ground for its belief and practice concerning this rite, which relieved it, as we shall see, of a difficulty met by Protestants, and especially by the Puritans, whose leading principle was that only the teaching and authority of Scripture gave sanction to faith. A candid and able divine of the English Church before quoted allows himself to express the following positive and unqualified statement: "Notwithstanding all that has been written by learned men upon this subject, it remains indisputable that infant baptism is not mentioned in the New Testament. No instance of it is recorded there, no allusion is made to its effects, no directions are given for its administration."[2] The Roman Church gives as its first reason for practising infant baptism, "a tradition which the Church has received from the Apostles." Other reasons are added. But when the authority of all traditions outside of the Scriptures was repudiated, and a warrant for all that was to be accepted for faith and practice was required to be found there, the way was opened for a most burning controversy on the proper subjects and mode of baptism. Its importance and efficacy were in no way diminished. If the baptism of infants had no warrant from Scripture, while baptism itself was an essential and saving

---

[1] The Catholic Christian Instructed.

[2] Ecclesiastical Polity of the New Testament, by Dr. Jacob, p. 270.

ordinance, it followed that the rite must in mature years be repeated for believers baptized in infancy who would secure the blessing from it. This *repetition* of the rite was Anabaptism. The term has no significance now as applied to "Baptists," who not having been baptized in infancy are baptized for the first time, if ever, in maturer years, when making a Christian profession.

The Puritan Standards and Confessions, both in England and in her colonies here, recognized —

"Baptism is a Sacrament of the New Testament, ordained by Jesus Christ, not only for the solemn Admission of the Party baptised into the Visible Church, but also to be unto him a Sign and Seal of the Covenant of Grace, of his ingrafting into Christ, of Regeneration, of Remission of Sins, and of his giving up unto God, through Jesus Christ, to walk in Newness of Life. . . . Dipping of the Person into the Water is not necessary; but Baptism is rightly administered by pouring or sprinkling Water upon the Person. . . . Not only those that do actually profess Faith in, and Obedience unto Christ, but also the Infants of one or both believing Parents are to be baptised."

In the Roman Communion, all parents having themselves been baptized in infancy were assumed to be members of the Church, so that all their children, as a matter of course, were entitled to the rite. The different principle and practice adopted here — as will be seen on a future page — occasioned in New England much controversy and strife, and was largely instrumental in bringing discomfiture on the system. In the Roman Church, baptism is essential to and insures the salvation of the infant. The Westminster Confession made a discrimination here, as follows:

"Although it be a great Sin to contemn or neglect this Ordinance, yet Grace and Salvation are not so inseparably annexed to it, as that no person can be regenerated or saved without it, or that all that are baptised are undoubtedly regenerated. . . . The Sacrament was to be administered only once to any person."

The church or congregation in which an infant had been baptized, was held through its parents to have come under the obligation of an oversight and responsibility for the child, and as having reason to expect that the child on growing up would complete its church relations by accepting the covenant for full membership.

The lack of direct, positive, quotable texts in the New Testament enjoining the baptism of infants was supplied mainly by ingenious inferences and deductions from the Scriptures. It was argued that children should accede to church privileges and responsibilities in their religious heritage through their parents, as they acceded through the same channel to civil rights and privileges. "The seed of Abraham"[1] became partakers of the covenanted blessing through the rite of circumcision performed on infant children. So the Puritans said, "We infer that baptism is designed to take the place of circumcision." The affectionate saying of Christ, "Suffer little children to come unto me," etc., gave an encouragement to infant baptism. It is rather through the tender and engaging appeal in these last words, than from the force of any positive command or a belief in the necessity of the rite for salvation, that Christian parents now offer their children in baptism as a dedicatory and grateful service, and as recognizing their own obligation and purpose for the Christian nurture of their children. Another inference was drawn in support of the Puritan custom from the mention in the Acts and Epistles of the baptism of a whole "household" when the head of it was the subject of the rite. The inference was that the household included children.

It was inevitable, however, that when, church authority being repudiated, each individual, with such ability, judgment, and intelligence as he might possess, brought his own acute and conscientious search to his own private interpretation of the Scriptures, he should be quickened or

---

[1] Genesis xvii. 7.

troubled, stirred to questioning or protesting, concerning the significance of baptism, the subjects of the rite, and the authority for its administration. A vast number of the innumerable polemical tractates of the age succeeding the Reformation are filled either with calm, learned, and able dealings with this subject, or with the wild utterances of enthusiasts and fanatics upon it.

It is curious to note the acuteness used in arguments, drawn by inferences, to justify the baptism of infants in the lack of direct Scriptural injunctions. Thus, Jesus had bid his Apostles go teach and baptize all nations. Now for an inference : —

"If a man should bid his servant go shear all my sheep and mark them, if that servant should shear all his sheep and mark them only that he had shorn, and not mark his Lambs, because he could not shear them, doth that servant fulfill his Master's command ? No more had the Apostles done if they had not marked his Lambs as well as his sheep : although they were not capable of teaching, yet they were capable of marking or baptising. Again, whereas our Lord commandeth, 'Suffer little children to come unto me, and forbid them not,' How properly can an infant come unto Christ but by Baptism ? Repent they cannot, believe they cannot, as the Anabaptists affirm. But by baptism they may come, where the minister in Christ stead receiveth them and blesseth them." [1]

But as if to revive the dreads connected with the avowal of Anabaptist opinions as associated with the lawlessness, immoralities, and extravagances of the old times in Holland and Germany, the attention of the authorities of Massachusetts was drawn to the appearance and organization of the faction in Rhode Island when that Colony was the harborage of " all sorts of consciences." Their diversities, eccentricities, and individualities of opinion had a free field and license. Winthrop writes during the summer of 1641 :

---

[1] Pagitt's Heresiography. London, 1661. p. 19. The writer was of the Church of England.

" Mrs. Hutchinson and those of Aquiday island broached new heresies every year. Divers of them turned professed anabaptists, and would not wear any arms, and denied all magistracy among Christians, and maintained that there were no churches since those founded by the apostles and evangelists, nor could any be, nor any pastors ordained nor seals administered but by such, and that the church was to want these all the time she continued in the wilderness, as yet she was." [1]

Here was enough to rouse the anxious watchfulness of the authorities of Massachusetts, to test the tolerance heretofore allowed for variances of opinion, and to prepare the way for harsh dealing with their avowal.

The variances of opinion on the subject of infant baptism which presented themselves were the most natural, and we may add the most reasonable, of all the factious dissensions which arose in the Massachusetts churches. Happily, the bitterness and severity of discipline which attended them were of brief duration, while the smart fell on but few victims. According to the Puritan view of the Scriptures, as furnishing the sole authority for all of religious belief and practice, and the means for ending all controversies, the lack in them of positive and direct injunctions for infant baptism should have prepared them for these variances of opinion, and secured for them a degree of tolerance. To a certain extent this tolerance was allowed; but it was for little more than private opinions, quietly and moderately expressed. But as the expectation and requisition of accord, harmony, and conformity in avowed beliefs and in church observances became steadily more rigid among magistrates and elders in the Colony, this tolerance was soon put to a strain. Cotton Mather more than once tells us that among the first comers to Massachusetts were many who held the special tenets of the Baptists, and that "they were as holy and watchful and fruitful and heavenly a people as perhaps any in the

[1] Winthrop, ii. 38.

world." But Mather also, as if to balance his encomium, quotes the opinion of one whom he calls " the noble martyr Philpot," that the Anabaptists " are an inordinate kind of men, stirred up by the Devil, to the destruction of the Gospel; having neither Scripture nor antiquity nor anything else for them but lies and new imaginations, feigning the baptism of children to be the Pope's commandment." [1]

At the Quarterly Court at Salem, Dec. 14, 1642, " The Lady Deborah Moody, Mrs. King, and the wife of John Tilton were presented for houldinge that the baptising of infants is noe ordinance of God." [2] Winthrop mentions this case as follows : —

" The Lady Moodye, a wise and anciently religious woman, being taken with the error of denying baptism to infants, was dealt withal by many of the elders and others, and admonished by the Church of Salem (whereof she was a member); but persisting still, and to avoid further trouble, etc., she removed to the Dutch, against the advice of all her friends. Many others infected with anabaptism removed thither also. She was after excommunicated." [3]

Lady Moody owned land at Swampscott. A neighbor of hers there, William Witter, next comes up for discipline at Salem Court, Feb. 28, 164¾, —

" for entertaining that the baptism of infants was sinful, now coming in Salem Court, answered humbly and confessed his Ignorance, and his willingness to see Light, and (upon Mr. Morris, our Elder, his speech) seemed to be staggered, Inasmuch that in court meltinglie Sentence, [*sic*] Have called our ordenance of God a badge of the whore, on some Lecture day, the next 5th day being a public fast, To acknowledge his falt, and to ask Mr. Cobbett forgiveness, in saying he spoke against his conscience, And enjoined to be heare next Court at Salem." [4]

---

[1] Magnalia, Amer. edit., ii. 532. [2] Lewis and Newhall, Lynn, p. 204.
[3] Winthrop, ii. 124. [4] Lewis and Newhall, Lynn, p. 219.

But the repentance and the sentence in his case were both ineffective; for, as appears from the following proceeding in the General Court, May 6, 1646, Witter had in the interval again been before the Salem Court: —

"Att the Courte at Salem, held the 18th of the 12th month, 1645, William Witter, of Lynn, was presented by the grand jury for saying that they who stayed whiles a child is baptised doe worshipp the divell. Henry Collins and Nath. West dealing with him thereabouts, he further sayd that they who stayed at the baptising of a child did take the name of the Father, Sonne, and Holy Gost in vayne, broake the Sabaoth, and confessed and justifyed the former speech. The sentence of the Court was an injunction the next Lord's day, being faier, that he make public confession to satisfaction in the open congregation, at Lynne, or else to answer it at the next Generall Courte; and concerning his opinion, the Courte exprest their patience towards him, only admonishing him till they see if he continew obstinate. The said Witter not appearing here according to order, itt is ordered that the major generall take order for his appearance at the next Court of Assistants, at Boston, there to answer, and to be proceeded with according to the meritt of his offence."[1]

There seems to have been an attempt at leniency in dealing with this offender, though he had made himself so obnoxious, not for holding, but for his rude way of declaring, an opinion.

The magistrates were persuading themselves that it was becoming necessary for them to have a law upon their statute-book enabling them, in keeping with their conservative and repressive policy, to deal with the extending and aggressive heresy of opposition to infant baptism. Before they did so, however, we learn from Winthrop of the case of another individual offender, as follows, July 5, 1644: —

"A poor man of Hingham, one Painter, who had lived at New Haven, and at Rowley and Charlestown, and had been scandalous

[1] Records, iii. 67, 68.

and burdensome by his idle and troublesome behaviour to them all, was now on the sudden turned anabaptist, and having a child born, he would not suffer his wife to bring it to the ordinance of baptism, for she was a member of the church, though himself were not. Being presented for this, and enjoined to suffer the child to be baptised, he still refusing, and disturbing the church, he was again brought to the Court, not only for his former contempt, but also for saying that our baptism was antichristian; and in the open court he affirmed the same. Whereupon, after much patience and clear conviction of his errour, etc., — because he was very poor, so as no other but corporal punishment could be fastened upon him, — he was ordered to be whipped, not for his opinion, but for his reproaching the Lord's ordinance, and for his bold and evil behaviour both at home and in the Court. He endured his punishment with much obstinacy, and when he was loosed he said, boastingly, that God had marvellously assisted him. Whereupon, two or three honest men, his neighbours, affirmed before all the company that he was of very loose behaviour at home, and given much to lying and idleness, etc. Nor had he any great occasion to gather God's assistance from his stillness under the punishment, which was but moderate, for divers notorious malefactors had showed the like, and one the same court." [1]

We may imagine that we hear the culprit, released from his scourging, boastfully cry out, in more reverent phrase, the same sentiment which a plucky boy after a whipping expresses in the defiance, — "Pooh! you have not hurt me much!" We note that Winthrop says, guardedly, that Painter was not scourged for "his opinion," but for disturbing the church proceedings, and for general misdemeanor. We shall find an attempt made at drawing the same distinction in the law now to be copied. This was drafted by the magistrates, and then submitted to the elders, "who approved of it with some mitigations, and being voted and sent to the deputies, it was after published." [2]

The allowance and tolerance of what were viewed as erroneous opinions on infant baptism, which has been

[1] Winthrop, ii. 175.   [2] Ibid., ii. 174.

before referred to, as granted to individuals, on implied conditions of moderation or silence, were found to be insufficient for protection against the working and insidious spread of the heresy. The Court therefore, in its watchfulness and presumed responsibility for protecting its constituency, passed the following law, Nov. 13, 1644: —

" Forasmuch as experience hath plentifully and often proved that since the first arising of the Anabaptists, about a hundred years since, they have been the incendiaries of commonwealths, and the infectors of persons in main matters of religion, and the troublers of churches in all places where they have bene, and that they who have held the baptising of infants unlawfull have usually held other errors or heresies together therewith, though they have (as other hereticks use to do) concealed the same till they spied out a fit advantage and opportunity to vent them, by way of question or scruple, and whereas divers of this kind have, since our coming into New England, appeared amongst ourselves, some whereof have (as others before them) denied the ordinance of magistracy, and the lawfulness of making warr, and others the lawfulness of magistrates, and their inspection into any breach of the first table, which opinions, if they should be connived at by us, are like to be increased amongst us, and so must necessarily bring guilt upon us, infection and trouble to the churches, and hazard to the whole commonwealth,

" It is ordered and agreed, that if any person or persons within this jurisdiction shall either openly condemne or oppose the baptising of infants, or go about secretly to seduce others from the approbation or use thereof, or shall purposely depart the congregation at the administration of the ordinance, or shall deny the ordinance of magistracy, or their lawful right or authority to make warr, or to punish the outward breaches of the first table, and shall appear to the Court wilfully and obstinately to continue therein after due time and meanes of conviction, every such person or persons shalbe sentenced to banishment." [1]

Several matters for passing remark are suggested by the terms of this law. We have already noted with what an

[1] Records, ii. 85.

obstinate and apparently perverse resolution a single religious opinion or belief, seemingly held in sincerity, and
peacefully, was associated with, and made accountable for,
any extravagances and dangerous practices, threatening
the fabric or good order of society, or running into disso-
luteness and immorality, which had accompanied the first
adoption or utterance of the heresy. The abominations of
impiety, and the outrages of decency, and the reckless
practices which had accompanied the wild enthusiasm and
fanaticism of those first known as Antinomians and Anabaptists, had attached to them for a century; and any one
who avowed the central matter of the heresy was suspected
of at least secretly tending to all the follies and vices that
ever accompanied it. So the terms of the law we have
copied intimate that those who object to infant baptism
have silently in reserve many other and more dangerous
errors, which they are watching an opportunity to insinuate when they can spy out a fit advantage. We have seen
how " inferences " supposed to be fairly drawn from opinions avowed by Mrs. Hutchinson, and her " revelations,"
were all the entailed burden from previous offenders. Another point is suggestive here. When Winslow was acting
as agent and defender of the Colony in England from imputations urged against it for its severity in this and other
of its laws, he pleaded that many among them known to
hold heretical or objectionable opinions were unmolested if
they kept them quietly and unaggressively to themselves,
without raising dispute or dissensions. But such individualities of opinion and scruples of conscience were not to be
restrained from a free and earnest utterance by the tongues
of men and women of the temper trained by Puritanism.
On many subjects that exercised them, they could relieve
their own uneasiness only by communicating it to others
around them. The unintermitted restating and rehearing
of the matters of creed and covenant could be kept from
becoming intolerable only by more than occasional ven-

tures of questioning and doubting. Of course, the Court could not presume to forbid the holding of certain opinions, nor perhaps would it censure their utterance in private intercourse; but if there was the scent of mischief in them, they were not to be ventilated among neighbors, but referred to the elders, or cautiously handled in the meetings of church members for discipline. Even the silent protest of leaving the assembly when an infant was presented for baptism was now forbidden.

A year after the passage of this law we have an intimation of the discontent it had excited, in the following action of the Court, Oct. 18, 1645 : —

"Upon a petition of divers persons, for consideration of the law about new-comers not staying above three weeks without licence, and the law against Anabaptists, the Court hath voted that the laws mentioned should not be altered at all, nor explained." [1]

But there were others who favored the law, as appears from the action of the Court, May 6, 1646, as follows : —

"The petition of divers of Dorchester, Roxberry, etc., to the number of 78, for the continuance of such orders, without abrogation or weakening, as are in force against Anabaptists, and other erronios persons, where by to hinder the spreading or divulging of their errors, is granted." [2]

One of the deputies of the Court from Dover, Edward Starbuck, had been fined for three weeks' absence. The Court in October, 1648 —

"being informed of great misdemeanor committed by Edward Starbuck, of Dover, with profession of Anabaptistry, for which he is to be proceeded against at the next Courte of Assistants if evidence can be prepared by that time," [3]

on account of the season and the distance, appointed two commissioners to send for witnesses and sworn testimony. We hear no more of this case.

[1] Records, ii. 141.   [2] Ibid., ii. 149.   [3] Ibid., ii. 253.

Recognizing the rigidity of discipline which the Court had adopted as its rule in matters concerning other persons' consciences, though in our judgments so mistaken and oppressive, we cannot but recognize also its persistency as shown in meddling with matters that alarmed them beyond their jurisdiction, which threatened mischief for Massachusetts. This is strikingly exhibited in the following letter addressed by the Court in October, 1649, to the Plymouth authorities. The letter will explain itself : —

"HONORED AND BELOVED BRETHEREN, — Wee have heard heeretofore of diverse Annabaptists, arisen up in your jurisdiction, and connived at; but being but few, wee well hoped that it might have pleased God, by the endeavors of yourselves and the faithful elders with you, to have reduced such erring men again into the right way. But now, to our great greife, wee are credibly informed that your patient bearing with such men hath produced another effect, namely, the multiplying and increasing of the same errors, and wee feare may be of other errors also, if timely care be not taken to suppresse the same. Perticularly wee understand that within this few weekes there have been at Sea Cunke thirteene or fowerteene persons rebaptized (a swift progress in one toune), yett wee heare not of any effectual restriction is entended thereabouts. Lett it not, wee pray you, seeme presumption in us to mind you heereof, nor that wee earnestly intreate you to take care as well of the suppressing of errors as of the maintenance of truth, God aequally requiring the performance of both at the hands of Christian magistrates, but rather that you will consider our interest is concerned therein. The infection of such diseases being so neere are likely to spread into our jurisdiction ; *tunc tua res agitur paries cum proximus ardet.* Wee are united by confoedaracy, by faith, by neighbourhood, by fellowship in our sufferings as exiles, and by other Christian bonds, and wee hope neither Sathan nor any of his instruments shall by theis or any other errors disunite us, and that wee shall never have cause to repent us of our so neere conjunction with you, but that wee shall both so aequally and zealously uphold all the truths of God revealed, that wee may render a comfortable accompt to Him that hath sett us in our places, and

betrusted us with the keeping of both tables, of which well hoping,
wee cease your farther trouble, and rest, Your very loving Freinds
and Bretheren." [1]

If there is bigotry, there is something other and better
than bigotry in that earnest and tender appeal to fellow-
exiles and fellow-believers in behalf of beliefs and principles
supremely precious to them. The dread of new dissensions
and divisions was for a long period the motive for stiffening,
instead of prompting a relaxation of, the attempt to secure
accord of opinion from " tender consciences." Massachusetts was aggrieved at the very slight response made by
Plymouth to the remonstrance and appeal. But an opportunity was now to present itself in which the authorities
would visit their discipline upon the prime agent in the
grievance which had drawn forth the above letter. This
was one Obadiah Holmes. He had joined the Salem church
on his coming hither, and being dismissed after seven years
of membership, in 1645, had become a member of the Congregational Church at Seekonk, or Rehoboth, the pastor of
which, an exiled Church clergyman, Samuel Newman, com-
piled the famous Bible Concordance which bears his name.
Some dissension arising in the church, Holmes with some
others seceded, and set up a Baptist Society, probably having procured baptism from Dr. John Clarke, pastor of the
Baptist Church in Newport. In response to the letter from
Massachusetts, Holmes was summoned by Plymouth Court
on June 4, 1650, and presented Oct. 2, 1650; but he does
not appear to have been sentenced. Dr. Clarke, a man
of great abilities and of a calm spirit and fine character,
after having practised as a physician in London, had come
to Boston just at the height of the strife with Mrs. Hutchinson, and marvelling that the excited parties could not
harmonize their variances, had moved to Rhode Island,
where at Newport he founded a Baptist Church, in 1644.

[1] Records, iii. 174.

He was also highly esteemed as a physician, and as Treasurer and Assistant of the Colony. Of a visit made by him
to Massachusetts, and the treatment he received there, we
have an account from his own pen, temperately but forcibly
related in a pamphlet entitled " Ill Newes from New England, etc.," published in London in 1652.[1] Backus, the
excellent historian of the Baptists, says that Clarke the
pastor, with two members of the church, Holmes and John
Crandall, were sent here by it on an errand of religious
sympathy to William Witter, already under our notice, and
that he was a member of their church. Clarke does not
mention this latter particular, nor does it appear how it
could have been so. Witter was infirm and nearly if not
quite blind. His membership may have been through
sympathy, correspondence, and recognition.

We will now follow Dr. Clarke's narrative, premising
that he and his companions were alike obnoxious to Massachusetts. Clarke sympathized fully in the conviction of
Roger Williams that the magistrate had no function in
matters of religious opinion, belief, or observance. He
said, " A sword of steel cannot come near or touch the
spirit or mind of man ; " and from the common armory
of Scripture for both sides in all controversies, quoted
the words of Jesus that the tares were not to be plucked
out, but left patiently to grow with the grain. Clarke
justifies the publishing his narrative on the ground that
an opportunity for open debate and argument having been
offered, was afterward denied to him. He had a strong
ground for rebuking the authorities of Massachusetts for
their compelling non-church-members and the unwilling
to attend upon their set services, and forbidding them to
meet in other congenial private assemblies. He objects
also that their churches were not " called together at the
command of the Lord," as at first, but by authority or allowance of the magistrates. He says he arrived in Boston, on

[1] This is reprinted in Mass. Hist. Soc. Coll., 4th series, vol. ii.

his first coming, in November, 1637, and being pained at the controversy about the two Covenants of Works and Grace, moved away for quiet and edification. On his visit with his companions on their errand of sympathy, July 19, 1651, " we lodged at a Blind man's house, by name William Witter." The next day was the first day of the week, when, " not having freedom in our Spirits for want of a clear Call from God to goe unto the Publick Assemblie," two miles distant, at Lynn, to declare their minds there, they held a service at the house where they lodged. Clarke says that four or five strangers came in unexpectedly midway in the services, and remained. This presence of outsiders, as we shall see, aggravated the charges against Clarke. The fact of the presence of the party must have been noised abroad; for while Clarke was preaching, two constables came in and served a magistrate's warrant for their arrest and presentment the next day. The constables being politely invited to listen till the exercises were closed, declined, and took the three to the ordinary, or ale-house. After dinner the officers proposed to take them to the place of worship, though Clarke warned them that if forced there they should in the meeting " declare dissent both by word and gesture." On entering the meeting, the congregation were uncovered and at prayer. Clarke says, " At my first stepping over the threshold, I unveiled myself, civilly saluted them, turned into the seat I was appointed to, put on my hat again, and so sat down, opened my Book, and fell to reading." The constable being ordered by the magistrate to remove Clarke's hat, did so. After the services ended, Clarke stood up, civilly asking if as a stranger he might propose a few things to the congregation, and waited a courteous reply. The pastor asked him if he was a member of a church, etc. Before he could answer, Mr. Bridges, the magistrate, said that if the congregation permitted he should be allowed, but not to make objections to what had been delivered. Clarke replied that he did not in-

tend to make such objections, but simply to explain his
gesture, showing lack of sympathy in coming into the
Assembly, " as they were strangers to each other's inward
standing with respect to God, and so cannot conjoyn
act in Faith.   And in the second place, I could not
judge that you are gathered together, and walk according
to the visible order of our Lord."   Mr. Bridges stopped
him there, saying that he had spoken that for which he
must answer.   The visitors were carried to the ordinary,
" watched over that night as Theeves and Robbers," and
next morning Mr. Bridges sent them by *complaint* to Boston
prison.   It would appear, from the charges in their sentence
afterward, as if they had held a meeting again at Witter's
on Monday morning.   The mittimus charged them with
holding a private meeting on the Lord's Day, exercising
among themselves, joined by some of the town's people, disturbing and contemning the public meeting, and " for suspition of having their hands in the re-baptising of one or
more among us."   On being brought to trial at the County
Court, July 31, Clarke denied the name of Anabaptist, with
which he was charged; for though admitting that he had
baptized many, he would not admit that it was a rebaptism,
because the former rite for them was null.   The offences
for which he was sentenced were, for preaching in a private
house on the Lord's Day where some of the inhabitants of
the town were gathered; for keeping on his hat during
prayer in the public assembly, and disturbing and professing against the church; and the next day, in contempt of
authority, and while in custody of the law, did again meet
at Witter's house, and there " administer the Sacrament of
the Supper to one excommunicate person, to another under
admonition, and to another that was an inhabitant of Lynn,
and not in fellowship with any church."   Other offences
in Court were, his adroit denial of having rebaptized some
who as infants had shared the rite, and his rejecting infant
baptism, and the ordinances and ministers, as nullities.

He was sentenced to pay a fine of twenty pounds, or give securities for it till the first day of the next Court, remaining in prison till then, " or else to be well whipt." Holmes was sentenced to a fine of thirty pounds, and Crandall of five, with the same alternative of being " well whipt." Clarke then asked if he might speak to the Court, alleging a promise made to him by Mr. Bridges that he should have that liberty. This being allowed, Clarke asked, as a stranger, to see the law by which he had been adjudged, quoting their own law warranting his demand. The Governor, Endicott, here

" being somewhat transported, broke forth, and told me I had deserved death, and said he would not have such trash brought into their jurisdiction ; moreover, he said, you go up and down, and secretly insinuate into those that are weak ; but you cannot maintain it before our Ministers : you may try and discourse or dispute with them," etc.

Though he was at once hurried off by the jailer, Clarke rightfully improved this taunt and challenge, by writing from his prison the next day to the Court, proposing to dispute with the ministers, and asking that a time be fixed for it. There was some playing fast and loose by the Court in the matter, the dispute being promised at a set time, and then by pretexts deferred. Clarke was told that he was not sentenced " for judgement or conscience, but for matter of fact and practice." But Clarke prepared his statement and propositions, and got them before one of the magistrates. Had he been permitted a fair field, those who coped with him would have needed to be keen and able. But the keeper of the prison received on the 11th of August an order for his release. His fine had been paid for him by some friends without his approval. The sincere man was sorely troubled that the proposed disputation, for which he says the expectation of the country was greatly raised, was frustrated. So he wrote at once before leaving

the prison a manifesto, expressing his regret that his fine
had been paid, and his readiness still to hold the disputation. The next day being Commencement at Cambridge,
it was rumored that Cotton had been selected to dispute
with him. This highly pleased Clarke, because he regarded
Cotton " as being the inventor and supporter of that way,
in these parts, wherein they walk." But the Governor,
deputy, and three of the magistrates here interposed.
They, by a letter to Clarke, charged him with misreport-
ing the fact. He had not been promised, and could not
have, a public disputation. It was to be private, and would
still be allowed on matters propounded by Clarke, with a
single elder, and before a moderator, Clarke to be harmless from civil process. He answered the letter from the
prison, August 14, insisting that he had represented truly
the promise made to him in the Court for a public dispute,
for which he was still ready, but declined a private debate.
The magistrates were doubtless wise on their own side in
avoiding the risks from " the infection " of the proscribed
opinions which would inevitably have attended any public
discussion. It was well known to them that very many of
the community alike in the larger towns and in every rural
settlement were as inflammable as tow when listening to
utterances involving novelties of opinion. The points contested in the controversy about the proper subjects and
method of baptism as the initiative rite of Christian discipleship, were more intelligible to the people in general
than were the abstruse and perplexing abstractions of the
Antinomian controversy. Matters of variance were to be
suppressed, if possible, by strict measures rather than by
fair and free debate. Some years afterward, on April 15,
1668, a public disputation was held by ministers in Boston,
represented by Whiting and Cobbett, with the defenders of
Baptist principles.

Dr. Clarke, burdened by the sense of the inhospitality
and indignity of his treatment, and still more by his hav-

ing been denied the much coveted opportunity of defending
his opinions, was called by his many responsibilities to
family, friends, and public offices, to return to Newport.
Holmes, the most obnoxious of all the intruders, suffered
the sentence of whipping. The thirty stripes laid upon his
bared body at the post, he says were severely inflicted by
the officers, but through the fervor and constancy graciously granted to him, " he told the Magistrates, you have
struck me as with Roses." Two of the spectators, who,
after the punishment, went up to him to take his hand
and express sympathy, were fined for so doing. The friend
for whom these sufferers were brought under the ordeal,
William Witter, was presented at Salem Court, Nov. 27,
1651, " for neglecting discourses, and being rebaptized." [1]

One who, in rehearsing the early history of Massachusetts, has set to himself the purpose of repressing the
utterances of regret, reproach, or indignation, for the severities of the Puritan rule, referring them all to a loyalty to their austere principles, will often find that purpose
put to a sharp trial. Most of the sufferers by these austerities, besides offering degrees of provocation, had a vigor
of self-assertion and solaces of their own to support them.
Their spirits were not broken, nor could they complain
that, having rendered some form of valuable service to the
community, they had received only wrong and ingratitude
in return. The treatment visited upon Henry Dunster,
the first President of Harvard College, for his avowed rejection of infant baptism, stands in many respects as a
special and peculiar illustration of the sternness of the
Puritan rule. But while our sympathies can hardly fail
to be warmly engaged on his side in his painful experience,
we must hesitate whether to visit our indignation on those
who so harshly dealt with him, or to recognize their sturdy
consistency with their own resolve to enforce impartially
their own intolerant principles. In the case now to be

[1] Lewis and Newhall, Lynn, p. 231.

rehearsed we are to bear in mind that Dunster was in full sympathy with the Puritan system, and its most trusted teacher, except on a single point of doctrine.

Dunster presents himself to us as one of the most engaging, lovable, and eminently serviceable men in our earliest annals. We have learned to reiterate, with all grateful regard and appreciation, our high tributes of respect to the founders of our State for their noble purposes in providing for a seat of learning in the first years of their wilderness life. The glory of our rich and revered University, the fountain of so much of blessing and honor to us, the favored deposit of our generosity and munificence, reflects back upon those who, with a single view to the welfare of their posterity, laid its foundations in the days of their extremest struggles and poverty. But to one man, its first President, we must assign the supreme tribute of our homage, for his eminent ability, his earnest devotion, and his wise administration, continued through fourteen years, in the organization of the College, in devising all practical plans for its studies and discipline, and in providing the method of its government and oversight, which in its best elements continues unchanged to this day.

The birthplace and the age of Dunster have not been positively certified to us. He received his two academic degrees at Magdalene College, Oxford, 1630-34. With the repute of eminent scholarship and an attractive character, he was warmly welcomed, on his arrival in Boston in 1640, by many of his former personal acquaintances and friends here. His coming, with the abilities and virtues which he brought with him, was most opportune for the Colony. The infant college, then but a school starting with a promise for its future, had been for two years committed to the charge of a most unworthy person as its head, and he had been summarily displaced in disgrace. Dunster was inducted as President, Aug. 27, 1640. He became a member of the church in Cambridge under the pastorship of Shepard, who died Aug. 25, 1649. In the relation of Dunster's religious experience on his admission to the church, we find an intimation of his views on a subject which had evidently been exercising his mind, and about which a subsequent change of opinion was to cause him much hard experience. He said, "There is something concerning sprinkling in Scripture, hence not offended when it is used." Dunster supplied the desk with great acceptance after the death of Shepard till the induction of Mitchell, Aug. 21, 1650. Mitchell had been brought here as a youth, and had graduated under Dunster's presidency in 1647. The pupil was soon, as pastor, put into embarrassing relations with his honored teacher. Dunster, in his preaching, had often declared his disapproval of infant baptism. On the birth of one of his own children in 1653, he forbore to present it for the rite, after the usual custom, in the meeting-house. There was much excited feeling in the church, and Dunster was earnestly advised to keep his opinions to himself. The young pastor pleaded for moderation and delay, but was urged on by others to the usual method of discipline. It was an embarrassing office for him, as in gravity, learning, and earnest but calm moderation in argument, the President was more than his match. Mitchell tried his utmost in a difficult work. He found scruples and misgivings arising in his own mind, as consequent upon the strong reasoning of Dunster, though he himself referred them to the promptings of the Evil One. Burdened night and day by the difficulty of the office he had undertaken, he was afraid of repeating his visits to Dunster, as he "found a venom and poison in his insinuations and discourses against Pædobaptism." Finding many of his own congregation halting and faltering on the subject, he preached many sermons defending infant baptism.

Early in 1654 the magistrates wrote to the ministers about the risk to the country and the college in this dissension, asking them to consider the matter and advise them what to do in the case. Accordingly, in February, nine of the ministers, two ruling elders, and Dunster met in a conference at Boston.[1] Dunster maintained the proposition, — " visible believers only should be baptised." Norton granted the proposition, but added the strange corollary, that " Infants of believing parents in church state are visible believers." This Dunster denied ; but with singular sweetness of pleading he said that infants were in no danger, as Christ gave them " a nearer access unto him and a nearer acceptance with him than children under the law." The aptness of this remark was in its meeting the notion of some of the elders, that infant baptism corresponded to circumcision under the law. Dunster then advanced this strong assertion, " All instituted Gospel worship hath some express word of Scripture. But Pædobaptism hath none."

The General Court had already passed an order in August, 1653, " that every person that shall publish and maintain any hoethrodoxe and erroneous doctrine shalbe liable to be quaestioned and censured by the County Court where he liveth, according to the merit of his offence." [2] And now, the ministerial conference having failed of its object, the Court, in May, 1654, passed the following : —

" Forasmuch as it greatly concerns the welfare of this country that the youth thereof be educated, not only in good literature but sound doctrine, this Court doth therefore commend it to the serious consideration and speciall care of the officers of the colledge and the selectmen in the severall townes, not to admitt or suffer any such to be contynued in the office or place of teaching, educating, or instructing of youth or child in the colledge or schooles, that have manifested themselves unsound in the fayth or scandelous in theire lives, and not giveing due satisfaction according to the rules of Christ." [3]

Dunster took the broad hint thus cast toward him, and sent in his resignation as President, to the Court, through

---

[1] The manuscript containing the minutes of the conference is in the cabinet of the Massachusetts Historical Society.

[2] Records, vol. iv. pt. i. p. 151.   [3] Ibid., iii. 343, 344.

the Overseers, dated June 10, 1654. On the 25th of the month the Court took the following notice of the matter:

"In answer to a writinge presented to this Court by Mr. Henry Dunster, wherein, amongst other things therin contayned, he is pleased to make a resignation of his place as president, this Court doth order that it shalbe left to the care and discretion of the overseers of the Colledge to make provision, in case he persist in his resolution more than one moneth (and informe the overseers) for some meete person to carry on and ende that work for the present, and also to act in whatever necessitie shall call for, untill the next session of this Court, when we shalbe better enabled to settle what shalbe needful in all respects in refference to the Colledge; and that the said overseers wilbe pleased to make returne to this Court at that time of what they shall doe herein." [1]

Whatever Dunster may have said in his letter of the reason for his resignation, no reference is made by the Court to the cause of it. The Overseers gave Dunster to understand that his service was so valuable and so highly appreciated that if he would keep silence he might remain. But he had his own conscience, which would not allow him to be guided by theirs. More than this. In order to show that he still held his convictions, on the occasion of an infant being offered for baptism in the meeting-house, July 30, 1654, he rose and bore testimony of disapproval. Of course the Court availed itself of its own order, assigning the dealing with such offences to the county courts. And so, eight months after the offence had been committed, and ten months after Dunster had resigned his office, we read the following record of the County Court, Cambridge: —

"April 3, 1655, Mr. Henry Dunster being presented to this Court by the Grand Jury for disturbance of the ordinances of Christ upon the Lord's day, at Cambridge, July 30, 1654, to the dishonor of the name of Christ, his truth and minister" —

[1] Records, iii. 352.

witnesses testified to the interruption which he continued when asked by the elder to forbear; affirming that
only visible penitent believers are the subjects of baptism ; that they were going to do something not conformed
to the institution or mind of Christ ; that the covenant of
Abraham is not ground for baptism ; and that corruptions
were coming in. The last point probably had reference to
the embarrassment already realized in the Colonies generally, coming from the growing up of so many unbaptized
persons, consequent upon the limitation of the rite to the
children of parents being church members. This embarrassment was soon to lead to the adoption of " the Half-
way Covenant."

The Court then ordered that by the ecclesiastical law of
1646, punishing the offence of contempt, Dunster should be
publicly admonished by a magistrate at the next lecture-
day at Cambridge, and give bonds for his appearance.
Dunster answered the next day, denying that he had done
anything in " contempt." He was firm but gentle in his
response, saying that he had spoken in the fear of God,
that he stood to what he had said, and wished a kind construction put upon his course. The admonition was in due
course administered on him in the meeting-house at Cambridge by the magistrate. It furnishes a scene for the
Alumni of Harvard who have cared to know the history of
the college which is their pride, and to trace its noble service in the enlargement and liberalizing of thought and the
advancement of truth. Here was this scholar and notable
trainer of scholars, probably the most learned man in the
Colony, as learning was then measured and valued, in the
glory of his ripe manhood and personal beauty, his auburn
locks not yet silvered, greatly beloved by all who knew him,
standing to be censured for a heresy. True, he had violated a law of the Colony, and by freeing his own conscience
in protesting offensively against a rite which he believed to
be meaningless and erroneous, he had wounded the con-

sciences of others, his friends, who grieved at his course.
But if the freedom of a true soul could not be allowed to
him, who could enjoy the right which all professed to value?
It was in the meeting-house, where Dunster's prayers and
his teachings on all other subjects had been received with
responsive assent and gratitude. Doubtless among the
spectators of that scene were some of Dunster's young
scholars. Would their immature judgments draw from it
an influence leading them in riper years to bigotry or scepticism? Yet the admonishers and the admonished were
alike sincere, "walking in the light" granted to each of
them. One is well disposed to recognize some other than
an angry or vengeful feeling in the inflictors of this
harsh discipline; for we know that only a stern fidelity
to their own convictions could prompt them thus to deal
with a revered man whom they all loved and highly
prized.[1]

Dunster had sent in a second resignation Oct. 24, 1654.
Nine days after this, November 2, the Overseers had elected
Charles Chauncy as his successor. He also was a heretic
on the subject of baptism, believing that though infants
were proper subjects of the rite, it ought to be performed
by immersion, not by sprinkling. On this, and on another
belief of his, namely, that the Lord's Supper ought to be
observed in the evening, he agreed to the requisition of

---

[1] In that precious publication, "New England's First Fruits," printed in
London, in an early year of Dunster's presidency, we read : " Over the College
is Master Henry Dunster placed as President, a learned, considerable, and in-
dustrious man, who has so trained up his pupils in the tongues and arts, and
so seasoned them with the principles of Divinity and Christianity, that we
have, to our great comfort, and in truth beyond our hopes, beheld their progress in learning and godliness also." Cotton Mather says of his removal from
office for his heresy : " He filled the Overseers with uneasy fears, lest the students, by his means, should come to be ensnared." The famous Bay Psalm
Book, printed at Cambridge in 1640, after it had passed the hands of the three
ministers who prepared it, was submitted to Dunster, "to use a little more art
upon it." Mather says Dunster "revised and refined the translation." Seeing that it is what it is after this process, what must it have been before it?

the Overseers that he would reserve expressing himself. He had been about returning to England.

The high-minded and patient Dunster had sent a letter to the Court Nov. 4, 1654, acquiescing in his lot. He was living in a house the means for building which for the use of the president had been largely secured by himself, from his special friends. It was provided with resources for the coming of a sharp New England winter. His wife was sick, as was his youngest child, seriously. His accounts, public and private, were unsettled. He desired the Court to consider these matters, and referring to his "extraordinary labors" for the college for fourteen years, he asks for a continued temporary use of the house. There are many papers preserved in our State Archives, which, had they been lost, though they might have left some gaps in our history, would have made unnecessary some of the blushes caused by the fathers for their posterity. Among them is one [1] containing a reply of the Court to Dunster's letter. Bellingham and Endicott were then Governor and Deputy. The reply sneers at Dunster's reference to his "extraordinary labors," asking what he had done except as belonging to his station. The house is refused to him while settling his accounts, because he might protract the matter indefinitely. On the 10th of the month Dunster again addressed the Court in reply to their curt answer to him. The "Considerations" which he offers concern most the season for a houseless and afflicted family. The close of it touches a tender point:

"The whole transaction of this business is such, which in process of time, when all things come to mature consideration, may very probably create a grief on all sides, yours subsequent, as mine antecedent. I am not the man you take me to be. Neither, if you knew what I hold and why, can I persuade myself that you would act as I am at least tempted to think you do." [2]

[1] Mass. Archives, lviii. 26.　　　　　　[2] Ibid., lviii. 30.

26

He was allowed to remain till March. Besides his own children, he had those of his wife by a former husband to provide for. His oldest child was nine years, the youngest thirteen months old. He went to reside at Scituate, the Old Colony being more tolerant; and here he did kind service in helping the minister. He never, like Roger Williams, submitted to rebaptism. His affairs occasionally calling him to Cambridge, where he still held church relations, a child was there born to him in December, 1656. For not offering it for baptism he was presented by the Grand Jury to the Cambridge Court, April 7, 1657, admonished, and required to give bonds to appear at the next Court of Assistants, for breach of the law of 1646. He died at Scituate, Feb. 27, 1659, and by his own request his body was brought for interment in sight of the hall where he had so devotedly labored and which he so fondly loved.[1] He kindly remembered in his will Mitchell and Chauncy.

There is no single exercise in our early annals more painful than is offered us in the case of Dunster, of the mixed authority, civil and religious, in what we have learned to regard as ways unjust, bigoted, and cruel in the treatment of matters of conscientious opinions. Its peculiar quality is that it emphasizes the fact that personal attachments and high public interests were here sacrificed, and held to be justly and necessarily surrendered, in order that an impartial and awful sternness of fidelity to a standard of religious obligation might not be violated. The Court and the Overseers seem to us to have been actually besotted

---

[1] Morton, in New England's Memorial, says : " He was embalmed and removed to Cambridge, and honorably buried." This embalming, which was done by filling the coffin with tansy and other herbs, helped in the identification of the remains of Dunster. The memorial stone first planted over them having decayed, and the inscription having disappeared, there had been some uncertainty as to the spot. This was removed by the search, the herbs still retaining their fragrance in 1845, when the Corporation provided a new and fitting monument.

in their course with Dunster. Not a single word to his discredit or disesteem is found on the record. They well knew his fitness and worth in his place. They put a just estimate upon his talents, his piety, the singular graces of his character, and his eminence in all that they prized as scholarship. That they should have dealt with him as they did is an apt illustration of the view taken of their ideal, design, and method of a Biblical commonwealth, in these pages. It is also an illustration of the fact that the spirit and type of their bigotry, however in part originating in the infirmities of human nature, drew some of its relentless severity from their creed.[1]

The Baptists were the first among the sects or denominations, breaking in upon the "standing order" of the Puritan church in Boston, to establish themselves as a separate congregation in the interest of the special tenet of their creed. The distinction thus won by the sect was honorably secured by patient, persistent fidelity and constancy under a severe ordeal of opposition. There was something far more significant in innovation, and in the direction of a radical, revolutionary change in the doctrinal platform of this fellowship, than in that of either of the other existing offshoots from the Congregationalism of the Calvinistic or Westminster pattern. To this fact we must refer the attempted repressive effort of the Court in its harsh dealing with the new sect. The old Congregationalism of the Colony is now represented by many separate fellowships still holding to the original policy of church institution and administration, but distinguished by degrees and shades of liberalism in doctrinal beliefs. The Baptists, however, struck at the most vital point in the Puritan method for the constitution and perpetuity of a church. The children of those already in covenant,

---

[1] Life of Henry Dunster, by Rev. Jeremiah Chaplin, D.D. Boston, 1872. This little volume is alike valuable for the authenticity of its matter and the impartiality of its spirit.

like the heirs of an estate, were to accede to the Christian inheritance. The rite of baptism was the initiatory seal of this heirship, and full possession would follow when in maturer years they came under the covenant of their parents. But neither the Court nor the elders could notice without anxiety and dismay the painful facts all too forcibly pressed upon their attention, that large numbers of children were growing up around them who had not been baptized because their parents had not been in covenant; and also that many baptized in infancy had, on reaching mature years, failed to become church members. The sad question naturally presented itself whether the community henceforward was to consist prevailingly of a heathen or a Christian population. The doctrinal position of the Baptists rather aggravated than relieved the anxiety and perplexities of the authorities in Church and State on this point. Making no account of any Christian birthright accruing to children from their parents, infant baptism was discredited, and it was left for each man and woman under religious experience to receive "believer's baptism," and that by immersion.

The house of worship now in succession occupied by the First Baptist Society in Boston, bears the inscription, "Organised in 1665." It is a peaceful way of stating an occasion which engaged many measures of ill-temper and intolerance. There were worthy persons then in the Colony who had been honored members of Baptist fellowships in England. Some had quietly held their convictions without obtruding them; others had adopted Baptist views while members of the Puritan churches, and some of these, who had given offence, had been under discipline. In the year just mentioned several persons, with the courage of their convictions, gathered in an assembly of their own, with ordinances. The General Court, in October, 1665, following the action of a previous magistrates' court, thus dealt with the leaders of the movement. The charge was of "a schismaticall rending from the communion of the churches heere, and setting up a publick meetinge in opposition to the ordinances of Christ here publicly exercised." They had persisted in the offence after warning. They were further charged —

"with prophaning the holy appointments of Christ, and, in speciall, the sacraments of baptisme and the Lord's supper by administring the same to persons under censure of an approved church among us, and presuming as a covert of theise their irreligious and pernicious practices, to declare themselves to be a church of Christ."

Notwithstanding another solemn admonition, the offenders refused to give up their meetings under a church form. For their "presumption against the Lord and his holy appointments, as also the peace of this government," they were sentenced to disfranchisement and committed to prison.[1] The next year, September, 1666, the Court allowed their discharge on the payment of their fines. It also provided for a large public meeting "with a great concourse of people," which the prisoners were required to attend, where "diverse elders" attempted to convince them of their errors. Of course it was in vain. So in May, 1668, the Court made a further effort. A long preamble describes the offenders as "obstinate and turbulent Anabaptists formed with others in a pretended church estate, without the knowledge or approbation of the authority here established, as the law requires, to the great griefe and offence of the godly orthodox." Some of them are excommunicated persons. They have chosen officers not conformable to the law which requires such to be "able, pious, and orthodox." They assert that their proceedings are "according to the mind of God," and they are not convinced to the contrary. They make —

"infaunt baptisme a nullitie, thereby making us all to be unbaptized persons, and so consequently no regular churches, ministry, or

[1] Records, vol. iv. pt. ii. p. 290.

ordinances, and also renouncing all our churches as being so bad
and corrupt that they are not fitt to be held communion with, —
thus setting up a free school for seduction into wayes of error,
and opening a door for all sortes of abominations to come in
among us, with contempt of our civil order, and the authority
here established," etc.

The Court, therefore, "judge it necessary that they be
remooved to some other part of this country or elsewhere." [1]
They are sentenced to imprisonment and banishment, but
without avail.

From fragments of information to be gathered from
sources outside of the Records, we learn that there was
much agitation of feeling and popular dissent and opposition of judgment as to the course pursued by the Court.
The complaint and the lament just quoted from the Records enable us to apprehend the dismay and consternation
felt by the authorities. The new sect, planting itself as
resolutely upon Scripture principles as did their opponents,
would not yield to dictation or prohibition. Yet, as the
Court rightly affirmed, their fundamental tenet, and the
practice conformed to it, dealt a fatal blow to the doctrinal
system of the "standing order." It made "infaunt baptisme
a nullitie;" it pronounced all the members of the churches
"unbaptized persons," and left them without a valid ministry and ordinances. The Baptists, as yet having no trained
and able ministers, were served by unordained lay exhorters,
who also ventured to officiate in the ordinances, thus opening "a free school for seduction into wayes of error." The
"great concourse of people" who had crowded to listen to
the debates between the elders and the new dissenters,
included many sympathizers with the latter, and of course
the number of them would increase. The Court was further greatly scandalized and evidently irritated by a petition from several considerable persons in Boston and
Charlestown, desiring favor for the Baptists under its dis-

[1] Records, vol. iv. pt. ii. p. 374.

cipline. The petition is said to have contained "many reproachfull expressions against the Court and their proceedings." Several of the signers were summoned, some of whom expressed their sorrow for their act, and were let off. The magistrates succeeded in ferreting out two "cheife promoters of the petition, who had gone from house to house to get hands to it." These refusing "to discover the first contriver thereof," were admonished and fined.[1]

But the Court was compelled to yield to the persistence, fidelity, and quiet patience of these "turbulent Anabaptists." Both the name and the epithet attached to it had lost all proper meaning. The Baptists, correctly so called, built their place of worship, contented themselves with such leaders in their services as they could procure, and did not have to wait long before they were well furnished with able and learned divines. Courtesies and acts of fellowship between the Congregational and the Baptist ministers of Boston were the means of a graceful reconciliation of a grievous strife.

One other struggle, and that the severest and most tragic of the efforts of the Biblical commonwealth to maintain its rule against an equally resolute opposition, is now to engage our attention. It will close the warfare of militant Puritanism.

[1] Records, vol. iv. pt. ii. p. 413.

XII.

THE INTRUSION OF THE QUAKERS.

THE first English settlers of the peninsula of Boston, with its northern extremity rising from the deep waters of the Bay, and its southern border united to the mainland by a long, narrow neck, approved of the site for two sufficient reasons, — the harbor waters left them free intercourse with the rest of the globe, and the slender neck might easily be fortified against an inroad of the savages. An early visitor here commended the situation also for the reason that the neck would keep out mosquitoes, as it made the peninsula, literally, almost an island. This last hoped-for advantage, as the inhabitants of the town ever since have had occasion to be well aware, was delusive. Mosquitoes have always had free access here, yielding only to the autumn frost. The savages, though more than once dreaded, never crossed the neck but as friends or diplomats. But the sea-waters were not so secure. Many a panic and thrill of dread struck through the hearts of the inhabitants, at intervals for more than a century and a half, on rumors that French men-of-war were hovering near the Bay, that Spanish cruisers, privateers, and pirates were at hand to cast their volleys or to levy contributions. But, considering the occasion of it and the lamentable issues to which it led, never was there a sharper shock or a more ominous consternation caused to the magistrates of the town than when, July 11, 1656, tidings were circulated that there was a ship in the harbor bringing two Quaker women from England by way of Barbadoes. Were it not for the tragic consequences, including the darkest stain, among many other lamentable incidents, upon the annals of the Biblical commonwealth of Massachusetts, which followed upon the arrival of those two female apostles of truth and peace, we might pause over the absurd and comic elements of the consternation and panic caused by the occasion to those grave magistrates.[1] The women, as a matter of course, were rightfully supposed to bring with them a good supply of those mischievous and explosive little tracts, the munitions of their sect, as dreaded as was French ordinance.

Before narrating the proceedings which ensued upon the spreading of these evil tidings, let us note the quality and energy of the two forces which were then brought into sharp collision. The strongest and the weakest points of attack and resistance of both the parties present themselves at the opening of the strife.

The Puritans and the Quakers at that precise period represented the two most discordant and antagonistic bodies, or sects, by which Christendom was divided. The attitude of hostility in which so-called Papists and Protestants stood to each other, could hardly show more of alienation, antipathy, and even rancor, than were drawn out when the Quaker defiantly faced the Puritan, claiming to have a special mission of rebuke to him from Heaven. All the differences of sentiment, belief, conviction, and conduct which attach respectively to idealists and realists, to conservatives and radicals, to literalists and spiritualists, would need to be set forth most distinctly and emphatically in order to show in full contrast the principles and methods of the Puritans of Boston and their dreaded visitors. And

---

[1] Bishop, addressing the magistrates, in his " New England Judged," writes: "Two poor women arriving in your harbor, so shook ye, to the everlasting shame of you, and of your established peace and order, as if a formidable army had invaded your borders."

what after all makes the tragic narration before us one
that will draw most severely upon our candor, impartiality,
and sympathy, is the undeniable, indeed the obtrusive fact,
that Puritans and Quakers alike held their principles and
convictions with equally intense and conscientious sincerity, and exhibited an equal constancy and self-sacrifice
in tenacity and in fidelity to them.

Our sympathies, as we look back upon the melancholy
narrative, go with the Quakers, as temporarily the weaker,
but finally the victors through their patient heroism. Besides this, the illuminating truths, the liberalizing spirit,
and the sturdy principles, with the amiable virtues, which
found their first earnest expression and consistent advocacy in the Quakers, make us ready and glad to affirm that
the right was on their side, and that they were on the side
of the right. But that had to be proved. It is not to
be assumed as apparent, and least of all as to have been
recognizable by the Puritans. It may well be asked if
some superficial readers of our history and some loving
champions of the Quakers have not lost sight of the fact
that the Puritans also had consciences and principles, —
not attractive to us indeed, but very constraining and very
precious to them, as bought with a price, and held by them
devoutly as by an actual covenant between them and God.
So inadequately has the intense sincerity of the Puritans
been appreciated by some of their censorious judges, as to
have allowed the assumption, with a marvellous compla-
cency, that they should at once have stricken their colors
at the first volley of the Quakers. We may well use that
word " volley " in description of the scornful, bitter, and
contemptuous tones, language, epithets, and peremptory
demands, with denunciations of Divine judgments hanging
over them, by which the Quakers challenged the Puritans
at once to give up and renounce all the beliefs and usages
approving them as in covenant with God. The Puritan
sermons, prayers, ministry, worship, and sacraments were

in the plainest and rudest terms of speech, with the glow
and passion of a burning zeal thrown into them, declared
to be the mere ritual of the devil. A striking illustration
of the fact that sympathy in feeling will engage partiality
in judgment, is offered when the champions of the first
Quaker intruders into Massachusetts express strongly
not only their complaints but also their amazement, that
they should have had such a rough reception. The intolerance of the Puritans, and their bigotry, were proper
subjects of rebuke by the Quakers. But when the Quakers
at once assailed with scorn and vituperation the religious
beliefs and methods of the Puritans, they themselves became intolerant. As the event has proved, the characteristic Puritan principles and usages which the Quakers so
reviled, — a paid ministry, prepared pulpit discourses, formal services, and the ordinances, — have survived the peculiarities of Quakerism. Renouncing the use of swords and
all other weapons, and non-resistants of all violence against
them, the Quakers, above all other contestants and assail-
ants, must be allowed to have waged the most galling warfare with the tongue. Before we bring the representatives
of these two sharply discordant parties into each other's
presence, we must inform ourselves, not only as to who and
what the strangers really were, but as to what, under the
circumstances, was of more consequence, — who and what
they were thought to be. The fact that alike here and in
England the Quakers first and most offensively presented
themselves by the extravagances of their earliest manners,
deprived their noble principles of a fair and candid hearing.

Brains, imaginations, impulses, dreams, emotions, consciences, and even the muscles and nerves of the body, had
each a part and place in the intense workings of the religious sentiment, freed from former restraints, in novel and
startling manifestations during the middle of the seventeenth century in England. Strangely enough, it was from
the convulsive agitations and workings of muscles and

nerves by a few enthusiasts when under the dealing of magistrates, that by a mere hap-hazard remark the disciples
of George Fox came to be known then, as afterward, as
Quakers. Their own chosen designation — one which then
and ever since best became them, in principle and in life —
was "the Society of Friends." In uttering their early
burdens and testimonies, they were observed to be exercised by violent shakings and tremblings of their limbs and
bodies. They explained the phenomena by saying that they
trembled and quaked under the power of the Spirit which
possessed them. "Then let them be called 'Quakers.'"
Those whom they offended and rebuked gave them the name
in derision. They made but slight objection to bearing it,
though they spoke of themselves as the people "in scorn
called Quakers." Soon they acquiesced in the common use
of the epithet.

Still more strange is it that this trivial incident, which
singled out the least significant and wholly indifferent phe-
nomenon of bodily quaking for inventing a name for the
new sect, serves as a specimen example to illustrate the
fact that for more than a score of years the mere oddities,
the offensive and aggressive behavior, and the intensely
extravagant and insolent language of the Quakers, were so
obtruded by them as wholly to hide from recognition the
lofty principles of truth and righteousness which are the
real glory of their fellowship. The Quakers, however, were
themselves rightly chargeable for this obscuring of their
own light, and blinding their opponents to its manifestation
in them. Their words and behavior were heard and seen to
be offensive and repulsive before those who withstood them
cared to be informed of their principles. As it proved,
these principles were in themselves so startling and obnoxious in their novelty and radicalism as to require all their
bold and heroic fidelity and constancy, even to gain them a
hearing. But having some grand illuminating and liberalizing truths as the staple of their principles, that fidelity

and constancy to them won them a triumph. The Quakers, from being the least understood and appreciated, and the most abusively and cruelly treated of all the contemporary sectaries, were the first of them all to secure large respect, immunity, and substantial independence. Before any other body of Nonconformists obtained even that measure of exemption from disabilities and penalties which arbitrary power at last yielded to them, the Quakers, partly from being winked at, overlooked, let alone, and partly from winning to themselves real respect, held their meetings unmolested, made affirmations instead of oaths, and solemnized their own marriages. And this success they gained without compliances or compromise. The very radicalism of their principles came rather to amaze than to shock or offend or irritate those who cared to inform themselves on the subject. But unfortunately our concern here is with those of the sect who first bore the name, and most offensively in speech and demeanor obtruded themselves, by their oddities and extravagances on men naturally most antagonistic to them. The Puritans, alike in Old England and in New England, regarded the first Quakers as — using familiar words now current — we regard " tramps " and " cranks ; " and this not without reasons furnished by the Quakers themselves. For they were roamers and wanderers from their own homes and country, seemingly dependent on chance fare ; they showed many signs of being " distraught in their wits;" they were uncivil and churlish, in substituting rude and blunt for courteous speech in addressing " superiors."

There are two quite distinct classes of publications making up the literature of Quakerism. The opinion which a reader in our time would be likely to form of the sect at its origin, of the character, spirit, education, and general demeanor and utterances of its members, will depend very much upon which class of these publications should chiefly engage his attention and furnish him with his information.

To the first class belong the original contributions to that
literature made by its first individual members. These are
chiefly small tracts containing journals, epistles, narratives
of individual experience in conviction, in travel, and under
opposition, trials before magistrates, and imprisonments.
These tracts came from the press voluminously, swelling
the flood of similar publications poured forth from the ferment working in the brains, hearts, and consciences of
people of all classes, especially of the middle class of England, in the seventeenth century. These original tracts are
not easily accessible except by readers who can avail themselves of the stores gathered on the shelves and in the
cabinets of libraries rich in that spoil of elder times.
Occasionally they may be picked up in the old book-stalls
of England, or turned out in searching garrets of ancient
dwellings. Only from these time-stained relics can one
catch the true aroma of the old spirit of those polemics.
They must be read in appreciation of, though not necessarily in sympathy with, the circumstances and the writers
which produced them. From perusing a considerable number of them one can easily inform himself as to the truth
about a question concerning which some differences of
opinion have found expression, whether the earliest Quakers were generally illiterate enthusiasts, intemperate in
controversy, and by their rude speech and unseemly behavior provoked the treatment which they received. Roger
Williams, the most trenchant and sharp-tongued of all the
opponents and disputants against Quakerism, says that he
had read George Fox's folio, and "above six-score books and
papers" relating to the sect. These of course were its
earliest literature. He gives his judgment and estimate
of this Quaker literature in these words: "Their many
books and writings are extremely Poor, Lame, Naked, and
sweld up only with high Titles and words of Boasting and
Vapour."[1] He adds, "that the Spirit of their Religion tends

[1] Publications of Narragansett Club, v. 5.

mainly to reduce Persons from Civility to Barbarisme."
Very many high encomiums have been passed by essayists
and literary critics, notably by Mr. Emerson, upon the rich
originality and vivacity of the religious genius of Fox, as
brightening the pages of his Journal and Epistles. But
Lord Macaulay, whose estimate of Fox is tart and flippant,
says that his "Journal, before it was published, was revised
by men of more sense and knowledge than himself, and
therefore, absurd as it is, gives us no notion of his genuine
style." [1] The historian does not give us his authority for
this statement, and I hesitate to accept it. I have before
me the folio edition of Fox's Journal published in 1694, four
years after his death, with fifty pages of prefatory matter by his devoted and ardent disciple William Penn; and
also the folio collection of his "Epistles to Friends," published in 1698, with a preface by his loving disciple George
Whitehead. Neither of these editors mentions any revision
of their originals, nor are there any tokens of a critical oversight. True, in reading the Epistles one may grow weary
over the very limited range of thoughts and ideas in them,
their lack of any glow of imagination, their repetition of a
few simple and gushing phrases of appeal and exhortation,
with an occasional intrusion of rant, and an almost maud-
lin liquidity of sentiment. But there are many passages in
Fox's Journal which have a marvellous vigor, sweetness,
and simple grace in the expression of the truths caught by
his spiritual insight. How could be expressed with more
comprehensiveness, force, and beauty, than in his words
following, the sufficiency to a believer, of Jesus Christ independently of forms, ordinances, ceremonies, priests, and
even Scriptures? Christ as the living and ever present
Head of the Church is "their Teacher to instruct them,
their Counsellor to direct them, their Shepherd to feed
them, their Bishop to oversee them, and their Prophet to
open divine mysteries unto them."

[1] History of England, chap. xvii.

Recurring to the original Quaker tracts which preceded the publication of Fox's collected works, though he himself sent forth several like single products of his pen, we may recognize in them all two general common qualities. Under quaint, often conceited, and often bellicose and vapory titles, not infrequently with rasping and objurgatory epithets, they contain the armory of sharp or defensive weapons against priests, opponents, and persecutors, vindications against misrepresentation and abuse, and narratives of knight-errantry on missionary work. Their other prevailing quality is an overgush of sentiment, in a few ever-recurring phrases of sometimes strong and tender, more often diluted and even unwholesome emotional fervors. They bear abundant evidence of sincerity and purity of experience, principle, and purpose, with joys and raptures of spirit over the deliverance from the fetters of literalism and formality, and the delights of free spiritual intercourse with God and with the new brotherhood. The range of thought and sentiment through which their testimonies and unstudied exhortations extended, made them very effective in speech and in devotional utterances over the hearts and minds of sympathetic hearers whose inner longings craved something more aglow with simple piety than they found in Puritan divinity with its ministrations. Travelling Quakers carried with them a full supply of their bellicose and their hortatory tractates, dispersing them freely as expositors of their principles, as denunciations of their persecutors, or as means of drawing others to their fellowship. When the obnoxious schismatics fell into the hands of the authorities, who regarded them as pestilent tramps and disturbers of the peace, these inflammatory tracts were taken from them and committed to the fire. I have several of them at my hand. It requires leisure and a special mood of mind to engage interest upon them. They mark faithfully a stage of progress in the emancipation of mind and spirit, in the middle classes of society,

from the cramps and fetters, the impositions and disabling
limitations of priestly sway, and the literalisms and formalities of the old religious rule. At the same time
these tracts reveal to us that the illumination and the
audacity requisite for the leaders in this special stage of
advance did not leave their own spirits wholly unclouded,
nor stop guardedly at the bounds where courage trespassed beyond order and decency.

The amount and comprehensiveness of what may be
called the Quaker literature may be inferred from the following titles of two considerable volumes; namely, " Bibliotheca Anti-Quakeriana;" or, A Catalogue of Books adverse
to the Society of Friends, — together with the Answers
which have been given to some of them by Friends and
others;" by Joseph Smith. London, 1873. 8vo. pp. 474.
" Bibliotheca Quakeristica: A Bibliography of Miscellaneous Literature, relating to the Friends. Chiefly written by persons not members of their Society;" by Joseph
Smith. London, 1883.

The compiler of these titles, with biographical sketches,
allows himself in both works a considerable range of liberty, as he includes many tracts and volumes having connection with the views and affairs of the Friends only very
indirectly, and principally as associated with the enormous
outpourings of the press on the subjects in discussion and
controversy with the utterers and antagonists of enthusiasm
and fanaticism of the time.

Nor should we fail to note that the most fiery and spicy
of the early tractates of Quakerism met with responses of
like character from the conservatives of the old rule whom
they aggrieved or outraged.

We can well understand what were the tone and contents of the contemporary tracts thrown back to the Quakers from those who scorned or dreaded them, under such
titles as these: " Hell Broke Loose ; or, an History of the
Quakers both Old and New;" by Thomas Underhill. 1660.

27

" Antichrist's Strongest Hold Overturned; or, the Foundation of the Religion of the People called Quakers, Bared
and Razed ;" by John Wiggan. 1665. " The Quaker
Catechism ;" by Richard Baxter. 1656. " Quakerism the
Pathway to Paganism;" by John Brown. 1678. Roger
Williams's pleasancy and piquancy led him to entitle his
onslaught upon Quakerism, " George Fox Digg'd out of
his Burrowes," thus paying his respects to Fox's able coad-
jutor, Edward Burroughs. The compliment was returned
in the answer to Williams entitled, " A New England Fire-
Brand Quenched." Morton, in his " New England Memorial," [1] says that President Dunster, in his retirement at
Scituate from persecution, " opposed the abominable opinions of the Quakers." Baylies [2] says that he was " vindictive " in his treatment of them. On the other hand,
General Cudworth, of Scituate, who, though not a Quaker, opposed their ill-treatment, said in a letter of 1658,
" Through mercy, we have yet among us the worthy Mr.
Dunster, whom the Lord hath made boldly to bear testimony against the spirit of persecution." [3] Something
more is to be said, further on, of the tongue rancor of
Roger Williams in his disputations against Quakers and
their ways.

The other class of Quaker publications, coming mainly
from those who had no share in their early contentions,
buffetings, and sufferings, but were in fellowship and
hearty sympathy with them, were the calm and intelligent
expositions of their principles, vindicating them from calumny, and proudly setting forth their purity, virtues, and
constancy. The fidelity and absolute truthfulness of these
writers may be implicitly relied upon. Nor is it strange
if their candor and impartiality are occasionally at fault.
They depend for the most part upon compilations and

[1] Davis's edition, p. 283.
[2] History of Plymouth Colony, ii. 50.
[3] Deane's History of Scituate, p. 248.

digests rrom the original Quaker tracts and journals. "New England Judged," by George Bishop, was the first of these secondary publications.[1] The best tribute that could be paid to the substantial excellence, veracity, and real practical value of Quaker principles, when freed from the crudity and extravagance of their original utterance and expression, was that during the lifetime of their first generation they should have found such able and adequate champions and exemplars as Besse, Sewall, Penn, and Barclay. Sewall's "History of the Quakers" was published in 1722. Besse's "Sufferings of the Quakers" was published in 1753. Robert Barclay, whose "Apology for the Church and People of God called in derision Quakers" we may even call the classical production of his fellowship, published his able work in 1676. The dates of Fox's two folios have already been given. The Friends have always been zealous in gathering, preserving, and editing the manuscripts of their members.[2]

From both classes of these original tracts — those of the Quakers and the anti-Quakers — we may well infer that the two parties were on a level in temper, effusiveness, and stinging volubility in the assault and defence. These characteristics are by no means restricted to this portion of the polemical literature of the time, but run through the whole of it. Fuller, if not richer, than the vocabulary of Shakspeare and Milton are these polemical fireworks in the sharp epithetical adjectives in which the English language abounds. Indeed, we learn its wealth in those terms

---

[1] Bishop's work was originally published in two parts, — the first in 1661, the second in 1667. The two, somewhat abridged, reappeared together in 1703, and bound with the volume is John Whiting's Answer to Cotton Mather's account of the New England Quakers, in his Magnalia.

[2] The first collection of these papers was made under the superintendence of Fox himself, at Swarthmore Hall, from 1651 to 1661. These are now preserved in the Friends' Depository, in Devonshire House, London. Joseph Smith published in London, in 1867, "A Descriptive Catalogue of Friends' Books," and in 1873, "A Catalogue of Books adverse to the Society of Friends."

of speech only after reading largely in the literature of sectarian controversy.

Quakerism, in its origin, was an eclecticism in tenets of belief and in principles of life and conduct. It did not originate as novelties either its eccentricities or its substantial principles, with the application of them. All the peculiarities of opinion and all the oddities and extravagances of demeanor first noticeable in the Friends had been adopted and exhibited by one or another of the extraordinary individuals or fellowships among the sectaries of the time. Edwards's " Gangreena," Pagitt's " Heresiography," Featley's " Dippers Dipt," and other similar summaries of novelties and extravagances of the time, show how those now identified with Quakerism had been anticipated. And this was in fact largely the occasion of the misconception, the ill-reception, and the odium which were concentrated upon the Friends. Their opinions and actions identified them with various types of fanatics and enthusiasts, who in their previous appearance had held these heresies in connection with some gross immoralities, some really malignant and defiant outrages and avowals which made them justly amenable to restraints and penalties. The Quakers really held none of these evil affiliations of heresy. They were, however, made responsible for them. One of these extravagances was a denial and contempt of civil magistracy, to which there are frequent references in these pages. The Quakers were charged with this lawlessness, but most unjustly. They objected only to the extension of the authority of magistracy over matters of religion and conscience, but in other respects were the most exemplary in their citizenship. This holding them as responsible for all the heresies in any way related to their opinions and principles, and what was really irritating, provoking, and offensive in their own rant of speech and unconventional and discourteous ways, were the chief occasions for the odium and violence visited on them.

Of George Fox, the founder — or rather organizer — of the Society of Friends, the best account we have is in his own words, as follow: —

A Testimony, how the Lord sent G. F. forth at first, in the Year 1643.

When the Lord first sent me forth in the Year 1643, I was sent as an Innocent Lamb (and Young in Years) [twenty years of age] amongst (Men in the Nature of) Wolves, Dogs, Bears, Lions, and Tigres, into the World, which the Devil had made like a Wilderness, no right Way then found out of it. And I was sent To Turn People from Darkness to the Light, which Christ, the Second Adam, did Enlighten them withal; that so they might see Christ, their Way to God, with the Spirit of God, which he doth pour upon all Flesh, that with it they might have an Understanding to know the Things of God, and to know him and his Son Jesus Christ, which is Eternal Life; and so might worship and serve the Living God, their Maker and Creator, who takes care for all, who is Lord of all; and with the Light and Spirit of God, they might know the Scriptures, which were given forth from the Spirit of God in the Saints and Holy Men and Women of God.

And when many began to be turned to the Light (which is the Life in Christ) and the Spirit of God, which gave them an Understanding, and had found the Path of the Just, the Shining Light, then did the Wolves, Dogs, Dragons, Bears, Lions, Tigres, Wild Beasts, and Birds of Prey make a Roaring and a Screeching Noise against the Lambs, Sheep, Doves, and Children of Christ, and were ready to devour them and me, and to tear us to pieces. But the Lord's Arm and Power did preserve me, though many times I was in Danger of my Life, and very often cast into Dungeons and Prisons, and haled before Magistrates. But all things did work together for good; And the more I was cast into outward Prisons, the more People came out of their Spiritual and Inward Prison (through the Preaching of the Gospel). But the Priests and Professors were in such a great Rage, and made the Rude and Profane People in such a Fury, that I could hardly walk in the Streets, or go in the High ways, but they were

ready oft-times to do me a Mischief. But Christ, who hath all
Power in Heaven and in the Earth, did so restrain and limit them
with his Power that my Life was preserved, though many times I
was near killed. Oh, the Burdens and Travels that I went under!
Often my Life prest down under the Spirits of Professors and
Teachers without Life, and the Profane! And besides the
Troubles afterwards with Backsliders, Apostates, and false Brethren, — which were like so many Judas's in betraying the Truth, —
and God's Faithful and chosen Seed, and causing the Way of
Truth to be evil spoken of! But the Lord blasted, wasted, and
confounded them, so that none did stand long; for the Lord did
either destroy them, or bring them to nought, and his Truth did
flourish, and his People in it, to the Praise of God, who is the
Revenger of his Chosen.

Fox, a son of "honest Christopher," a weaver, was born
at Drayton in July, 1624, and died Feb. 13, 1690. The
above account of himself was evidently written as a retrospect of the past. The reference which he makes to the
troubles which he had had with "Backsliders, Apostates,
and false Brethren" should fix our attention, because the
least offensive of the Friends suffered by not being distinguished from these unworthy pretenders and fanatics.

But Fox does not here tell us why he was so wondered
at and ill-treated, though his Journal affords a full explanation of the matter. As already stated, he and his brethren
were first known by what was simply whimsical, offensive,
and obtrusive in their ways,— their incivility, rudeness,
and seeming insolence and impudence. After Fox, in his
religious musings, had tried in vain to find spiritual help
from priests, professors, doctors of divinity, and dissenting
teachers, he came to the conclusion that they had none
to give him, had not even any themselves, but were all
"in the Dark." And soon he began very frankly to tell
them so, with rebukes and reproaches, thus bringing them
into contempt with those whose respect and confidence
they desired. As his life was a wandering one, he had

made himself a pair of "leather breeches," and was soon widely known by an epithet drawn from that part of his apparel. When it was noised abroad that "the man with leather breeches" was near by, a crowd was soon attracted. He visited "steeple-houses" to challenge and rebuke the priest. When brought before magistrates he refused to remove his hat, as this would signify deference or worship, or the acknowledgment of a superior, giving to men the honor that belonged only to God. For the same reason he used "thee" and "thou," instead of the usual plural pronoun, in addressing an individual. It may have been that Fox had read no other book than the Bible. If so, he illustrates a familiar saying, that a full knowledge of the English Bible is an education. Fox being asked his "warrant for the hat," that is, Scripture authority for keeping it on in the presence of magistrates, master as he was of the letter as well as the spirit of Scripture, he instantly quoted the only place where the word appears, — Daniel iii. 21, — of the three Jews who were bound before Nebuchadnezzar "in their coats, their hosen, and their hats," to be cast into the furnace.[1] So he proscribed

---

[1] Two missionary Quakers, Fisher and Stubbs, sent in to the Prince Elector Palatine of the Rhine, through his secretary, word that they "had a message for him." He received them courteously, and both at this interview, and at the supper with his nobles to which he invited them, the Quakers found much satisfaction in keeping on their hats, though all others were uncovered. There may have been brains under those hats, but the fact was not proved by this whimsey of the wearers, which, however, may have afforded as much amusement to the host and his guests as it did of conscientious comfort to the Quakers (Bishop, p. 17). I have somewhere met with an anecdote to this effect. A Quaker approaching to address Charles II., at ball play in the Park, kept on his hat. The King, with affected deference, removed his own plumed head-gear. The abashed Quaker remonstrated, saying, "Friend, thee need'st not remove thy hat." "Oh, no matter," replied the volatile monarch; "only, when a subject is conversing with the King, it is usual for one of them to be without his hat." Some of our magistrates seem to have caught discourtesy from the Quakers. Randolph, in his report to the King, of his reception by the Council for presenting his Majesty's letter, in 1676, writes : "At the beginning of the reading, the whole councill being covered,

"bowing," as the woman in the Gospel who "had a spirit of infirmity was bowed together by the Devil," but straightened up when delivered. Seeming to imagine that the people were aware of their paganism in using the names of heathen gods for the days of the week and the titles of the months, he bade them distinguish by numbers. He proscribed a knowledge of Latin, Greek, and Hebrew for a minister, as "tongues began at Babel." But these crotchets would have been small capital on which to start a new sect, and the offence going with them was trivial to all but precisians. Fox's own Journal tells us that —

"when the Lord sent me forth into the World he forbad me to put off my Hat to any, High or Low. And I was required to Thee and Thou all Men and Women, without any respect to any Rich or Poor, Great or Small. And as I travelled up and down, I was not to bid People Good-Morrow or Good-Evening; neither might I Bow or Scrape with my Leg to any one."[1]

He testified also against "Wakes or Feasts, May-Games, Sports, Plays, and Shews."

"But the black, Earthly Spirit of the Priest wounded my Life: And when I heard the Bell-toll, to call People together to the Steeple-house, it struck at my Life. For it was just like a Market-Bell to gather People together that the Priest might set forth his Ware for Sale. Oh the vast sums of Money that are gotten by the Trade they make of selling the Scriptures!"

Feeling such a burden in his soul, Fox could not restrain it there. Macaulay says that Fox, so far from being skilled in the languages, "did not know any language."

I put off my hat, whereupon three of the magistrates tooke off their hats and sate uncovered; but the governor with the rest continued to keep their hats on" (Hutchinson's Collection of Papers, p. 504).

[1] It is with no intent of flattery, as Fox thought, that in English idiomatic speech the plural "you," as in German "they," is used in addressing an individual. Indeed, the address "thou" seems to be much more stately in tone, as reserved for the Deity.

Fox well knew his own mother tongue, and it would be difficult to find in any writer — except it may be in some of the authors of the tracts that have been referred to — a more copious and varied supply of epithetical adjectives, abusive, contemptuous, objurgatory, and insulting terms, than Fox uses against the priests and magistrates. These invectives fired and gave a sting to the testimonies which he delivered in the steeple-houses, and in his confronting priests wherever he met them. It was for these, and not for his "theology" that he was buffeted and imprisoned. The Quaker historians are exhaustively faithful in the statistics of their sufferers by persecution in England and in New England. One hundred and seventy of such sufferers are charged upon New England under fines and various penalties. In England, Scotland, and Ireland there are enumerated 13,258, who bore more or less of these inflictions; 219 were banished at one time from Bristol alone; 360 died from prison inflictions and distempers, some having been confined eight or ten years.

Under the light and freedom of our own times humanity asserts its claims in restraining the penalties inflicted upon all classes of offenders. This constitutes the principal if not the only difference between the judicial proceedings of former ages and our own. If a zealous Puritan of the native stock in this city — whether to be regarded as sane or insane, according to the view taken of his action — should on a Sunday morning rush into the Roman Catholic Cathedral, when crowded with worshippers, and should there utter fervent protests against "the superstitions, blasphemies, and idolatries" of the service, he would be seized, and as it might happen, with or without rough treatment, depending upon the hands into which he fell, he would be locked up in a station-house. On Monday he would be brought before a magistrate and sentenced to imprisonment or a fine. On a repetition of the offence the penalty would be increased. If when released he

should still insist upon bearing his testimony, he would
be permanently committed to an asylum as insane. Here
would be a deprivation of liberty without bodily infliction,
now disused, not because undeserved, but because barbarous. In this last respect alone we note the difference.
In the age with which we are dealing, scourgings, mutilations of the body, and cruel treatment in loathsome dungeons were additional punishments visited upon all classes
of offenders, whether men of rank and office like Prynne,
Burton, and Bastwicke, or common vagabonds.[1] That
excellent English country gentleman, John Evelyn, Esq.,
pure and elevated in his character, who, contemporaneously
with the famous roué and worldling, Samuel Pepys, was
writing so unlike a Journal, gives us, under date of July 8,
1656, while he was in Ipswich, the following entry : —

"I had the curiosity to visite some Quakers here in prison ; a
new phanatic sect, of dangerous principles, who show no respect
to any man, magistrate or other, and seeme a melancholy, proud
sort of people, and exceedingly ignorant. One of these was said
to have fasted twenty daies ; but another endeavouring to do the
like perished on the tenth, when he would have eaten but could
not." [2]

The Platonic divine, Henry More, who should have
appreciated the ideality of the Quakers, was impressed by
what he called their "Pharisaical Sourness," and by their
being "undoubtedly the most Melancholy Sect that ever
was yet in the world."[3]
It was with apostles of this strange and odious sect,
whose extravagances for the time obscured their noble

---

[1] Arthur Christopher Benson, in his "Study of the Life and Character of
Archbishop Laud," referring to the severity of the sentences pronounced by
that prelate in the Star Chamber, so dreaded by the Puritans, says : "We
must remember that the shearing away of ears was in the style of the time,
and did not seem to be any violation of the principles of humanity" (p. 161).

[2] Journal, ii. 114.

[3] Enthusiasmus Triumphatus, p. 19.

principles, that the Puritan magistrates of Massachusetts were now to be confronted. It was strange that a visit from them should have been so long deferred. For the majority of the first disciples of the sect, under the glow and joy of their new illumination, were prompted to wide missionary wanderings beyond the bounds of Protestantism, and even of Christendom, to communicate their messages. Twelve years had passed since Fox had begun his travelling ministry. But the authorities of Massachusetts, though so long spared their presence, were thoroughly informed, through correspondence and books, of the phenomena of the sect in England, and had the utmost dread of them, as bent on mischief of the most alarming and dangerous character.[1] Books of a similar sort with those of the Quakers, such as the writings of the mystical enthusiasts John Reeves and Ludwick Muggleton, "the two last Witnesses," known to be circulating in the Colony, had been proscribed by a law in 1654. A month before the arrival of the Quakers a solemn Fast Day had been observed, "to seek the face of God in behalf of our native countrie, in reference to the abounding of errors, especially those of the Ranters and Quakers." There was no law as yet on the statute-book concerning them, and they could legally be got rid of only by an application of the law against strangers passed in the Antinomian struggle. The charges which the Quaker historians visit upon the Puritan magistrates for all their severities against the intruding Quakers begin at this point: that before they had com-

[1] It is possible that the first reports which had been received here about the Quakers in England soon after their appearance, may have prompted the use of some peculiar expressions in the elaborate ecclesiastical laws passed by the Court in November, 1646. In imposing a fine for non-attendance on, and for disturbing, worship, the law refers to such as "renouncing church estate or ministry, or other ordinances dispensed in them, either upon pretence that the churches were not planted by any new apostles, or that ordinances are for carnall Christians, or babes in Christ, and not for spiritual and illuminate persons," etc. (Records, iii. 100).

mitted any offence, and while there was no law by which they could be so summarily dealt with, they were treated, as it were by anticipation, as culprits. The first comers suffered no bodily infliction, save confinement to prevent the "infection of their principles." Punishment indeed, in the form of fines, and a bond to carry away their unwelcome passengers, were, as we shall see, exacted of the master mariners who had unwittingly brought them here. There is no evidence on the Records that the magistrates felt any embarrassment about the matter. They found in their charter a provision which, as they interpreted it, would fully warrant their proceedings. This provision made it lawful —

"for the governors and officers of the said Company, for their special defence and safety, to incounter, repulse, repell, and resist, as well by sea as by land, all such person and persons as shall attempt or enterprise the destruction, invasion, detriment, or annoyance to the said plantation or inhabitants."

Nor were the magistrates troubled by any misgiving that they were trespassing beyond their bounds of accordance with the laws of England. For, either with or without law, saving only in the execution of the last penalty, the magistrates simply followed ample English precedents in their treatment of the Quakers.

The claim of the magistrates by their Charter to exclusive rights of territory and habitancy passed for nothing with the Quakers. They regarded themselves as Apostles of the Light, and so, like the sunbeams, they had eminent rights of entering and domain over Christendom and heathendom. The magistrates from the first, and continuously, tried to distinguish in their legislation and treatment between those whom they insisted on regarding as strangers, strolling vagrants, with no errand here but one of discord and mischief, and such as might catch the infection among their own people. But it proved impracticable to follow the distinction in inflicting penalties, save that neither of the four whose lives were taken from them were resident here. The Quakers, with many other troublesome intruders, insisted that as free-born Englishmen they had a right to enter and traverse any portion of the realm. But we should be wholly inappreciative of the spirit of the time and of those whom it stirred, to expect of the authorities to wait for any special enactment in the emergency. They proceeded exactly as does the Board of Health in its summary measures on learning of the arrival in the harbor of infected persons, not waiting to see if harm would come from their presence.

Now, as we have the full, intelligent, and judicial privilege of thoroughly understanding and appreciating the motives, views, and principles of both the parties who were to come into collision, — as neither of them did those of the other when they were confronted, — let us try, with all the candor and impartiality we can summon to guide us, to put ourselves into their respective positions. What was the state of mind, the intent, the attitude of each of them? Allowing for the heat and elation of zeal and the possible spiritual conceit of the first Quakers here, we must recognize in them a thoroughly sincere, pure, unselfish, and heroic prompting. They knew very well, what was so rife in England, that there was in Masssachusetts a rule of the most oppressive and unrelenting severity both in civil and religious administration. The English Court and Council had been beset by the complaints of sufferers, and one might meet in the streets with those who, in telling their grievances, would bitterly portray the harshness, bigotry, and cruelty of " the rule of the Saints." The Quakers, by tests satisfactory to themselves, trusted themselves in distinguishing between the promptings of mere inclination and ordinary motives, and their direct impulses, monitions, and inspirations from God. They were " free " or " not free " to do this or that. Their own wills were held or controlled by a power outside of them. The Puritans and the Quakers, with equal sincerity and fidelity, acknowledged this controlling sway over them, with this extremely diverse source of it: with the Puritan it was the letter of the Bible; with the Quaker it was the illumination of the Spirit. The Quakers could judge when they had a Divine call to go or stay, to wander or abide in their places. They affirmed that they came here in "the movings of the Lord." Messages also were committed to them to be communicated, and few of these were agreeable to those who received them. They had "burdens of the Lord," to be relieved only by denunciations of judgments and calamities. Under this divine prompting, successive Quakers, single or in companionship, were "moved of the Lord to go to Boston," there to confront the authorities and to bear testimony against the austerities and formalism, literalism, deadness, and rottenness of Puritanism. They had large, free, enlightening liberalizings, and benedictive truths and principles, to announce. They were well aware what a reception they would meet, and what treatment they would receive; and they were well prepared for it. They would be blameless and harmless in their relation to civil law, non-resistant under violence; would pay no fines, swear no oaths, make no pledges, yield no willing obedience to unjust commands, and bear their testimony till conscience within gave them a full discharge.

The buffetings and inflictions which their fellow-believers were meeting in England assured them that those who dared to face the concentration and intensity of Puritanism here would have a hard warfare. The only weapon of offence or defence they could employ was the tongue. And this, with the language which it might use, they did not receive as their own; for while the Puritans regarded their utterance as "set on fire of hell," the Quakers believed it to be taken into the service of God. Such was the Quakers' view of their errand and duty here. Most faithfully and heroically did they discharge it. Their minds and consciences had been opened to what they believed to be the shameful and startling fact that the religion of their time, which pretended to stand for Christianity, was the merest sham and hypocrisy. The plainest teachings and doctrines of Jesus Christ, like non-resistance to evil, unworldliness, seriousness of life, simplicity of speech, a prohibition of war, offensive or defensive, were with a cool effrontery pronounced to be only " counsels of perfection " utterly impracticable in actual life. The Quakers set themselves to carry out those counsels of perfection, and to allow that the very least portion of literal Christianity is impracticable of obedience. In the spirit of sincerity, of fidelity, constancy, and purity, which animated and guided them, the Friends, as a fellowship, have come the nearest, both in spirit and in practice, to conformity with the Christian rule of life, of all the sects which have borne the title of disciples. Had they, here or elsewhere, sought to establish a theocracy, unlike that of the Puritans, it would have found its model in the New Testament, not in the Old. As the oddities, eccentricities, and extravagances, which, so unfortunately for them, introduced them to ridicule and ill treatment, have gradually been dropped as purely trivial and wholly distinguishable from the vitalities of their system, the lofty principles and truths for which they secured an appreciation have been assimilated with the tenets and practices of other Christian fellowships.[1]

On the other hand, how stood the Puritans to meet and

[1] On Sunday, Aug. 23, 1887, the writer, in attendance at the Friends' worship in their old meeting-house in Newport, R. I., where the yearly meeting of the Society is held, would have found it difficult to distinguish the place and the services from those of many other worshipping congregations. There was no pulpit, choir, or musical instrument. But there were raised seats from which two men and one woman offered earnest exhortations and prayers, with Scripture readings, while three different individuals, in intervals of silence, sung hymn and psalm, others joining in. But in the considerable congregation no one of either sex had any distinguishing garb.

deal with the encounter before them ? They also had consciences and convictions, most intense in their action and
assurance. They believed they had the long start and advantage over the Quakers in having entered into a covenant
of their own with God, through the guidance and pledge
of a sacred book. They had a heritage to defend and enjoy.
At their own charges they had become possessed of certain
rights of property, territory, and authority. For more than
a score of years they had been laying the foundations of
order and government in one patch of a vast wilderness,
meeting a constant succession of harassing and threatening experiences. They had planted themselves upon a
solemn purpose of a commonwealth administered by " the
laws, statutes, and ordinances of God," and, still in the
first stage of the experiment, had as yet no misgiving that
it was to fail. The all-essential condition of their security
and success was in a general if not a unanimous adhesion
to their covenant, and so to each other, without discord or
schism. What they had most to dread was contention
among themselves, contempt of authority, and sedition.
They would not go out of their bounds to molest others ;
and the wide-reaching continent afforded to others free
opportunities for trying their own experiments.

Such were the Quakers and the Puritans as they met in
an antagonism fully understood and appreciated by us,
but not at all so by each other. The Quaker came, with
no intent whatever of peaceful and permanent residence
and citizenship, or to cast in his lot and interest with the
colonists. His errand was a transient one, and the avowed
purpose of it was sure to rouse ill-feeling, bad passions,
distraction, and a revolutionary convulsion in society. If
Winthrop said truly of the Antinomians, that their spirit
and principles were such that they could not peaceably
abide here, what was to be said of wandering Quakers who,
after bearing their testimony and scattering their inflammatory books, should watch to see the mischief that would

follow ? The alternative seemed to the authorities in possession here a very simple but a very peremptory one.
Either they must at once abandon their precious, endeared,
and consecrated system, — their covenant and recognition
of it in worship, — their prayers, sermons, church relation and ordinances, baptism and the Lord's Supper, their
educated ministry and their weapons of defence, or say to
the intruders, " Go away, and stay away. We have no
place for you here. Go unharmed now ; but if you persist
in annoying and exasperating us, it shall be at the peril of
your lives." The Quakers chose to meet that peril, and
they triumphed gloriously over it.

It would be equally out of place and wholly futile to introduce the narrative that is to follow, with an attempt to
suggest anything in relief or justification of the measures
of repression and infliction so fatuously adopted by the
magistrates in dealing with the dreaded intruders. By
our standard of right, justice, and expediency, thrown back
nearly two and a half centuries, not a word can be said
even in palliation of the course pursued. The prompting
comes to all of us, under our enlightenment and enfranchisement, to ask, Why were not the intruders allowed
to come on shore, bear their testimony, and scatter their
tracts ? Their message would have been soon told. If there
had been a prospect of its being kindly received, it might
have been more courteously spoken, and would certainly
have done the Puritans much good. But that question put
to the magistrates at the time would have been very much
as if one should ask those of our time, Why not allow a
ship-load of immigrants infected with the small-pox to
land and circulate through our streets ? Tasking as the
effort is, we must endeavor to appreciate the view of their
obligations taken by the magistrates themselves as set to
administer a Biblical commonwealth. During the intermission of the General Court all responsibility lay with
them. We give them the benefit of all the grace possible,

when we recognize their own resolute and dogged purpose
at all costs and hazards to do what they regarded as a
clear and positive duty, assumed by oath for an imperilled
community. We can easily detect how soon and how
fatally there mingled with this sense of the duty of magistracy an exasperated passion, coming in through the ever-
open inlets of human nature, at the bold contempt and
defiance of their authority. The discomfiture of the experiment in government which they were trying, august
and righteous as they regarded it, could come only through
its proved impracticability, as involving the harshest
bigotry and a barbarous cruelty.

As there was no special law yet on their statute-book
against Quakers, — except as inferential from that passed
in the Antinomian troubles, — the magistrates, in a declaration published three years afterwards, avowed that they
proceeded upon the full knowledge, derived from what had
transpired in their mother country, of the character and
the pestilent principles of the Quakers. On a Fast Day,
observed twenty years afterward, in the desolation of King
Philip's War, one of the preachers ascribed the calamities
of the country as a judgment of God on it for not having
dealt more severely and thoroughly with the Quakers.

The two women in the harbor were Ann Austin, described as " stricken in years, and the mother of five children," having left her family in England for her mission,
and Mary Fisher, " a maiden Friend." Though the reception of the latter in Boston was to be only inhospitable,
her previous sufferings in England had been protracted and
very cruel. She had appeared there in 1652, when about
thirty years of age, as a minister among the Friends ; and,
for addressing a public meeting, had been imprisoned in
York Castle sixteen months. And again, for preaching
with another woman at the gate of Sydney College, in 1653,
she and her companion were whipped " until the blood ran
down their bodies." After two more imprisonments for

speaking in "steeple-houses," Mary Fisher had "a religious call" to go to Barbadoes. A letter from her, written from that place, to George Fox, addressed "My Dear Father," and expressing her zeal for her work, is extant. As she never returned here after her banishment, reference may be made to her interesting subsequent career. Being carried from here to Barbadoes, after a visit to England in 1657, and another in the next year to Barbadoes, she started in 1660 for her mission, on a perilous and difficult journey to the Orient. She found her way to Adrianople, where she gave her testimony, through an interpreter, to the "Grand Turk," the Sultan Mahomet IV. She was civilly treated by him, the assumption being that she was insane, and therefore, as the Turks believed, inspired. She parried with skill the test question, What she thought of Mahomet? by replying that she did not know him. Returning safely to England, she labored long and zealously in her Society, and was twice married, coming with her second husband to America. She is mentioned as living in Charleston, S. C., in 1697, then a widow.[1]

Ann Austin was imprisoned "in a filthy gaol" in London in 1659, and died there of the terrible plague in 1665.

As Governor Endicott was absent on the arrival of the vessel, Lieutenant-Governor Bellingham sent an officer on board, who brought the women with their effects on shore to the prison. About a hundred books or tracts were taken from them, which were burned by order in the market-place. In conformity with the dismal superstition of the time in all Christendom that such persons as the prisoners might be bewitched, some women were sent to the jail on the revolting errand to follow the usual English judicial process in searching their bodies for evidence that the Evil One stately drew nutriment from them. A wart or a mole was a perilous disfigurement in those times. Happily no such blemish was found.

[1] Bowden's Society of Friends in America, i. 31.

I have before me a manuscript of some hundred and fifty pages, containing a transcript made by me many years ago from a collection of loose papers gathered into a volume, now among the archives in the State House, of legal proceedings against the Quakers. The Quaker historians do not seem to have had knowledge of these papers. They supply many interesting facts, of which I shall make use. The first of them gives us the action of the Council, which had authority when the General Court was not in session, taken immediately on the known presence of the Quakers; as follows : —

11th July, 1656. Voted by the Council. Present, the Governor, Deputy-Governor, Sam'l Symonds, Capt. Gookin, Major Willard, Major Atherton.

Whereas there are several laws long since made and published in this Jurisdiction, bearing testimony against heretics and erroneous persons, yet notwithstanding, Simon Kempthorne of Charlestown, Master of the Ship Swallow of Boston, knowingly hath brought into this Jurisdiction from the Island of Barbadoes two women, who name themselves Mary Fisher, and Anne, the wife of one Austin : being of that sort of people commonly known by the name of Quakers, who, upon examination, are found not only to be transgressors of the former laws, but do hold many very dangerous, heretical, and blasphemous opinions, and they also acknowledged they came hither purposely to propagate their said errors and heresies, bringing with them and spreading here sundry books wherein are contained many most corrupt, pernicious, heretical, blasphemous doctrines, contrary to the truth of the Gospel professed among us: The Council, therefore, tendering the preservation of the peace and truth enjoyed and professed in this country amongst the Churches of Christ, do hereby order, 1. That all such corrupt books as shall be found upon search to be brought in and spread by the forenamed persons, be forthwith burnt and destroyed by the common executioner. 2. That the said Mary and Anne be kept in close prison, and none admitted to communication with them without leave from the Governor, or Deputy-Governor, or any two Magistrates, to prevent the spreading of their corrupt opinions, until such time as they be delivered by the authorities aboard some vessel to be transported out of the country. 3. That the said Simon Kempthorne is enjoined speedily and directly to transport or cause to be transported the said persons from hence into Barbadoes from whence they came, defraying all the charges of their imprisonment: and for the effectual performance whereof he is to give Security to the Secretary in a bond of £100 Sterling, and upon his refusal to give such security he is to be committed to prison till he do it.

E. R., Secretary.

The Council seem to have assumed that Kempthorne knew the offensive character of his two passengers.

The women were not scourged. As they " were not free in mind" to work for the jailer for their subsistence, nor allowed to buy food with their own money, they were in danger of famishing. When brought before the magistrates' Court, their " Thee and Thou" was held to be sufficient proof of who and what they were, and they were replied to with rude and harsh words. Then at once the authorities had to meet the first manifestation of what they greatly dreaded as an "infection," — sympathy engaged for the sufferers on the part of citizens and church members. None of this was shown by the jailer, who was both of these. But so also was a worthy man, Nicholas Upshall, sixty years of age, with a family, respected in the community. He made a protest, at first privately, and afterward publicly, for which he was rebuked. He did more; for he gave the jailer five shillings a week for being allowed to give food to the prisoners. Upshall is worthily remembered by the Friends as being the first in a number steadily increasing, to the great annoyance of the authorities, of those among the inhabitants who showed this sympathy.[1]

---

[1] His wife, however, did not accord with him. In the State Archives, as addressed to the Court of Assistants, in 1658, is "The humble petition of Dorothy Upshall. Humbly sheweth, That whereas your petitioner's husband, in October, 1656, did not only unadvisedly, but sinfully, reproach the honored

To them, either as boldly questioning and rebuking, or as quietly discountenancing the cruel treatment of the Quakers, as we shall see farther on, and not, as has been assumed, to the interposition of the King, Charles II., is to be ascribed the curb put upon the will of the magistrates. The women were in prison five weeks before the sailing of their ship. But one week before their release another vessel had brought eight more Quakers, four men and four women, who were imprisoned in like manner for eleven weeks by those whom Bishop calls " the refuse of mankind,"—a complimentary description of the Puritans. For two successive days the magistrates and Elder Norton held conferences with these prisoners, the discussion bearing principally on the point, Whether the Scriptures are the only rule and guide of life, or subordinate to the quickenings of the Inner Light? Norton seems to have been more docile than were the magistrates under the Quakers' pleading. The captain of the vessel was put under bonds to remove them and to bring no more. One Richard Smith, of Long Island, a fellow-passenger, reputed a " Proselite," venturing to speak in the meeting-house after service, was imprisoned and sent home by water. A fine was imposed upon ship-masters who should bring any known to be Quakers. They were released from this fine on showing that they had erred in ignorance.

On the meeting of the General Court, Oct. 14, 1656, was enacted the first law against the intruders.[1] Parts of this must be verbally quoted, if only that its epithets may serve as the embers of the fire.

magistrates, and spake against that wholesome law to prevent the coming in amongst the good people of this land such as are notable deceivers," etc. She expresses her own warm satisfaction " with the truth and ordinances here profest, so dear and precious to her soul," etc. She is distressed in the support of her family, and in providing for the support of her husband, banished and fined £20. The magistrates agree that the remainder of the fine not yet paid, shall be settled on the petitioner, not to go for the use of her husband.

[1] Records, vol. iv. pt. i. pp. 277, 278.

"Whereas there is a cursed sect of haereticks lately risen up in the world, which are commonly called Quakers, who take uppon them to be immediately sent of God, and infallibly assisted by the spirit to speake and write blasphemouth opinions, despising government and the order of God in church and commonwealth, speaking evill of dignities, reproaching and reviling magistrates and ministers, seeking to turne the people from the faith and gaine proselites to theire pernicious waies, this Court, taking into serious consideration the premises, and to prevent the like mischiefe as by theire meanes is wrought in our native land, doth heereby order, and by the authoritie of this Court be it ordered and enacted, that any commander of a vessel that shall bring into this jurisdiction any knowne Quaker or Quakers, or any other blasphemous haereticks as aforesaid, shall pay the fine of £100, except it appeare that he wanted true knowledge or information of theire being such; and in that case, he hath libertie to cleare himself by his oath, when sufficient proofe to the contrary is wanting;" for default of payment or security to be imprisoned; then to give bonds to carry them to the place whence he brought them.

"Any Quaker coming into this jurisdiction shall be forthwith committed to the house of correction, and at their entrance to be severely whipt, and by the master thereof to be kept constantly to worke, and none suffered to converse or speak with them during the time of their imprisonment, which shall be no longer than necessitie requireth. . . . And further, it is ordered, if any person shall knowingly import into any harbor of this jurisdiction any Quakers' bookes or writings concerning their divilish opinions, shall pay for every such booke or writting, being legally prooved against him or them, the somme of five pounds; and whosoever shall disperse or conceale any such booke or writing, and it be found with him or her, in his or her house, and shall not immediately deliver in the same to the next magistrate, shall forfeit and pay five pounds. Any person proved to have the haeretical opinions of the said Quakers, or their books or papers, shall be fined forty shillings; for the second offence four pounds; for still offending, to be imprisoned till banished. Lastly, it is heereby ordered, that what person or persons soever shall revile the office or person of magistrates or ministers, as is usuall with the Quakers, such person or persons shalbe severely whipt, or pay the somme of five pounds. This order was published 21 : 8 m. 56, in severall places of Boston, by beate of drumme."

The next order to this in the Court Book, is one giving to the President and Fellows of Harvard College authority to punish the misdemeanors of the youth by fine, or by whipping in the hall.

As the drummer passed the house of Upshall proclaiming this law, he uttered a bold protest against it, for which, as previously mentioned, he was fined, imprisoned, and banished.

The conditions to which prisoners, like the Quakers, were subjected, may be inferred from the following provisions. A few months before the first coming of Quakers the Court had ordered that the selectmen of each town should provide for the prison or county house of correction a stock of hemp, flax, or other materials, the value of the labor on which done by the prisoners should accrue to the use of the master. Out of this he was "to allow only so much as will keepe the delinquent with necessary bread and water, or other meane food, as four pence out of the shilling earned by his or her labour." On coming into the prison the delinquent was to receive ten stripes, and then to be employed by a daily stint. "If he or she be stoborne, disorderly, or idle," the master should "abridge them of part of their usuall food, or give them meet correction." The Quakers refused to work for the benefit of the jailer while receiving such poor commons.[1]

Next appeared Ann Burden, coming from England, as she said, to collect dues of her husband. With her was Mary Dyer, "passing through to Rhode Island," whither she had gone from Boston in the Antinomian times. Winthrop described her then as " a very proper and fair woman, much infected with Mrs. Hutchinson's errours, and very

[1] Records, iii. 399.

censorious and troublesome, she being of a very proud spirit, and much addicted to revelations." [1] She had become an object of dread in Boston, because of the fright connected with a misfortune in maternity. She is yet to appear tragically in this record. Both these women were imprisoned and sent away. August 29, Mary Clark, leaving her family in England, had come here, as she said, with " a message from the Lord." She fared all the worse for that claim, receiving twenty stripes and being sent off. Sept. 21, 1657, Christopher Holder and John Copeland " bore testimony in Salem Church," after the service, and received violent personal treatment. Being sent to Boston prison, they each suffered thirty stripes, and were confined nine weeks, nearly famished and without fire in wintry weather. A sympathizer in the meeting, Sam Shattuck, was imprisoned in Boston, whipped, and banished. Laurence and Cassandra Southwick, of Salem, " an aged, grave couple," church members, for " entertaining two strangers," and the wife for approving " an heretical paper," were imprisoned. Richard Dowdney, coming from England, was arrested at Dedham, taken to Boston, received thirty stripes, was deprived of his tracts, and sent off with four others, threatened with loss of ears, after the English fashion, if they returned.

Sympathy for the sufferers was rapidly strengthened at Salem, dividing the flock in the meeting-house, so that the Friends began to hold worship of their own in the woods and at private houses. They were followed up there by the magistrate Hathorne, and by the law of 1646 were fined five shillings a week each for absence from the assembly. Bishop informs his readers that Queen Elizabeth had been content with exacting only twelve pence a week for this offence. Many of these Salem Friends were imprisoned in Boston, and confined when they were most needed at home for farm labors, while distraint was laid upon

[1] Winthrop, i. 261.

their property for payment of fines. Even the purpose was entertained by the Court in May, 1659, of selling one or more for transportation to Virginia or Barbadoes; but it failed of execution, for no mariner would take them. "Horred Gardner, mother of many children," came with a nursing babe from Newport to Weymouth, and with her servant-girl was imprisoned in Boston, receiving ten lashes. Sarah Gibbens and Dorothy Waugh, April 13, 1658, "spoke in Boston meeting." They were imprisoned, famished, and whipped. Thomas Harris, coming from Barbadoes through Rhode Island, "spoke in Boston Meeting," denouncing Divine judgments. He was imprisoned, whipped, and "would have starved," had he not been fed through the window at night by sympathizers. William Brend and William Leddra, "moved of the Lord," after visiting Salem, "had a conference with a priest at Newbury," and with others were sent to Boston prison and whipped. The people protested so strongly against the unmerciful castigation of Brend, that the jailer was saved from process only by the intervention of Elder Norton. The Boston Thursday Lecture furnished a favorite opportunity for the harangues of the Friends, men and women, who insisted upon appearing there, though protesting that they could not join in the worship. The magistrates became exasperated beyond measure, and were at their wits' end by being so defied. Their law had provided for a riddance from their tormentors only for such as came in by sea. But when they flocked in from Rhode Island, as "a back door," no one was chargeable for removing them. We have to look to the original Quaker tracts for details, facts, and speeches not to be found in the historic compends, to apprehend fully the goadings, insults, extravagances, and denunciations by which magistrates, ministers, and congregations were infuriated against the intruders. As was remarked before, the early Quakers, either from choice or from circumstances, were known and made odious by their

crotchets and oddities.   Undoubtedly these stood in the
way of many who observed their fantastic ways, and prevented even a patient, much more a receptive, spirit in
listening to the noble lessons, the large and edifying truths
from Quaker lips, which they had themselves reached.   The
Puritans looked with utter contempt upon the "theology"
of the Quakers, and did not think it worth listening to.
Associating theology, as the Puritans did, with profound
linguistic learning in the rigid literalism of the Scriptures,
they were confronted by those whom they most unjustly
regarded as only ranters and scoffers for claiming a spiritual illumination as a key to opening those Scriptures.
The two methods of dealing with the Book were radically
opposite and irreconcilable.   The Quakers were never
permitted, as the Antinomians and Baptists had been, to
have anything like a free hearing or debate, at church
meetings, in a synod, or in the Court.   This was withheld from them for two reasons.   First, those other heretics were residents, citizens, and church members, otherwise in good standing, while the Quakers were strangers,
"roaming vagrants."   And again, the illiteracy, the offensive language and behavior of the Quakers made them
personally so odious, and the wild notions "broached" by
them were so exasperating, as to make the Puritans unwilling to put themselves on the level of a discussion.
The assertion of the Quakers that their journeys, errands,
and messages were assigned to them by private, direct
personal inspirations from God, was to the Puritans simply blasphemous.   They themselves could know "the mind
of God" only through a channel common to them and
to all others, — the Bible.   But no single grievance fills
so large a place in the altercations of both parties as
the importance assigned to the "Hat."   The Quakers in
their tracts earnestly and often peevishly complain that
the keeping on of their hats in courts and meeting-
houses, before they had even opened their lips, or their

opinions were really known, was enough to insure for
them condemnation and abuse. It was so, and it was
because they chose to have it so. The hat seemed to
signify defiance and contempt, as if it said, "I am as
good as you are: I owe you no respect or deference, and
I will prove this by insulting you." The habit and the
attitude were taken as a gross breach of manners, or gro-
tesqueness of costume; it would in our time mark a fool,
a crank, or an insane person. As to the "testimonies"
borne by the Quakers in meeting-houses, courts, and other
places, taking only their own reports of them, we can well
understand how the truth and fresh inspiration of some of
the utterances would pass for nothing because of the rant,
the bitterness, the scorn, the fierce and withering denunciations connected with them. The most offensive epithet
to be used for an elder or minister was that of "priest."
Because the Puritan worship proceeded by form and routine, it was pronounced "lifeless, dead, Pharisaical, and
without power to instruct or edify." The "ordinances,"
the most sacred rites of the Puritans, — baptism and the
Lord's Supper, — were spiritualized by the Quakers into
disuse. Wandering through lonely woods, with his musings, and reaching stopping-points for mission-work in his
Heaven-guided journeys, the Quaker would appear on the
scene, with a fervor and elation of spirit, to give forth his
repressed exaltation.

What utterances would come from the mouths of those
whose pens wrote matter like the following, may be readily
inferred from a tract, whose title is here given, with extracts from it, from a copy which I transcribed from the
original in the British Museum : [1] —

"*N. England's Ensigne:* It being the Account of Cruelty, the
Professors' Pride, and the Articles of their Faith, Signified in
Characters written in Blood, wickedly begun, barbarously con-

[1] Collection marked $\frac{493\text{-}h}{6}$.

tinued, and inhumanly finished (so far as they have gone) by the present power of darkness possest in the Priests and Rulers in N. England, with the Dutch also inhabiting the same land.   In a bloody and cruel birth which the Husband to the Whore of Babylon hath brought forth by ravishing and torturing the seed of the Virgin of Israel.   Happy are they who are blest out of the hands of Hypocrites, by whom my Saviour suffered.   This being an account of the sufferings sustained by us in N. England (with the Dutch), the most part of it in these last two yeers, 1657–58. With a letter to John Indicot and John Norton, Governor and Chief Priest of Boston, and another to the Town of Boston.   Also, the several late conditions of a friend upon Road Island before, in, and after distraction; with some Quaeries unto all sorts of People, who want that which we have.   Written at sea by us whom the Wicked in scorn call Quakers, in the 2d month of the year 1659."   London, 1659.

The Preface describes the people of New England as " Cruel English Jewes, the most vainest and beastliest place of all Bruits, the most publicly profane, and the most covertly corrupt," etc.   The treatment of the writer up to the date already reached is related.   The sufferings of Robert Hodgstone, from the Dutch at Hempstead, L. I., are described.   He was beaten with a pitched rope, one hundred blows, and chained to work with a wheelbarrow in a hot sun.   " Yet his mouth was opened to such as came about him."   We may be sure of that.   " 15th of 6th month, 1657, two of us, Holder and Copeland, were moved of the Lord to go to Martin's Vineyard.   After the Priest, Thomas Maho [Mayhew], had done his speech, one of us unspake a few words."   They were thrust out, and the next day were sent off and landed by an Indian at Sandwich, causing great excitement.   A warrant was issued against them as " extravagant persons."   Copeland had a dispute with Stone, " the Priest of Hartford."   We then have the following description of a New England church member, which doubtless had its counterpart in life :

" A man that hath a covetous and deceitful rotten heart, lying lips, which abound among them, and a smooth, fawning, flattering tongue, and short hair, and a deadly enmity against those that are called Quakers, and others that oppose their wayes, — such a hypocrite is a fit man to be a member of any New-England Church. And touching the matter and manner of their worship, it is most like the rigid Presbyters, so called, but a little differing from the late Bishops, onely they use not their blind service and surp-cloaths. J. Rouse and H. Norton were moved to go to their great meeting-house at Boston upon one of their Lector dayes, where we found John Norton, their teacher, set up, who, like a babling Pharisee, run over a vain repetition near an hour long (like an impudent smooth-faced harlot who was telling her Paramoors a long fair story of her husband's kindness, while nothing but wantonness and wickedness is in her heart) ; when his Glass was out he begun his sermon, wherein, amongst many lifeless expressions, he spake much of the danger of these who are called Quakers : some of his hearers gaped on him as if they expected honey should have dropped from his lips ; and amongst other of his vain conceits he uttered this (whereby he plainly discovered the blindness and rottenness of his heart), that the Justice of God is the Armor of the Devil, the which, if true, then is the Devil sometimes covered with Justice, which is more than ever I heard any of his servants say in his behalf before," etc.

" On the 13th of 2d month, 1658, S. Gibbens and D. Waugh [two women] spoke at Lecture."

I do not know whether these Quakers spoke the words, or whether they are the report of Bishop, in the terse English sentence, — " They heard the Grave uttering her voice, and Death feeding Death, through your painted Sepulchre, John Norton." [1]

The circulation of copies of Norton's book, which is referred to by his name in the Records, as might be expected, inflamed to bitterness the resentment of the Court.

Thomas Newhouse gave his " testimony " in Salem meeting, " where, having spoken to them what was with him,

1 Bishop, p. 72.

and having two Glass Bottles in his Hands, dashed them to pieces, saying to this effect, That so they should be dash'd in Pieces."[1]   Newhouse was whipped.

But the "infection" spread rapidly and became more virulent. The means taken to suppress it gave it vigor. Many of the ministers preaching sharply against Quaker- ism, misrepresenting and caricaturing its real principles, excited curiosity and interest in it, and won for it disci- ples in their own flocks. Some keenly discerning persons, wearied or repelled by the reiteration of literalisms and Calvinistic dogmas, began to see behind the fantastic and grotesque obtrusions of Quakerism the vital and elevating principles of higher truth. These consequences caused not only alarm, but passionate indignation among the magis- trates and deputies, who as church members could alone make and execute the laws. Not all of these, however, were of the same mind.

The General Court, Oct. 14, 1657, tried to strengthen its legislation by the following provisions. A fine of £100 was imposed, with imprisonment till paid, on every one who should bring into the jurisdiction " a known Quaker, or other blasphemous haeretick." Forty shillings for each hour of entertainment of any such, by an inhabitant, with imprisonment till paid, was the penalty for that offence. A male Quaker returning here after having been once dealt with, should have one ear cut off, and be kept at work in the house of correction till he could be sent away at his own charges, and for again returning, should lose the other ear, etc. " Every woman Quaker so returning shall be whipt and kept at work in the house of correction till re- moved at her own charge ; " and so for repetition. Every Quaker, " he or she," returning still a third time, should have the tongue bored through with a hot iron, and be again sent off. The same treatment was now to be visited upon Quakers arising among ourselves as upon strangers.[2]

[1] Bishop, p. 431.   [2] Records, vol. iv. pt. i. p. 308.

Under this law, Sept. 16, 1658, three men, Christopher
Holder, John Copeland, and John Rouse, had each one ear
cut by the hangman;[1] but no tongue was bored. The
only instance of branding in New England — so often practised in England — was that of Humphrey Norton, in New
Haven, who had the letter " H " burned in his hand for
" Heresie."

Still another law passed by the Court, May, 1658, provided that " all persons who by speaking, writing, or by
meeting on the Lord's day, or any other time, to strengthen
themselves or seduce others to their diabolicall doctrine,"
for attending such meeting shall be fined each time ten
shillings; for speaking at such meeting, five pounds each
time, with whipping and work in the house of correction,
till giving pledge with bonds " not any more to vent their
hatefull errors, nor use their sinfull practizes," or else depart the jurisdiction at their own charges, subject, if returning, to the former laws against strangers.[2]

But even the penalties carried up by legislation to this
point, while not availing against the subjects of them, fell
short of what some — happily it soon proved to be only a
minority in the Puritan State — desired and were ready to
approve. " All that a man hath will he give for his life,"
is a Scripture sentence, though spoken by Satan. Some
of the people wished to put it to trial in the case of the
Quakers, and they had occasion to learn that the sentence
came from " the great liar." Among the papers in the
State Archives is a document which I have seen nowhere
else, indorsed, " Boston Petition, entered freely with the
Magistrates, October, 1658, which is past." It is addressed
"To the Honored General Court now assembled at Boston,"
and bears the signatures of twenty-five prominent citizens.

---

[1] The mutilation was done by clipping the rim of the ear. One of the
three eminent sufferers by this process in England, before named, by a second
sentence had the operation repeated upon him.

[2] Records, vol. iv. pt. i. p. 321.

The burden of it is to ask for even severer laws against the Quakers. It begins by acknowledging the pious care and fidelity of those "who have sat at the helm," and by God's blessing have secured the State in civil and religious interests, though Satan has never given over his wiles and plottings against them. Yet notwithstanding all their repressive and punitive measures against "the prodigious insolency of the Quakers," the petitioners are moved to offer some propositions for their serious consideration: (1) The malignity of the Quakers against the establishment of civil government shows them to be "professed enemies of the Christian Magistrate and seducers of the people," — they break the fifth commandment; (2) "Under pretence of new light they subvert the very body of religion, — denying the Trinity, the person of Christ, the Scriptures as a rule of life, the whole Church institution of the Gospel, and the ordinary means appointed for the conversion and edification of souls;" (3) Whether the increase and strengthening of their obduracy, perversity, and malignity does not give reason for apprehending a renewal of the spirit of Muncer, or John of Leyden, and justify, as in other commonwealths, a rule for self-defence against the incorrigible, and require that the penalty of death be inflicted upon those returning from banishment, as well our own people as strangers?

The Court at once gave heed to the third of these propositions. Previously, however, — in a document found in the same collection of papers, but not in the Records, — it gave order for issuing "A Manifesto," to hinder the spread of the Quaker doctrines, dated Nov. 6, 1658, when it appeared after the passage of the law next to be given. This Manifesto provides for a Declaration to be written by Mr. Norton, stating in review the efforts of the magistrates to repress and punish the persistent heresies and ill practices of the Quakers, and the increasing mischief of their activity. At the second session of the Court, Oct. 19, 1658,

29

Puritan legislation passed an enactment by which, in consequence, three men and one woman, all of unsullied life, constant, heroic, resigned, triumphant even in spirit, yet with no declamatory or unseemly boastfulness, were hanged from a gallows on Boston Common. With shame and regret, unrelieved and unrelievable, must the historian for all time read, write, and comment on that melancholy episode. All recognition of, all admiration for, some of the noble qualities of our Puritans, and all allowance for the exigencies and straits of their position, must pause at this point and refuse to justify or palliate. If it were conceivable that one of those relentless magistrates could as a shade confront the writer of the preceding sentence, asking, "What could we have done else, — beset, defied, blackguarded, and outraged as we were in our attempted rescue of our jurisdiction from utter lawlessness and wreck?" one could but answer, "Anything, rather than what you did. Your gallows was only for criminals, not for those who in calm constancy of spirit were following their consciences." The magistrate, however, would rejoin that the Quakers were executed as criminals. This was in fact the plea offered in justification by the Court to their own constituency and to the King, — that these victims suffered, not as Quakers or heretics, but for a defiance and contempt of law which would prostrate civil government.

It is under the guidance of this plea, with all the patience and candor that we can exercise, that we must follow the course of the magistrates in making and executing this fatal law. All that can be said for them is what was said by themselves. It was enough to justify them in their own eyes, but not enough for us. Happily a gleam of relief presents itself to one who searches sharply and penetrates to the inner revealings of the thoughts and feelings working profoundly in many minds and hearts at the time, very soon to find avowal and strong assertion to the effect of interdicting any further like outrages of humanity. The fatal law, as we shall see, barely secured an enactment, by a majority of one in the Court, and then only by being modified by the introduction of a provision not found in its original draft. It was resolutely opposed at every stage. Very shrewdly, and with calculating policy, had the sternest of the magistrates and ministers been preparing the way to having the proposed enactment recognized as vitally necessary. It is not uncandid to suppose that they had themselves prompted the petition just referred to, asking them to enact severer laws, including the death penalty. Their request also that an elaborate Declaration should be prepared, stating and vindicating the grounds and methods of their proceedings against their troublers from their first appearance, shows their nervous unrest under a relenting and opposition which they well knew to be working in the minds of many honored members of their community.

The plea of the magistrates being that henceforward they were to regard the Quakers as criminals, their character as heretics was subordinated to this view of them as the agents of sedition and lawlessness, planning the ruin of the commonwealth. Heretofore the magistrates had in every case found that a sentence of banishment from their jurisdiction was obeyed, if not respected. Even Roger Williams, with all the humility of a petitioner, will not venture within the limits from which he has been expelled, merely for a point of embarkation for a voyage to England, without asking and receiving permission. But some of the Quakers first and most defiantly flung contempt upon the sentence of banishment, though others of them had respected it and complied with it. Like wilful children, or rather like bold and stubborn asserters of their immunity from the restraints of the law, they insisted that the inspiration which moved them, discharged them from obedience to man's statutes. Under these perplexities the magistrates

asked what they were to do. Should they abdicate their
offices, give place to the will and rule of these "criminals,"
or make yet one more effort, in their sworn trust, to save
the State?[1] The new law is introduced by a fresh recital of their grievances: —

"Whereas there is a pernitious sect, commonly called Quakers,
lately risen, who, by word and writing, have published and maintained many daingerous and horrid tennetts, and do take upon them
to chainge and alter the received laudable customes of our nation
in giving civill respect to æqualls or reverence to Superiors, whose
actions tend to undermine the authority of civill government, as
also to destroy the order of the churches by denying all established
forms of worship, and by withdrawing from the orderly church assemblies, allowed and approved by all orthodox professors of the
truth, and instead thereof and in opposition thereunto, frequenting
private meetings of their owne, insinuating themselves into the
minds of the simpler, or such as are lesse affected to the order and
government in church and commonwealth, whereby diverse of our
inhabitants have been infected and seduced, and notwithstanding
all former lawes made (upon experience of their arrogant, bold obtrusions to disseminate theire principles amongst us) prohibitting
their coming into this jurisdiction, they have not binn deterred
from theire impetuous attempts to undermine our peace and hasten
our ruine," —

[1] The following report of a conference at a dinner of the Council is found
on a paper in the State Archives. "March 9, 16⅝⅜. Major Hawthorne, at
dinner with the Gov. and Magistrates at a Court of Assistants, said that at
Salem there was a woman, called Cassandra Southwick, that said she was
greater than Moses, for Moses had seen God but twice, and his back sides
[Exodus xxxiii. 23], and she had seen him three times, and face to face, instan-
cing the places ; i. e. her own house one time, and in such a swamp another
time, etc. Also he said that a woman of Lynn, being at the meeting when Wm.
Robinson was there, who pressed much the seeking for the power within, she
asked him how she could come to seek that power within. He told her that
she must cast off all attendances to ordinances, as public preaching, praying,
reading the Scriptures, and attending to times of God's worship, and then wait
for the communication of this power. And he added, that he that will so do,
it will not be long that the Devil will appear either more explicitly, or at least
implicitly, to communicate himself."

The Court proceeds to order and enact that all such intruders shall be imprisoned till brought before the next Court of Assistants, and —

"then, having had a legal trial before a special jury, if convicted, shall be sentenced to banishment upon pain of death. And every inhabitant taking up, publishing, and defending the horrid opinions of the Quakers, or by stirring up mutiny, sedition, or rebellion against the government, or by taking up their absurd and destructive practices, namely, denying civil respect and reverence to æqualls and superiors, withdrawing from our church assemblies, and instead thereof frequenting private meetings of their own, approving Quaker tenets or practices opposite to the orthodoxe received opinions and practices of the godly, and endeavoring to disaffect others, and condemning the practice and proceedings of this Court against the Quakers," etc., — upon legal conviction, shall be committed to close prison for one month, and then, "unless they choose voluntarily to depart the jurisdiction" shall give bonds for their appearance before another Court, and if not retracting, shall be banished upon pain of death.[1]

No inhabitant but only strangers, regarded as "vagabonds" and "criminals," suffered the extreme penalty. Up to this point the Court might claim to have followed English precedent and practice in dealing with the Quakers. But though the Quaker historians give us the names of near twoscore persons of their sect, with the circumstances, who died in English prisons and dungeons from abuse, privations, and cruelty, no one was capitally punished there.

Reference has been made to a gleam of light shining upon this proceeding. Deacon John Wiswall, one of the deputies from Dorchester in the Court, was strongly opposed to the intended enactment. He was ill at the time, and being unable to attend, had had the promise of another deputy that he should have warning if his presence was needed. But as the dissenting deputies thought they could vote down

[1] Records, vol. iv. pt. i. pp. 345–347.

the law, he was not sent for. After the magistrates had passed the law, it came to the deputies. The speaker, Mr. Richard Russell, and eleven others were in the negative, while thirteen were in the affirmative. When Deacon Wiswall heard the result he was sorely troubled, saying he would have crept on his hands and knees to have prevented it. The two Boston deputies, Hutchinson and Clark, entered their protests. As the law first passed, it was without provision for a trial by jury. The twelve dissentients threatening to withstand the law as in this respect repugnant to the laws of England, the magistrates, fearing a complete break-down, consented to insert it. Yet the provision amounted to but little, as the jury would have to decide merely upon the fact of the accused being a Quaker.

There is further evidence of the nervous anxiety of the magistrates to hold to the point reached, and to keep the people who were on their side resolute and watchful.

The Quaker historians follow the narration of the proceedings against the Quakers from Massachusetts, where they began, into the other New England Colonies, and into the Province of New York, then under Dutch rule. It would be aside from our limits, as concerned only with the affairs of the Biblical commonwealth of the Bay Colony, to make any reference to these extended proceedings, were it not for the fact that Massachusetts did so much toward instigating them. Under the title of the " United Colonies of New England," Massachusetts, Plymouth, New Haven, and Connecticut had entered into a confederacy. The first suggestion for some such union had come from Massachusetts, in June, 1638; it was not effected, however, until May, 1643. In her relations with her sister New England Colonies, Massachusetts too often, and generally, allowed herself to assume a dominant and dictatorial spirit. Two reasons may have prompted this course : First, there was a weight and positiveness of character in her leading men,

helped by superiority in wealth and means, which seemed
to justify her pre-eminence and to make it natural for the
other Colonies to recognize it; Second, Massachusetts very
soon developed a policy in her affairs which clearly defined
to herself and others what she was aiming for in a strongly
grounded system of government, with the method and appliances requisite to secure it, while the other Colonies
were only feeling their way. Massachusetts readily affiliated with Plymouth, though occasionally moved to interfere
with suggestions and advice, and to administer reproofs
for laxity in administration. The confederacy was to be
represented by two commissioners, chosen by the General
Courts of each of the four Colonies, meeting successively
in each of them. The articles recognize their common ends,
— "to advance the Kingdome of our Lord Jesus Christ,
and to enjoy the liberties of the Gospell in puritie with
peace." They refer to the "sad distractions in England"
in the time of civil strife, and to their own exposure,
"dispersed upon the Sea Coasts and Rivers further than
was at first intended." They are "encompassed with people of severall nations and strang languages, who have
formerly committed sondry insolences and outrages upon
them." They therefore "enter into a firme perpetual
league of friendship and amytie, for offence and defence,
mutuall advice and succour upon all just occations both
for preserving and propagateing the truth and liberties
of the Gospell, and for their owne mutuall safety and
wellfare."

Massachusetts made haste to avail herself of this covenant under her consternation at the intrusion of the
Quakers within her bounds. The commissioners met in
turn at Plymouth, Sept. 4, 1656. A letter was there
read, sent by the governor and magistrates of Massachusetts, who had just passed their first enactment against the
Quakers. It opens with a reference to their covenant "for
maintaining Religion in its puritie," and after rebuking

Plymouth for slackness in its encouragement "of a pious Orthodox Minnestrey," it comes to the point thus : —

"Heer hath arived amongst us severall persons proffessing themselves quakers, fitt Instruments to propagate the kingdome of Sathan ; for the Securing of ourselves and our Naighbours from such pests, wee have Imprisoned them till they bee despatched away to the place from whence they came."

One of these was returned to Southampton, and Connecticut is reminded to look after him. The commissioners are asked to commend to each General Court rules " to prevent the coming in amongst us from foraigne places such Notorious heretiques as quakers, Ranters," etc. The commissioners applaud the zeal of the Massachusetts, and make the desired recommendation to the Courts.

William Coddington, Governor of Rhode Island before its charter and its incorporation with Providence Plantations, had, in 1648, petitioned the commissioners that his Colony might be received into the confederacy. This was refused, on the ground that the island should properly put itself under the jurisdiction of Plymouth, and also because it was full of confusion and distraction from dangerous persons and culprits who used the place " as a City of Refuge."

The next year, in September, 1657, the commissioners, meeting in Boston, addressed a letter to the government of Rhode Island to this effect: They had information that during the summer some Quakers had been entertained at the island who might prove dangerous to their neighbors, and the islanders are told of the advice given by the commissioners of the previous year " that all quakers, Rantors, and such notorious heretiques " coming from abroad, or rising up here, should be sent off. The islanders are solicited to follow this advice, with an intimation that if it is neglected something may follow.

Among all the dismal documents for one's reading on this subject, it is refreshing to come upon a paper which by its naïveté and humor gives momentary relief. Rhode Island had become known as " a harborage for all sorts of consciences." The uniformity sought for in Massachusetts may be likened to the cording of sticks of wood, each straight and all of equal length. One however would have been puzzled to deal in that way with the material for consciences in Rhode Island at that time, which presented itself in the form of those roots of forest trees used for making a " Virginia fence," with gnarled and crooked prongs in all directions. Benedict Arnold, President of Rhode Island, and for his associates, replied as follows to Massachusetts Court, Oct. 13, 1657 : —

" Please you to understand, that there hath come to our view a letter subscribed by the honoured gentlemen commissioners of the united coloneys, the contents whereof are a request concerning certayne people caled quakers, come among us lately.

" Our desires are in all things possible to pursue after and keepe fayre and loving correspondence and entercourse with all the Colloneys, and with all our countreymen in New England; and to that purpose we have endeavoured (and shall still endeavour) to answere the desires and requests from all parts of the countrey coming unto us, in all just and equall returnes, to which end the coloney have made seasonable provision to preserve a just and equal entercourse between the coloneys and us, by giving justice to any that demand it among us, and by returning such as make escapes from you, or from the other coloneys, being such ·as fly from the hands of justice, for matters of crime done or committed amongst you. And as concerning these quakers (so-called) which are now among us, we have no law among us whereby to punish any for only declaring by words their minds and understandings concerning the things and ways of God as to salvation and an eternal condition. And we, moreover, finde, that in those places where these people aforesaid in this coloney are most of all suffered to declare themselves freely, and are only oposed by arguments in discourse, there they least of all desire to come ; and we are informed that they begin to loath this place, for that they are not opposed by the civill authority, but with all patience and meeknes are suffered to say over their pretended revelations and admonitions, nor are they like or able to gain many here to their way; and surely we find that they delight to be persecuted by civill powers, and when they are soe, they are like to gaine more adherents by the conseyte of their patient sufferings than by consent to their pernicious sayings. (And yet we conceive that their doctrines tend to very absolute cutting downe and overturning relations and civill government among men, if generally received. But as to the dammage that may in all likelyhood accrue to the neighbour colloneys by their being here entertained, we conceive it will not prove so dangerous (as else it might) in regard of the course taken by you to send them away out of the countrey as they come among you. But, however, at present we judge itt requisitt (and doe intend) to commend the consideration of their extravagant outgoings unto the generall assembly of our coloney in March next, where we hope there will be such order taken as may, in all honest and contientious manner, prevent the bad effects of their doctrines and endeavours; and soe, in all courtious and loving respects, and with desire of all honest and fayre commerce with you and the rest of our honoured and beloved countrymen, we rest, Yours in all loving respects to serve you." [1]

Roger Williams, whose vigorous disputation with Quakers at Newport and Providence will be referred to on a later page, gives this account of the impression which they made upon him : —

"They are insufferably proud and contemptuous. I have, therefore, publicly declared myself, that a due and moderate restraint and punishment of these incivilities, though pretending conscience, is so far from persecution, properly so called, that it is a duty and command of God unto all mankinde, first in Families, and thence into all mankinde Societies." [2]

At the meeting of the commissioners in Boston, September, 1658, the whole eight, with an exception to be noticed,

---

[1] Hutchinson's Hist. Mass., vol. i. appendix xi.
[2] George Fox Digg'd out of his Burrowes, p. 200.

agreed to recommend to the several General Courts the enactment of a measure which begins with a recitation: " Whereas there is an accursed and pernitious sectt of heritiques lately risen up in the world, who are commonly called Quakers, who do take upon them to bee immediately sent of God and Infallably assisted," etc. Reference is then made to the dangerous character of their tenets and their offensive practices, and to the laws already passed, and the efforts made in vain to suppress them. The measure proposed is that the Quakers be banished from the several jurisdictions, under pain of severe corporal punishment if they return, and on a second return be put to death. John Winthrop signs with this condition, " Looking att the last as a query and not an Act: I subscribe." [1]

It is grateful to assign to John Winthrop, Jr., of Connecticut, the esteem he deserves from us for his pronounced dissent from the extreme course of the Massachusetts authorities toward the Quakers. He said he would go on his knees before the magistrates to arrest their execution. Another friend they found whose interposition might have been of service. Col. Sir Thomas Temple, who, in 1656, had purchased Nova Scotia from De la Tour, and had been made Governor of the Province by Cromwell and Charles II., proposed to the Court of Massachusetts, at his own charge to transport the Quakers there, and to maintain them for a time. The magistrates approved, but the deputies rejected the proposal. Reference is made to the subject in a letter from Rev. John Davenport to Winthrop, Jr.: —

" I am very sorry that the General Court at Boston did not accept Colonel Temple's motion, which had bene a cleare way, and incomparably the best expedient for freeing all the Colonies from the Quakers, who would have feared that kind of banishment more than hanging; it being a real cutting them off from all

[1] Records of Commissioners (1658), vol. ii.

opportunities and libertie of doing hurt in the Colonies by gain-
ing proselytes, which would have bene more bitter than death
to them." [1]

Neither of the other Colonies passed a capital law, as did
Massachusetts. In Plymouth very severe proceedings were
adopted against the Quakers, with warm protests from
those who sympathized with them. Connecticut dealt with
the Quakers so leniently that they did not much annoy that
Colony. In New Haven much sharper treatment was visited upon them, and of course their own words and acts
were more defiant and troublesome. In the Dutch Colony
of New York individuals and meetings of them were
treated with extreme violence. But these references are
outside of our subject.

A whole year passed after the enactment of the capital
law before it found the first two victims of its penalty. In
the mean while, however, seven persons, who had returned
after being banished with the sentence of death should
they be found again in the jurisdiction, were amenable to
the law, and were in prison. How it would have fared
with them had they not finally agreed to go away, may
be doubtful. Nor may we charge either of the seven
with a failure of firmness in courage or resolve in releasing themselves from the direful trial of their constancy.
Grateful, rather, should we be to them for finding in their
spiritual reckonings with themselves a prompting to go
rather than to stay. The first of the seven, subject to
condemnation, William Brend, who had been a grievous
trial to the magistrates, "felt at liberty" to leave, and
went to Rhode Island. Six more, arraigned May 11, 1659,
were to be on trial for life if not gone within a month.
Three of them went to Barbadoes, two to Shelter Island,
and one to Rhode Island. Two others, young persons,
were intended to be sent to Barbadoes or Virginia, after

[1] 4 Mass. Hist. Coll., vii. 509.

a usage of the time, to be sold for their fines. But no mariner would transport them, so they were left to take care of themselves. If the magistrates encouraged themselves from these voluntary departures that the terror of death on the gallows would henceforth be their security in all cases, they were soon brought to realize their error.

William Robinson, a young English Friend, who, after an imprisonment of six months in Virginia, had been travelling here on a mission, hearing that the sentenced persons just referred to had found release, felt "that the Lord had laid the burden upon him" to put the law to trial in his own person. In company with an English farmer, Marmaduke Stevenson, who "had been required of the Lord to leave my dear and loving wife and tender children, under a secret message to my heart, 'I have ordained thee a prophet unto the nations,'" came to Boston. Two others put into prison with them were Mary Dyer — on her second venture to Boston — and Nicholas Davis. Being brought to trial, they were sentenced, Sept. 14, 1659, to banishment and to death if they did not depart within two days. Davis left the jurisdiction, and Mary Dyer "felt liberty" this time to go home to Rhode Island; but soon after, "feeling a religious restraint," she came back to Boston, October 8. Robinson and Stevenson, who, instead of leaving the jurisdiction, had been on a missionary tour, holding meetings in it, again boldly presented themselves in Boston, and were committed to prison with the resolute and unquailing Mary Dyer, whose spirit could find no rest while the atrocious death penalty hung over any of the Friends whom she knew to be the "most innocent, pure, and harmless" of all who then lived around her. The woful tragedy had reached its fifth act. In the Court, Oct. 18, 1659,—

"Itt is ordered that William Robbinson, Marmaduke Stephenson, and Mary Dyer, Quakers, now in prison for their rebellion, sedition, and presumptuous obtruding themselves upon us, not-

withstanding theire being sentenced to banishment on paine of
death, as underminers of this government, shall be brought before
this Court for their trialls, to suffer the poenalty of the lawe (the
just reward of their transgression) on the morrow."

Then, on the trial, they acknowledged themselves to be
the persons banished, — the point on which the jury was to
pass; and, on a full hearing, Governor Endicott, having
put the question to the Court, with its approval, pronounced against each of them the sentence for execution.
The Secretary was ordered to issue his warrant to the
Marshal-General, Michelson, to take from the prison the
three condemned, October 27, and —

"by the aide of Capt. James Oliver, with one hundred souldiers,
taken out by his order proportionably out of each company in
Boston, compleatly armed with pike and musketteers, with pouder
and bullett, to lead them to the place of execution, and there see
them hang till they be dead, and in theire going, being there, and
retourne, to see all things be carried peaceably and orderly."

Such entertainment as, under their grim circumstances,
the prisoners would most relish was provided for them by
the Court, in sending to them the two elders, Symmes and
Norton, to "tender theire endeavors to make the prisoners
sencible of their approaching danger by the sentence of
this Court, and prepare them for theire approaching ends."
They would even then have been allowed to depart had
they consented to do so. Thus the issue was fairly drawn
between the magistrates, standing for their authority, and
the Quakers, standing for conscience. We know nothing
about the interview, but may be sure that the Quakers,
wholly indifferent to what the two "priests" might urge
upon them, spoke their own minds with all plainness.
Though the Court had sentenced Mary Dyer to execution,
yet on the intercession of her son she was allowed forty-
eight hours in which to be taken from the jurisdiction,
to be closely imprisoned until removed, and "to be forth-

with executed if she returned. In the mean while she was to go with the other two condemned to the place of execution, and to stand upon the gallows with a rope about her neck till her companions were executed."

There are many tokens that the magistrates were aware that they were about to submit their doings to a severe ordeal in boldly defying the known disapproval and the possible opposition of a large number of the people, especially of the " uncovenanted." Captain Oliver was ordered to place thirty-six of the soldiers about the town as sentinels, to preserve the peace while the execution was going on. The selectmen of Boston were required to press ten or twelve able and faithful persons every night to watch the town and the prison while the Court was sitting.[1]

It was after the Thursday Lecture, Oct. 27, 1659, that great multitudes of people gathered in the town to witness the tragic spectacle. The condemned took an affecting leave of their fellow-prisoners, with embracing and joyful outpourings of their constancy and assurance, and then they were taken " like Innocent Lambs out of the Butcher's Cub to the Slaughter."[2] The procession went by the " backway, lest the people should be affected too much if it went by the foreway." The drummers were placed close to the prisoners to drown their voluble and triumphant utterances. Mary Dyer walked between the men, " as to a Wedding day," with a serene and lifted spirit, and with beaming features, joining her hands in theirs, though jeered by some for this familiarity with two young men. The victims bore themselves with a seemly dignity. Mr. Wilson, the Elder, casting aside all that became his profession and self-respect, addressing Robinson " in a light Scoffing manner, said, Shall such Jacks as you come in before Authority with your Hats on ? " Still the hat ! — the idol equally of both parties. The gallows seems to have been a ladder rising above a branch of a tree, from which

[1] Records, vol. iv. pt. i. p. 384. [2] Bishop.

a rope was attached to the victims one by one, and then the ladder was removed. The bodies, without any covering, were put into a hole in the earth, which was soon covered with water. Some sympathizing friends had brought into the town linen for their shrouds. The bodies were disinterred to allow of this covering, but coffins were forbidden, and the Quakers murmured that they "might be preyed upon by Bruit Creatures." A striking token of the long surviving animosity to the first Quakers in the town is furnished in the Journal of Judge Sewall. The Quakers had a meeting-house — the first one in the town built of brick — and a burial-ground in Brattle Street in 1694. A new one was substituted for this in 1708, in Congress Street, then called Quaker Lane; but their meetings have been long discontinued. The Judge records, under date of June 17, 1685, —

"A Quaker or two goe to the Governour and ask leave to enclose the Ground the Hanged Quakers are in under or near the Gallows, with Pales: Governour proposed it to the Council, who unanimously denied it as very inconvenient[1] for persons so dead and buried in the place to have any Monument."[2]

The Quaker historians note among the "providences" marking the treatment of their friends, that as the crowd returned from the execution of Robinson and Stevenson, a portion of the drawbridge — it crossed a creek in the present North Street — broke down, injuring many persons, some fatally.

Mary Dyer had been pinioned and raised on the ladder. When released, she said she was "not free" to come down, and left it to the officials to relieve her. She addressed papers to the magistrates, expressing her discontent at receiving her life at their hands, and was carried from the

---

[1] The Judge, throughout his Journal, uses the word "inconvenient" in the sense of unseemly, improper, inconsistent.

[2] Sewall Papers, i. 82.

jurisdiction by a body of horsemen. All the condemned, with many other prisoners, addressed letters of remonstrance, or testimonies to their faith and their principles, from the jail to the magistrates. These papers are among the State Archives. They are all of an earnest and becoming tone and tenor, filled with the simplicities of piety and the joys and fervors of full conviction.

The next measure of the tormented magistrates was to spread upon their records, and to circulate — one by the press, the other in writing, to the various towns — the two preferred out of several papers that had been sent to them, as "Declarations," rehearsing and justifying their proceedings against the Quakers, including the capital law and the two executions under it. Their tone and pleading are pitiful and painful to readers of our time. Nothing of statement, argument, or vindication is found in them which has not been already brought to the notice of the reader. We are, however, bound in justice and candor, with whatever of reluctance and antipathy the effort may cost us, to endeavor to read ourselves — we cannot do more — into the intent and position, the outlook, and the assumed obligation of the pleaders. The papers cover six solid quarto pages. They begin by affirming that so far from offering an apology for their last proceedings, they may rather look for encouragement and commendation "from all prudent and pious men." Therefore they address themselves —

"to men of weaker parts, who, out of pitty and commiseration (a commendable and Christian virtue, yet easily abused, and susceptible of sinister and dangerous impressions), for want of full information, may be lesse satisfied : and men of perverse principles may take occasion hereby to calumniate us, and render us as bloody persecutors ; to satisfy the one, and stop the mouths of the other, wee thought it requisite to declare — "

Then follows a review of the legislation of the last three years. They had had warning of the pernicious and dan-

gerous principles and practices of the Quakers, expressed
with all the harsh and shuddering epithets attached to them,
and identifying them with the fanatics, "their predecessors in Munster." Successive efforts, at first not punitive,
then by gradation of penalties, had been tried in vain for
protection and security, till they had at last been driven
to pass a law of banishment on pain of death, "according
to the example of England, in their provission against
Jesuits." They had been compelled, after the failure —

"of gradual proceedings, to offer the points, for our own just and
necessary defence, which these persons have violently and wilfully
rushed upon, and thereby have become *felons de se.*"

Six grounds of their proceedings are then methodically
stated : 1. "The doctrine of this sect of people is destructive to fundamentall trueths of religion," with particulars
and arguments in proof of the assertion. 2. "It is the
commandment of the blessed God that Christians should
obey magistrates." This is abundantly traced through the
Scriptures. But the Quakers deny honor and reverence to
magistrates. "They show contempt against them in theire
very outward gestures and behavior, and (some of them at
least) spare not to belch out railing and cursing speeches.
Witness that odious, cursing letter of Humphrey Norton."
3. "The story of Solomon and Shimei (1 Kings ii.) is
a warrant for banishment. And banishment is a lighter
infliction than confinement, as it leaves a man free for
and in all places but one." 4. This proposition elabo-
rates with much force and precision the favorite plea of the
magistrates of their exclusive territorial rights, as absolute
proprietors of this jurisdiction, precisely like those of a
housekeeper, with consequent power to expel interlopers
and unwelcome strangers. 5. Heads of families have a
right and duty to protect themselves from all pernicious
companionship and teachings, and to secure them like
sheep and lambs from destroying wolves. 6. The Lord

commanded his disciples if persecuted in one city to flee to another. Scripture is largely cited to show how all "true saints" complied with this command. The Quakers disobey it.

This Declaration is followed by two orders, — one for the strengthening of the fence round the prison and house of correction, to debar intercourse with the prisoners; the other to arrest those who had lodged Quakers. The Court also dealt with Christopher Holder, who, having been sent to England without punishment, and having returned without leave, had three days allowed him to go back in a ship about sailing, or to be banished on pain of death. In November the Court awarded five hundred acres of land to Mr. Norton in return for his having written, as requested, his "tractate refuting the daingerous errors of the Quakers." It is entitled, "The Heart of New England rent by the blasphemies of the Present Generation." Fines were imposed on seven persons for entertaining Quakers, and other like culprits were summoned. Edward Wharton, who had "pilatted" Quakers, was imprisoned, and received twenty stripes. Ten more Quakers, men and women, "absenting themselves from theire family relations, for their disorderly practices and vagabond life" were whipped.

And now again appears Mary Dyer, for the fourth time since her first banishment from Boston as an Antinomian. Reprieved and sent off on the last 27th of October, she returns and is brought before the Court on the 30th of the next May. She had been carried away under the burden of having failed of her full mission, and she invited an opportunity to crown it. If that woman was sound in her mind, — and the intensity and fervor of her spirit, however it may have swayed and driven her, is no proof that she was not, — she had a grand nobility of nature, firm in nerve, with a calm earnestness of soul, and the force which goes with a gentle and heroic constancy. To the magistrates, however, she was a persistent and pestilent tormentor, under whose teasing aggravations they had been smarting for twenty years. Of her whereabout during the seven months since her reprieve we are informed only imperfectly, in a letter from her husband, William Dyer, Secretary of Rhode Island, dated Portsmouth, May 27, 1660, and addressed to Governor Endicott. The original is in the State Archives, and one reading it in these days will be moved to add to the tears which the writer plainly let fall upon it. It is evident from it that he was not in sympathy with the views and the conduct of his wife; and it would seem that, as she had abandoned her home, he had not seen her since her reprieve. This pathetic appeal from a deserted husband is as follows: —

HONORED SIR, — It is no little grief of mind and sadness of hart that I am necessitated to be so bould as to supplicate your honored self, with the Honb^le Assembly of your Generall Court, to extend your mercy and favor once agen to me and my children. Little did I dream that I should ever had had occasion to petition you in a matter of this nature; but so it is that throw the divine providence and your benignity my sonn obtained so much pity and mercy att your hands as to enjoy the life of his mother.

Now my supplication to your Honors is to begg affectionately the life of my deare wife. 'T is true I have not seene her above this halfe yeare, and therefore cannot tell how in the frame of her spirit she was moved thus again to run so great a hazard to herself and perplexity to me and mine, and all her friends and well-wishers; so it is, from Shelter Island about by Pequid, Narragansett and to the town of Providence, she secretly and speedily journied, and as secretly from thence came to your jurisdiction. Unhappy journey may I say; and woe to that generation, saye I, that gives occasion thus of grief and trouble to those that desires to be quiet, by helping one another (as I may say) to hazard their lives for I know not what end, or to what purpose. If her zeale be so greate as thus to adventure, oh, let your favour and pitye surmounte itt, and save her life. Let not your forwonted compassion be conquered by her inconsiderate madness; and how greately will your renowne be spread, if by so conquering you become victorious. What shall I say more? I know you are all sensible of my condition, and let the reflect be, and you will see what the petition is and what will give me and mine peace. Oh, let mercie's wings once more soar above justice' ballance, and then whilst I live shall I exalt your goodness. But otherwise 't will be a languishing sorrowe, yea, soe great that I should gladly suffer the blow att once much rather. I shall forbear to trouble your Honors with words, neither am I in a capacitye to expatiate my-selfe at present. I only say this : your selves have been and are, or may be, husbands to wife or wives, and so am I, yea, to one most dearlye beloved. Oh, do not you deprive me of her ; but I pray give her me out again, and I shall bee soe much obliged for-ever, that I shall endeavor continually to utter my thanks, and render your Love and Honor most renowned. Pitye me. I beg it with tears, and rest

Your most humble suppliant, W. Dyer.

Most Honored Sir, let these lines by your favor be my petition to your Honorable General Court at present sitting.

Yours, W. D.

Among the papers in the State Archives is one recognizing the receipt of Mr. Dyer's letter : —

The Magistrates desire their brethren the Deputies would please give them a meeting about two hours hence, and that Mary Dyer be sent for out of prison, to appear before the whole Court.

Assented to by the Deputies.

Boston, 31st of May, 1660.

Probably at this meeting Mrs. Dyer was offered a release at the intercession of her husband, as she had received it previously at the intercession of her son, if she would consent to leave the jurisdiction, and that she refused to do so.

If her husband could have answered for his wife, she would have lived. Most gladly would the magistrates have welcomed one word from her own lips, that she would no more exasperate and defy them, but would keep out of their jurisdiction. But she spoke quite other words.

"She gave no other answer but that she denied our lawe, came to bear witnes against it, and could not choose but come and doe as formerly." She was sentenced, according to the previous October warning, " for her rebelliously returning into this jurisdiction, notwithstanding the favour of this Court towards her," to die on the second day following, — June 1.

There were further proceedings at this Court, with a show of clemency in them, against Quakers returned from banishment.[1] Mrs. Dyer calmly and triumphantly met her fate. There was to be still one more, the fourth victim to the capital law. This was William Leddra. He had been long and often scourged and imprisoned, here and in Plymouth, and was one of the most pertinacious, and, as the magistrates viewed him, the most insolent of those who defied them by returning from banishment. With the same parade of soldiers and drummers, he was executed after the lecture, March 14, $16\frac{60}{61}$. His friends were allowed to take away his body for interment, so that he was not thrown into the ground with the others on the Common.[2]

[1] Court Records, vol. iv. pt. ii. p. 419.

[2] It may be that the following reference in the Journal of Judge Sewall (Sewall Papers, i. 91) is to the grave of Leddra : —

"Aug. 5, 1685. After Dorchester Lecture, going to Mr. Stoughton's, I saw a few feet of ground enclosed with Boards, which is done by the Quakers out of respect to some one or more hanged and by the Gallows ; though the Governor forbad them when they asked Leave."

An epistle which Leddra wrote in the jail before his execution, addressed to " The Little Flock of Christ," is a characteristic paper (State Archives). Here are extracts from it : —

"MOST DEAR AND INWARDLY BELOVED, — The sweet influences of the morning star, like a flood distilling into my habitation, have so filled me with the joy of the Lord in the beauty of holiness, that my spirit is as if it did not inhabit a tabernacle of clay, but is wholly swallowed up in the bosom of eternity, from whence it had its being. Alas ! Alas ! what can the wrath and spirit of man, that lusteth to envy, aggravated by the heat and strength of the king of the locusts which came out of the pit, do unto one that is hid in the secrets of the Almighty ? Oh, my beloved, I have waited like a dove at the windows of the ark. As the flowing of the ocean

Winlock Christopherson, who was under sentence of death if he returned from banishment, had ventured to present himself at the trial of his friend Leddra. No one of all those who were in peril of their lives was more stout, resolved, defiant, and denunciatory than he, — generally called Christison. He said he was ready to meet his threatened fate. Being brought to trial in May, 1661, the Court, now greatly weakened in its severity, faltered about passing sentence. Endicott was so provoked by this weakness that he absented himself for two days. He was induced to return to his place, on the promise that the work should proceed. Finding the Court still hesitating, he took upon himself to sentence Christison to death on June 13. Being the last to receive that sentence, he delivered himself from having to suffer by it. Among the papers in the State Archives before referred to are the following : —

I, the condemned man, do give forth under my hand, that if I may have my liberty, I have freedom to depart this jurisdiction, and I know not that ever I shall come into it any more.

From the Goal in Boston, the 7th day of the 4th mo. 1661.

WINLOCK CHRISTISON.

Upon the motion of Christopherson, the prisoner, in making known his freedom to depart, the Deputies do hereby grant him liberty, he departing this Government, when he shall be let out of prison, as soon as may be : with reference to the consent of our honored Magistrates hereto.

WILLIAM TORREY, *Cleric.*

Consented to by the Magistrates.

7 (4) 1661.   ED. RAWSON, *Secretary.*

The Quaker historians do not mention this case of compliance with what the Court wished and proffered for all

doth fill every creek and branch thereof, and as it then retires again towards its own being and fulness, and leaves a Savour behind it, so doth the life and virtue of God flow into every one of your hearts, whom He hath made partakers of his Divine nature."

the imprisoned intruders upon them. It has been said that after all Christison's bravery and bluster "he showed the white feather." It is not necessary, however, to suppose that his pluck and courage failed him in view of the gallows. A divine prompting, which he claimed had brought him here, might also release him from bearing any further testimony.

But the people would allow no more of this death penalty. Happily, this resisting attitude of the community and the breaking down of the Court seem to have been contemporaneous with a relaxation of obduracy in the imprisoned Quakers themselves. The magistrates had with great concern and anxiety noticed the rapidly increasing manifestations of discontent with their proceedings, and of sympathy with the Quakers. This was shown by many who could not approve the behavior or the principles of the Quakers, but believed they would be harmless if let alone. Their fines were paid and acts of kindness done them by these sympathizers. We must remember that the whole power of government was with the small minority as church members. So far, then, from concluding that every one of general Puritan principles was a persecutor, it would rather be reasonable to infer that the majority of the people disapproved of the extreme proceedings. This state of public feeling was coincident with an evident disinclination on the part of the Quakers, under sentence, to carry their provocation any farther. Whether they were honorably released from further defiance by a satisfied conscience, or by the dread of the gallows, they made the full concession required of them.

It is a relief to come in the Records upon this provision for a general jail delivery: thus, granting the petition of the Quakers : —

"October 16, 1660. In answer to a motion of the Quakers now in prison that they may have theire liberty to goe for England, the Court judgeth it meete to declare that all the Quakers now in prison shall forthwith have their libertie to goe for England in this ship now bound thither, if they will; and for such as will not goe for England, they shall have liberty forthwith to depart this jurisdiction within eight days, so as they solemnly engage, under their hands, delivered by them to the Governor or Dep. Gov., that they will not return into this jurisdiction without leave from the Councill or Generall Court first by them obtained." [1]

At the same Court Joseph Nicolson and Jane his wife, in prison for having returned after banishment on pain of death, having expressed their willingness to depart for England, were allowed to do so.[2] As soon as they reached England they were imprisoned in Dover Castle for refusing the oath.

To some who have followed up to this point the narration of a harrowing conflict between antagonistic consciences, it may seem as if it had ended in the complete triumph of the magistrates. All the Quakers under duress, twenty-seven in number,[3] besides the three who were doomed to the gallows, had agreed voluntarily to leave the jurisdiction. This was all that the magistrates had ever required of them. Holding firmly to their own conviction that these intruding strangers, alleging a divine mission to come and overthrow all civil and social order in the country, were fanatics and nuisances of the most pestilent character, they ordered them to leave the jurisdiction where they had no right to abide. They thought that if the Quakers regarded themselves as wronged, they should obey the command of their Master, and when persecuted in one place should go to another. There had come to be three parties to the conflict: the magistrates, charged with the defence of the commonwealth; the majority of the people, who were opposed to any further capital proceedings; and the Quakers, the cause of so much annoyance. It would seem as if all these three parties had occasion

---

[1] Records, vol. iv. p. ii. p. 433.   [2] Ibid.
[3] Bishop gives their names (p. 340).

to be satisfied.   The will of the magistrates had prevailed
by the recognition of their authority ; the people were to
be spared any more scenes on the scaffold ; the Quakers,
convinced by their own methods of illumination and divine
promptings, felt that they were in conscience discharged
from any further " testimony," and " had freedom to
depart."   The general jail delivery was to be welcomed,
through whatever agency it had been effected.   It is always, however, to be remembered that it was the unflinch-
ing and heroic constancy of the four victims that had won
the people to the resolve that, whatever else should be done
with the Quakers, no more of them should suffer the death
penalty.

The General Court, meeting Dec. 19, 1660, voted an Address to King Charles II., on his restoration, which is spread
on the Records.   It contains a plea for the preservation
of their colonial rights and liberties, and a defence against
the machinations and complaints of their enemies near
the throne.   They well knew that among these were the
Quakers, to whom the following reference is made in the
Address : —

" Concerning the Quakers, open and capitall blasphemers, open
seducers from the glorious Trinity, and from the Holy Scriptures
as the rule of life, open enemies to government itself as established
in the hands of any but men of theire owne principles, malignant
and assiduous promoters of doctrines directly tending to subvert
both our churches and State, after all other meanes for a long
time used in vaine, wee were at last constreined, for our owne
safety, to passe a sentence of banishment against them upon paine
of death.   Such was their daingerous, impetuous, and desperat tur-
bulency, both to religion and the state civil and ecclesiasticall, as
that, how unwillingly soever, could it have binn avoyded, the magistrate at last, in conscience both to God and man, judged himself
called, for the defence of all, to keepe the passage with the point
of the sword held towards them.   This could do no harme to him
that would be warned thereby ; theire wittingly rushing themselves

thereupon was theire owne act, and wee, with all humillity, conceive a crime bringing theire blood on theire owne head. The Quakers died, not because of theire other crimes, how capitoll soever, but upon their superadded presumptuous and incorrigible contempt of authority; breaking in upon us notwithstanding theire sentence of banishment made knowne to them. Had they not binn restreined, so farr as appeared, there was too much cause to feare that wee ourselves must quickly have died, or worse: and such was theire insolency, that they would not be restreined but by death; nay, had they at last but promised to depart the jurisdiction, and not to returne without leave from authority, wee should have binn glad of such an oppertunity to have said they should not dye." [1]

The view which the magistrates took of their own course and responsibility is asserted with the utmost strength which they could give to it. We are left to decide as intelligently and as shrewdly as we are able, whether their plea in self-defence expresses the blind and relent- less severity of bigotry, exasperated by defiance, or an honest and sincere conviction that such defiance of their authority really threatened the wreck of govern- ment.

Was it with sham pretence, or with reason grounded on apprehensions, that the authorities alleged that beyond their heresies the Quakers were to be dreaded as enemies to the peace and security of society? That able Quaker cham- pion, Edward Burroughs,[2] in his appeal to the King in their behalf, writes: " Did ever these poor people whom they con- demned and put to a shameful death lift up a hand against them, or appear in any turbulent gesture towards them? Were they ever found with any carnal weapon about them?" etc. And Mr. Doyle[3] calls it a " flimsy and dishonest ex- cuse that the Quakers were dealt with not as heretics, but as enemies to civil order." The explanation of this is to be inferred from preceding statements. The Quakers never

[1] Records, vol. iv. pt. i. p. 451.
[2] Collected Writings, p. 756.   [3] Puritan Colonies, ii. 171.

committed, or even threatened, any act of violence, nor raised a carnal weapon; nor were they, as already stated, in any way opposed to lawful magistracy within its province. Nevertheless, it was not their hands nor their weapons which the magistrates dreaded, but simply their tongues, the burdens which they uttered, their contempt of the orders and laws of the magistrates. These truculencies of speech and conduct the magistrates insisted on regarding as dangerous instruments of sedition and anarchy as firearms would have been. It is difficult to believe that the repeated declarations of the magistrates to this effect were hypocritical.

We must keep in mind that the magistrates, some of the deputies, and such of the freemen, church members, as felt most outraged by the persistency of the Quakers, and were still disposed to treat them with the utmost severity, were now placed in a position of extreme embarrassment. They well knew that a spirit of opposition to their harshest proceedings, and a spirit of sympathy and commiseration, even of admiration, for the Quakers, were rapidly strengthening in the community. No more capital punishments would be tolerated. What then should the magistrates do in this dilemma? The Court, May 22, 1661, passed a new law: —

"This Court, being desirous to try all meanes with as much lenity as may consist with our safety to prevent the intrusions of the Quakers, who, besides theire absurd and blasphemous doctrine, doe, like rouges and vagabonds, come in upon us, and have not been restreined by the laws already provided, have ordered that every such vagabond Quaker found within any part of this jurisdiction should be taken before a magistrate, and being adjudged to be a wandering Quaker,— namely, one that hath not any dwelling or orderly allowance as an inhabitant of this jurisdiction, — and not giving civil respect by the usuall gestures thereof, or by any other way or meanes manifesting himself to be a Quaker, shall by warrant to an officer be stripped naked from the middle upwards, and tied to a cart's tayle, and whipped " from town to town, by the constable of each, till out of the jurisdiction.[1]

This punishment to be repeated on a second and a third return. On a fourth return, at the discretion of the magistrate, to be branded with the letter " R " on the left shoulder, and again whipped and sent away. Returning yet again, " then to be proceeded against as incorrigible rogues and ennemies to the common peace," to be imprisoned and tried under the law of banishment on pain of death. This was for vagabond intruders or strangers. For Quakers arising here the penalties were substantially the same.

All Quakers then in prison were to be informed of this law, and to be released, passing unharmed from constable to constable out of the jurisdiction, and if they returned, to be dealt with according to the above provisions. Two of the prisoners who had stood mute before the Court, refusing to give any answer, were sentenced to be whipped both in Boston and Dedham, and then sent out of the jurisdiction.

Some of our writers, alike in prose and in poetry, have assumed, and have written on the assumption, that the deliverance of the Quakers was effected by the interposition in their behalf of King Charles II.[2] It will appear, from a clear statement of the facts of the case, that the interposition of the King, instead of relieving the Quakers from such penalties as the Court would inflict upon them, proved most harmful to them. As Mr. Doyle very forcibly puts it, the Quakers having asked, and supposing they had received, the protection of the King, were to their sorrow reminded of the warning, " Put not your trust in princes." Long

[1] Records, vol. iv. pt. ii. p. 3.

[2] The writer of these pages some years ago gave a degree of assent to this view. See " Memorial History of Boston," i. 187. But a stricter attention to dates and to the fact that popular feeling here had anticipated the command of the King, satisfied him of his mistake.

fellow, in his New England Tragedy, " John Endicott," puts into the Governor's mouth, addressing his Deputy Bellingham the order for the release of the imprisoned Quakers, these words : —

> " But see that none of them be sent to England
> To bear false witness, and to spread reports
> That might be prejudicial to ourselves."

Now, so far were the magistrates from fearing any harm to be done them by Quakers reporting their doings in England, and from restraining their going thither, that, as we have read in the Court order, they were released from prison on the express condition of their promise to go there. Any one who has read diligently the Records of the General Court of Massachusetts at that period, will find matter alike of amazement and amusement in the hardly disguised adroitness and truculency with which the authorities treated the anointed monarchs successively occupying the throne. There is adulation, something that looks very much like fawning, and hypocritical deference and flattery to the King in their words, while utter disloyalty and disobedience were in the hearts of the magistrates. They cared nothing for the ill reports which the Quakers might spread of them in England, for they knew they could tell their own side of the story, and they were well informed as to the virulent treatment of the Quakers there. Indeed, it is exceedingly doubtful whether Endicott, Bellingham, and their associates would not have found some ingenious method of disobeying a positive command of the King if it thwarted their own purpose. At any rate, in the case before us the direction of the monarch had been anticipated.

Edward Burroughs, an English Friend, learning of the just quoted Address sent by the Court to Charles II. on hearing of his restoration, wrote a very sharp and able answer to it, which is supposed to have reached the knowledge of the monarch. He also obtained an audience, and by his earnest pleading drew from the monarch a letter to the magistrates which he allowed to be sent in a private vessel, provided by the Quakers, to Governor Endicott. Samuel Shattuck, a banished Salem Quaker then in London, was the bearer of the letter. Wearing his own hat, while Endicott removed his to receive " a message from the King," the Quaker had a brilliant triumph. After a conference with his deputy, Bellingham, the Governor said, " We shall obey the King." This is said by the Quaker historians, but not by Shattuck.[1]

The royal letter, which follows, had, as we have seen, been substantially anticipated as to its principal demand by the action of the Court. The general jail delivery of thirty-one Quakers, including the three under the death sentence who had voluntarily agreed to go off, was ordered by the Court in October, 1660. The King's letter was dated at Whitehall a year afterward. Let us claim whatever of relief we can find in reminding ourselves that it was the stern opposition and protest of the majority of the people of the Puritan Colony, and not the King's command, that had opened the gates of mercy.

CHARLES R.

TRUSTY AND WELL-BELOVED, — We greet you well. Having been informed that several of our Subjects amongst you called Quakers have been and are Imprisoned by you, whereof some have been Executed, and others (as hath been represented to us) are in danger to undergo the like, We have thought fit to signifie Our Pleasure in that behalf for the future ; and do hereby

---

[1] Shattuck sent a letter to his friends in England describing his voyage and reception by Endicott. It is without the dramatic features given by the Quaker historians, — save the restoration to him of his hat, which had been taken from him before his message was delivered. It is pleasant to have in the letter the recognition by Shattuck of the sympathy of the people with the errand on which he came : "The moderate sort rejoiced to see me ; the truth had gotten prety much ground of the Adversary." He remained between shipboard and on land, and visited some friends in jail. The letter is in Aspinwall Papers, 4 Mass. Hist. Soc. Coll., ix. 160–162.

require, That if there be any of those People called Quakers amongst you, now already Condemned to suffer Death or other corporal Punishment, or that are Imprisoned and Obnoxious to the like Condemnation, you are to forbear to proceed any further therein, but that you forthwith send the said Persons (whether Condemned or Imprisoned) over into this Our Kingdom of England, together with the respective Crimes or Offences laid to their Charge, to the end such Course may be taken with them here as shall be agreable to Our Laws and their Demerits: And for so doing, these Our Letters shall be your sufficient Warrant and Discharge. Given at Our Court at Whitehall, the ninth day of Sept. 1661.

By his Majesty's Command,

WILLIAM MORRIS.

There is some confusion as to what followed the immediate reception by the magistrates of this royal letter. John Whiting, in his Reply to the account of the Quakers given by Cotton Mather in his Magnalia,[1] says that when the jailer was called upon by Friends to release some then in prison, according to the King's command, he replied that "it was not for them," and that the magistrates were still urging jury trials for capital cases. Of later date, and not till after the meeting of the Court, Nov. 27, 1661, we find this order to —

WILLIAM SALTER, keeper of the prison in Boston, — You are required, by authority and order of the General Court, to release and discharge the Quakers who at present are in your custody. See that you do not neglect this.

EDWARD RAWSON, *Sec.*

BOSTON, 9th December, 1661.

Whiting does not explain to us who the prisoners were whom the jailer refused to release on the ground that "the order was not for them" as Quakers. Nor can I clear the perplexity. In the interval after the jail delivery, it may

[1] In Bishop, p. 96.

have been that some new-comers or sympathizers were under restraint.

Before the meeting of the General Court to take action on the letter of the King, a rumor was in circulation that he had granted certain immunities to the Quakers. A paper in the State Archives informs us of the notice taken of this rumor on June 4, 1661, by the deputies, before the King's letter was written, though their proposition was not assented to by the magistrates. The paper recites: —

"Whereas it seemeth at present to this Court, by such intelligence as we have, to be uncertain what persons (whether Quakers or others), under pretence of authority from England, may attempt to publish or act in this Jurisdiction during the vacancy of the General Court [it is ordered that all persons putting forth any writing or acting anything (under pretence of authority from England or elsewhere) against the existing laws], especially that against a conspiracy for altering this government, shall be arrested by a magistrate and imprisoned without bail."

The Governor, Endicott, summoned the Court to meet in Boston, Nov. 27, 1661. The critical character of the occasion was fully realized, as appears by another interesting paper in the State Archives, showing deliberation in proceedings when the Court's authority was under question. The paper is entitled, "Answer of Elders to the Questions of the General Court relative to the Quakers."

The Elders being called to attend the Honored General Court at a Session held at Boston, Nov. 27, 1661, have unto certain queries then and there proposed to them returned their Apprehensions as followeth:

Quaery 1. Whether the execution of our Laws referring to the Punishment of the Quakers as such shall be suspended *pro tempore*, or what else to be done therein?

Ans. Upon his Majestie's letters we conceive it expedient that Execution of death, or corporal punishment, according as is expressed therein, be suspended *pro tempore*. Provided that some effectual course be also taken in the interim for the restraint of turbulencies in church or state, which the King's warrant, to our apprehension, no ways inhibits, but rather encourageth thereunto.

Qu. 2. Whether the Quakers in Prison should be sent for England with their accusations, or otherwise released out of prison.

Ans. We think it much better that the Quakers in prison should be sent for England with their accusations, than that they should be released out of prison.

Qu. 3. Whether this Court is called to make a humble address by petition to his Majesty, in answer to his letters now brought concerning the Quakers?

Ans. To this 3d Qu. we answer affirmatively.

The fourth and fifth queries, and the answers to them, ask and assent to the fitness of sending one or more agents to England with provision to act in the country's behalf.

Another paper in the Archives is entitled " Votes as to Laws against Quakers."

1. *Qu.* Whether the Execution of our Laws referring to the Quakers' corporal punishment shall be suspended *pro tempore ?* The Deputies have voted that it be suspended till the next Court of Election.

The Magistrates dissent.

2. Whether the Quakers now in Prison shall be sent to England with their accusations? The Deputies have voted in the Negative.

The Magistrates consent hereto.

4. Whether this Court will send an Agent to England to prosecute our affairs there? The Deputies have voted in the Negative. The Magistrates have voted in the Affirmative.

5. Whether there should be monies raised to effect the same ? The Deputies have voted in the Negative. The Magistrates have voted this also in the Affirmative.

The 3d Question [relating to " an Humble Address "] not being agreed on, is further to be considered of.

WILLIAM TORREY, *Cler.*

Afterwards, Magistrates and Deputies both consent to an Address to his Majesty. EDW. RAWSON, *Secretary.*

Previous to the receipt of the King's letter about the Quakers, the Court had on Aug. 7, 1661, indited another letter to him, the strain of which is fawning and hypocritical in the most offensive degree. A portion of it may be given here, premising that the reference in it to Venner, the leader of the Fifth Monarchy fanatics in London, who had been a cooper in Salem, Mass., adroitly suggests "that he had come to us before he went from us."

To the high and mighty prince, Charles the Second, by the grace of God King of Great Britain, France, and Ireland, Defender, etc.

ILLUSTRIOUS SIR, — That majestie and benignity hath sat upon the throne whereunto your outcasts made their former addresse, witness this second eucharisticall approach unto the best of kings, who, to other titles of royaltie common to him with other gods amongst men, delighted therein more peculiarly to conforme himself to the God of gods, in that he hath not despised nor abhorred, etc. This script, gratulatorie and lowly, is the reflection of the gracious rayes of Christian majestie, etc. We are deeply sensible of your majestie's intimation relating to instruments of Satan acted by impulse. Diabolicall Venner (not to say whence he came to us) went out from us because he was not of us. God preserve your majestie from all enemies agitated by an infernall spirit, under what appellations soever disguised. Luther sometimes wrote to the senate of Mulhoysen to beware of the woolfe Muncer.[1]

The Address of the Court in answer to the letter of the King, of Sept. 9, 1661, is as follows : —

" The just and necessary rules of our government and condition for preservation of religion, order, and peace, hath induced the authority here established from time to time to make and sharpen lawes against Quakers in reference to their restles intrusions and impetuous disturbance, and not any propensity or any inclination in us to punish them in person or estate, as is evident by our graduall proceeding with them, releasing some condemned and

[1] Records, vol. iv. pt. ii. p. 32.

others liable to condemnation, and all imprisoned were released and sent out of our borders; all which, notwithstanding theire restless spiritts, have mooved some of them to returne, and others to fill the royall eares of our soveraigne lord the king with complaints against us, and have, by their wearied solicitations in our absence, so farr prevayled as to obteine a letter from his majesty to forbeare their corporall punishment or death. Although wee hope, and doubt not, but that if his majesty were rightly informed he would be farr from giving them such favour, or weakening his authority here so long and orderly setled, yet, that wee may not in the least offend his majesty, this Court doth heereby order and declare that the execution of the lawes in force against Quakers, as such, so farr as they respect corporall punishment or death, be suspended untill this Court take further order." [1]

Magistrate Bradstreet and Elder Norton were sent on their agency to England with many instructions on various matters.[2] The one of concern here was, that they should "indeavor to take off all scandall and objections which are made or may be made against us." [3]

Meanwhile, pending the issue of the two addresses made to the King, the Court, by an order of May 7, 1662, which, though not mentioning the Quakers, included them under " the vagrant and vagabond persons, as well inhabitants as forreigners, that wander from their families, relations, and dwelling-places," still provided for their corporal punishment from town to town.[4] Without looking outside the Records, we see the evidence of a feverish excitement in

---

[1] Records, vol. iv. pt. ii. p. 34.

[2] These agents might have had a perilous experience in England had it not been for the forbearance and magnanimity of some of the Friends, who personally challenged them for their share in the proceedings here against their brethren. The father of their victim, Robinson, was prompted to bring a complaint. Fox advised that they be left to "the dealing of the Lord." He gives in his Journal a charmingly characteristic account of an interview with them ending in their discomfiture. The agents had ventured to plead that the Quakers had been dealt with as English law dealt with Jesuits. "But," replied Fox, " you know they were not Jesuits."

[3] Records, vol. iv. pt. ii. p. 37.   [4] Ibid., p. 43.

the community, marking this as a crisis for the more reso‐
lute of the magistrates in maintaining their defied author‐
ity. They complained that Quakers, hoping to receive
protection from the interposition of the King, roamed
about the towns and villages, finding lodging and food
with sympathizing inhabitants, drawing multitudes away
from their necessary employments, breaking the quiet of
the Lord's Day, and causing frights and panics for nervous
people by their denunciatory prophesyings in the meeting‐
houses. So the magistrates pertinaciously held to their
course of severity. They were evidently in no fear of the
King. Knowing well that hundreds and thousands of
the Quakers were at the time meeting the penalties of the
law, suffering from mobs, and rotting in jails in England,
they would not believe that they would be forbidden self‐
protection from these offenders here, where disorder and
sedition were more threatening. A ship-commander had
unwittingly, not knowing the character of his passenger,
brought into the town a woman Quaker, " a decrepit per‐
son, a notable and fitt instrument of that cursed sect, to
divulge their tenents, and came furnished with many blas‐
phemous and haereticall bookes, which she had spread
abroad." The captain professed his sorrow for his act,
and promised to keep her on board and to return her
whence she came. His fine of one hundred pounds was
remitted, on his giving a barrel of powder.[1] Stiffening in
its purpose, on Oct. 8, 1662, the Court announced that —

" for some reasons inducing, it had judged meet to suspend the
execution of the lawes against Quakers, so farr as they respect
corporall punishment or death, during the Court's pleasure. Now,
forasmuch as new complaints are made to this Court of such
persons abounding, especially in the easterne parts, endeavoring to
drawe away others to that wicked, — the law, title, Vagabond
Quakers, of May, 1661, shall henceforth be in force in all respects,
provided that theire whipping be but through three townes." [2]

[1] Records, vol. iv. pt. ii. 55.   [2] Ibid., p. 59.

These brutal scenes at the cart's tail — so in keeping with the police system of those days in England, so revolting as to be impossible of enactment in our own times — had their aggravation or relief, according to the measure of barbarity or humanity in the officer, and the behavior, whether passionate in remonstrance or sympathizing, of the lookers-on. The people of Dover — now New Hampshire — petitioned the Court for more severity "against the spreading of the wicked errors of the Quakers amongst them," and the local magistrate was instructed to execute the laws.[1] Oct. 21, 1663, the Court ordered, —

"Whereas, it is found by experience that there are many who are inhabitants of this jurisdiction which are ennemies to all government, civil and ecclesiasticall, who will not yeild obedience to authority, but make it much of theire religion to be in opposition thereto, and refuse to beare armes under others," — combining in some towns to make parties and influence elections, and abstain from public worship, — "be made uncapable of voting in all civil assemblies," and be fined.[2]

At length the Court received the expected answer from the King. His letter contained other matters which will be referred to in another connection. The following passage in the letter concerns the matter now before us : —

"Wee cannot be understood hereby to direct or wish that any indulgence should be granted to those persons commonly called Quakers, whose principles being inconsistent with any kind of government, wee have found it necessary, by the advice of our Parliament here, to make sharp lawes against them, and are well contented that you doe the like there." [3]

The Quakers had appealed to the King against the magistrates of Massachusetts. Most disastrous was the result for the sufferers. The Quaker historians give us the former letter of the King; but whether from disappointment,

[1] Records, vol. iv. pt. ii. p. 69.   [2] Ibid., p. 88.   [3] Ibid., p. 165.

or some other feeling, they suppress this. Considering that capital proceedings had been already abandoned, not because of the prohibition of the King, but by the breaking down of the Court through the protest of the people,[1] the magistrates now felt that they had the royal sanction for "sharp lawes" against the Quakers, like his own.

The facts relating to the interposition of the King in behalf of the Quakers appear from the Records to be as follows: No prisoners, with the charges against them, were sent by the Court to England, as the King had ordered. Such of them as voluntarily chose to go there were at liberty to do so. The prisoners under capital sentence had previously consented to leave the jurisdiction. While some of the magistrates would still have been willing to inflict the death penalty, the protest of the people and the breaking down of the Court had disabled them. If other corporal punishments were temporarily suspended, they did not cease at the command of the King, and were afterwards renewed as by his sanction in his second letter.

The most offensive and extravagant of the eccentricities of deportment in individual Quakers occurred after the harshest severity of the treatment of them had been much relaxed, and popular respect and sympathy had been largely drawn to them. It is fitting to state, however, that the cases to be mentioned were exceptional ones. The morals, behavior, manners, and speech even of the rudest of the Quakers were always rigidly conformed to decency and purity. In no single case did they furnish occasion for scandal. Not a reproach for any moral offence rests upon any one of them; and this is true, notwithstanding the fact that individuals of either sex wandered about together in their

[1] Mr. Doyle (Puritan Colonies in New England, ii. 172) writes: "Inasmuch as the Court of Massachusetts had already changed its policy towards the Quakers, it is clear that they were moved by the dread of royal interposition, and not by that interposition itself." In saying this he seems to have overlooked the opposition and disgust of the majority of the people which compelled the failure of the sanguinary law.

missions, and their sentimental relations were fond and gushing. The wife of Eliakim Wardel, of Hampton, described as a "chaste and tender woman," of "exemplary modesty," five years after the last execution in Boston, having embraced Friends' principles, had forsaken public worship, though often asked to attend and give reasons for her course. At last she startled the congregation at Newbury by going through the aisles of the meeting-house wholly unclothed. The Quaker historians explain her "prophetic act" as a testimony against the immodest exposure of the females made by the magistrates when they were stripped to the waist to be scourged.

About the same time Deborah Wilson, described as "a young woman of a very modest and retired life," went through the streets, without clothing, for like testimony. Both these women suffered scourging. In 1677 Margaret Brewster, of Barbadoes, came to Boston, "having a foresight given her of a visitation of the black pox, which required her to proclaim it during public worship." So, with three other women and a man, she entered the South Meeting-house in Boston, on Sunday, "in Sackcloth, with Ashes upon her Head, and barefoot, and her Face blacked." [1] She caused great consternation and horror, so affrighting some females as to lead to serious consequences for them. This case may be an illustration of what the Puritans believed to be a spirit of fanaticism roused in the Quakers in their ecstasies and broodings over supposed promptings from God. She told the Court that she had been brought near to death because she had had this divine monition for three years and had neglected it. She received twenty lashes for her act. Within a few days twenty-two Quakers were scourged for attending their meetings. Protests from abroad and at home were so disapproving and indignant that this was the last occasion in which the lash was used here against Quakers. And

[1] Besse, ii. 260.

from this date, notwithstanding the exceptional cases just mentioned, the more objectionable manifestations of the Quakers began to diminish.

That a portion of the Court retained all its bitterness against the Quakers when it could no longer visit its direst penalties upon them, appears from the following reference to them in the summary review of public woes during the Indian War. In November, 1675, the Court declares : —

" Whereas, it may be found amongst us, that men's thresholds are sett up by God's thresholds, and man's posts besides God's posts, espeacially in the open meetings of Quakers, whose damnable hoerisies, abominable idolatrys, are hereby promoted, embraced, and practised, to the scandall of religion, hazard of souls, and provocation of divine jealousie against this people ; for prevention and reformation whereof, it is ordered by this Court that every person found at a Quakers' meeting shall be apprehended and committed to the house of correction, and there to have the discipline of the house applied to them, and to be kept to worke with bread and water for three days and then released," [1] or pay as fine five pounds.

As had been the case with the Baptists, so it was with the Quakers. Firmness and persistency, with support and sympathy in tolerance and kind acts from individuals in every place who still attended the regular meeting-houses, encouraged the dissenters to assemble in private houses or in the woods, and then to provide their own places for assembly and worship.

The Quakers, as is the experience of all other sects, soon began to meet differences of opinion and practice arising among themselves, threatening division. As soon as they could, they held in peace a meeting at Salem. John Perrot had persuaded some Friends there, that there was a " testimony " to be made by keeping on their hats even

[1] Records, v. 60.

in prayer. The solemn broad-brim, which had been substituted for the gayly plumed cavalier head-gear, had an
important place in the symbolism of Quakerism. John
Burnyeat, with two English Friends, coming to Salem, by
a well-managed " meeting " repressed this heresy, and allowed worshippers in homage to the Deity to uncover their
heads, as they would not before any of their fellow-men.
The plainness of the Quaker garb had more significance
as " a testimony " when it was adopted than it has had at
any time since. It was then in most broad rebuking contrast with the cavalier and court array, with " slashed "
apparel, laces, ribbons, buttons, and elaborate costume.
But William Penn allowed himself in such matters more
conformity with the world. He had in him a fund of
humor which he indulged. By ingenious circumlocutions,
he avoided in his correspondence with those not of his sect
the use of "thee" and "thou." He wore buckles and wigs;
he used silk and damask; used a rich coach and a stately
barge; and kept pomp and ceremony, without a water diet,
in his household.

Reference has been made to a doubtful charge against
President Dunster in his retirement at Scituate, — that
though himself a sufferer from intolerance, he encouraged
severity against the Quakers. However it may have been
in his case, the spirit of dislike, contempt, and scorn exhibited toward them, their tenets and principles, by Roger
Williams ran to such excess of bitterness, that a reader
of his controversial assaults who might be moved to protest is more likely to find in them matter of merriment.
Quakers soon abounded all around him in Providence, and
in their period of freshest zeal and spirit of proselytism,
making as he thought very shocking parodies of Scripture
and theology, they gave him material for the most lively
exercise of his most contentious qualities. He would not
have harmed a single hair of the head of any one of them,
but his tongue and pen were free in the whole range of

raillery, satire, and rasping invective. Not satisfied with conference and quarrel with such of the heretics as fell in his way at his home, in field, or by fireside, " his spirit was stirred within him " on hearing that George Fox himself, the prime heresiarch of the sect, had arrived on a missionary journey at Newport, in 1672. He drew up as a challenge " fourteen Propositions," half of which he offered to defend respectively there and at Providence in open discussion with Fox. With a keen zest for the coming encounter, this vigorous contestant of all opinions but his own — though these were not always the same — prepared himself for the only sort of fray which he ever enjoyed, but which was the delight of his spirit. Though he had passed his threescore years and ten, he tells us that, setting out alone to row himself for thirty miles in an open boat down Narragansett Bay, " God graciously assisted me in rowing all night with my old bones, so that I got to Newport toward midnight, before the morning appeared." Fox had not received his challenge, and had gone away. Williams never could be convinced that Fox had not run off, in dread of his formidable antagonist. However, the proposed disputation went on with other Quakers, in both places. We have the results, and the castigation which Williams in return received, in the two volumes already referred to.

With these encounters of peaceful pugnacity between two parties who had caused such distraction in Massachusetts, we close the review of the Martyr Age of the Colony.

XIII.

THE DOWNFALL OF THE COLONY CHARTER.

THERE were several effective causes which worked together in bringing about the annulment of the Charter of
the Colony of Massachusetts Bay, and, as a consequence,
the prostration of the theocratic basis of government.
The vital and essential principles of this theocracy' had,
however, received a disabling and almost fatal blow, in
the extension of the franchise, while the Charter still
held to its threatened life. The proceedings under *quo
warranto*, against the Charter, had been begun in July,
1683, in the Court of King's Bench, but were transferred
by the Crown lawyers to Chancery. Thence the fatal
decree went forth October 23, 1684. This gives us a
period of fifty-four years, combining a part of the years
of active life of men of two generations. The Charter
government and the theocracy were so far identified, that
the latter could not sustain itself without the authority
of the former. But the theocracy was made to yield;
was humiliated and disabled twenty years before the
Charter was annulled.

We are now to review the causes, agencies, and methods
which brought about those two results. We have to remind ourselves that the events were always imminent, and
to be looked for as such by those having most reason to
dread them. It is rather a matter of surprise that the
results were so long delayed, held in arrest; for the movements which at last effected them had existed and had been

working actively from the first. From the ineffectual process of *quo warranto* against the Charter in 1635 till the
actual enforcement of it fifty years later, busy enemies of
the theocracy first, and then of the Charter itself, had never
rested in their efforts. If anything were necessary to
assure us of the seeming sincerity with which the authorities interpreted the Charter as securing to them the rights
which they claimed and exercised under it, especially their
theocratic administration, we should find it in marking the
almost defiant resolution, the tenacity and persistency, even
the lingering death-grasp, with which they stiffened themselves against royal demands, and the well-nigh baffled
requisitions of royal commissioners for subverting it.

Before distinguishing and defining the hostile influences
which aided in bringing about the catastrophe, we may start
with a frank recognition of the one general, comprehensive,
and of itself all-sufficient reason for it, and in which all the
other helping agencies found their occasion and impulse.
That was the actual impracticability, as well as the civil injustice and the religious intolerance involved in the scheme
itself.

I said on an early page of this work, that among the ideal
and more or less visionary schemes for the planting and administering of social and civil government in a community,
it was natural, and to a degree reasonable, that that of a
theocracy, with the Bible for its statute-book, should have
its turn for trial. The most opportune time for it would
come when there was found an associated company of men
profoundly moved by a deep, earnest, and implicit belief, a
reverent and constraining conviction, that the Bible was not
only adapted to the use to be made of it, but positively imposed a demand that it should be so used. I have all along
sought, not excuses nor palliations for, but simply explanations of, the zeal and resolution, and the high-handed course
of those who had pledged themselves to try the experiment.
The two requisite conditions would be the full sincerity and

loftiness of purpose which consecrated it to them, and their ability, by authority, legislation, and administration, to enforce theocratic principles of government upon the rest of their community. With such charitable indulgence as our common humanity compels us to yield, we may allow that the former of these requisite conditions, notwithstanding some interminglings of ill passions, was substantially satisfied till the Charter was annulled.

It was the second of those conditions which failed. The disfranchised and unchurched members of the community, subjected to disabilities and burdens under each of those deprivations, were constantly increasing their proportion in the population, and proclaiming their grievances. The theocracy would have fallen even if the Charter had retained its life. The colonial government had abundant occasions for severe self-questioning as to its proceedings, for reconsidering the fundamentals of the scheme, for stopping in its course, and, taking thought from the severity of its rule, for asking, Are we acting wisely; are we not on the wrong lead, defying right, truth, justice, and mercy? Williams published his "Bloody Tenent of Persecution" in 1644, twelve years before the inroad of the Quakers. The vigor and cogency of his arguments, with their quaint directness of rhetoric in presenting truths of reason as sharply-pointed weapons of logical temper, were sure to be read, and as sure of impressing liberal views on receptive minds. But they wholly failed of effect on one of such a mind as Cotton, whose answer was nerveless and weak, because fallacious. He thought he could wash that "Bloody Tenent;" and he succeeded in making it "more bloody," in his attempt to make it pure and white in "the Blood of the Lamb." And these occasions for reconsidering the foundations of their scheme as impracticable and involving injustice, did not fail of being pressed upon the magistrates, alike by friends, like the noble-spirited Saltonstall, and by a whole series of complainants and sufferers at the English Court. This impracticability and tyrannous injustice of their scheme, to which they themselves should have opened their eyes, was the most effective agency, working in each of the special influences now to be mentioned, that brought about the deprivation of the Charter. For fifty years they had held to that patent — and to their own construction of their rights under it — against all challenges, hostilities, and tentative processes of the home government. Their most artful and effective method for parrying strokes against them had been found in temporizing, with delays and evasions, pausing on contingencies, or, as they expressed it, "referring their cause to God," and waiting to see what way he would open out of a strait place. The lengthened interval of convulsions and distractions in the civil and religious strife in England, had directly served them by giving temporary power at home to those in sympathy with their principles, in allowing them intervals of relief from interference, and a time for turning fibre into gristle. The success which had so far been mastered by them had nerved them with fresh resolve, taught them skill in fencing off opposition, and persuaded them that like constancy would continue their triumph. There are good grounds for believing that there were happy opportunities in which, if they had sagaciously consented to drop from their scheme the elements of it which were manifestly impracticable, oppressive, and unjust, they might substantially have retained self-government. As we are soon to take notice, the interposition of royal authority in their affairs was strictly confined at first to a demand for the disuse of their theocratic principles, and, indeed, so far from threatening their Charter left it in full force, even with a suggestion of enlargement of privileges. But this was without avail. Their theocracy stood with them as the life-blood of their Charter. If their cause had been less unjust and unrighteous, one might admire the resolve and constancy with which the authorities, having in their charge, as they asserted, sacred rights, stood unquailing and unyielding to the last. They never budged, nor flew to covert : they took back nothing, abated nothing, never apologized, and never repented. Those of the old original fibre who survived the loss of their Charter were never reconciled, but lived and died as mourners. And, as we shall see, their last desperation to retain it was the song of the swan in death.

Sufficient place has already been given on previous pages to the assurance with which the General Court administered the government, under either the conviction or the assumption that the Charter secured to them the rights which they claimed. But the authorities had never, so far as we are informed by the Records, given any deliberate consideration, by discussion, and the weighing of diverse opinions, to the terms of their relation to the home government, in deference, dependence, or subjection to its intervention in matters of policy and local administration. Nor do the Records furnish us with the detailed information we might desire on an interesting and pregnant episode in the public councils, for our fuller knowledge of which we have to look to Winthrop, who devotes several pages to it.[1] The time and circumstances both here and in England made the discussion to be mentioned of critical significance. In the prostration and abeyance of the kingly rule, preceding the execution of the royal culprit, Parliament was trying its hand at colonial as well as home administration. It is observable that in the correspondence and intercourse that followed between Parliamentary commissioners and the authorities of Massachusetts there are exhibited sympathetic complacencies, and complimentary exchanges of regard, as between those who are alike rather dubious of their grounds and position. Equally observable it is that our authorities were inclined by some emboldenment of spirit to treat the Parliament with somewhat more of a nonchalant familiarity than they did the King. Several complications and annoyances combined

[1] Vol. ii. pp. 278-284.

to vex our authorities on this special occasion. Complaints and grievances had been brought before Parliament against Massachusetts by Gorton and others of Rhode Island, as well as by Dr. Child and his fellow-petitioners, as already mentioned, in the matter which had roused the ire of our Court. At its session in November, 1646, an order was read which had been received from the Commissioners for Foreign Plantations, under date of Westminster, May 15, 1646, relating to the petitioners about the Narragansett. The Commissioners courteously affirm that their action does not assume the truth of the charges brought against Massachusetts, "we knowing well how much God hath honored your government, and believing that your spirits and affairs are acted by principles of justice, prudence, and zeal to God," etc. Several critical questions were opened in this order for the astute members of the Court, keenly watchful about every token of a trespass on their liberties and self-sufficiency, without allowing appeals from their decisions. So "such of the elders as could be had were sent for, to have their advice in the matter."

The full subject "propounded to consideration was in what relation we stood to the state of England; whether our government was founded upon our charter, or not; if so, then what subjection we owed to that state." The magistrates first gave their minds, that the elders might be helped in giving their advice. It being agreed that the Charter was the foundation of the government, some thought that we were so subordinate to the Parliament that it might countermand our orders and judgments, and therefore that we should petition for an enlargement of power. Others thought that though, as we had before professed, we owed allegiance and subjection, yet the charter gave us "absolute power of government; for thereby we have power to make laws, to erect all sorts of magistracy, to correct, punish, pardon, govern, and rule the people absolutely," etc., — all implying a self-sufficiency not needing the help of any supe-

32

rior power to complete the government. As to petitioning for " enlargement," grave objections were offered, especially that it would peril the present Charter. With the case thus presented, the elders, after deliberation, rendered their advice. A scruple had arisen as to acknowledging the title of the Commissioners. But this was shrewdly disposed of by the reminder that in any answer given to them, " if their stile were not observed, it was doubted they would not receive it." The elders admitted dependence upon and due allegiance and fidelity to England, as having derived our Charter from her, and being dependent upon her " for protection and the immunities of Englishmen; " that our powers of government are so full that there should be no appeal from, or interruption of, our proceedings; that our agents and defenders abroad must do the best they can in justifying our proceedings against complainants, " but if the Parliament should be less inclinable to us, we must wait upon providence for the preservation of our just liberties." We may give to the Commissioners " such titles as the Parliament hath given them, without subjecting to them in point of our government." Finally, the elders, as professionally bound, advise to the churches " a solemn seeking of the Lord for the upholding of our state and disappointment of our adversaries." The Court acted substantially upon this advice. It was proposed that Winthrop should go to England as agent. He would have consented, though reluctantly, but was happily relieved by a substitute, through whom a most elaborate reply and justification was sent to the Commissioners, with specific answers to the complaints of Child and the other petitioners, who, meanwhile, were sternly dealt with here by heavy fines.

This mention of what was in fact an embassy from the Court to England prompts some further remark upon the matter here.

Besides the temporizing shifts and devices of the Court, its politic delays and mystifying evasions, it had naturally had recourse to the sending of agents to defend it before King and Council, to subvert inimical plots and enemies, and to win friends to its interests. From the earliest years of the Colony down to the opening of the War of the Revolution, Massachusetts was represented by a succession of such agents. It is safe to say that, though it was on a smaller scale, no intricacies, ingenuities, and arts of diplomacy between sovereign nations ever drew more heavily upon the wits and resources of ambassadors, than in the cases of these Massachusetts emissaries. There is this distinction, however. The persons and the personal rights of real ambassadors are sacredly secure. But the Massachusetts agents, not being assured of official recognition, might risk their own liberty, be held as hostages, or even as victims. There never was any strong craving here for these quasi-ambassadorial functions, — at least among such as the Court would regard as most competent and fitting for them, though enough would have been ready to assume them. If space permitted, a lengthened, and indeed a lively review might be spread forth here, from the Records, of the diplomatic history of the Court of the Bay Colony. Measuring exactly by the emergency and the stringency of each occasion, there was an increased difficulty to find the qualified person, and to win his consent to the call. And it may be added, the more faithful the agent, and the more sagacious and prudent he was in adapting himself to the hard exigencies of his mission, accepting the best terms he could secure, the more ungrateful and resentful were his reception and his treatment on his return. No allowance was made for the difference in the atmosphere and surroundings of the Puritan and the English Courts. The Court would have long debates, with the advice of elders, on each occasion for sending an agent, and longer ones on his instructions. The most emphatic of these were, never to commit the Court beyond the letter of them, to hedge and parry within them, and when hard pressed, to assert the limitations upon him and to reserve the privilege of communicating with his principals. Norton and Bradstreet had run a serious risk of being challenged and proceeded against in England by relatives of the executed Quakers. In the last attempts to avert the blow against the Charter, it was only with extreme effort, and after protracted delay, and then with embarrassment in providing supplies, that competent agents were secured. What there was for them to do we can better appreciate by returning now to note the reasons and agencies which imperilled the Charter. Were it of sufficient importance, one might expand at length, beyond the brief mention of them, which is all that is necessary, three special causes, all included in what we have already recognized in the impracticability of the theocratic experiment, which effected its discomfiture. These were—dissension, discontent, alienation, and sharp variances arising among those who formed the government in State and Church, from its own ill-working; active assaults upon it from outsiders and sufferers; and political changes in the mother country.

1. In following out the administration under the charter with that construction of it which the authorities maintained as of right, we have had constant occasion to note the ferment which was working within. An increasing severity of rule by the covenanted church members, over an ever-enlarging proportion of the disfranchised, unchurched, unbaptized, and those denied the religious ministrations which they preferred, while they were compelled to support such as they disapproved, was the occasion of internal discord. It was not only as it was intended to be, the rule of saints over sinners, but it was the oppression by the few, with self-assumed privileges, over the liberties and rights of all. In every case of dissension, followed by infliction of discipline, the authorities intensified the ill-feelings against themselves and called out sympathy for their victims. In their proceedings against Roger Williams and the Antinomians they had promoted a troublesome colony on their borders, al-

ways afterward a source of annoyance to them. They had turned some of those in full fellowship with them into converts for the Baptists and Quakers. When some of the most excellent and honored of those in church covenant with them espoused the cause of the Quakers, the Court could not long venture to treat them as it had dealt with the strolling " vagabonds " coming from abroad. The magistrates found their severe measures constantly thwarted. Differences arose between them and the deputies, and the arbitration of the elders was not always effective.

2. These dissensions among themselves were actively promoted by the agents in the second of the causes which accomplished the vacating of the Charter. Beginning with the Browns, Gardiner, and Morton, and closing with the Quakers, all who had grievances against the Court brought them before the authorities in England, and together they formed a formidable body of bitter and persistent enemies. The mother country had all the means of knowing with full warning what was being done on this side by the intractable and truculent founders of what they called a " state," or a " commonwealth," which issued processes in its own name and not in that of the King; which had had the effrontery to trespass on the royal prerogative by coining money in its own mint; by disregarding the navigation laws of the realm, and by denying all appeals from its very peculiar laws to England. Besides the numerous body of complainants for the wrongs they had suffered from the government of the colony, there were others, like Gorges and Mason, who, as patentees of territory, maintained a vigorous hostility not only against the grasping measures of Massachusetts in extending its own bounds, but also against the validity of its Charter.

3. To these two direct agencies in fomenting mischief for Massachusetts must be added a third one, in the really awakened attention of English statesmen given to the Colony, when the restoration of Charles II. seemed to present

occasion and opportunity for settling some of the confusion which had been working in distracted times. The King's letter of June 28, 1662, received by the returning agents Bradstreet and Norton, and acknowledged by the Court, Oct. 8, 1662, was not put upon record till the session of May, 1665.[1] I have quoted from that letter only the passage in which the King authorized the Court to pass "a sharpe law against the Quakers, as he had himself done." The letter contained other grave matters, now to be noticed. On the whole, it is in its tenor most kind and conciliatory, accepting the professions of loyalty of the anxious but not frightened magistrates for more than they were worth. The King writes of his " good subjects," —

" wee receive them into our gracious protection, and will cherish them with our best encouragement, and wee will preserve and doe hereby confirme the patent and charter heretofore granted unto them by our royall father, of blessed memory, — and that wee will be ready to renew the same charter to them, under our great seale of England, whensoever they shall desire it."

Referring to " the licence of these late ill times in England," as to an extent relieving the mismanagement in the Colony, the King grants his full pardon for all crimes and offences committed there against himself, excepting only those attainted of high treason who may have transplanted themselves, who must be delivered into the hands of justice. His allusion is to the regicides Whalley and Goffe, who were known to be in New England, but who were secreted, befriended, and never betrayed. His Majesty requires that all laws or ordinances contrary or derogatory to his authority and government be annulled, that the administration of justice be according to the Charter and in his name, and that the oath of allegiance to him be taken. Then comes the graver matter. The King — through the pen of his adviser — taking " liberty of conscience " to be

[1] Records, vol. iv. pt. ii. p. 164.

something quite different from what it was to those whom he was addressing, adds : —

"And since the principall end and foundation of that charter was and is the freedome and liberty of conscience, wee do hereby charge and require that that freedome and liberty be duely admitted and allowed, so that such as desire to use the Booke of Common Prayer, and performe their devotions in that manner as is established here, be not debarred the excercise thereof, or undergoe any prejudice or disadvantage thereby, they using their liberty without disturbance to others, and that all persons of good and honest lives and conversations be admitted to the Sacrament of the Lord's Supper, according to the Booke of Common Prayer, and their children to baptisme. [Then follows the allowance of "a strict law" against the Quakers, and permission to reduce the Charter number of the Assistants to not more than eighteen nor less than ten.] Wee assuring ourself, and obleiging and commanding all persons concerned, that, in the election of the Governor or Assistants there be only consideration had of the wisdome, virtue, and integrity of the persons to be chosen, and not of any affection with refference to their opinions and outward professions; and that all the freeholders of competent estates, not vitious in conversation, and orthodoxe in religion (though of different persuasions concerning church government) may have their votes in the election of all officers, both civill and military." [1]

Though, as before said, this letter of the King was not entered on the Records till two and a half years after its reception by the Court in October, 1662, the Court then ordered the "publication" of it, — whatever that might have meant, — and at once provided, in compliance with one of its demands, that all processes should henceforward issue in his Majesty's name. But the graver matters were dealt with as follows : —

"And forasmuch as the said letter hath influence upon the churches as well as the civil state, itt is further ordered, that all manner of actings in relation thereunto be suspended untill the

[1] Records, vol. iv. pt. ii. p. 165.

next General Court; so that all persons concerned may have time and oppertunity to consider of what is necessary to be doune in order to his majesty's pleasure therein." [1]

The Court appointed the first Wednesday of the November coming, for Thanksgiving for mercies at home and abroad, and also the first Wednesday of December for a day of Humiliation on account of the " prevailing power of Antichrist abroad, together with some public rebukes of God among ourselves."

At the next meeting of the Court in May, 1663, after " long and serious debate in refference to his majesty's letter," a committee of thirteen, magistrates, deputies, and elders, was charged to examine the several parts of it and to report at the next Court. Evidently there was no intention to hurry matters, for temporizing had often done good service. The crucial point concerned " extending the liberty of certeine of the inhabitants in point of elections ; " so elders, freemen, " and other inhabitants " were invited to give the Court, or the committee, " their owne understandings in writing." We may well conceive that the public in Church and State, and outside of both, had lively times and themes in discussion.

In the Records of the Court in May, 1664, we find this very significant entry, suggestive of the same human device in another range of interests, of the sagacity of a child who hides a toy which he fears may be taken from him : —

" Forasmuch as it is of great ccncernment to this commonwealth to keepe safe and secret our pattent, it is ordered the patent, and duplicate belonging to the country, be forthwith brought into the Court, and that there be two or three persons appointed by each house to keepe safe and secret the said patent and duplicate, in two distinct places, as to the said committees shall seem most expedient."

[1] Records, vol. iv. pt. ii. p. 58.

Four persons, magistrates and deputies, were appointed, who received "the grand patent from the secretary, to dispose thereof as maybe most safe for the country."[1]

This stratagem shows how dear and precious the hidden parchment was to the Court; but the trick was of no avail against a process in Chancery. Recourse was had to this concealment because of a rumor of the coming of some royal commissioners charged to examine complaints, who, it was feared, might demand the surrender of the Charter. The committee on the King's letter had not reported when these Commissioners arrived in July, 1664, bringing another royal epistle, to institute their searching inquisition into affairs, and to carry on a contest with the Court, in which the latter, with tough, adroit, and persistent courage and skill, parried the attacks of the former with a degree of success. The documents containing the controversy and wrangling fill nearly six-score pages on the Records.[2]

The Court, Aug. 3, 1664, modified the law restricting the franchise to church members, by enacting, —

"That from henceforth all Englishmen presenting a cirtifficat, under the hands of the ministers or minister of the place where they dwell, that they are orthodox in religion, and not vitious in theire lives, and also a certifficat, under the hands of the selectmen, that they are freeholders [ratable for ten shillings], or that they are in full communion with some church amongst us, it shall be in the liberty of every such person, being twenty-four years of age, householders and settled inhabitants of this jurisdiction, to present themselves for admittance to the freedom of this commonwealth, and put to vote in the Generall Court for acceptance to the freedome of the body polliticke by the sufferage of the major parte, according to the rules of our pattent."[3]

The reader may at his choice mark either the stubbornness or the ingenuity of this seeming concession to the

---

[1] Records, vol. iv. pt. ii. p. 102. The parchment is now in the Secretary's office in the State House.

[2] Ibid., pp. 157–273.　　　　　[3] Ibid., p. 118.

requisition of the King while still conserving in its terms
the exclusiveness of the franchise. In his letter he had
asked the extension of the franchise only to persons " orthodox in religion," though his standard of " orthodoxy "
was quite different from that of the Court. The Court
had evidently persuaded itself that the relations of Conformists and Dissenters in England were directly inverted
here. The King required for those who dissented from
the established order here, rights and privileges which in
England were forbidden to Dissenters there, who were
burdened by many disabilities and exactions. An example of securing the franchise by the new enactment is
as follows : —

At the Court, Oct. 11, 1665. "On cirtifficat from the selectmen of Springfield, and Mr. Pelatiah Glover, minister there, that
Thomas Merrick, a setled inhabitant there, is, according to law,
rateable, orthodox in religion, of pious and laudable conversation,
the Court allowes and approoves of him to be a freeman of this
jurisdiction." [1]

It may have been, though not avowed, in the astute
minds of some of the magistrates here, in drawing the line
of privilege between church members of their own standing order and outsiders, or " dissenters," to give a significant hint to their foreign dictators about the beam in their
own eyes, in the disabilities imposed upon Nonconformists.
It is, however, an interesting coincidence that Episcopalians did not secure their rights in Massachusetts till the
grievous penalties for Dissenters had been removed in England. The strength of the Puritan principles consisted in
the singleness, definiteness, and, as they believed, the absolute rightfulness and practical value of the one rule by
which the standard for the reforming process should be
chosen and applied. They could not accept any purely
arbitrary methods or limits, any devices, adaptations, selec-

[1] Records, vol. iv. pt. ii. p. 285.

tions, or preferences, by which the reconstruction and purification of the ecclesiastical and civil system under which
they were to live was to be effected. That was a bold and
logical, though a wholly disloyal position on which the
Massachusetts authorities planted themselves at this time.
The King and his agents thought they were uttering a
simple axiom in affirming that the religion and mode of
worship established in the realm should have at least a
respectful recognition in a colony of that realm. But two
reasons of sufficient weight with our magistrates invali-
dated that claim. The first was that, standing by their
original Nonconformist principles, they regarded the institution and the ritual of the English Church as unscriptural,
and of human invention. The second reason for their
alleged contumacy was that their Charter committed to
them certain powers and prerogatives among which was
the right, under their remote exigencies and circumstances,
to do for themselves, through their Court, very much what
the English Parliament did for the people of the realm, in
all that concerned the administration of religion and a
form of worship. Looking back to the long and sharp
conflict which their Puritan predecessors had carried on,
in endeavoring that the work of reformation should be
thorough and Scriptural, they had found their side worsted
simply by the engagement of the civil preference and
authority in favor of conformity. The prelates, divines,
and communicants of the English Church at that time,
as has been the case ever since, having no advantage
or superiority in scholarship, piety, capacity, fidelity, or
efficiency in the ministry, over the Nonconformists, had
simply just that favoritism which privilege and patronage
conferred by Parliament secured to them, — all as of a
worldly premium. Through nearly three centuries the
Dissenters in England, nearly dividing its population, sup-
porting at their own charges their educational institutions,
their chapels and charities, while sharing the cost of the

Establishment besides, have naturally protested against this State favoritism of conformity. This ancient and grievous oppression and injustice seems now to be in a way of redress. Something like it was attempted in the shape of an English Church establishment in Virginia and New York. The Puritans of Massachusetts, having the wit to devise it and the resolution to enforce it, chose to have an establishment of their own, in which their chartered Court stood for the English Parliament at home.

The five New England Colonies, including Massachusetts, had addressed Charles II., asking security in their privileges, and in four of these letters complaints had been made of the Bay Colony. The letter of the King brought here by the commissioners was the third of his epistles to our magistrates. His attention had been at once drawn, on his restoration, to the spirit of restlessness, insubordination, and, indeed, of independence, manifested here; and his Chancellor, Clarendon, with his Council, — as the method and tenor of his third letter and of his instructions to his commissioners abundantly prove, — had given earnest and keen inquisition into the actual state of affairs in the Colonies, and especially in Massachusetts. The royal documents show a wonderful fulness and accuracy of information about the aims and disposition of leading men, the matters of party variance, the occasions of grievances, the weak points in administration, and the methods of self-defence which would be availed of.

Considering the real attitude and behavior of the Massachusetts, and the full knowledge of particulars possessed by Clarendon and the Council, one who now reads their communications in the name of the King, notes with a degree of surprise and admiration their dignity, mildness, and quiet courtesy of tone, their gentleness, and even forbearance of censure, and their absolute freedom from all threatenings, though a reserve of what may follow if this method fails is mildly intimated. The method of communication was avowedly chosen, as a way of "insinuation" of the King's feelings and intentions, rather than one of provocation. And, on the other hand, the reader notes with equal appreciation and admiration the caution, the acumen, the perfect self-possession, the adroitness, and the stiffness of resolve shown in the documents which went forth from the Court. Sagacious minds and sturdy spirits, employing an able pen, were put to its service. The disputations between the commissioners and the Court were tediously protracted, and shifted rapidly from one subject to another, as the former began with surface-work and shrewdly advanced step by step to the serious issues. The Court well understood the strategy, and was never once beguiled or put off its guard. As the result proved, they could not prevent the commissioners from finding sufficient and grievous matter for their messages of discomfiture to the King; but in not a single point of graver import did the commissioners succeed in circumventing or constraining the action of the Court. The Charter was yet to have a score more of years of vitality for itself, and for the adolescence of the commonwealth.

We may trace with brevity the course of this lively contest. The King in each of his letters, especially in that brought by the commissioners, had in the kindest terms and with the most positive assurances referred to the Colony Charter given by his father, "of blessed memory," as not only to be sacredly ratified and continued by him, but had even offered to enlarge the privileges which it conferred. His declarations, and the emphasis of them, furnished a whole armory of defence and of offence to the Court, giving it all it wanted, even the means of challenging, of protesting, and of resisting any measures of interference which came from the same royal source through his commissioners. So long as the Company could maintain their Charter, which they well understood how to use to cover all that they claimed under it, they were safe.

As soon as the Court had knowledge of the expected arrival of the commissioners, it made provision for their courteous reception, appointing two honored gentlemen to render them " such civilities as the people and place were capable of." The commission consisted of four members, — Col. Richard Nicolls, a sort of chief or chairman, Sir Robert Carr, and George Cartwright and Samuel Maverick, Esqs. The last named, on the arrival of Winthrop's Company, had been found seated on Winnisimmett. He was an Episcopalian, but was made a freeman in October, 1632, and had been a constant trouble and vexation to the Court, the records of which describe him on his coming as a royal commissioner, as " our known and professed enemy." The two frigates which brought these gentlemen were the first vessels of the royal navy to appear in the waters of our Bay. Nicolls and Cartwright arrived at the opening of the Puritan Sabbath, Saturday evening, July 23, 1664. It may be mentioned here that Endicott, then Governor, died on the 15th of the following March. His repute with the English Council had made him so obnoxious that the commissioners were instructed to seek his displacement from office. At their request Endicott ordered a meeting of the Council of Magistrates on July 26, before which the King's letter of April 23 and the commission of his emissaries were read. All through the course of the hearings and controversies which followed, as at the beginning of them, the commissioners asked that the whole General Court might be convened for business with them. This the Council always refused, stating that the Charter fixed the dates on which that body should be convened, while at the same time insisting that its legal presence and authority were necessary to entertain such business as the commissioners had to bring before it. Besides their commission, these gentlemen had two sets of " instructions," concerning one set of which they were to exercise their discretion as to communicating

them.   The Council wished to know the whole of them,
but could draw them out only by piecemeal.   Various matters were covered by these instructions, as relating to the
other Colonies, questions disputed about boundaries, war
with the Dutch of Manhattan, etc., compelling the commissioners to absent themselves at intervals, making return visits to Boston.   I shall remark almost exclusively
upon their business with the internal affairs of this Colony.
The royal letter was kindly and conciliatory in its opening.
It even complimented Massachusetts as having given "a
good example of industry and sobriety" to the other Colonies, and as having prospered above them.   The King
now intends no harm or injury to the Colony, but fully
confirms to them the Charter from his father, and is ready
to grant further favor.   He wishes to discountenance all
the jealousies and calumnies of which he has heard.   The
commissioners are to confer on the King's letter of June
28, 1662, sent by Bradstreet and Norton, and the Court's
reply to it, of November 25, "which did not answer our
expectations, nor the professions made by your messingers;" and he requires that his commissioners be treated
with respect.   The Council, taking the royal letter into
consideration, marked the compliance they had already
made in extending the franchise, but found in its other
contents peril to their Charter rights.

The Court, on assembling, agrees to reply in an Address
to the King.   This document shows in its composition and
tenor that it had engaged the advice, ingenuity, and acuteness alike of magistratical and clerical co-laborers.   Its
tone opens plaintively and pleadingly, as from a body of
suppliants poor, and remote from the fount of mercy.   The
"first undertakers" of the plantation, relying upon the
royal covenant in their Charter, had borne the cost and
charges of their hazardous enterprise.   For more than
thirty years they had struggled with but moderate thrift.
Quoting the King's previous promises about their Charter

rights, they murmur that he should now send "four strangers," who, keeping back some of their instructions, are
ominously intermeddling with the affairs of the Colony.
The commissioners manifest such a spirit as to lead the
Court to dread a subversion of all their solemnly covenanted rights, with such results of confusion and disorder
as may compel the colonists to seek out a refuge in a new
dwelling-place, or to faint under discouragements. As to
the complaints that have been made against them to the
King, the Address boldly asserts: "The body of this people
are unanimously satisfied with the present government,
and abhorrent from change; but few among us are male-
content, and fewer that have cause to be so." The Court
perhaps assumed for their monarch a familiarity like their
own with Scripture, when reminding him, "It was Job's
excellency when he sate as king among his people, that he
was a father to the poore." [1]

Three of the commissioners having been absent on a
visit to the Dutch, returning to Boston, Feb. 15, 166$\frac{4}{5}$,
and meeting with some of the magistrates, asked that a
map of the bounds of the Colony be provided for them. In
this request they were gratified. They announced their
wish that on their return from a short visit to Plymouth, a
mass-meeting of all the inhabitants might be summoned to
Boston on the day of the election. This request of the
commissioners was evidently founded on the belief that
among the inhabitants at large, including non-freemen and
non-church-members, there would be a considerable if not
quite a large body of sympathizers to encourage and support their own demands, and so to further embarrass the
magistracy. The latter, of course, were not inclined to
risk this inlet for dissension. The magistrates refused the
request, saying that anybody who pleased might come, but
that all the people could not be summoned to leave their
home duties, wives, children, and the aged, to the mercy of

[1] Records, vol. iv. pt. ii. pp. 172, 173.

the Indians and the neglect of the labors of the season. The commissioners, not liking this rebuff, took upon them to address circulars of call to leading persons, some of them not freemen. They also nullified some of the doings of the Court with other Colonies, and revoked some of its grants of land. They gave offence by discourtesy as to hospitalities provided for them. The refusal to summon the Court on other than its Charter seasons, so stiffly maintained, called out further remonstrances. The commissioners deigned to deny certain calumnious rumors in circulation about their errand and purposes, as, for instance, that they were to demand a revenue of five thousand pounds for the King, and intended to impose a land-tax.

All this, however, was preliminary skirmishing. The commissioners next brought out their instructions upon three points in the King's previous letter which the Court had neglected to notice; namely, his demand about the Book of Common Prayer, the bold sheltering of the Regicides, and the breach of the Navigation Laws. To the King and his commissioners nothing could seem more reasonable than the request that such of his subjects resident here as might choose to do so, should in their service of worship use the Prayer Book of the Church established in the realm. But that book had come to be to the exiled Puritans the symbol of many other things connected with it, against which their prejudices, convictions, and practices had been strengthened by indulgence. To have allowed schism among them, the setting up of rival worshipping assemblies, and the consequent partition of the support raised for the ministry, presented practical difficulties. The use of that book, it might be feared, would bring in its train Church days and ceremonies, especial privileges to Episcopalians in the government, demands for endowment, and possibly even the importation of bishops, with such blended temporal and spiritual powers as they exercised

33

in England. The Court could not contemplate such consequences without the gravest apprehensions. So to the demand of the King and his commissioners that the Book of Common Prayer be in free use here, the Court replied, not curtly with the monosyllable No! but with the same negative written out at length, thus: —

"Our humble addresses to his Majesty have fully declared our maine end in our being voluntary exiles from our deare native country, which wee had not chosen at so deare a rate, could wee have seen the word of God, warranting us to performe our devotions in that way and to have the same set up here; wee conceive it is apparent that it will disturb our peace in our present enjoyments."

Which means, that as the Bible did not warrant their performing their own devotions by book, so it would not warrant their allowing other persons to do so. The same Bible also contained warnings against the betrayal and delivery of such hunted wanderers as the Puritans believed the regicides Whalley and Goffe to be.[2] So the Court, knowing very well where those condemned traitors were, was content with affirming that it had issued a warrant for their apprehension if in its jurisdiction. They suffered no harm here, but were sheltered till they died in peace. As to the Navigation Laws, the colonists had some convenient methods of their own which they were not disposed greatly to modify.

The commissioners next demanded to have before them a copy of "the Booke of the Generall Lawes and Liberties" of the Colony, to see if there was in them anything derogatory to the King and his authority; also a full account of the constitution of the government, civil and ecclesiastical, of the taxes and revenue, the military, forts, shipping, etc. Of these last matters the Court gave such information as it thought best to communicate. The commissioners

---

[1] Records, vol. iv. pt. ii. p. 200.   [2] Isaiah xvi. 3, 4.

went through the " Book of Lawes " very much as a peda-
gogue examines the composition of a schoolboy.   They
suggested twenty-six amendments, the principal being as
follows : They required that the King should be declared
in the title of the book to be, by the Charter, the source of
all authority, and that all writs and acts should issue in
his name.   The King's arms should be exhibited in every
court-room, and the English colors on every vessel and in
every military foot company.   The word " Commonwealth"
should be stricken out wherever it appeared, and " His
Majesty's Colony " be substituted.   It may have been a
sense of propriety, or a piece of cool and impudent effrontery, that prompted the commissioners to say —

"There ought to be inserted and ordeined to be kept the 5th of
November and the nine and twentieth of May, as dayes of thanksgiving : the first for the miraculous preservation of our king and
country from the gunpowder treason, the second for his Majesty's
birth, and miraculous and happy restauration to his crownes upon
the same day ; as also the thirtieth of January, a day of fasting
and praying, that God would please to avert his judgements from
our nation for that most barbarous and execrable murder of our
late soveraigne, Charles the First." [1]

The commissioners understood too well the temper of
those whom they were addressing, to suppose for a moment
that they would give any heed to these suggestions, or
construct a calendar for such observances.   It is possible
that some wag in the Court might have proposed, by an
aside, that two of the occasions be taken up, with an in-
version of their observance, — the execution of Charles I.
being made an occasion for Thanksgiving, and the restoration of his son an occasion for Fasting.   Probably every
member of the Court regarded the decapitated monarch as
" a perjured traitor to the rights and liberties of the people
of England, and a convicted dissembler and liar."   The

[1] Records, vol. iv. pt. ii. p. 212.

commissioners required the repeal of the penalty for keeping Christmas.

It is unnecessary, for our purpose, to follow up in particulars the sharp and embittered contention of the two parties in this undecided issue. The commissioners constituted themselves together, and even individually, a court of appeal, not only between the Colonies, but between the Court and private offenders justly under its discipline and condemnation. The Court stoutly resisted all such claims and pretences, falling back on the Charter and the King's assurances under it, which precluded his empowering his commissioners with such functions as they claimed. Baffled at nearly every point, the commissioners say —

"We have thought it necessary to reduce all the discourse hereof into one question, whereunto wee expect your possitive answer, which wee shall faithfully report to his Majesty: Whither doe you acknowledge his Majesty's commission, wherein wee are nominated commissioners, to be of full force to all the intents and purposes therein conteyned?"

To this categorical question the Court replies: —

"Why you should put us on to the resolve of such a question, wee see not the grounds thereof. Wee have only pleaded his Majesty's royall charter to us, — it being his speciall charge to yourselves not to disturbe us therein." [1]

The commissioners complain that in reimposing the oath of allegiance the Court had fettered it with provisos; also, that in the pretended extension of the franchise to non-church-members, — demanding a rate of ten shillings, — while "not one church member in an hundred pays so much; scarce three members in a town of an hundred inhabitants." The commissioners reported it as the desire of the King that the Court should send over to him four or five of its leading men, one of them to be the Governor, for

[1] Records, vol. iv. pt. ii. pp. 204-206.

information and direct conference.   Under the circumstances this would not have been an attractive agency, even if of personal safety, to the messengers.   The Court affirmed that its direct communications by correspondence would meet all that such agents could effect.

Both the parties to the contention sent home their respective reports, with charges, criminations, and recriminations, so that both sides of the shield were fully shown. The Court addressed the King in a very able and ingenious paper.   They did a further act, the ingenuity as well as the generosity of which was well appreciated.   Knowing the exigencies of the royal navy at the time, they sent to the King a present of timber, principally masts, at an expense to the colonial treasury of two thousand pounds.   Pepys, then in the Admiralty, knowing and appreciating the value of the gift, wrote in his Diary, under Dec. 3, 1666 : —

" There is also the very good news come of four New England ships come home safe to Falmouth with masts for the King; which is a blessing mighty unexpected, and without which (if for nothing else) we must have failed the next year.   But God be praised for thus much good fortune." [1]

It must have been with a degree of satisfaction that the Court replied to certain queries put by the King in his instructions to the commissioners, asking —

" What progresse hath beene towards the foundation and maintenance of any colledg or schooles for the education of youth, and in order to the conversion of infidells, and what success hath attended their pious endeavours of that kind," etc.[2]

---

[1] In October, 1677, under its new vexations from the troubler Randolph, the Court repeated its courtesies to the monarch by sending him some of the country produce.   " It is ordered that the Treasurer doe forthwith provide tenn barrels of cranburyes, two hogsheads of speciall good sampe, and three thousand of cod fish, to be sent to our messengers, by them to be presented to his Majesty as a present from this Court " (Records, v. 156).

[2] Records, vol. iv. pt. ii. p. 190.

The answer in full, given to these queries by the Court, is one which those of Puritan lineage may read with pleasure : —

" You may please to take notice that there is a small colledge in this jurisdiction, at the towne of Cambridge, called Harvard Colledge, the first and principall benefactor and founder thereof being of that name. There hath beene and is severall summes disbursed by the treasurer of this jurisdiction, both for the building and maintenance thereof; some small additions likewise have beene cast in from the benefficence of some well disposed persons.

" Wee have appointed the praesident, fellowes, and treasurer of the said colledge to give you a particular account thereof, if you desire it, and through the blessing of God, wee may say (and that without boasting) that at least one hundred able preachers, phisittians, chirurgeons, and other usefull persons, that have been serviceable in his majesty's dominions, have issued thence. Touching other schooles, there is by law enjoyned a schoole to be kept and maintained in every towne, and for such townes as are of one hundred families, they are required to have a grammar schoole. The country is generally well provided of schooles. Concerning the civillising and instructing the Indians in the knowledge of God and humaine learning, there is a smale colledge of fabricke of bricke erected in Cambridge, peculiarly appropriated to the Indians, which was built on the accompt and by the order of the corporation [meaning that in England]. There are eight Indian youths, one whereof is in the colledg and ready to commence batchiler of art, besides another, in the like capacity, a few months since, with severall English, was murdered by the Indians at Nantucket; and at other schools some ready to come into the colledge, all which have been and are mainteyned on the state's [!] account and charge. There are six townes of Indians within this jurisdiction, who professe the Christian religion, who have lands and towneships set forth and appropriated to them by this court. There are also persons appointed to govern and instruct them in civillity and religion, and to decide controversies amongst them : the Sabaoth is constantly kept by them, and they all attend to the publicke worship of God. They have schooles to teach their youth to read and write in severall of their townes, and many of their youth and elder persons can read and write." [1]

Did space permit, these modest statements made by the Court on the single subject of the provisions for education in the Colony would suggest a line of interesting observations. A very able and original sermon by the late eminent Dr. Horace Bushnell had for its title, " Barbarism the First Danger." Its theme, suggested by the rapid rush of large numbers of our population into the western spaces of our country, was of the risks and perils attendant upon the removal of individuals and companies of men from civilized and well-ordered states of society into untamed regions, there amid rude and rough conditions to bear the deprivation of safeguards and civil and social restraints. The danger was of a relapse to barbarism, to rough, uncouth, and lawless ways of life. Signally secured from these risks of deterioration was even the first generation born from the settlers of Massachusetts. As remarked on a previous page, they were even more narrow and rigid in their ways, less polished and refined in manners and gentle influences from the English home, than were their parents. But there was among them no sinking into illiteracy, coarseness, or vulgarity of life, no decay of domestic or social virtue, no relapse in the nobler qualities of manhood and citizenship. Their parents had gathered around them safeguards in home, school, town meetings, and churches. So they tided over the perils of degeneracy. I have quoted the bold assertion of the Court that the people of the Colony were uncomplaining and content, and it may be affirmed that there was no other community then on the earth more healthfully held to task-works of industry, or better rewarded by thrift, family comfort, intelligence, and sobriety, than the people of the Massachusetts towns and villages. The inhabitants of Charlestown, for example, enjoyed no

[1] Records, vol. iv. pt. ii. pp. 198, 199.

peculiar privilege. Yet in a petition which its freemen addressed to the General Court in 1668, they describe themselves as "the most happy people that they knew of in the world."[1] We may be sure that the generally quiet, contented, orderly, and thrifty state of all classes in Massachusetts of that generation averted much mischief that might have resulted from the intermeddling errand of the commissioners. The people in the towns generally must have found satisfaction in the resolve and skill by which their deputies had maintained their immunities.

After this long struggle with the emissaries of the Chancellor Clarendon and Charles, the Colony, having magnified its Charter by the firmness with which it had stood for it and the amount of privilege and securities which it had found in its parchment covenants, had a breathing period of relief for about ten years. Then came the direful struggle, amid massacres, conflagrations, and frontier desolation, known as Philip's War. The wilderness nursing which the first generation of the English born on this soil had received, made them more fitted than would have been their fathers to meet the exigencies of that fearful conflict. It was from the perils and atrocities of Indian warfare at that period that our ancestors learned lessons on which they were to practise for more than a century following. It was from those experiences also of the stratagems and the exquisite skill and ingenuity of the savage barbarities of torture, that our people conceived that merciless spirit toward their red foes, which so far from remaining a mere tradition among us, has been kept in living activity to this day. More than half of the fourscore towns of what is now the State of Massachusetts shared in degrees of desolation, from total destruction by fire and carnage down to such exhaustion and dread as compelled the remnant left in them to abandon them for the safer settlements.

[1] Mass. Archives, lxvii. 57.

A tenth part of the full-grown male population fell in open fight, were picked off in their field work, or, being carried away as prisoners, met their shuddering fate at the gauntlet and the stake. The cost in money to Massachusetts was nearly a quarter of a million of our present money, at its then eight-fold standard of value. The Court records are filled for some years with petitions for relief from the wounded, the widows and orphans, and other individual losers and sufferers by the catastrophe.

It was before the war had closed, and amid the exhaustion, depression, and dismay of its later stages, that the Court, under the governorship of that sturdy Cromwellian soldier, Leverett, was called to meet and tussle with the initiation of those measures so skilfully prompted and guided by their arch-mischief-maker, Randolph, which, protracted for ten years, resulted in the vacating of the Charter.

Randolph first appeared here in the middle of June, 1676, with letter and instructions from the King, through the Council for Plantations, as its messenger. His two chief points of inquiry concerned the known trifling with and defiance of the Navigation Law of the realm by our traders, and the complaints of Gorges and Mason, as land patentees, of trespasses by Massachusetts on their bounds. It is observable that from this time very little reference is made from abroad to grievances arising from the stern rule of the theocracy; while our authorities found themselves occupied with many malcontents among themselves. A monitory letter from the King in the spring of 1666 had received but slight attention, and no reply, from the Court. But more than " an hundred of the principal inhabitants " of the Colony had petitioned the Court in October, advising deference and caution in its proceedings.[1] This, too, was slighted. We are fully informed of Randolph's reception by the magistrates, — he had no opportunity to meet the

[1] Hutchinson Papers, p. 511.

General Court, — and of his course of proceedings in intrigue, keen inquisitorial investigations, and attempts to sow discord, by two full and elaborate reports which he made to the Council and the King.[1] The magistrates kept him at bay, telling him the matters of complaint were trivial, and could be easily disposed of. They offered him no access to the Court, and would not even send back by him such reply as they might make to the King.

Randolph spent a little more than six weeks in the country; and never did a fomenter of discord and mischief use time and opportunity, wit and skill, more diligently than he did. The authorities, wishing to be rid of him, and not intending to use him as their messenger, suggested his return in the ship within the month. But he said he was not ready to go — had other business — and the King had allowed him two months' stay. In the interest of Gorges and Mason he went to New Hampshire and Maine, for evidence of real or alleged grievances from people there from the usurpations of Massachusetts beyond their bounds, and busied himself in combining and instigating the malcontents in opposition. These boundary troubles were finally disposed of by money purchase and diplomacy. But all the annoyances, discords, and legal proceedings which resulted in the vacating of the Charter of Massachusetts, after protracted altercations and attempts to avert the catastrophe, may be traced to the agency of Randolph in this the first of his repeated visits. When he next came, in February, 168$\frac{1}{2}$, it was with a commission as Collector of Boston; and this office intimates to us that his keen inquiries had specially been engaged upon the thriving and illegal commerce from our ports extending to all points of the compass, with profits from exports and imports defying the navigation laws of the realm, and even pretending and boasting of authority from the Charter.

Randolph had been charged to report, under several

[1] Hutchinson Papers, pp. 477–511.

heads of inquiry, concerning the present state of New England. His papers are of interest as furnishing a contemporary account on many subjects relating to the then condition of the country, — the mode of government; the laws as conformed or derogatory to those of England ; the population and its elements; the military with its officers ; the castles and forts; the reputed boundaries and contents of land; relations with the French and New York ; the causes of the existing war with the natives ; the products, the trade, and commerce of the country ; taxes and duties ; the state of parties and their feelings toward England; the ecclesiastical government and the college, with support of the ministry, etc.   Randolph certainly picked up a large amount of detailed information, with facts and statistics ; though as a matter of course under the circumstances his reports are not always correct nor free from malignant insinuations.   It did not take him long to learn that

" the plantation of the Massachusetts bay, commonly called the corporation of Boston, is the most flourishing and powerfull, and at the present gives lawes to a great part of this country, by a pretended charter from his late Majesty."

Randolph was especially bent upon finding disaffected persons weary with government in its rigidness, and ready for a change.   Nor was he unobservant of the nonchalance and superciliousness of the authorities toward himself and his errand.

Intimations were given by some of the discontents to Randolph, which he heartily approved, that the way of relief would be for the King to assume the direct control of the Colonies, and to settle their differences by sending over a General Governor.   When the wily messenger, whose qualities as a nuisance rather than abilities for mischief had attracted the notice of the magistrates, was on his return voyage, the Governor summoned the Court, which confined its attention to the complaints from Gorges

and Mason, and to the demand of the King for agents to
be sent to him. Elders were called in for advice whether
the Court should send agents or trust to a written address.
The elders, laying stress on the demands of courtesy, advised the sending of messengers, and fortified their advice
by Scripture, as Rom. xiii. 5 ; Titus iii. 1 ; Judges xi. 14.
The Court was not wholly pleased with this advice, but
after some delay it was concluded to send an Address to
the King, to be carried by Stoughton and Bulkeley, as representing different party views. Their instructions, as
usual in such cases, bound them within very strict limits
and to specified matters of business, making them dependent upon further advices from Massachusetts, as their
reports from time to time should make necessary. The
agents, sailing on the last of October, 1676, arrived in England three months after Randolph. They did not reach
Boston, on their return, till December, 1679. During this
whole interval they were fretting under the restraints
and annoyances of their mission, longing for release and
for their home. Randolph, with his reports and machinations, was a thorn in their flesh. After debates on their
affairs, and offensive measures against Massachusetts proposed in the Council, or by law officers, they would be summoned for information, or to meet charges. They used
much adroitness, not a little casuistry, and a degree of
special pleading. But their task was beset with vexations ;
for the actual lack of real loyalty, and the matured spirit
of independence and self-sufficiency in Massachusetts, could
not be concealed by any blinds they could interpose. The
Court, to which they faithfully communicated information,
asking from it further instructions, was impatient for their
return. A treasury exhausted, and crushing indebtedness
incurred by the Indian War, made their support burdensome. But, notwithstanding, the Court could summon resources of money to meet an emergency. The agents had
been secretly instructed that if pecuniary purchase would

alone buy off the claims of Gorges to Maine, to avail themselves of the opportunity. This was accordingly done,
by the payment of twelve hundred pounds, much to the
chagrin of the King, who was contemplating the acquisition
of the province for his natural son, Monmouth.

As preliminary to what was further to follow, the King
had written in April, 1678, to the Court, rebuking it for
connecting with the oath of allegiance to himself one for
" fidelity to the country." This was derogatory to him,
and must be withdrawn. The Court, in reply to this and
other royal injunctions through the agents, had expressed
its readiness to comply. But to the very end of the contest they were now maturing to its unavertible result, they
stoutly insisted upon their Charter rights as to the admission and qualification of freemen. One of the last resolute
utterances of the authorities asserted with emphasis that
view of the intent of their enterprise in coming into this
wilderness, which has been accepted all through these
pages. The Court will do anything to meet his Majesty's
wishes about their laws, " *except such as the repealing
whereof will make us to renounce the professed cause of our
first coming hither.*" [1]

The discovery and prosecution of the Popish Plot gave
another breathing space for the interests of Massachusetts,
by engaging the attention of the Council on other matters.

The returning agents, utterly wearied out and in disgust, brought with them another letter from the King,
dated July 24, 1679.[2] In this, referring to the limited and
unsatisfactory agency of Stoughton and Bulkeley, he requires that two more agents, properly qualified, be sent
within six months. The following sentence of the letter
would startle the Court: "For since the charter, by its
frame and contents, was originally to be executed in this
kingdom, and not in New England, otherwise than by
deputation," a perfect settlement of difficulties can be

---

[1] Records, v. 201.　　[2] Hutchinson, Collection of Papers, p. 519.

made only in England.   What might be said on this point
has been already anticipated.   The King expresses his satisfaction that his order about the oath of allegiance has
been complied with.   He repeats his injunction, —

" in respect of freedom and liberty of conscience, so as those that
desire to serve God in the way of the Church of England be not
thereby made obnoxious or discountenanced from their sharing in
the government; much less that they, or any other of our good
subjects (not being Papists), who do not agree in the congregationall way, be by law subjected to fines or forfeitures, or other
incapacities, for the same; which is a severity to be the more
wondered at, whenas liberty of conscience was made one principall motive for your first transportation into those parts : nor do
wee think it fitt that any other distinction be observed in the
making of freemen, than that they be men of competent estates,
rateable at ten shillings; and that such, in their turnes, be also
capable of the magistracy, and all lawes made voyd that obstruct
the same."

We must again remind ourselves that the sense in which
the King uses the phrase, " liberty of conscience," and in
the meaning which it had for him, he utterly, though un-
intentionally, misrepresented the intent and design of those
whom he addressed. \The phrase with the latter signified
the privilege — rather, the obligation — to govern themselves by a rule made obligatory to them by the Bible.
They had seen too much of other exercises of the " liberty
of conscience " to dispose them either to claim or to
allow it.

These last injunctions of the monarch fell disregarded
by the Court.   So long as the Charter was retained with
the privilege which it granted of making freemen on its
own terms, the Court did not believe that the King had
any right to make even a suggestion in the matter.   So,
till the Charter was voided, the theocratical rule was not
in any way relaxed ; and dissenters from the civil religious establishment here continued to be taxed for its

support precisely as, the parties being reversed, was the case in England. The King adds: "Wee have appointed our trusty and well-beloved subject, Edward Randolph, Esq., to be our collector, surveyor, and searcher — for all New England," the object being to insure observance of the acts of trade and navigation. The letter closes with two reprimands, — one for the surreptitious purchase of Gorges' province, which the King claimed should be made over to him on reimbursement of its cost; the other, that the Court recall all commissions it has granted for government in Mr. Mason's province.[1]

One may begin at this point in our history and read onward to the opening of the War for Independence; or he may invert the process, and beginning with the latter era may read backward to the date of these royal interferences with the autonomy of Massachusetts, and the relations of cause and effect will by either method be equally well opened before him. With Charles II. began that course and series of measures which found their natural issue in the policy of George III.

Would it not have been wiser for Charles, averse as he was to all annoyances and perplexities of business, and having enough of trouble and anxiety on his own side of the sea, to have given over all attempts at intermeddling with his intractable colonial subjects? Suppose he had left them to themselves to manage their own affairs, would he not have saved for himself and his successors much fruitless controversy, diplomacy, and treasure, with final and humiliating discomfiture? The territorial claim of the throne of England to a transatlantic region, whose coast had been sighted by an English subject, would have been fully and consistently recognized in the establishment upon it of thriving colonies of Englishmen, leaving their relations with the parent state to the natural development of mutual interests. If it be answered that the Colonies

[1] Hutchinson, Collection of Papers, pp. 519–522.

needed the protection and patronage of England, the reply is ready. They had never asked for nor received any
such help, but were shrewdly cautious against seeking or
sharing it. The enterprise of the colonists was solely at
their own charges. As to their collisions with their French
and Dutch neighbors, these were mainly the consequences
of broils of the parent countries at home ; and so far as
was unavoidable, the colonists could have disposed of their
share in them here as they did in sharp work with their
savage foes. But what we now read as history was to be
the actual, if not the natural or the preferable, development of events.

Randolph, who had kept so keen a scrutiny upon the
doings of the colonial agents in England, followed them
home, arriving in Boston, Jan. 28, 1680, a month after
them, having previously attended to some business in New
Hampshire. The sagacious and more moderate of the
rulers of Massachusetts were well aware that affairs were
working toward confusion and disaster. There were many
causes for depression and anxiety. Following the exhaustion and debt of Philip's War, a disastrous fire in Boston, Aug. 8, 1679, had destroyed property of a value of
two hundred thousand pounds. Two successive General
Courts disposed of some of the lighter business required by
the King's letter. But concerning " liberty of conscience "
to dissentients, the old arguments were stoutly stood for.
The matter of greatest embarrassment was the sending of
more agents or messengers, the difficulty of finding fit persons willing to go, the risk they would run personally, the
probable futility of their errand, and its cost. So the
Court apologized to the King for delay, and pleaded its
reasons and misfortunes. We had at the time no strong
party of friends in England, and a few letters of entreaty
were written to men in power. The usual consequences
of such a crisis in affairs followed here, — variances and
antagonisms of opinion, party animosities or preferences,

vacillations and hesitations, both among magistrates and deputies. By order of the King, the number of the magistrates had been raised to the Charter provision, and some of them were temporizers.

Randolph at once began his official enforcement of the laws of trade, but was obstructed and baffled in his seizure of delinquent vessels by the intervention of courts and juries. The best evidence of his temper and purpose at this juncture is found in his " Representation of the Bostoneers," made to the King in 1680, as follows : —

" 1. That the Bostoneers have no right either to land or government in any part of N. England, but are usurpers, the inhabitants yielding obedience unto a supposition only of a royal grant from his late Majesty.

" 2. They have formed themselves into a commonwealth, denying any appeals to England; contrary to other plantations, they do not take the oath of allegiance.

" 3. They have protected the murtherers of your royal father in contempt of your Majestye's proclamation and letter.

" 4. They coin money of their own impress.

" 5. They put your Majestye's subjects to death for religion.

" 6. They did voyalantly oppose your Majestye's Commissioners in the settlement of N. Hampshire, by armed force.

" 7. They impose an oath of fidelity upon those that inhabit within their territories, to be true and faithful to their government.

" 8. They violate all the acts of trade and navigation by which they have ingrossed the greatest part of the West India trade, whereby your Majesty is damnified in the customes, £100,000 yearly, and the kingdom much more.

" All which he is ready to prove." [1]

And all which he might prove, because the charges were true, excepting the first, and by qualification the last. With such a resolute and able agent of mischief on the spot, — and not without sympathizers, — the prospect for Massachusetts was indeed dark. Randolph's charges to the King were made the grounds of his advice that a writ of *quo warranto* be

[1] Hutchinson, Collection of Papers, pp. 525, 526.

issued against the Charter. His bitterness and malignity were intensified by the contempt and hate which he received. The Court denied him an attorney. His servants, watching a warehouse, were mobbed and driven off. His deputy was turned out of doors. A vessel that he had seized was towed away by Boston men, while he had the Governor's warrant for his act. He tells the King that his letters here are of no more account than " a London Gazette." He seems to have been frightened away from Boston for a while by fears of imprisonment. His reports sent home led the King, in spite of the slight cast upon his letters, to write another, dated Sept. 30, 1680. It is a mixture, in tone and matter, of forbearance, chiding, and rebuke, and requires agents to be sent in three months with full instructions and powers for settling all difficulties. It ends with a threat.[1] The Court had sought to stiffen itself and its constituency for what might come next, by appointing Nov. 25 and Dec. 16, 1680, as respectively a day for Thanksgiving and for Fasting, and had rearranged its military organization.

On the receipt of the letter of the King last mentioned, brought by John Mason, the complainant, a special meeting of the General Court was summoned Jan. 4, $16\frac{80}{81}$, before which the letter was read. The Court, adjourned from day to day through a week, made some feint about Mason's business, acknowledged its dilatoriness in the revision of the laws as dictated from England, chose by ballot William Stoughton and Samuel Nowell to go abroad as its agents, and adjourned to February 22. Meeting that day, the Court adjourned again to March 16. We are left to imagine the increasing lack of harmony as to the course to be pursued in the impending crisis; for the Court engaged itself only with less important matters, and the single entry of interest on the record is the substitution of John Richards in place of Stoughton as agent, the latter being too sagacious to venture on the errand. The agents were in

---

[1] Hutchinson, Collection of Papers, pp. 523-525.

no hurry to start on their mission ; and the Court, June 3, 1681, addressed a letter to one of the Secretaries of State, accounting for the delay and pleading for consideration. Randolph had got back to England by April 16, 1681, fully charged with ill reports and malicious advice. He found the Privy Council engaged upon a proposition of a General Governor for New England, to be paid by the King. Randolph had begun to recognize what he calls " an honest party " in Massachusetts, — meaning those whom he was using as his tools. It is unnecessary to trace in detail every incident and measure which prepared for or delayed the final blow against the self-government of Massachusetts. Randolph, with complacent self-confidence, advised the King to a series of proceedings in the effecting of which he proposed himself as the medium. The principal of these were the setting of a General Governor over New England, — his candidate for the office being Culpepper, then in Virginia, — and the prosecution of Massachusetts by a writ of *quo warranto*. He speaks with great confidence of the party in his interest here.

Meanwhile the General Court, meeting in May, 1681, with apparent coolness, after transacting much miscellaneous business, gave its attention to the objections against some of its laws raised by legal officers in England. Assenting to some alterations, — like making highway robbery a capital offence, that " the law against Christmas be left out," and exempting banished Quakers from death if returning, — the Court declined to change its marriage or its Sabbath laws. That Monsieur Tonson Randolph appears in Boston again December 17. Good Judge Sewall tells us of something which he ought not to have seen, when, recording that Randolph " and his new wife and family " attended the South Meeting-house on the 25th he adds, " Mrs. Randolph is observed to make a curtsey at Mr. Willard's naming Jesus even in prayer-time." [1]

[1] Journal, under date.

Randolph brought with him an additional commission for himself in the revenue office, and another letter from the King, dated Oct. 21, 1681. This in severe and rebuking tones reiterated all former complaints and made additional ones, demanding again that fully empowered agents be forthwith sent to him, "in default whereof we are fully resolved, in Trinity Term next ensuing, to direct our Attorney General to bring a *quo warranto* in our Court of King's Bench, whereby our charter granted unto you, with all the powers thereof, may be legally evicted and made void."[1] The King had then rid himself of a Parliament, and was to be feared. The Court, assembling Feb. 15, 168$\frac{1}{2}$, at once addressed the King, beginning with conciliatory and courteous terms, again referring to the straits and hardships of their enterprise, stating the changes made in their laws in compliance with orders, and that, in obedience to his letter of October, 1681, they had despatched Dudley and Richards as messengers. The ·agents, however, did not sail till the last of the following May. The instructions they received before departing were carefully drawn and guarded. They were to apologize for the minting of money in the Colony as a matter of necessity. In a previous communication to the King on this subject, the Court had asked liberty to continue this minting, and had suggested to him to offer a stamp or device for the coins. The agents were to report, —

"That wee have no law prohibbiting any such as are of the perswasion of the church of England, nor have any ever desired to worship God accordingly that have been denied. For liberty of conscience wee have been, as wee then conceived, necessitated to make some severe lawes to prevent the violent and impetuous intrusions of the Quakers at their first coming into these parts, and our proceedings thereupon were approved by his majesty in his gratious letter of June 28; which also for divers yeares have been suspended, upon the signiffication of his majesty's pleasure

1 Chalmers, Annals, p. 443.

therein; and as for the Annabaptists, they are now subject to no other poenal statutes than those of the Congregational way.

"For admission of freemen, wee humbly conceive it is our liberty, by charter, to chuse whom wee will admit into our owne company, which yet hath not binn restryned to Congregational men, but others have been admitted, who were also provided for, according to his majesty's direction, by a lawe made anno 1664 in answer to his majesty's letter of June 28, 1662; and the law restreyning freemen to church members only, is repealed."

Other instructions refer to matters of trade, appeals, Mr. Mason's and Mr. Gorges' affairs, etc. The King having said something about "the regulation of the government," as he had promised "not to violate or infringe our charter," the agents are not to consent to anything of that tendency, and are to say that, having received no instructions, they cannot entertain the matter.[1]

Considering the weighty business on which the agents had gone, the Court appointed June 22, following their departure, for a Fast Day. Randolph, who had been watching the efforts of the Court to avert his own plottings, and who had acquainted himself with the instructions to the agents, sent further despatches of his complaints in the vessel with them. In one of these he had the effrontery to suggest to the Bishop of London that some of the funds of the English Charitable Society, for the benefit of the Indians, be used to support the worship of the Church of England in Boston. He intimated the pliability and subserviency of a substitute agent, — Dudley. His judgment of this degenerate son of the stiffest and most bigoted of the first company of exiles here, Gov. Thomas Dudley, was abundantly confirmed by his later course. Born when his father had passed his seventieth year, he lived to be a servant and agent of, if not an effective instrument in bringing about, the changed form of government for the Colony, of which his father

[1] Records, v. 346–349.

was one of the boldest and sternest spirits. He stands in
our histories with stains upon his manhood and good fame.
It may be that his pliancy was not all from self-seeking,
but can in a measure be referred to policy when he
discerned clearly that the forfeiture of the Charter was
inevitable.

The agents, bent on their futile errand, had a tedious
voyage of nearly three months. They presented their case,
as instructed, before the Privy Council, excusing their delay, and defending the Colony and its government against
such charges as they were permitted to refer to by the
authorities behind them. They said that the Colony was
under a crushing debt of twenty thousand pounds from the
Indian war; that the Liturgy might now be used in worship by such as wished it; that Church of England men
could hold office; and that the Acts of Trade and Navigation were in force. The Records of the Court, beginning with $168\frac{2}{3}$, are crowded with the tokens of distress
and discomfiture, of baffled efforts, and of apprehensions
that what was dreaded was certain to befall. And as
strongly marked in these Records are the evidences of a
still resolute will, of nerve and constancy, of a determina-
tion to hold out in the struggle, to prolong it in order to
defer the fatal blow, — the only hope being that some
trouble or complication at home, as had heretofore favored
them, might interpose for their relief. Randolph, through
the whole critical period, passed to and fro, the diligent
agent of mischievous or of loyal machinations on both
sides of the water. He crossed the ocean at least fourteen
times. He informed himself thoroughly of all the elements, the personal and party relations, the public interests, the individual intrigues and ambitions, which entered
into the strife, and found delight, as was believed, in the
simple exercise of his malignity.

He remained long enough at intervals here to watch the
working of the perplexities and dissensions he had already

provided for the authorities, trying to probe the secrets of the vacillating, and to acquaint himself with the restricted instructions given to the agents. He would most diligently write letters, filled with his mischief, to go by every outward bound vessel, till he thought it necessary to make a return voyage that he might personally watch, embarrass, and circumvent the agents, as his schemes and plots matured. Meanwhile those two agents, under all their limitations and annoyances, were not of one mind. They had been specially matched by the Court as an offset to each other, by their opposite proclivities, temperaments, and party relations. Randolph was sure that he would find, if not a helping, yet not an obstructive, instrument in Dudley; while Richards was stoutly patriotic to the Colony, and incorruptible.

Nor was there by any means perfect harmony, unity of purpose, accord in judgment, or resolution for the same ends of patriotism, among the authorities and the people here. The simplicity, austerity of manners, and characteristic Puritan spirit of the first age had become sensibly qualified, in Boston especially, and among magistrates and others in office. It was not so, or to any such extent, in the rural parts of the Commonwealth, where the primitive tone and habits were rather strengthening than relaxing their sway. So the magistrates and the deputies were not in full harmony. Englishmen only transiently resident here for trade and commerce, and some of our enriched citizens, had introduced the dangers and fascinations, as well as the amenities, of luxury and ease.

The Governor communicated to the Court in February, 168$\frac{2}{3}$, a whole Pandora's box of troubles, — a letter of a threatening tone from the King, with other documents, copies of Randolph's complaints, and laments from the agents. The Court, receiving the whole in a mass, had but to adjourn day by day for deliberation, in order to deal with each subject in detail. Meanwhile the familiar effort for relief and renewal of resolve was sought in the appointment of a Fast. A law passed in October, 1673, enjoining a delay of a year for allowing the voting of a freeman other than a church member, was repealed. From this time onward, till the dreaded blow fell, each address and appeal of the Court contained a more and more emphatic, often pleading and pathetic, reference, with urgent insistence to the primary purpose and motive of the first patentees, to plant a Colony here, as dissenters from the Church of England, under their own scheme of a Biblical commonwealth. This was asserted to the last.

Thus, in a humble address — adulatory, gratulatory, and in a supplicatory spirit — now sent to the King, praying for consideration and delay in judgment, the Court insists upon its covenanted Charter rights. The agents also are further instructed, "joyntly, and not severally," to go the utmost lengths in compliance and concession, — " to accept of and consent unto such proposalls and demands as may consist with the mayne ends of our predecessors in their removall hither our charter," [1] etc. They were not to consent, under any stress, to any alteration of the fundamentals of that Charter. Again, in further instructions of March 30, 1683, we read : —

" Whereas, in our commission and power sent to you, one generall limitation is the saving to us the main ends of our coming over into this wilderness, you are thereby principally to understand our liberties and priviledges in matters of religion and worship of God, which you are therefore in nowise to consent to any infringement of." [2]

Still further private instructions bid the agents observe that the King's avowed purpose " of the regulation of this government" cannot mean " an abolition of our charter, or any essentiall part of it." Yet, " if nothing will satisfy but the nulling our charter, or imposing of appeales," then

[1] Records, v. 386.　　　　[2] Ibid., 390.

they have liberty, "but are to be slow" in using it; "to tender the Province of Maine, or give up any thing else, but what our charter will not warrant our keeping." Yet if the worst comes to the worst, and a *quo warranto* is to proceed, they must take advice whether they will resist and make dispute, — "be sure you spend little or no money therein, unless you cann have very good assurance that it may be substantially made and mainteyned by law." [1]

These instructions were accompanied by a petition subscribed by the inhabitants at large in three of the counties of the Colony, addressed to the King, the presenting of which was left to the judgment of the agents. This petition, tender and earnest in its supplication, asks "that they may not be deprived of those liberties and privileges which they hold in such high esteeme, and have themselves and progenitors been at so great hazard and charge, and encountred with such extream difficultyes for the injoyment thereof." [2]

To complete here what is further to be said as to this pleading with the King on the ground of the religious intent in the settlement of the Colony, I will anticipate by quoting from the Records two more strong expressions of it. In an "humble petition and address to the King," October, 1684, the Court pleads : —

"The cause and ground of our fathers (and of some yet living) leaving all that was deare to them and us in England to come into this wildernesse, a land then not inhabited (but by the Indeans, of whom wee purchased the right), was not out of dislike to the civil government, which wee always highly prized, and accounted at the least aequall to the best in the world, nor of the doctrine of the church of England, which, for the substance thereof, we owne, embrace, and professe ; but to avoyd the severity then exercised in many places, because their consciences could not permit them to conforme to some ceremonies of the church strictly imposed, accounted by some indifferent things, but to them otherwise. And

[1] Records, v. 391.   [2] Ibid., 388.

therefore, to avoyd giving offence to his majesty, or undergoing that burthen they were not able to beare, they chose rather, in a quiet, orderly manner, to leave their dearest native country, committing themselves to the Providence of the Most High, to encounter the difficulties both of the sea and the wildernesse. This his Majesty Charles the First, of happy memory [!], well understood, who freely and graciously granted them a patent for this place, with the priviledges therein conteyned, to them and their successors for ever: and upon the confidence and security of that royall grant, transplanted themselves, where they and wee have lived as exiles and great sufferers, grapling with many difficulties, daingers," etc.[1]

These certainly are strong, and apparently perfectly sincere, affirmations, made as stating the ruling motives of the founders of the Colony. Those who see any reasons for impugning this sincerity are at liberty, if they judge it right to do so, to suggest that these affirmations are ingenious after-pleas adroitly urged beyond the limits of the truth.

Yet once more. At a session of the Court, July 21, 1685, on tidings of the death of Charles II., a petition is addressed to his brother and successor, James II. Beginning with respectful recognition and sympathy, the petition recites: —

" Our fathers, and some of us with them, left their native land, with all their pleasant and desirable things therein [with the usual references to the ocean, the wilderness, the Indians, hardships, perils, poverty, etc.], and for the space of fifty years and upwards, — all this was donne and suffered that our fathers, and wee their children after them, might worship God according to the dictates of our consciences, founded upon the sacred Scriptures, which liberty of our religion wee esteeme more deare to us than our lives: nor did they come hither but with the approbation and princely encouragement of your majestie's royall ancestors, declared in their letters patents, and afterwards often rattefied by the word of a king," etc.[2]

---

[1] Records, v. 456, 457.   [2] Ibid., 495.

For the sake of bringing together these reiterated appeals for warding off the dreaded stroke, I have slightly anticipated the main current of the narration. At the opening of the General Court, Nov. 7, 1683, the Governor communicated the doleful tidings. The harassed and disheartened agents had got back to Boston, October 22. Four days afterward Randolph arrived, elated with the consciousness that after his long enmity and plotting he had triumphed in his purpose. Before his return to England again, December 14, he had communicated his fatal papers, now on the Records,[1] which the Court were then to entertain. They included the writ against the Massachusetts Charter, which had issued June 27, notifying the Company of the *quo warranto*, and summoning the defendants to meet it at the Court in London. Randolph brought with him two hundred copies of all the proceedings against the Charter, which he was to distribute, and also a Declaration of the King promising certain favors on certain concessions. After watching the effect of these missiles, Randolph was to return and make report. The colonial agents in England, not being willing or able to undertake the defence of their cause, had been allowed to go home,— not, however, to sail till after Randolph, as it was desired that he should reach here before them. Randolph had sought in vain to have a frigate and some military demonstration to accompany him, actually or feigningly suggesting some possible resistance. It is not strange that some of the firmest patriots in the Colony muttered mysterious suggestions about seeking to put themselves under the protection of some foreign friendly power.

The reader is referred to fuller historical narrations than the limited scope of these pages allows, if he would follow the details closing the chartered existence of the Bay Colony, and would trace the futile efforts of the distressed but still desperately resisting authorities to avert their fate.

[1] Records, v. 421–423.

Times and men, influences and agencies, on both sides of the ocean, had undergone great changes from the conditions under which, in previous threatenings of calamity, the Court had averted it, by its stoutness, its policy, and its acute ingenuity of resource. The King, now supreme in his arbitrary prerogative, rid of the hampering restraints of Parliaments, with the ready countenance of his advisers could work his will. The Puritan party, the great and noble leaders of which were dead, and the remaining sympathizers with which in the lower ranges of society and influence were powerless, could no longer, as in the years of the Commonwealth, shelter and strengthen the self-sufficient Colony. The pristine vigor, the harmony of spirit and purpose, the general equality of condition, the principles, habits, and simplicity of life, and the resolute independence of the early years of the Colony, had all yielded to deteriorating influences. The official and the private papers relating to the crisis reveal to us so fully the incidents, passions, and feelings of the passing years, that the reader is well-nigh made to share the anguish and dismay of the rumors, the experiences, and the alarms of the people, and to watch the distrust and bitterness of alienated sentiments attached by the patriot party to those who openly or privately counselled submission to the King. Dudley had either by such reckoning with himself as satisfied his judgment, — not to say his conscience, — or by the lures of place and ambition, committed himself against the spirit of his father and former favoring friends. Seated among the magistrates on his return, he won a majority of them to compliance. This upper body of the Court voted another humble Address to the King, and a commission to more agents instructed to yield submission, without contention with the King at law, confiding in his pledge that his intent was only to *regulate* their government, not to destroy it. Some of the deputies were ready to consent; but a majority resisted, offering strong reasons and protests, and plying Scripture texts against the sin of self-destruction either by suicide or fatal concession. So Randolph had to carry back with him the return that the Court rejected the royal proposal. The Court, Dec. 5, 1683, commissioned Robert Humphreys, an eminent London lawyer, as their attorney, to make defence in order "to save a defult and outlawry for the present." The Court also made trial of some legal quibbles. It further instructed Humphreys "to spinn out the case to the uttermost," and to retain counsel, adding another appeal to the King. But the case had been already spun out till the tenuity of its thread had been broken. Dudley received a private letter in October, 1684, informing him that a *scire facias* had been issued from Chancery against the Company, to which answer was to be made within six weeks. The Court made publication, Jan. 28, 168$\frac{4}{5}$, that the Charter had been condemned, and considering the "sad and awfull circumstances," appointed a day of humiliation, and sent another letter to the King from "his poore and distressed subjects." Charles died Feb. 6, 168$\frac{4}{5}$. The event was announced in the Court, May 7, and James II. was proclaimed in Boston, April 20. The letter addressed to him by the Court has already been referred to. Final judgment was entered against the Charter, Oct. 23, 1684. Humphreys sent to the Court a copy of it in the following May. For a long period of uncertainty, of deep distress and increasing dissension, the people waited for what was to follow. Dudley, associated with others as a commission, was appointed by the royal Council to the headship of affairs in the prostrated Commonwealth. It was with the bitterness of pain and resentment that the Court, meeting May 20, 1686, complained that the communication made to them by the commission was not addressed, as of old, to the Governor and Company of Massachusetts Bay, but to "some of the principall gentlemen and chief inhabitants." "A royal covenant was broken."

Thus after a practical trial of a little more than half a century, the experiment of a theocratic form of government, to be administered by statutes and ordinances gathered from the Bible and digested into a creed covenanting the administrators of it, was brought to a close. It was terminated, not directly by the exposure of its impolicy and injustice, nor by the failure of the will, purpose, and ability of its administrators still to maintain it, but by the interposition of external authority. I stated in the beginning that the founders and legislators of Massachusetts had sought to establish a wholly original form of government, with novel conditions of citizenship. Nowhere in the world — not even in any part or age of Christendom — had there been a precedent for it. If enough has not been already said about the good faith and the thorough sincerity of purpose with which the scheme was devised and put on trial, this would be shown to appear in the unyielding firmness and persistency with which it was maintained, not only against those who opposed and impugned it, but also against difficulties and a succession of frustrated efforts to enforce it, which, as we view the case, might have induced even its fondest approvers to abandon it. But so far was this from being true, that the authorities never lost faith or heart in it; they mourned their own discomfiture, and alleged that the royal covenant so solemnly plighted to them had been meanly dishonored. And so, not in championship, or defence of these Puritan legislators, but recognizing simply the originality, the novelty, the wholly unique and peculiar qualities of their model for government and their qualification for citizenship, it would seem that we ought in fairness to adjust our judgment of them. Our early Puritanism, limited and transient as it was, covering only one of our five half-centuries, has attached an historic repute to our whole history. It is from this brief period of theocratic and Bible rule that, not so much in grave and sober histories, as in light popular essays and windy and flashy speeches, with their gibes and satires, our State has been put under reproach. In many cheap flings from ill-informed and superficial declaimers, the dark and dismal period of our history is presented, and even that with exaggerations, as if it were the whole of it. As by English law traitors went to the block and heretics to the stake, so many of us have heard from our orators that Massachusetts *burned* Quakers and witches. But how stands the case in general history, and in our own history? There was not at the time, nor had there ever been, a civil government in any State in Christendom which did not legislate for and enforce doctrines and practices of religion, upheld by penalties. The whole question for us concerns the novel and peculiar way in which that religious legislation was devised here. Our early Puritanism differed in spirit and discipline from other forms of religion under Papal and Protestant rule, not in being any more or any less intolerant or persecuting than they were, but in the motive, method, and direction of its intolerance. Seemingly, Puritanism would have more to say for itself in defending its intolerance, in that, instead of planting its authority on ghostly claims of priestly and superstitious sanction, utterly incapable of being certified, and to be accepted only by faith or credulity, it appealed to divinely attested writings, readable and intelligible, which all Christian people professed to acknowledge and revere.

In these passing days we find occasion to affirm that while dissent, anarchy, and nihilism may make resistance against arbitrary and despotic governments, they should be silent under citizenship in a constitutional republic where organic and statute law receives its authority from its own members. It would seem that the Puritan founders of Massachusetts recognized the same distinction for their rule by an acknowledged code. Under the Papal and Prelatical sway they affirmed that human inventions, sacerdotal and despotic enactments, and ghostly assumptions claiming a

Divine authority, rested wholly upon the caprice or interests of those who devised them, and could not be verified
by tests of historic proof or processes of impartial judgment or reason. These were airy, floating, and sandy
foundations, and could not compel devout, free, and earnest men to build upon them. But Papists and Prelatists, as well as Puritans, believed that the Bible was the
word of God, "a sure testimony," offering them a constitution under which they were all citizens. The corollary
then followed: persecution and intolerance were unlawful
and wicked when exercised under Papal or Prelatical authority; but they were justifiable, or rather ceased to be
persecution and intolerance, when the magistrates of a
Christian commonwealth required of its citizens to obey
"the Statutes, Laws, and ordinances of God." Puritanism held its citizens to obedience and allegiance to the
Bible, just as the civil government assumes that all citizens know the law and are bound to conform to it. These
intolerant principles in the methods of all religion mark
stages in the struggles of progressive liberty, light, and
knowledge. We must certainly admit that an advance
was made, when the right of using intolerance and restraint was withdrawn from the support of priestly and
human inventions in religion, and was claimed to be allowable only according to the rule of the "Word of
God." They answer in many points of resemblance to
the traditions, experiments, and errors in the theory
and practice of the healing art. The Antinomians, Baptists, and Quakers, under spiritual treatment here, had
their counterparts at the time in invalids and patients
under the hands of the doctors, with pills and purgings,
suffering exhaustive bleeding, and denied air and water
on their fevered beds. Physicians of our time are prime
offenders against the commandment to honor their fathers,
if it is to be taken in the Westminster covenant sense of
respect and deference to authorities.

Having thus painfully, and with a purpose of fidelity, traced the Puritan rule of our first half-century, we may naturally ask if the residuum and deposit and aftermath of Puritanism, its principles and its habits, have not left us something more and better to appreciate, esteem, and honor ? As has been stated on an early page of this volume, the influx of foreign and uncongenial elements in this place "for the publique meetings" of the Puritan settlers, has made it impossible for us to trace what would have been its development here if the indigenous and homogeneous stock of its population had been left to itself. The heritage was strictly one of Puritanism for two hundred years. The last half-century has wrought a change. The problem presented to those who highly esteem their Puritan heritage, and who do not welcome, but endeavor peacefully to acquiesce in the ascendency of these uncongenial elements, is, whether the vitality and power of the best elements of Puritanism can retain and exercise a sway that will neutralize what is hostile, and assimilate what is harmless and good, in this infusion of foreign agencies and influences. What, then, are the characteristics of those qualities and principles of Puritanism which survive among us and have retained their ancient virtues ? Some might question whether there is a survival of any true Puritanism among us.   But in answer to this intimation, it might fairly be pleaded that any reductions, limitations, and liberalizings of the spirit and usages of the old Puritanism, which fairly resulted from the development of its own free principles, or from latent tendencies not at first recognized in active exercise in it, would still leave its essential identity unimpaired. The Puritanism of to-day, like that of the Reformation era, protests against and rejects the whole spirit of mediævalism, all class distinctions and privileges founded on prerogative and artificial rank, and all the assumptions and tyranny of ecclesiasticism and sacerdotalism. The leaven introduced by Massachusetts Puritanism has proved the most effective of all agencies in excluding those once supremely potent influences from the portion of this new continent governed by the organic and constitutional laws of our nation, distinguishing it in these respects from most of the other governments of Christendom. What Puritanism did not originally bring here of the full energy of these principles, has been wrought out by its own earliest provisions for popular education and for individual independence, and the rights of each for self-government. Even that element in the early Puritan legislation and administration which, in all the criticisms upon them, ranging from grave discussions and objections down to satirical and contemptuous reflections, has received the severest condemnation, has been most strangely misconceived and misrepresented. That element, as assumed, was the supreme sway by dictation and authority of the clerical order. The elders are alleged to have been the legislators and rulers of the Massachusetts theocracy. If what has been set forth from our most authentic and instructive records as defining the real position, agency, and influence of those elders does not fully expose the error of that assumption, I have no disposition or purpose to challenge it any further. In a Biblical commonwealth, whose magistrates were the " Ministers of God," it was but natural that the religious teachers, the expounders of the Scriptures through their special learning and knowledge, should be consulted by those magistrates, and that so far as they could throw light upon any question submitted to them, their word should have weight. From first to last, the Puritan elders had no other authority or influence than this. The Protestant clergy, who succeed them now all over this country, have precisely the same sort of authority and influence, — subject only to the essential qualification that the civil government and the people do not accept the Bible as the statute-book, and so do not depend upon clerical help for its interpretation.

The respect and deference paid to these early elders was secured by them through their character and abilities. It was solely by these that they were put into office; and the functions of that office, with its privileges, were rigidly conditioned upon those qualities in the men. Great as their influence was among a people so much of whose life and thought were engaged with religion, it cannot even then be called professional or official, and it was as remote as are the poles from including anything of a priestly or sacerdotal character. There was a radical and a world-wide difference between a Puritan elder, " a minister of God's word," and every claimant of a priestly prerogative, Papal or Protestant. The minister was but the mouth-piece of an assembly in pronouncing a sentence of admonition or excommunication. He repudiated the priestly pretence that the benefit or efficacy of a sacrament depended upon the official character of the administrant of it. He denied that anything he might do or leave undone, anything he could say or leave unsaid, of blessing or cursing, would affect the relation between a human being and his Judge. He was himself utterly powerless, individually, to impose sentence or judgment. He had no right to demand that confession should be made to him, nor would he venture to offer absolution. Had an instance ever presented itself in which a Puritan elder had presumed, standing by the death-bed of a sinner, to deny to him prayer and mercy, to inflict on him the curses of sacerdotalism, and to interdict him the hope of Divine grace and forgiveness, that elder would have come under civil process, and been made to smart for his offence.

So we may easily trace down from the Puritan elder the succession in position and influence of the clerical order all over our land, as well as in this commonwealth, save as new influences have come in with imported foreign elements, which the Puritans had discredited and left behind them. When the Colony Charter was outlawed, the King did not impose upon Massachusetts the institution, discipline, and ritual of the Church of England; he simply enjoined that all of his subjects who desired to do so should be free to engage in its communion and worship, without prejudice to their civil rights. 'Substantially under the form of government substituted for the colonial, what is called the voluntary system in religion received its sanction. This system, imposed on provincial Massachusetts by authority from without, and afterward adopted and approved by independent State legislation from within, has resulted, by the development of time, experience, and the progress of practical wisdom, in the complete divorce of Church and State. The voluminous pages of our statutes, showing the processes by which that result has been reached, are interesting and instructive. The old, rigid, compulsory legislation for religion slowly lingered in its traditional hold upon the community, bracing itself for a time on the plea of its necessity to sustain civil order and to promote good morals. Having once required that all the people should be taxed for and should respect the ministry and dispensation of religion under one and the same form, it paused awhile on the compromise of freedom to support any preferred form, provided that it were some ministration respectably recognized. Then, within the lifetime of those now on the stage, the citizen received full freedom, in thought, observance, and purse, to look upward and inward for his religion. Such would long since have been the result in the mother country, had the principles of Nonconformity prevailed there. Meanwhile the clergy in Massachusetts retain and exercise all that was best, or only good, in the influence of their Puritan predecessors. Character and abilities are still the conditions of their accepted service, while their official prestige is a nullity. True, our modern elders are not called in to "advise" the magistrates; but they find their representatives as chaplains and members in the legislature, in constitutional conventions and in electoral colleges, and in the opening of civil courts and the inauguration of municipal governments.

The natural and logical results of the independency and of the educational institutions of our old Puritanism have wrought in two opposite directions. One of these has been in the extremes of individualism, with every form of dissent, variance, and freedom in belief and speculation: the other is in a reversion, a looking back for mental peace and spiritual resource to ancient beliefs and sanctities of observance. There are those, even of Puritan lineage, though with adopted views alien from their inheritance, who view this fragmentary, scattering division of what they believe should be one fold of inclusive discipleship as, to use their own term for it, a " scandal " to all " who profess and call themselves Christians." Reference has been made in an earlier page to a kindly intended, however hopefully advised, scheme proposed by some of these for a reconciling process in the interest of what they suppose to be implied by " Christian unity." The last census gives us rather more than three thousand clergy of the Protestant Episcopal denomination owing " canonical obedience " to some fifty " bishops." The proposition is, that the sixty or seventy thousand other ministers of the various Protestant denominations should go to those bishops to receive from their hands the tactual impress which shall convey to them the sacramental grace, " the gift of the Holy Ghost," and the power to exercise " a valid ministry." Those who are now in life may not expect to see that exorbitant proposition accepted. Some of these bishops are the sons, or from the families, of reverend men, who fulfilled a faithful ministry without this " sacramental grace." It is conceivable that one or more of these elders might have survived to find their sons invested with the prelatical office. Then it would have been a spectacle to see the aged parents kneeling before their children to have a defect in their official ministry supplied. Yet the Episcopal denomination may naturally make the most of what is substantially its only distinguishing claim. Our Protestant bishops are but the shadows of English prelates, and for the rest their fellowship has yielded to the modified Puritan Congregationalism. No patron, not even a bishop, has " the right of presentation " to a parish. Each congregation has an independent action in the choice, the tenure of office, and the removal of its minister. The laity divide with the clergy all the business of its conventions. It may be well also that if, in the one Christian Church represented in our country by so many branches and twigs, there is an exclusive claim to the vital sap, there should be a rivalry among the claimants. So as the old sacerdotalism in its full vigor has been imported into our country, reduced manifestations of it may serve as checks and safety-valves.

But this reversion to the spirit and practice of the old sacerdotalism will turn the thoughts of many serious and earnest persons of kindly and generous breadth of spirit to quite a different conception of " Christian unity " than that of an organic ticketing and labelling by one official mark of those who may partake of " one spirit" under so " diverse operations and manifestations." The preceding pages have shown us how men and women, profoundly and intently exalting religious belief and observance into the all-absorbing interest of their life, exceptionally pure in morals and habits, and with kindly hearts and helping hands in all neighborly offices, wellnigh made a pandemonium of a little struggling town on the edge of a wilderness. It was all because, instead of being drawn into unity by the like virtues and graces just recognized in them, they thought they ought all to believe together, or to quarrel together, on a few points of belief or observance which differently engaged their consciences or judgments. And such will ever be the result — though never again with legal penalties of fine, banishment, the prison, and the gallows — of all attempts to force doctrinal or ritual observances upon men and women of intelligent minds, whose proclivities, temperaments, tastes, ranges of thought, imagination, and fancy decide for them their preferences among all the phases of truth and the attitudes and reverences of faith and worship.

We have well learned, or ought to have learned, the lesson that inborn or inherited qualities, tastes, and temperaments, with differences of strength, freedom, and confidence in the exercise of the intellectual powers, courage or fear in trusting to the ventures of inquisitive reason, and facility or difficulty in the tendencies of the believing faculty, will inevitably result in wide divergences in all that concerns religious belief and observance. The ritualistic temperament and the Quaker temperament are still reproduced in living generations. As Sewall has told us, poor Mrs. Randolph, in her drear and cold surroundings in the South Meeting-house, amid the bare rigidity of its services, took a gleam of satisfaction in courtesying at the name of Jesus in the elder's prayer. It was on Christmas day, which passed wholly without recognition. She missed all that was dear and wonted to her in her sweet method of devotion. One of inborn Quaker temperament, attending upon a modern ritualistic service, with his free and restless spirit, would see only what was formal and mechanical — he might even pronounce it lackadaisical — in the changing of attitudes, the intervals of silence, the responses of the worshippers, and the gliding of surpliced priests across the chancel, one after another, to divide between them the sentences and paragraphs of prayer, collect, lesson, Gospel, and Epistle. The Quaker's questions would be, Might not one do all this without distraction or parade ? Does this formality look toward God, or men ?

The early colonists of Virginia, such as they were, with

no Puritanical scruples, used the service-book of the English Church, constraints and punishments no less severe than those in force in Massachusetts being used to compel attendance. Our Puritans, leaving that book behind them, and becoming wonted to their different worship, worked themselves up to a disesteem and contempt of it which led them to forbid its use. A strange exhibition of erratic human nature! Yet their own way was wisely conformed to their needs and exigencies. Many of those who have been trained by a liturgical service connect with it the fondest, tenderest attachments, and would be desolate without it. Those who know the service only by occasional observance are perhaps the most impartial in their judgment of its use and sufficiency. They appreciate its richness and beauty of tone, sentiment, and language, its calm dignity and its devoutness of spirit, and the compass of its devotional range and expression. But the Puritan estimate, free of their grievance about it, is still entertained, and with reasons for it. The formal, unvaried service finds its fit and helpful use in the placid routine of life, in the orderly refinements and dignities and comfort of settled times. But as the Puritans found it, it seems painfully inadequate in critical and distracting experiences, where spontaneity, fervor, and yearning sympathies between men and women, and between men and women in their seeking for God, crave the familiarity of unstudied utterance. One of the most objectionable elements of the Book Service to those who occasionally participate in it is the blind and superstitious reading by rote the whole of the Book of Psalms. Why, because in that strangely miscellaneous gathering of psalmody there are strains of most sublime and tender devotion, the very anthems and raptures of piety, should the whole of it be held sacred? There can be no edifying nutriment for heart or mind in its obscure, meaningless, and heathen ingredients, its unchristian, vindictive, and imprecatory contents.

Our narration began with the strong and passionate assertion of the spirit of Nonconformity, against principles and usages of human device and imposition, in religion. That spirit drove those whom it mastered into exile in the wilderness, that they might make trial of methods which their consciences constrained them to follow. Our narration closes with the enforced teaching to those exiles of some further lessons, in the impracticability and wrong of their own imposed Conformity. The struggle that advanced here was but another phase of the issue opened in England at the Reformation between the obedience which was enjoined as of divine right, and the freedom that was claimed as of human right. Only here the claim was shifted from an appeal to divine right as set forth by a Church to the authority found for it in a Holy Book. So I have ventured on a previous page to state as one of the results of the failure on trial of a Biblical commonwealth here the demonstration of a truth which will startle and offend some persons, and which therefore I hope may not be misinterpreted. That demonstrated truth I understand to be, that no organic form of civil government and administration can wisely or safely base itself on religion, unless it may be that religion be taken in the broadest and vaguest sense which it might have in an infinite diversity of interpretations. By this is meant that statutes and laws must be content with claiming only a human and mundane authority. Behind their wholly secular phrasing and defining there may be in the hearts and minds of those who enact them, and of those held in obedience to them, any degree and amount — and the more the better — of a reference to an assumption and belief of a divine sanction for them. It would have been well for all Christendom had it always proved true that " rulers are ministers of God for good." But experience has compelled us to interpret the assertion as meaning that it is *intended*, or *desired*, or *fitting*, that rulers should be such representatives of Deity.

The rulers of Massachusetts, like so many others, fell short of this lofty ideal. And now, as taught by experience, we have learned that not "Moses his Judicials," nor even the "Precepts of Jesus Christ," can be enacted or enforced in civil government. And this for two reasons, if for no other, — that those who are to be governed, or to govern themselves, are not agreed as to the authority of those religious codes; and that those who own that authority differ most widely in interpreting them. Laws to be compulsory in their authority, and to be enforced by penalties, must confine themselves to secular interests and sanctions. It is the province of religion to do its work on the purposes, motives, and judgment of those who make the laws, that they may be just and reasonable, and to induce obedience to them.

The whole tendency of all the free, vitalized, earnest, and unchallengeable working of thought, speculation, and fancy now is to promote individualism and independence in the full range of matters in which uniformity or unity was once demanded and enforced by penalties. The thousand little rills and streams of thought and belief which once served for isolated communions and sects, have found their way to rivers which lead on to the ocean, where navigation is no longer by landmarks, but by the piloting of the open heavens. Meanwhile that this disintegration and individuality in religion are rendering chimerical any fond scheme for restoring an "organic unity" in belief and observance, the spirit of a broad and sympathetic humanity in its manifold workings, in all its agencies of reform, renewal, redress, purification, and benevolence, is drawing human hearts to a unity which human intellects will never realize. The noblest service done by the Quakers was in demanding recognition for some of the most vital and benedictive forces of the Christian religion which were latent in it but unrecognized. There are more such inspirations which are finding their prophets and missionaries. Among them is one presenting to us in the Gospel record the sublimest figure of impersonation to be found in all literature, where the great Teacher, " and all the holy angels with him," seated upon " the throne of his glory," dispenses eternal allotments, not for beliefs or conformities, but according as humanity in its woes and straits and needs has or has not been ministered to.

NOTE ON THE "SALEM WITCHCRAFT."

THE limitations of time and of subject-matter proposed for rehearsal in this volume would not have required any reference to the tragic and appalling incidents through a portion of a single year, in one of our villages, which have passed down into history under the darkest shadows of our first century. The trials and executions for alleged witchcraft in Salem, in 1692, have no direct connection with the theocratic government of Massachusetts, nor with anything special or peculiar in the characteristics and legislation of the Puritan colony. The loss of its first Charter had, after a troubled, unsettled, and revolutionary interval of some seven years, found the former Colony a province of Great Britain. Under its new Charter the people were deprived of the right of self-government. It was under the administration of the first of the provincial governors, and by a special court appointed by him, the legality of which has always been questioned, that those trials and executions, under the dismay of a sporadic delusion and frenzy, visited their sad experiences upon some twenty victims. The Governor, a rough and illiterate, though a marvellously fortunate, adventurer, with not so much knowledge of affairs of civil government as he had of astronomy, — for he was a good navigator, — had just acceded to office, through luck and favoritism. The exercise of sound discretion and decided caution in him might have smothered the frenzy at its outburst; but having allowed the spark to kindle, he left the province temporarily on official business, and on his return put an arrest upon the dreadful proceedings, seemingly moved to interpose chiefly because his own wife had been "cried out upon" as one of the culprits. The reference which I shall make to this direful subject will be brief. Indeed, I should have wholly passed it by, were it not that I find in it a very striking illustration of the strange and perverse way, the crookedness of opinion, and the falsity of judgment with which many matters of early Massachusetts history have been treated by sciolists, by very ignorant and superficial critics, and by some uncandid, not to say ill-tempered commentators. What passes for history, and what serves for many keen gibes of reproach in tradition and popular amusement, have found material for a revel of license in dealing with the theme of Salem witchcraft.

No one would be moved to put in a plea or to raise a protest in dealing with this subject on any such ground as that of misstatement, exaggeration, or over-darkening of the cruel and iniquitous proceedings at Salem under the delusions and frenzies of a panic. The veritable history of the event and its incidents is unrelievable in its horrors. Whenever reader or historian, moved by a sense of painful interest or duty, acquaints himself with the facts of the case and brings before him the pangs and woes of innocent victims, there is no occasion for stirring him to indignation against the actors, or to sympathy with the sufferers ; and he may even feel the risings of a desire to visit some post-mortem penalties upon the prime wrong-doers. There is no need of retelling the story to reduce its distressing melancholy, nor to lighten the burden of reproach and condemnation which must rest somewhere and upon some agents in those harrowing incidents. But there is one signal wrong and error connected with many rehearsals of the story, for a participation in which those who are either with or without the candor or the information requisite in such a case are justly to be rebuked. This censure is deserved by all those who speak of Salem witchcraft as if it were a special, peculiar, and unique product of the Massachusetts theocracy, the flowering out and full fruitage of Puritanism. The delusions and atrocities connected with that distressing episode in our history had no relation whatever to the distinctive qualities of Puritanism, but involved in a common share in superstitions and cruelties all classes and ranks of men and women, of every party in religion, Papal or Protestant, and of no religion. Philosophers and physicians, popes, prelates, divines, statesmen, judges, and monarchs, were in full harmony of belief all over Christendom with those who were parties to what transpired amid the forests and the clearings of a farming village in New England.

A thought and suggestion have come to my own mind in reflecting upon this repulsive subject, which I have never found to be expressed or intimated by any who has written upon it. It seems to me so natural and obvious that I will venture to utter it. It is this. Taking into view all the facts and circumstances of the case, Massachusetts may be regarded as having been most marvellously and propitiously, we may even say with partiality and favoritism, dealt with in the apportionment to her of so small a share in the horrors of a world-wide and cruel superstition. One who has been at pains to inform himself, in particulars and details, concerning the peculiar conditions and experiences of private, domestic, and social life in the Massachusetts towns during our first century, will, I am persuaded, find much reason for wonder, congratulation, and even boastfulness, that while this Colony, as was inevitable, caught from the Old World a spark from the universal combustion working there at that period, the flame was so confined in space, and so restricted in time, when it broke out here. Most merciful and lenient was the visitation upon Massachusetts of the delusion which so ravaged with barbarous and revolting inhumanity nearly every scene of human life in the mother country. For myself, I am deeply impressed by the contrast between what was realized and what might most naturally have been experienced here. Consider the circumstances and conditions of life in our early rural settlements, and the marvel will be that witchcraft was not an universal, indigenous, inveterate, and chronic infliction in every one of them. There was in each of them solitariness and isolation, sharp deprivation, and hard experience. There were lonely hours for individuals, for much brooding over a limited range of thoughts. The scenes of Nature around were full of gloom. The rigors of winter were stern and of long duration. The woods were filled with savage forms, whom many regarded as imps and agents of the Evil One, and who were believed to be, through the Powwows and sorcerers, his worshippers. There were no means and no allowance for relaxation, amusement, or jollity. The lines of a familiar modern hymn, —

> " Religion never was designed
> To make our pleasures less," —

had not then been sung, and the pleasurable quality of Puritanism was not presented in prayer, sermon, or psalmody. Under these circumstances one might have expected to find a widely extended, and as I have said, a chronic presence of the phenomena of witchcraft. We might have come to take it as a matter of course that each of our many scores of town histories should have devoted an early chapter to the cases of witchcraft that had been noted and dealt with in it, the names of culprits, and the death penalties. If the history of every town in England and Scotland, to say nothing of those on the Continent, had been written with the same minuteness of detail, the exceptions would have been very rare to the universal recognition of the presence of witchcraft, and the atrocious proceedings against the victims of the delusion. The number of such victims on the records of those two countries exceed thirty thousand, and, taking those on the Continent into the count, run up into hundreds of thousands; and the delusion with the woful and appalling frenzies, panics, and judicial cruelties which it involved held its terrible sway for several centuries. Sir William Blackstone gave his full countenance to the reality of witchcraft seventy years after the Salem tragedies had closed, and the statutes of England still recognized it as a punishable crime.

All the circumstances and conditions which furnished the phenomena of reputed witchcraft in the towns, villages, and hamlets of England and Scotland might well have been supposed to present themselves in Massachusetts. A lonely, deformed, or ill-favored old woman, unwedded, sour and woe-begone by some bitterness in her lot, might here as well as there have cast an "evil eye" or muttered a malediction which caused a neighbor's cow to cast her calf, or the dough in the kneading-pan to lose its sweetness, or one of a hundred mishaps and maladies to fall upon any one of those whom she envied or hated. The gossip of neighbors, helped by credulity and dreary superstitions, would readily catch and intensify the rumor of such malignant influences. All mysterious and startling events, the repetition and succession of calamities in one household or community, infelicities of domestic life, accidents and portents, which furnished the accusation of demoniac spells all over the homes of Europe, might have found their material and opportunity in every village of Massachusetts. Everywhere in Europe the tests, the kind of evidence required, the modes of proceeding for dealing with witchcraft, and the judicial processes and shocking tortures and executions were always kept in ready and efficient use. How was it that Massachusetts was to such an extent and degree delivered from a full proportionate share in such horrors? The question is really worth pausing upon. Should we not refer the exemption of our towns to such an exceptional extent to the kindly neighborly relations, the sympathetic ties, the mutual interest, confidence, and helpfulness of the people? There were unfortunate persons, men and women, deformed, ill-tempered, unlovable, half-witted specimens of humanity in most of these towns, but they were commiserated or borne with perhaps even more tolerantly than often in these days.

In view, then, of what might have been, and what the people of our first century would have regarded only as their share in a universal exposure to the wiles and machinations of the Evil One, the tragic events which transpired in Salem Village ought not to be rehearsed in historical relation, as they too often have been, as a signal monstrosity of Massachusetts Puritanism. Everything that occurred there in the paroxysm of a panic, in outrages upon a common humanity, in the alarm and consternation of a community, in the mockery of judicial proceedings, and in the execution of innocent victims, might be paralleled in every feature and incident in hundreds of places in the Old World. What indeed should seem startling or deplorable that transpires when Satan is believed to have borne down upon a group of households, putting his venom and malignity into the hearts of little children and their parents, and poisoning the springs of love and trust and mercy? Anything special, peculiar, or intense in the phenomena of the delusion in Salem may be considered as to a degree offset by the concentration there alone, and within seven months of a single year, of the share of Massachusetts in the visitation of a world-wide calamity which lingered in Europe long after its terrors had ceased here.

There had been four executions for reputed witchcraft in Massachusetts previous to the Salem tragedies. They were those of Margaret Jones in 1648, of Mary Parsons in 1651, of Ann Hibbins in 1656, and of Goody Glover in 1688. These cases in no respects differed from those common to Christendom. The ingredients mingled in the witches' caldron at Salem Village were of the uncanny sort which needed only to simmer together, stirred by malignant hands, to effect their baneful spells.[1]

Some petty feuds and bickerings, with gossip and grudgings between neighbors in a partially reclaimed wilderness village, with controversies about local rights, had prepared material for mischief, awaiting a provocative agency for fomenting it. An ill-tempered and ill-balanced minister in contention with his flock which wished to be rid of him, though not the prime, was a secondary agent in

[1] There is no subject for a monograph in the history of Massachusetts which has been treated so ably, fully, and faithfully as has the distressing delusion in Salem, by one remarkably qualified with all the faculties, means, and opportunities for obtaining and presenting exhaustive information concerning it. This was the Rev. and Hon. Charles W. Upham. After a score of years of service as minister of the First Church in Salem, he resigned his office on account of the loss of his voice. After a period of rest, he continued for thirty years, to the end of his life at the age of seventy-three, in the pursuit of his labors as a diligent and accomplished scholar, and as an earnest and patriotic servant of the public. He represented Salem three years in our Legislature, was in the State Senate three years, two of them as its president, and a Representative in the Thirty-third Congress of the United States. He was a most honored citizen of Salem, thoroughly versed in its history, proud of the traditions of its old-time local importance as the birthplace and home of scholars, jurists, and eminent merchants, whose commerce was carried on over the whole world. He felt very deeply the scandalous injustice by which the village suburb of the town of Salem had in reputed history been made so signally to bear the odium connected with the witchcraft delusion, as if its horrors and tragedies there had not been experienced all over Christendom. It was not to clear or relieve the town of the ill-report of what had really transpired there under the frenzy of a short-lived panic, but to expose the folly and falsehood of the distinctive reproach attached to it, as if the melancholy detail of what had occurred there were not paralleled in every feature of horror in every country of Europe for a period of two centuries. Thus he was prompted to give years of diligent study, research, and labor to the preparation of his profoundly instructive work entitled "Salem Witchcraft: with an Account of Salem Village, and a History of Opinions on Witchcraft and Kindred Subjects." (Two Volumes. Boston, 1867.) So thoroughly, judiciously, and impartially, and with such wealth of learning and compass of sound philosophy, does the author deal with his repulsive but compulsory theme, that no further treatment of it is requisite or desirable. Its documentary materials, its local identifications, its minuteness of details, and the calm, candid, and catholic spirit in which the work is written, claim the gratitude of its readers.

that mischief. He had in his family two native African slaves, husband and wife, John and Tituba, — the latter a name to conjure with, — both skilled in the "sorcery, necromancy," and superstitions of their race. A circle of young girls, unwatched and wilful, more than one of them depraved, had spent many dreary winter evenings at the minister's house with his daughter, a child of nine years. They practised palmistry and fortune-telling, and seem to have become experts in some of the tricks of the séances and "materializations" of our day, which mark the donkeydom or asshood stage in our social development. Surprises, relations, delusions, frauds, minglings of audacious lyings and malignity, were all thrown into the caldron. Marvels of invention and exaggeration were added, and the report went forth of " afflicted children " pinched and tortured by invisible hands. It was not a minister, but a physician, who being called in for advice, first spoke the ominous word " witchcraft." The Evil Hand, with its demoniac cunning and its mocking triumph for a season over all the power and resources of common sense, intelligence, and agencies of sober piety in the little community, had got the mastery. The consternation spread over an extending circle. Imagination wrought in its wildest license in conjuring spectres in homes and fields, in highways and churches, by the table and the bedside. Satan had been allowed for a time to throw off the shackles of his pit, and to go abroad getting signatures of blood in his book. Some, not always weak-minded persons, were so bereft of wit and their real personal consciousness, as to believe that they had a duplex existence, and confessed to having made covenant with the Devil. Circumstances, scenes, incidents, and the same inextricable interminglings of delusion, falsehood, and malignity which characterized the witchcraft panics the world over, and the same judicial proceedings, with a besotted contempt of all rules and safeguards in receiving sworn testimony, were repeated here, the judges and courts following English precedents. The subject neither invites nor demands further relation. The very intensity and agony which marked the spell of frenzy in this community, stamped out the superstition and the enormities of inhumanity which enshrouded it here, and gave us an immunity while Europe continued under its gloom.

The dismay and insensate panic of this short-lived delusion here have been often paralleled in all their features at other times and in other places. They were aggravated tenfold in the Gunpowder and the Popish Plots in England. Incidents in our American history most nearly resembling the tragic experiences in Salem are the two so-called "Negro Plots" in New York, occurring respectively in 1712 and 1741, — the victims in each of them exceeding in number and in the barbarity of the penalties and sufferings inflicted upon them the score of those in Salem. The panics in New York, which well-nigh crazed or paralyzed the whole body of the citizens, originated in alleged plots of slaves to burn and plunder the city. In 1712, twenty-one victims were executed. Some were burned at the stake, one was broken on the wheel, one was hung in chains to die of starvation. In the second alleged plot, in 1741, the Supreme Court and jury, like the people, seemed to be swept and stunned as by a tornado, from April to October, when a Thanksgiving for relief was observed. One hundred and fifty negroes were imprisoned, fourteen were burned at the stake, eighteen were hanged, two were gibbeted, and seventy-one were transported. Four white men were executed. In New York, as in Salem, the first alarm came from a lying and perjured girl, and a minister of religion, wholly innocent, was among the victims. Satan was outdone in his demoniac rage in Salem by a more effective human diabolism in New York.

But while, as has here been strongly affirmed, allowing for the unique conditions and circumstances of a neighborhood of farmers in rude and simple times, there was nothing at all distinctive or peculiar in the share visited upon Salem Village of its dismal experience in the universal delusion of witchcraft, there are three facts connected with the harrowing subject which deserve emphatic mention. They present themselves as cheering, though not atoning for, the wrongs and miseries of the experience when time, with its compunctions and regrets, had led to a waking penitential retrospect of the nightmare visitation. That waking excited sentiments tenderly and poignantly melancholy and self-accusatory.

Four years after that in which dismay and frenzy had done their cruel work, the whole community was exercised by a profound sorrow, a conviction that an irreparable injustice had been done, which had violated and tortured the most sacred affections of private hearts and homes. The names of innocent sufferers were recalled with unavailing pity, when locked and troubled breasts ventured to break an ominous silence, which could not bring oblivion. It was the well-nigh universal sentiment that the whole community should join in a public expression of humiliation and penitence. So a day was set apart for solemn fasting and confession in homes and meeting-houses. The occasion was made deeply impressive when one of the judges in the trials rose and stood in his place in the sanctuary while the minister read aloud a note which he had handed to him, asking that in the general prayer his own individual petition be offered, imploring forgiveness for the wrong which he had personally committed in his high office. His prayer was that his error might not be divinely visited upon him, his family, nor the public.

A third incident, intended to give expression to this general penitence and commiseration, was the distribution from the public treasury of considerable sums, in compensatory allotments, wholly inadequate, indeed, but kindly designed, to the representatives of some of the sufferers from losses, disabilities, or scandals.

Was there a single other community, State, province, county, or town in Christendom, numbering the victims of the delusion by scores, hundreds, or thousands, that signified its relief from a dismal superstition by either of these penitential or compensatory acts?

INDEX.